DIY Citizenship

DIY Citizenship

Critical Making and Social Media

Edited by Matt Ratto and Megan Boler

The MIT Press
Cambridge, Massachusetts
London, England

This book was set in Stone Sans and Stone Serif by the MIT Press. Printed and bound in the United States of America.

Library of Congress Cataloging-in-Publication Data

DIY citizenship : critical making and social media / edited by Matt Ratto and Megan Boler.
pages cm
Includes bibliographical references and index.
ISBN 978-0-262-02681-9 (hardcover : alk. paper)—ISBN 978-0-262-52552-7 (pbk. : alk. paper) 1. Citizenship. 2. Civil society. 3. Political participation. 4. Social media. I. Ratto, Matt, 1969– II. Boler, Megan.
JF801.D59 2014
323.6—dc23
2013022297

10 9 8 7 6 5 4 3 2

Contents

Foreword

Throughout history, the invention of new information and communication technologies has brought with it inflated hopes for liberation and democracy, only to have those hopes punctured by the inevitable crush of state and corporate power. Is the Internet an exception?

This question has animated new media scholars and activists alike ever since the first email lists and bulletin boards were used to organize and disseminate information at the dawn of the Internet age. There can be no doubt that the Internet and its related tools, like social networking and mobile computing, have placed powerful capabilities in the hands of individuals who collectively have used them in innovative ways to break free of powerful forces, expose corruption, and even bring down regimes once thought immoveable. The dramatic Arab Spring, fueled by social media empowered activists, is the most oft-cited of this type of "do-it-yourself" citizenship, but there are a multitude of other "springs" out there that follow the same playbook: individuals, networked together through distributed means of communication, outflanking and exposing the entrenched systems of power. As the many chapters in this volume reveal, DIY means taking matters into your own hands, not leaving it for others to do it for you. It means making decisions without the gaze of those in power saying what's right and what's wrong, what's allowed or what's not. A decentralized medium of communications alongside ad hoc, leaderless, "cloud-like" social movements, the Internet and DIY seem like the perfect match and a recipe for freedom and democracy.

The Citizen Lab, which is an interdisciplinary research laboratory at the University of Toronto that I have directed since its inception in 2001, is another example of the power of DIY and the Internet working hand in glove. In our case, we have deliberately borrowed the methods of state intelligence agencies—specifically, the combination of human-based and technical investigations with open source information gathering—and turned them on their heads to watch the very agencies from whom we have liberally borrowed. We employ wide-area scans of the Internet in conjunction with field research undertaken by partners in dozens of countries to "lift the lid" on the hidden exercise of power beneath the surface of cyberspace.

But what we have found has been disturbing—indeed, calling into question the very liberating potential of the Internet itself. Whereas activists, citizens, and others have employed the Internet and new media to further democratic empowerment, we have reason to believe that the powers that be have quietly and effectively used them to do the opposite: to censor, monitor, and even disable and silence Internet-enabled social movements. We have tracked a growing market for sophisticated products and services that are sold to autocratic and repressive regimes, which use them to track dissidents, infiltrate opposition, and limit access to information and freedom of speech.

These disturbing findings of the Citizen Lab have been reinforced by the recent revelations of the National Security Agency (NSA) whistleblower, Edward Snowden. As Snowden has confirmed, the very social media upon which citizens depend, most of which are operated by US-based corporations who have for years been colluding with a secretive and mostly unaccountable US intelligence agency, can be a source of insecurity as much as liberation, of control as much as freedom. Every bit and byte of information we exchange, it turns out, are open for collection and analysis—a detailed record of our social networks, our trusted contacts, our movements and habits, even our innermost thoughts.

Whether the many forms of DIY highlighted in this excellent volume can eventually muster the energy and persistence to reign in growing state power in cyberspace is an open question. But ultimately, the answer to that question is up to all of us. Like all technologies before it, the Internet is what we make of it. It is ours. We need to remember that before it slips through our grasp.

Ron Deibert, Director of the Citizen Lab,
Munk School of Global Affairs, University of Toronto
August 2013

Introduction

Matt Ratto and Megan Boler

DIY—do-it-yourself—no longer just describes the weekend warrior struggling to install their own bathroom tiles or build their own deck. Instead, DIY increasingly constitutes our lived, daily experiences, in particular those that involve media and communication systems. And increasingly, the DIY ethos has seismically reshaped the international political sphere, as can be seen in ongoing global uprisings and the uses of media and communications within a "logic of connective action" (Bennett and Segerberg 2012), a kind of "collective" or "networked" individualism (Rainie and Wellman 2012) constituting new hybrid social movements and practices of horizontal, participatory, and direct democracy (Boler 2013; Boler and Nitsou 2014). The Occupy Wall Street movement that began in September 2011—inspired by Los Indignados Movement in Spain, following the "Arab Spring"—represents just one example of such emergent, DIY political activities.

This volume brings together scholars, artists, and activists who are exploring the nature of DIY activity, discovering the potentials and the problems of digital and digitally mediated forms of making. The contributions address making as a "critical" activity, an activity that provides both the possibility to intervene substantively in systems of authority and power and that offers an important site for reflecting on how such power is constituted by infrastructures, institutions, communities, and practices. Critical makings (Ratto and Hoekema 2009; Ratto 2011a, 2011b)—such as low-power FM stations, video productions, civic rituals, community gardens, and octogenarian tidal power systems—are reviewed and examined in the chapters that follow. Critical making signals the ways in which productions—whether of video, web-based communications, gardens, radio transmitters, or robots—are understood as politically transformative activities by the individuals and groups described in each chapter. Critical making also signals the integration/simultaneity of processes and practices, the act of *making "things,"* and suggests that practices of "making" are potentially

Figures I.1 and I.2

Images of Occupy movement. Boler personal archives.

linked to critically-infused reflection about aspects of the process itself, Critical making invites reflection on the relationship of the maker to the thing produced, reflection on how elements (whether nuts and bolts, bits, and bytes, or breath, blood, flesh, brain, and neurons) work together—in short, consideration and awareness of the mediated and direct experiences of interacting with the material world. In turn, our subtitle "critical making and social media" articulates the point of inquiry around the increasingly technologically and digitally mediated experience of our everyday lives, of labor in an information economy.

Offering another concept as a point of entry, Steve Mann (chapter 1) defines "maktivism" as a practice straddling hacking, making, DIY, and DIT, implying as well the intersections of the proprietary and the free, copyright, and copyleft: "Maktivism often involves the moral, ethical, and lawful ('white hat') elements of the 'hacker' ethos, but not necessarily the illegal 'cracker' ethos. Maktivism combines the DIY (do-it-yourself) ethos of home renovation with the DIT (do-it-together) ethos of the GNU Linux and Free Software movement." In his chapter, Mann also mentions "tinquiry": "tinkering as inquiry," another way of depicting the multi-layered nature of critical making and DIY citizenship.

Each contribution is conceptualized through the lens of "DIY citizenship," a term intended to highlight the diversity of ways citizenship is enacted and performed. While DIY activity had previously been characterized primarily in terms of youth subcultures (McKay 1998), digitally mediated DIY practices have recently become more mainstream. Terms such as "social media," "web 2.0," and "user-generated content" have become buzzwords, and platforms such as Twitter and Facebook are being used for overtly political purposes. The most obvious examples of these political shifts includes the so-called Facebook revolution that followed the 2009 Iranian presidential elections, or the "Twitter revolutions" that helped to end the rule of Zine El Abidine Ben Ali in Tunisia and Hosni Mubarak in Egypt in 2011. Such events constitute new modalities of political participation—"DIY government"—or, at least, such are the hopes and claims of many protestors and observers.[1]

Less overtly political are the large numbers of "modders," hackers, artists, and activists who redeploy and repurpose corporately produced content or create novel properties of their own, often outside the standard systems of production and consumption. This activity is not relegated to the sphere of the digital but also includes communities of self-organized crafters, hackers, artists, designers, scientists, and engineers. These groups are increasingly to be found online exchanging sewing and knitting patterns, technical

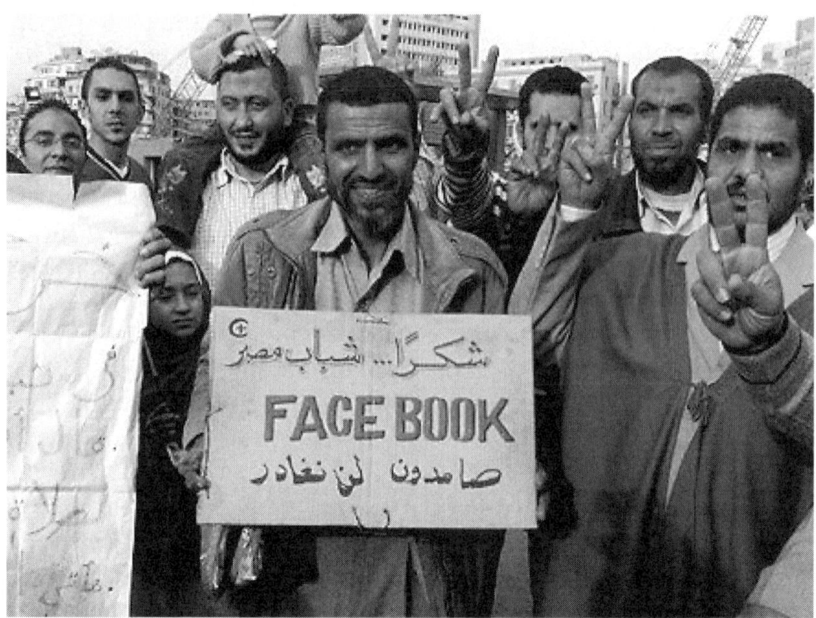

Figures I.3 and I.4
Images of Facebook, Egypt. Some rights reserved by Interact Egypt—Play Innovation.

data, circuit layouts, detailed electronics tutorials, and guides to scientific experiments, among other forms of instruction and support. Such activities can also be understood as political in the sense that they potentially challenge existing systems of authority—questioning ownership rights to media, for instance, or putting to the test traditional systems of peer review. Many of these "maker" activities begin to take on additional importance as dominant institutions, such as the military, corporations, and governments, increasingly recognize the ways in which DIY activities challenge traditional hierarchies of authority and the existing status quo.[2]

We suggest that these emergent communities of "critical makers" and political protestors that organize on- and offline are aptly described as "DIY citizens." As noted by Hartley (1999), these are individuals and social groups who, in becoming producers as well as consumers, are "making themselves up as they go along." DIY democracy perfectly describes the horizontal processes of leadership and consensus engaged in the Occupy Wall Street (OWS) movement. OWS participants patently rejected traditional assumptions, identities, and practices associated with "democracy" and instead conscientiously created and developed distinctly DIY organizational processes, values, and norms.

This self-creation can be seen in a positive light—for instance, as a reaction against the regulation of identity that can constitute the lived experience of a totalitarian government. However, it can also be understood as part of a hegemonic acceptance of the breaking apart and individualization of civil society. In fact, Rosenberg (2005) has called this the "diyization of modern society," pointing to IKEA as the most visible manifestation of the increasing privatization and individualization of the public realm. DIY citizenship, therefore, sits at the intersection of a series of tensions: between consumers and citizens, between experts and novices, between individuals and communities, and between politics as performed by governments and politics and DIY grassroots democracy. The authors in this collection take up the themes of social groups, competence, capacity, and the (often hidden) costs of participation. DIY citizenship potentially invites us to consider how and when individuals and communities participate in shaping, changing, and reconstructing selves, worlds, and environments in creative ways that challenge the status quo and normative understandings of "how things must be."

For example, in chapter 4, "Radical Inclusion? Locating Accountability in Technical DIY," Christina Dunbar-Hester explores how media activists negotiated maker identities and traditional associations between technical work and gender and race as part of their DIY activities. For the groups

Figures I.5 and I.6

Images from Maker Faire 2012. Ratto personal archive.

Dunbar-Hester studied, DIY was not just about building alternatives to corporate radio stations, but also a means of addressing the ways in which technical expertise was unevenly distributed in their community. Thus, in order to enact their overtly political activity of creating alternatives to mainstream media, they had to work to develop and enhance the technical abilities of female and nonwhite members, goals that were somewhat contradictory to each other. For this group, DIY citizenship is about technical proficiency, which is understood as being linked to political power.

Similarly, chapter 19, "Citizen Innovation: *Active*Energy and the Quest for Sustainable Design" by Ann Light, reviews a participatory project that involves somewhat nontraditional makers. This group, the Geezers Club, is a group of men between sixty and eighty years of age with little or no formal training in engineering or related fields. With the support of researchers from the University of London, the Geezers Club has been designing and building alternative energy systems based on the use of tidal power from the Thames River—an inspiring story about technical capacity-building for amateurs, social intervention, and participatory political power.

Throughout this volume, DIY citizenship provides a conceptual thread for relating diverse practices and domains—allowing us, for example, to compare Dunbar-Hester's media activists to Light's Geezers Club, and to see their identities and practices as related. These examples, like others in the volume, demonstrate a shift in the possibilities of political participation. To be a citizen is no longer merely about the standard political activities of voting, advocating for policy changes, and protest. Now, as the chapters in this volume highlight, citizen action is diverse, participatory, and discoverable in unexpected locales. These broadened concepts of citizenship call into question the traditional notions of the public sphere as performed through either rational deliberation (Habermas 1962/1989) or contested debate (Mouffe 1992). In other words, DIY citizenship draws attention to nondiscursive activity and "direct action" (McKay 1998; Doherty, Plows, and Wall 2003) as socially interventionist. Creating community gardens, filming personal music videos, and even knitting can in this light be understood and evaluated as emergent modes of political activity.

Origins and Organization

The ideas for this collection originated from a 2010 conference on DIY Citizenship convened by the editors.[3] This international conference brought together diverse participants—scholars, artists, practitioners—representing a wide range of disciplines (including communication and media studies, education, science and technology studies, geography, architecture, information studies, and sociology) with shared interests in the notion of DIY citizenship.

During the three-day conference, participants sometimes heatedly engaged in debate and discussion regarding the term "DIY" as well as "citizenship." These debates are reflected within the chapters in this book; authors emphasize different aspects of and questions about DIY and citizenship. With respect to word choice, one must immediately query "DIY": are we not talking, often, about DIT, or do-it-together? Might not the spirit of much that falls under DIY be associated more with "DIO"—do-it-ourselves, emphasizing the collective and collaborative action of the individual and atomistic invocation of a self that acts? As Reilly (chapter 8) notes from his interviews with tactical media pranksters the Yes Men: "Bichlbaum argues . . . this DIY ethic is only truly effective when actions take on a cohesive collaborative bent; to pull off these labor-intensive hoaxes requires 'the assistance of huge armies of individuals.' We playfully noted that DIY might best be described as do-it-*yourselves* (pl.), given the often large number of group members needed to carry out a particular action." Reilly describes a wide diversity of work that sees itself under the DIY umbrella.

Similar to the diverse concepts of DIY expressed by conference participants, the notion of "citizenship" raises myriad questions. With its connotation and realities of inclusion/exclusion and related forms of violence, "citizenship" is a problematic and loaded term given its implications and histories. Nonetheless, the term arguably merits reclaiming and repurposing; our choice of the term "citizenship" for the 2010 conference and for this book seeks to raise questions regarding new forms of participatory engagement and world-making. Traditionally, the concept has invoked notions of membership, rights, and belonging, all of which have been curtailed and limited by nation-states. But new ways of considering citizenship are emerging. In an illustrative account, Stoker et al. (2011) examine the limits of citizenship as it is enacted within an increasingly global society, but also provide updated conceptions of what citizenship practices may look like in their best sense. They note the continuing debate within political theory over whether citizen participation has intrinsic or instrumental value, and they emphasize that most theorists currently "place a premium on increasing citizen participation as a way of ameliorating the disconnect . . . between citizens and those who make decisions in their name" (Stoker et al. 2011, 33). In their account, they note five challenges to robust citizenship: (1) differential rates of participation across social groups; (2) the competence of citizens to make reasoned judgments; (3) the capacity of citizens to influence or control political decision making; (4) the costs borne by citizens and public authorities; and (5) the extent to which participation can be embedded at significant levels of governance (Stoker et al. 2011).

Finally, four broad and overlapping themes emerged from this event, which serve to organize the chapters into four parts:

Part I: DIY and Activism: New Modes of Civic Engagement and Participatory Politics
Part II: DIY and Making: Learning, Culture, Hacking, and Arts
Part III: DIY and Design: Opening the Black Box and Repurposing Technologies
Part IV: DIY and Media: Redistributing Authority and Sources in News Media

Each part begins with a short introduction to the general similarities and differences between the chapters within the given section. The book's structure highlights how DIY practices are evolving through the engagement of technologies and media with social and cultural arenas—arenas ranging from activism and media to design hacking, arts and culture, and education. Each area of cultural production is increasingly shaped by uses of technologies and media, sometimes developed specifically for the particular cultural arena and more often "repurposed" to align a corporate produced technology or media platform with an unintended use or practice. But ideas of DIY and of citizenship—and their conjoining in this portmanteau phrase—are not taken for granted by the authors in this volume but are explored through their own conceptual and empirical examples.

In the next sections, we unpack further some of the conceptual histories and implications associated with "citizenship," "DIY," and "DIY citizenship."

Origins of DIY

The earliest uses of DIY can be seen as prescient forecasts of the anti-consumerist values that continue to fuel contemporary DIY cultures. The term "DIY" came to be associated with the counterculture of the late 1960s. Gauntlett discusses the connections between emerging countercultural critiques of the formal educational system[4] and thinkers who emphasized needs for experiential and do-it-yourself modes of alternative schooling (Gauntlett 2011, 50). He characterizes the central theme of all DIY practices as the "rejection of the idea that you overcome problems by paying somebody else to provide a solution" (Gauntlett 2011, 56). Leveraging thinkers such as Alan Watts, John Holt, and Ivan Illich, Gauntlett provides a historical and conceptual point of departure for DIY activities. Equally, Stewart Brand's *Whole Earth Catalog* provided a fixed origin for a wider cultural appreciation of DIY sensibility. First published in 1968, the *Whole Earth Catalog* provided a key touchstone for many countercultural movements and communities that continued to develop into the 1980s.

By the late 1980s and early 1990s, DIY culture had evolved with the innovative emergence of "zines," a significant cultural production practice of both punk and third-wave feminist cultures.[5] Amy Spencer's book *DIY: The Rise of Lo-Fi Culture* (2005) provides some of the history and details regarding these activities, noting in particular the ways proponents of lo-fi culture emphasized low cost and DIY alternatives to mainstream forms of media production. George McKay's edited collection *DiY Culture: Party and Protest in Nineties Britain* (1998) brings together a number of contributions exploring the raves and protests that characterized 1990s activism in the UK and elsewhere. People around the globe were enacting forms of protest and direct action that increasingly wedded "art" and "politics." As John Jordan writes in his oft-cited contribution to McKay's volume:

> Since the beginning of this century, avant-garde agitational artists have tried to demolish the divisions between art and life and introduce creativity, imagination, play, and pleasure into the revolutionary project. Inspired by and following in the footsteps of the protest movements and counter cultures of the sixties, seventies, and eighties, the diy protest movement is finally breaking down the barriers between art and protest. It seems that at the close of the century new forms of creative and poetic resistance have finally found their time. (Jordan 1998, 129)

Indeed, this conjunction of art and protest has only snowballed over the ensuing decades; feminist artists working in craft and activism have coined the term "craftivism," which continues the legacy of DIY culture. Key texts such as Levine and Heimerl's *Handmade Nation: The Rise of DIY Art, Craft, and Design* (2008) and Tapper and Zucker's *Craft Activism: People, Ideas, and Projects from the New Community of Handmade and How You Can Join In* (2011) provide detailed stories and examples from practitioners of craft-based lifestyles.[6] Like the lo-fi movement before them, these individuals and social collectives find value in the self-production of craft objects and understand this work as a protest against the increasing commodification of society.

We now turn to an examination of how the concept of DIY citizenship has been articulated and used, discussing the advantages and limitations of its early articulations. We suggest that, moving forward, conceptions of

DIY citizenship require a more robust account of power relations to avoid familiar and empty invocations surrounding "democracy" rhetoric that too easily slide into liberal assumptions of individualized agency.

Hartley's DIY Citizenship

The specific articulation of "DIY citizenship" is one of two notions John Hartley adds to Thomas Marshall's citizenship "types"; civil, political, and social (Jacka 2003). To these, Hartley adds a fourth—"cultural"—and a fifth, what he calls do-it-yourself (DIY) citizenship. As Jacka summarizes:

> For Hartley (1999), cultural citizenship has to do with "identity" in the sense of identity politics—the "politics of the internally colonized demographics of modernity" (the poor, women, people of color) (p. 167). The second—DIY citizenship—supersedes (but continues to coexist with) the first. It is based on difference rather than identity and consists in the "practice of putting together an identity from the available choices, patterns and opportunities on offer in the semiosphere and the mediasphere." (Jacka 2003, 185)

According to Hartley, the DIY citizen is one who creates their identity and individuality through a process of choosing from the semiotic material on offer. This understanding of identity construction is resonant with recent notions of "self-branding" (Hearn 2008) and the production of self-identity seen by Giddens as one of the constitutive elements of late modernity (Giddens 1991). But Hartley takes this further, equating such processes with the production of citizenship as well: "'Citizenship' is no longer simply a matter of a social contract between state and subject, no longer even a matter of acculturation to the heritage of a given community; DIY citizenship is a choice people can make for themselves. Further, they can change a given identity, or move into or out of a repertoire of identities. And although no one is 'sovereign' in the sense that they can command others, there's an increasing emphasis on self-determination as the foundation of citizenship" (Hartley 1999, 178).

Hartley's articulation comes under some scrutiny and critique for two primary reasons: first, his definition appears to assume the problematic atomistic individual long associated with liberalism. This is a conception of self deeply rooted in Western thought, which sees individual choice being able to supersede realities of social hierarchies, power differentials, and the uneven playing field on which—despite the best rhetoric of liberal democracy—individuals do not start out with equal handicaps. The notion of DIY raises—and may beg—a host of questions about the ways in which these potentially "radical" practices may align with or be appropriated by an emphasis on liberal individualism. To value "doing it oneself" sounds very much like "pulling oneself up by one's bootstraps" and results in a continued privileging of the individual. One need merely consider general notions of the "digital divide" to see that questions of access, power, and social and cultural capital challenge any generalized or universal concept of DIY citizenship.

A second and related problem is highlighted by Jacka: "it is difficult to see the difference between Hartley's account of DIY citizenship and mere consumerism—that is, the freedom to choose products that will situate the buyer in a semiotic landscape of 'style'" (Jacka 2003, 185). This critique points out again the overvaluation of individual choice and underestimation of the realities of late capitalist consumer society. As Jacka states:

> The kind of democracy Hartley (1999) had in mind is not political democracy but semiotic democracy—what Hartley called "semiotic self-determination," also known as DIY citizenship. Democratization of semiosis leads to a "truly sovereign community," a population "among whom relationships, decisions and ideas are negotiated and arbitrated." It is the "citizenship of the future; decentralized, post-adversarial, based on self-determination not state coercion" (p. 161): a truly panglossian vision. (Jacka 2003, 186)

While Jacka applauds this panglossian vision, we would suggest that Hartley's outline of DIY citizenship is even further vulnerable to the sorts of critiques levied against the Habermasian vision of the public sphere. "Semiotic self-determination" assumes, like Habermas's public sphere, an ideal set of conditions in which every voice is welcome at the table; all voices carry equal weight; and everyone is heard on the terms of their rational contribution to the conversation. These assumptions of deliberative democracy and public sphere have been thoroughly criticized since the 1990s for ignoring the realities of social hierarchies of power that determine who can participate in public sphere debates, whose voice is recognized, and thus who is heard. A more comprehensive examination of the critiques of the public sphere is illustrative as a point of departure for thinking through the claims of DIY citizenship.

DIY Citizenship and the Public Sphere

Concepts of deliberative democracy are frequently used as a stand-in for debate about the viability of public spheres. For Habermas, a liberal democracy ideally requires the formation of "public spheres," sites that provide citizens space to deliberate, debate, and discuss matters of public interest outside of formal governmental processes. Habermas's first major work, *The Structural Transformation of the Public Sphere: An Inquiry into a Category of Bourgeois Society* (Habermas 1962/1989) explored the development of this sphere, originating from a bourgeois liberal constitutional order that provided opportunities for critical reflection on its role in society. For Habermas, the key to a properly functioning public sphere involved spaces in which "rational-critical discourse" could take place: "The ideal of the public sphere calls for social integration to be based on rational-critical discourse. Integration, in other words, is to be based on communication rather than domination. 'Communication' in this context means not merely sharing what people already think or know but also a process of potential transformation in which reason is advanced by debate itself" (Calhoun 1992, 29). However, critiques and debates about the viability of a democratic public sphere continue; Nancy Fraser's renowned critique of the Habermasian ideal serves as a case in point (Fraser 1990). Fraser focuses her criticisms on the actualities of power relations, exploring inclusion and exclusion as they play out in Western societies. She notes how the Habermasian ideal of a public sphere is founded on strict divisions of public and private, a division that has served historically to exclude women's participation in the public sphere. The gendered requirements to serve in the private domestic sphere as mother, wife, and domestic laborer have served to disenfranchise women from deliberative democracy. More fundamentally, Fraser criticizes the Habermasian public sphere as requiring problematic processes of consensus building, processes that require agreed-upon definitions of common concerns and the bracketing of identities as well as ignoring systematic inequalities within the artificial zone that constitutes the space for deliberative debate. Additionally, achieving consensus and deliberative democracy in the Habermasian public sphere privileges rational (i.e., masculine) as opposed to emotional (i.e., feminine) discourse and debate, which further diminishes women's legitimacy as authoritative participants. Finally, Fraser illustrates how assumptions about participation in the public sphere overlook hegemonic exclusion and dominance that institutionally disenfranchise and silence perspectives that don't reflect normative or dominant cultural values.

Fraser's critique (alongside more recent discussions by political theorists including Jacka [2003], Gitlin [1998], and Mouffe [1992]) reveals the stark realities surrounding citizenship: namely, clear distinctions about who is allowed to participate in public debates, who is heard, and when, how, and whether the concerns and experiences of non-dominant groups and classes hegemonically erased, denied, and silenced are included. These critiques of oversimplified invocations of public sphere participation serve as an invaluable warning while more robust conceptions of DIY citizenship are further developed.

The liberal individualism presumed by ideals of the public sphere is further challenged by the more recent work of Hardt and Negri (2001, 2005), and in particular by their defining of the notion of the "multitude," a concept they see as providing an alternative to traditional notions of political power that presume shared identities, goals, or necessary unity:

> One of the recurring truths of political philosophy is that only the one can rule, be it the monarch, the party, the people, or the individual; social subjects that are not unified and remain multiple cannot rule and must be ruled . . . The concept of the multitude challenges this accepted truth of sovereignty. The multitude, although it remains multiple and internally different, is able to act in common and thus rule itself. Rather than a political body with one that commands and others that obey, the multitude is living flesh that rules itself. (Hardt and Negri 2005, 100)

The concept of the "multitude" as differentiated yet able to "act in common and thus rule itself" resonates with characterizations of the DIY communities studied by the scholars in this volume. However—as another warning to those developing new conceptions of participatory DIY democracy—Hardt and Negri come disturbingly close to erasing difference for the sake of defining the multitude: "When we say that we do not want a world without racial or gender difference but instead a world in which race and gender do not matter—a world in which they do not determine hierarchies of power—this is a desire for the multitude" (Hardt and Negri 2005, 100). Despite their desire to avoid the liberal democratic model of "bracketing identities," upon which a Habermasian public sphere is predicated, there is no clear sense of how in fact a model of participatory democracy in which race and gender do not matter might function.

A further troubling matter is Hardt and Negri's category of precarious and affective labor, which potentially ends up designating women's unpaid labor as of a different order than the labor recognized in the (masculinized) public sphere. As renowned autonomia theorist, anarcha-feminist scholar, and activist Silvia Federici writes: "My concern is that the Negrian theory of precarious labor ignores, bypasses, one of the most important contributions of feminist theory and struggle, which is the redefinition of work, and the recognition of women's unpaid reproductive labor as a key source of capitalist accumulation" (Federici 2008).

Given the challenges, we suggest that the work of Jacques Rancière, among others, provides a valuable direction for theoretical exploration of new understandings of public sphere and participatory democracy. Of particular concern in the work of Rancière are the "unheard," those who have "no part," those without a so-called political voice in democracies. The moments of interruption or intervention—the eruption of the unheard into what he terms the "police order"—is precisely what constitutes "politics" for Rancière. Politics are the dynamic events and exchanges in which those without voice in the dominant culture express and make heard, or "sensible," what has been repressed, precluded, or censored within political regimes. For Rancière, disagreement signifies the importance of radically different registers in which citizens make sense of their world and of power and authority—different registers that, unlike those in the Habermasian ideal public sphere, cannot always be rectified for the sake of consensus and agreement. Quite significantly (though the purview of this introduction does not permit full explication), the value of engaging Rancière's understandings of the representational regime as contrasted with the potentially more radical aesthetic regime (2004, 12) is that it effectively describes the significance of DIY citizenship as a hybrid of art and politics, a mode of political poesis that can challenge stratified political structures that exclude and that seek to render interruptions and interventions "unhearable."

According to Rancière, "Political activity is whatever shifts a body from the place assigned to it or changes a place's destination. It makes visible what had no business being seen, and makes heard a discourse where once there was only place for noise" (1999, 30). This "politics of aesthetics" Rancière terms the "distribution of the sensible" (2004, 7). We suggest that DIY citizenship and critical making enact this "redistribution" of the sensible, thereby pointing toward "disagreement" and the "politics of aesthetics" as an extremely rich theoretical framework for future explorations of DIY citizenship.

Reclaiming DIY Citizenship

Despite its vulnerability to these myriad critiques, the concept of DIY citizenship is creatively augmented and amplified by different authors in our volume. Rather than come to an authoritative definition of the term, the authors collectively address a range of related questions.

Key Questions for Understanding DIY Citizenship

While the book is divided into four sections, there are also six key questions that thread across the chapters.

Who is the DIY citizen? A number of chapters explore the subjectivities of DIY identity. Using examples from actual communities and contexts, the authors explore the nature of DIY participation and action. Rather than define an authoritative description, the chapters together create a composite image of the activities, memberships, and cultivations from and through which the DIY citizen emerges. For example, in "Fan Activism as Participatory Politics: The Case of the Harry Potter Alliance" (chapter 3), Henry Jenkins explores the identities and subjectivities of the DIY citizen. He describes some of the campaigns of the Harry Potter Alliance, a nonprofit organization started by fans. As Jenkins describes, this group utilizes metaphors and images from the Harry Potter books to create a platform for civic engagement. Organizing online through websites and fan fiction forums, members of the group rewrite aspects of Harry Potter to instigate political change. These DIY citizens blend their identities as fans and their identities as activists in order to form hybrid subjectivities.

What are the tools and practices of DIY citizenship? Across the volume, authors provide specific examples of DIY activities and the objects, systems, and technologies that facilitate practices of participation in social systems. For example, in "The Growbot Garden Project as DIY Speculation through Design" (chapter 17), Carl DiSalvo explores "DIY speculative design" as a form of political action. Using his experiences with the growbot project from the 2010 01SJ Biennial, DiSalvo reveals how tinkering, redesigning, and imagining serves as a novel way for publics to engage materially in important social issues, but also raises the question about what should come after these imaginations. Is speculation enough or is a further step necessary?

Is DIY essentially liberatory? This question signals a debate we hope readers will consider throughout their reading of this book. A number of chapters detail how and in what ways DIY fails to live up to its hype, illustrating such concerns as the hidden labor of DIY, technological determinisms frequently assumed, as well as the corporate interests embedded within many of the platforms and systems appropriated for DIY purposes. For example, chapter 18, "Doing It in the Cloud: Google, Apple, and the Shaping of DIY Culture" by Michael Murphy, David J. Phillips, and Karen Pollock, foregrounds the quid pro quo of social media. Through a close examination of the agreements people must sign to make use of their respective systems, as well as the ways user-created data is utilized by Apple and Google, the authors explore how these private companies shape DIY culture. The authors illustrate the contradictions and tensions between public and private infrastructures, which are nonetheless productively utilized for DIY activities. Through their examinations of these conflicting values embedded in primary systems such as cloud computing, we are warned that, contrary to the opinion of John Perry Barlow, information does not just want to be free.

What and where are the spaces and communities of DIY Citizenship? Joshua McVeigh-Schultz's "Redesigning the Vox Pop: Civic Rituals as Sites of Critical Reimagining" (chapter 23) broadens both the idea of DIY and the concept of design through attention to what he terms "civic rituals." Situated literally in the streets, his project "Synaptic Crowd: Vox Pop Experiments" exemplifies critical making to defamiliarize the common "vox pop" media ritual (on-camera interviews with passers-by) and thereby reimagines the role of media in identity formation. McVeigh-Schultz troubles what he sees as Hartley's romanticized notion of DIY citizenship and critiques the idea of semiotic self-determination as both a fantasy and as a matter for concern.

What are the roles of social media in DIY citizenship? As noted in many of the chapters, participation in public debate is an important driver of DIY citizenship. In chapter 26, "Critical News Making and the Paradox of 'Do-It-Yourself News,'" Mike Ananny examines citizen journalism as an alternative to mainstream forms of media, revealing the ways publics are reconstituted within DIY journalism. Graham Meikle uses the failures of *Kony 2012* to address the possibilities and challenges of "*distributed citizenship*, in which individuals from across the globe were to engage in a collective project for political change. . . . Distributed citizenship is a political possibility of the network society in its shift from what Castells terms the space of places to the space of flows" (chapter 27). Chris Atton explores the "incorporation of media production into the routines of everyday life; the site of production in a domestic setting; and the depiction of everyday activities in the content of the media itself." His analysis of such everyday productions as the "personal home page," "perzines," and "fanzines" illustrate how these "mundane media" draw on the resources of capitalism while simultaneusly revealing the (political) identities and sociality of productions by the "silent majority."

What is the role of making for DIY citizenship? Many authors explore the materialities and the processes of DIY construction and demonstrate how this work provides new modes and possibilities for political and social engagement. Steve Mann's chapter highlights practices such as "maktivism" and "tinquiry," illustrating these novel conceptualizations with critical projects of his own design and making such as the "Griefcase" and the "License to Sit." In "Woven Futures: Inscribed Material Ecologies of Critical Making" (chapter 13), Daniela K. Rosner and Miki Foster link work with electronics to knitting practice, examining how participants in an after-school program use shared making as a way to overcome social hierarchy and discover shared ground for collaboration. Here, making as a critical activity is foregrounded and its connection to politics as social relations is demonstrated. As Kate Milberry writes: "Activist-designed and built technologies are therefore disruptive tools that destabilize trends toward a closed, privatized, economically striated and commercially oriented Internet. By designing software that meets their practical needs and social justice goals, tech activists contribute to the democratization of the Internet. As a 'practical means of resistance,' this kind of critical making can be deployed in the blind spots inherent in systems of surveillance and social control, where there is always 'space to manoeuvre' (Marx 2003, 372)" (Milberry, chapter 2, this volume). DIY practices ideally create "maneuvering" space, encouraging us to rethink binary distinctions such as cultural/political and amateur/professional that reductively constrain the ways in which scholars across the arts, humanities, and social sciences understand the relationship of individuals and networks to the boundaries of cultural production and politics. Understanding these boundary-blurring practices as constitutive of DIY citizenship is, we suggest, of paramount importance.

Conclusion

New forms of transnational, cosmopolitan, or global citizenship are increasingly the focus of much scholarly and popular attention. As noted by Stoker et al. (2011), "The technologies of globalization have facilitated new forms of political expression and created new or alternative public spaces and possibilities of citizen engagement" (n.p.). DIY citizenship, we suggest, can be understood as a twenty-first-century amalgamation of politics, culture, arts, and technology that in turn constitutes identities rooted in diverse making practices. In contrast to earlier studies of fans and consumers that positioned them as passive receivers of popular culture, technologies, and media, DIY is characterized by its emphasis on "doing" and the active roles of interventionists, makers, hackers, modders, and tinkerers. Dunbar-Hester's analysis of the indy radio collective Pandora illustrates this explicitly:

The media activists sought to cultivate a particular mode of "maker" identity. They presented technical engagement as a strategy for leveling expertise and increasing political participation. In this, they recognized that tinkering is as much a form of cultural production as a technical one; the activists sought to produce not just technical artifacts but egalitarian social relations by eroding boundaries between experts and laypeople. Activists suggested that demystification of technology through widespread hands-on making could provide an alternative to prevalent technical cultures in which authority is not distributed, but resides exclusively with experts. (Dunbar-Hester, chapter 4, this volume)

One may envision the DIY citizen on a continuum, with one end representing the overtly political/interventionist and the other end representing those simply channeling creativity and a kind of poesis into everyday practices. In this collection of essays, the individuals and groups described by authors for the most part understand their work to be socially interventionist. Through diverse interventionist practices of design, development, and exchange, DIY citizenship challenges traditional divides between production and consumption and corresponding power differentials built into technologically mediated societies.

Such work, seen en masse and across different material and social domains, provides important guidance for questions regarding public participation in both politics and technology. Langdon Winner has noted, "Because technological things so often become central features in widely shared arrangements and conditions of life in contemporary society, there is an urgent need to think about them in a political light" (Winner 1992, 343). Winner deplores the lack of public engagement around the politics of mediated society, noting that most moves in this direction fall into a "technocratic" pattern. He follows with the important question: "How can and should democratic citizenry participate in decision making about technology?" (343)

The contributors in this volume turn Winner's question on its head, asking instead, "How do we engage with society politically through technology?" Their answers chart a space for DIY citizenship, a productive practice in which ethical and social interventions cross through a number of different modalities and materialities. In their discussion of how citizens can resist and take control of the ways that ID cards and sensitive personal information are required and used by the state and corporations, McPhail et al. bring attention to the concept of "responsibility":

DIY citizenship as we practice it takes seriously the concept of responsibility—not just the responsibility to follow the rules and accept legitimately imposed limits on our participation in society, but *the responsibility to hold our governments accountable for*

> *making rules to reflect the kind of society in which we want to live.* DIY citizenship as we approach it in our research about identification and identification documents is active, engaged, and sometimes critical citizenship. It has the potential to reveal and push the kinds of societal limits that we often take for granted. (McPhail et al., chapter 5, this volume; emphasis added)

Finally, given the intersecting media and economic landscapes that increasingly redefine the traditional identities associated with nation-states, "distributed citizenship" as introduced by Graham Meikle (chapter 27, this volume) suggests a promising direction for rethinking the historically overdetermined meanings of "citizenship."

The social implications of the shift to DIY citizenship are readily apparent. We contribute this collection of critical theorizations of making, in hopes of providing a starting point for others to extend such practices and as a foundation from which to examine the implications of DIY citizenship.

Notes

1. For an overview of the claims and critiques associated with democracy and social media, see Boler 2010.

2. We should also add that dominant institutions may also be working to appropriate the processes and outcomes of DIY activities. A case in point is the recent funding of Maker activities by DARPA and the participation of military personnel at the New York Maker Faire 2012 depicted in figure I.6. Such instances point to a somewhat different politicization of DIY than is typically considered by DIY enthusiasts and indicate a need for increased reflection of the type demonstrated by some chapters in this collection.

3. DIY Citizenship: Critical Making and Social Media conference, November 12–14, Toronto, Ontario. Video archive at http://www.diycitizenship.org.

4. These ethics of questioning educational practices and values come forward in this collection most prominently in part II.

5. For more on zines in this volume, see Chidgey, chapter 6, and Reitsamer and Zobl, chapter 24.

6. For more on craft in this volume, see Orton-Johnson, chapter 9, Kafai and Peppler, chapter 12, and Rosner and Foster, chapter 13.

References

Bennett, L., and A. Segerberg. 2012. The Logic of Connective Action. *Information, Community and Society* 15 (5): 739–768.

Boler, M., ed. 2010. *Digital Media and Democracy: Tactics in Hard Times*. Cambridge, MA: MIT Press.

Boler, M. 2013. Occupy Patriarchy: Will Feminism's Fourth Wave Be a Swell or a Ripple? In *Women in a Globalizing World: Transforming Equality, Development Diversity and Peace*, ed. Angela Miles, 582–590. Toronto: Inanna Press.

Boler, M., and C. Nitsou. 2014. Social Media and Global Protest: Hybrid Social Movements and Politics as the "Redistribution of the Sensible." Forthcoming in *Cyberactivism 2.0*, ed. Martha McCaughey. New York: Routledge.

Calhoun, C. J. 1992. *Habermas and the Public Sphere*. Cambridge, MA: MIT Press.

Doherty, B., A. Plows, and D. Wall. 2003. "The Preferred Way of Doing Things": The British Direct Action Movement. *Parliamentary Affairs* 56 (4): 669–686.

Federici, S. 2008. Precarious Labour: A Feminist Perspective. http://inthemiddleofthewhirlwind.wordpress.com/precarious-labor-a-feminist-viewpoint/.

Fraser, N. 1990. Rethinking the Public Sphere: A Contribution to the Critique of Actually Existing Democracy. *Social Text* (25/26): 56–80.

Gauntlett, D. 2011. *Making Is Connecting*, 1st ed. Cambridge: Polity Press.

Giddens, Anthony. 1991. *Modernity and Self-identity: Self and Society in the Late Modern Age*. Cambridge: Polity Press.

Gitlin, T. 1998. Public Sphere or Public Sphericules? In *Media, Ritual and Identity*, ed. Tamar Liebes and James Curran, 168–174. London: Routledge.

Habermas, J. 1962/1989. *The Structural Transformation of the Public Sphere: An Inquiry into a Category of Bourgeois Society*. Cambridge: Polity Press.

Hardt, M., and A. Negri. 2001. *Empire*. Cambridge, MA: Harvard University Press.

Hardt, M., and A. Negri. 2005. *Multitude: War and Democracy in the Age of Empire*. New York: Penguin Books.

Hartley, J. 1999. *The Uses of Television*. London: Routledge.

Hearn, A. 2008. Meat, Mask, Burden. *Journal of Consumer Culture* 8 (2): 197–217.

Jacka, E. 2003. Democracy as Defeat. *Television & New Media* 4 (2): 177–191.

Jordan, J. 1998. The Art of Necessity: The Subversive Imagination of Anti-road Protest and Reclaim the Streets. In *DiY Culture: Party and Protest in Nineties Britain*, ed. G. McKay, 129–151. London: Verso.

Levine, F., and C. Heimerl. 2008. *Handmade Nation: The Rise of DIY, Art, Craft, and Design*. Princeton: Princeton Architectural Press.

McKay, G. 1998. *DiY Culture: Party and Protest in Nineties Britain*. London: Verso.

Mouffe, Chantal. 1992. Democratic Citizenship and the Political Community. In *Dimensions of Radical Democracy: Pluralism, Citizenship, Community*, ed. Chantal Mouffe, 225–239. London: Verso.

Rainie, L., and B. Wellman. 2012. *Networked: The New Social Operating System*. Cambridge, MA: MIT Press.

Rancière, Jacques. 1999. *Disagreement: Politics and Philosophy*. Trans. Julie Rose. Minneapolis: University of Minnesota Press.

Rancière, Jacques. 2004. *The Politics of Aesthetics: The Distribution of the Sensible*. Trans. Gabriel Rockhill. London and New York: Continuum.

Ratto, M. 2011a. Critical Making: Conceptual and Material Studies in Technology and Social Life. *Information Society* 27 (4): 252–260.

Ratto, M. 2011b. Open Design and Critical Making. In *Open Design Now: Why Design Cannot Remain Exclusive*, ed. P. Atkinson, M. Avital, B. Mau, R. Ramakers, and C. Hummels, 202–209. Amsterdam: BIS Publishers.

Ratto, M., and S. Hoekema. 2009. Flwr Pwr: Tending the Walled Garden. In *Walled Garden*, ed. A. Dekker and A. Wolfsberger, 51–60. Rotterdam: Virtueel Platform.

Rosenberg, B. C. 2005. Scandinavian Dreams: DIY, Democratisation and IKEA. Transformations, Issue No. 11—Edges and Centres: Contemporary Experience and Lifestyle. http://www.transformationsjournal.org/journal/issue_11/article_02.shtml.

Spencer, A. 2005. *DIY: The Rise of Lo-Fi Culture*. London: Marion Boyars Publishers Ltd.

Stoker, G., A. Mason, A. McGrew, et al. 2011. *Prospects for Citizenship*. London: Bloomsbury Publishing PLC.

Tapper, J., and G. Zucker. 2011. *Craft Activism: People, Ideas, and Projects from the New Community of Handmade and How You Can Join In*. New York: Potter Craft.

Winner, L. 1992. Citizen Virtues in a Technological Order. *Inquiry: An Interdisciplinary Journal of Philosophy* 35 (3): 341.

I DIY and Activism: New Modes of Civic Engagement and Participatory Politics

DIY ethos and culture provide a compelling and coherent framework for understanding contemporary forms of activism and collective identities. The chapters in this section illuminate new hybrid forms and modalities of activism and digitally mediated networks where real/virtual, direct/mediated experiences are no longer distinguishable; online and offline activities meld and morph within our distributed networks afforded by mobile devices, social media, and information and communications technologies (ICTs). Due to the blurring of social and political practices and identities within our hybridized everyday lives, hybridity is redefining traditional understandings of the "political" and "politics" and enabling new modes of civic engagement and participatory politics.

The intersection of DIY and activism represented in part I highlights several recurrent themes that straddle the key question outlined in our introduction: How do different "maker identities," DIY citizens, and spaces of practice help us understand the necessary elements for liberatory and radical DIY citizenship? The chapters in this part illustrate diverse maker identities ranging from the fan activist (Jenkins; Burwell and Boler), to feminist zine makers (Chidgey), to tactical media activists like the Yes Men (Reilly), to indy radio collective activists (Dunbar-Hester) and hacktivists/maktivists (Mann; Milberry; McPhail et al.).

In chapter 1, Steve Mann outlines the hybrid modalities of activism, hactivism, and making, enabling him to contribute the valuable concept of "maktivism": "Maktivism often involves the moral, ethical, and lawful ('white hat') elements of the 'hacker' ethos, but not necessarily the illegal 'cracker' ethos. Maktivism combines the DIY (do-it-yourself) ethos of home renovation with the DIT (do-it-together) ethos of the GNU Linux and Free Software movement."

Milberry (chapter 2) outlines the historical context in which these modes of activism need be understood, emphasizing prefigurative politics, open source movements, and uses of technology to challenge capitalist norms:

> With the emergence of global justice movement(s) in the mid-1990s, tech activists began remaking the Internet in the image of the just society they pursue. Using free and open source software (FOSS), tech activists continue to build the digital infrastructure of the "newest social movements," developing *technologies of resistance* to support activists online. The newest social movements are contemporary, broadly anti-capitalist social movements that organize loosely around anarchist politics, informed by emancipatory theory. . . . By designing values into technology that are consonant with movement goals, tech activists engage in prefigurative politics. This self-reflexivity invokes the spirit of critical making as both an activity and a site for deepening a transformative sociotechnical praxis. In deploying FOSS across an increasingly commercialized and privatized web, tech activists enact their politics at both a technological and social level. Drawn from the free software and global justice movements, these values—including freedom, decentralization, heterarchy, autonomy, self-determination, collaboration, collectivism, and mutual aid—challenge capitalist norms that dominate the social factory both online and off.

Without a doubt, mediated networks and DIY culture are spawning new modalities and expressions of political and civic engagement. Before the Occupy Wall Street (OWS) movement of 2011 that swept North America and the globe following the Arab Spring, dominant discourses framed young people of this generation largely as disaffected, disenfranchised, and/or apathetic. As Jenkins (chapter 3) notes: "Existing literature suggests that young people are most apt to become politically involved if they come from families with a history of citizen participation and political activism, if they encounter teachers, especially in the civics classroom, who encourage them to reflect on and respond to current events, if they attend schools where they are allowed a voice in core decisions, and if they participate in extracurricular activities and volunteerism that gives back to their community."

This momentous historical period of uprisings around the globe reflects—among other radical shifts in global and local networked DIY protest—the political engagement and awakening for hundreds of thousands of first-time activists. These first-time activists of the twenty-first century include everyone from the millions of people who participated in global uprisings to the various fan activists discussed within these chapters. Adamant about new understandings of participatory democracy and thus central to any updated conceptions of DIY citizenship, the OWS movement's commitments to "horizontal leadership" and consensus decision making reflect a profoundly DIY ethos. The OWS movement exemplifies DIY citizenship in its refusal of existing hierarchical practices in favor of attempts to embody the utopian ideals of radically different processes of social organization, decision making, and leadership (Boler 2013; Boler and Nitsou 2014).

Another noteworthy instance of widespread, "first-time" activism was demonstrated in the record-breaking turnout for the 2010 Rally to Restore Sanity and/or Fear sparked by fake news pundits Jon Stewart and Stephen Colbert, which brought nearly half a million people of all political stripes to rally on the National Mall in Washington, DC, demanding responsibility and sanity on the part of corporate-owned media. This turnout of a civic-minded fan base of diverse ages mainly consisted of those who had never been to a political event or rally before (Reilly and Boler 2014). And while the majority of those attending the Rally to Restore Sanity and/or Fear do not identify as "activists" per se, the shared concerns for a "saner" world and the call for accountability from media and elected politicians demonstrate the kinds of hybrid activism that concern Jenkins's "Fan Activism as Participatory Politics: The Case of the Harry Potter Alliance" (chapter 3) and Burwell and Boler's "Rethinking Media Activism through Fan Blogging: How Stewart and Colbert Fans Make a Difference" (chapter 7).

Emergent forms of fan activism represent novel and quintessential examples of DIY citizenship. While activism has of course existed in myriad forms long before the advent of digital and social media, we are witnessing a sea change (one with which scholars can barely keep apace) in the blurring of the social and political, the political and personal. Global, and ubiquitous popular cultural engagement alongside participatory media enables unprecedented accessibility to the means of production and circulation, resulting in unpredictable and emergent forms of hybrid fandom. "While many other forms of DIY culture have sought to establish autonomy from mainstream culture, fandom exists at the intersection of grassroots and commercial media," writes Henry Jenkins. These chapters contribute innovative studies of how hybrid fandom constitutes new modes of civic engagement and redefines participatory politics.The globally networked fans united by popular cultural productions reflect DIY "maktivist" identities and definitively blur traditional distinctions between the social and political.

In contrast to traditional conceptions of activism, fan-based activists of the Harry Potter Alliance (Jenkins) and *The Daily Show* and *The Colbert Report* (Burwell and Boler) characterize the emergence of distinct, fan-based "maker identities." In the opening of chapter 3, Jenkins writes, "Fan cultures have long been cited as textbook examples of the larger phenomenon of DIY media production, and fan activism represents an exemplar of the ways that such creative communities might evolve their own models of political and civic participation."

Jenkins's (chapter 3) description details the close relationship between commercial ownership and grassroots. Indeed, this tension between corporate ownership and values and interventionist DIY ethos animates all of the practices considered in this part.

> Historically, fans have often entered civic discourse when they assert their collective rights as the most active and engaged segments of the media audience. *While many other forms of DIY culture have sought to establish autonomy from mainstream culture, fandom exists at the intersection between grassroots and commercial media.* Given this unstable positioning, the fan identity is often an embattled one, and efforts to save shows from cancellation or to rally support for a film project have helped to cement social ties between fans, define their shared interests, and shape their public status. *By the time these fan groups had defined an issue, identified decision makers, developed tactics, and educated and mobilized supporters, they had done all of the steps required for activism.* (emphasis added)

In her chapter on feminist zines, Chidgey (chapter 6) also notes the centrality of the intersection of commercial and grassroots in contemporary activist practices:

> As a form of alternative media, zines inevitably create different modes of production, representation, and consumption to those found in mainstream media industries. Yet they're not entirely separate entities—the skills learned through DIY media making can be brought into makers' professional lives and zinesters often appropriate and reuse materials from popular culture in their publications. As social documents of lived experience and cultural ephemera, zines are increasingly finding their way out of fringe communities and into libraries, archives, publishing houses, and classrooms. They provide excellent sites of narration around grassroots and DIY political identities, activism, and agendas.

DIY activities constitute modes of political intervention undertheorized by current concepts of civic engagement such as that of the public sphere. The chapters in part I thus serve both as sites for examining DIY and activism as well as arguments about new ways to conceptualize modern politics. As Burwell and Boler (chapter 7) conclude on this point:

> By thinking about fan *practices of making* (archives, blogs, websites, networks, communities), we also came to see that fans worked to *make a difference* (to other fans, to media power differentials, to untenable political situations) and to *make sense* (of technological change, of unreliable media accounts, of a world gone mad). In a project dedicated to "rethinking" media, politics, and citizenship, the questions that fan production generated constantly pushed us to rethink fundamental building blocks of contemporary citizenship practices and what counts as "political" engagement.

Two chapters in part I address the challenges of "leveling the playing field" of access to and confidence with tools of activism. Dunbar-Hester (chapter 4) describes the challenges faced by the Pandora Radio Project:

> The media activists sought to cultivate a particular mode of "maker" identity. They presented technical engagement as a strategy for leveling expertise and increasing political participation. In this, they recognized that tinkering is as much a form of cultural production as a technical one; the activists sought to produce not just technical artifacts but egalitarian social relations by eroding boundaries between experts and laypeople. Activists suggested that demystification of technology through widespread hands-on making could provide an alternative to prevalent technical cultures in which authority is not distributed but resides exclusively with experts.

Just as this collective struggled with the unequal social capital and hence confidence with which participants approached the creative activist possibilities, so does Reilly (chapter 8) emphasize the challenge of encouraging more populist and widespread DIY engagement of Yes Men media hoax tactics and practices:

> [Could] everyday citizens . . . replicate the Yes Men's successes, or [are] figures like Andy Bichlbaum and Mike Bonanno . . . truly exceptional individuals who pulled off hoaxes far beyond the reach of the uninitiated[?] . . . In a time of real political foment, the Yes Men are now training and mentoring groups to participate in the creation of media spectacles designed to highlight social justice issues and political struggles of great civic importance. The Yes Lab offers a bridge between the media hoaxing actions of a much-revered group and DIY citizens and groups who lack the knowledge, wherewithal, or infrastructure to see these hoaxes to fruition. The effort marks an important shift in their work, demonstrating how an already successful mode of activism can be taken up to facilitate the transmission and reproducibility of inspiring work. *What have the Yes Men taught me? If there's no application process to participating, we should really just do it ourselves.* (emphasis added)

References

Boler, M. 2013. Occupy Patriarchy: Will Feminism's Fourth Wave Be a Swell or a Ripple? In *Women in a Globalizing World: Transforming Equality, Development Diversity and Peace*, ed. Angela Miles, 582–590. Toronto: Inanna Press.

Boler, M., and C. Nitsou. 2014. Women Activists within the Leaderless Occupy Wall Street: Consciousness-Raising and Connective Action in Hybrid Social Movements. Forthcoming in *Cyberactivism 2.0*, ed. Martha McCaughey. New York: Routledge.

Reilly, I., and M. Boler. 2014. The Rally to Restore Sanity, Pre-politicization, and the Future of Politics. Forthcoming in *Communication, Culture and Critique*.

1 Maktivism: Authentic Making for Technology in the Service of Humanity

Steve Mann

Maktivists are social makers—people who make things for social change. Maktivism brings together the technology and media-technology activists as discussed by Milberry (chapter 2, this volume) and Dunbar-Hester (chapter 4, this volume); content-activists, as discussed by Jenkins (chapter 3,this volume), Chidgey (chapter 6, this volume), and Burwell and Boler (chapter 7, this volume); policy-activists, as discussed by McPhail et al. (chapter 5, this volume); and artists as discussed by Reilly (chapter 8, this volume). As such, Maktivism is not just making things that change/preserve/save the world/planet. A Maktivist is a maker who is authentic—not a poseur (Bricmont and Sokal 1998) or someone just following a trend or doing it for money, to get tenure, or to be popular. A Maktivist has a high degree of personal involvement and commitment in the existemological (existential epistemology, i.e., "learn-by-being" [Mann 2006]) sense. DIY maktivism was introduced in Toronto in 1998 by way of two courses: ECE1766 and ECE385—making material things and hacking GNU Linux device drivers to make those material things work in an Open Source cloud-computing mobile/portable/smartphone environment. The emphasis was on "tinquiry" (tinkering as inquiry) and spontaneous participatory "hacks" using found objects, in contrast to the more "professionalized," organized, and carefully planned approach to engineering that other professors usually teach.

In this framework, examples I used to teach "tinquiry" included a chair that had spikes that only retracted when a credit card was inserted in order to download a "License to Sit" (Mann 2001c); and Griefcase™, a briefcase equipped with a fingerprint scanner that can be opened by anyone other than its owner. Both these projects taught DIY "hacking" principles—each student obtained a surplus card reader and fingerprint scanner, and was taught how to reverse engineer these products and write GNU Linux device drivers for them. Griefcase was designed for encounters with security guards who demand to search briefcases upon exiting public libraries. The case included fingerprint scanners and wireless communications, arranged in such a way that the owner could not open the case, but anyone else could. In order for the owner of the case to submit to being searched, then, the guard had to submit to being fingerprinted (see figure 1.1; picture Copyleft S. Mann, 2000).

Over the past fourteen years, by way of these maktivism courses, I've taught hundreds of students how to salvage computers from dumpsters, how to hack ID card readers, fingerprint scanners, smartphones, etc., and how to write GNU Linux device drivers and cloud-based computing applications for surplus junk. My aim has been to teach technology as "intervention by users, rather than a mysterious black box" (Milberry, chapter 2, this volume), in order to "resist" the hegemony of what would otherwise be surveillance technologies (Milberry 2012). This understanding of the normally closed-source world of surveillance technologies aims to "liberat[e] human beings from all circumstances that enslave them" (Horkheimer 1982, 244)—opening up the "black boxed technologies hidden within contemporary identification practices" (McPhail et al., chapter 5, this volume).

Maktivism often involves the moral, ethical, and lawful ("white hat") elements of the "hacker" ethos, but not necessarily the illegal "cracker" ethos. Maktivism combines the DIY (do-it-yourself) ethos of home renovation with the DIT (do-it-together) ethos of the GNU Linux and Free Software movement. In that spirit, *this chapter you are now reading was written using LaTeX on a computer running GNU Linux, rather than Microsoft Word, partly*

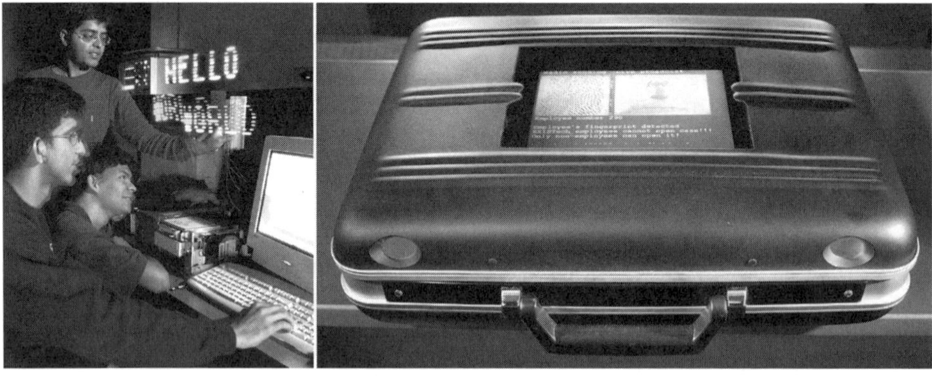

Figure 1.1
Griefcase

because Microsoft is so anti-DIY, that many of us are opposed to Word on moral and ethical grounds, and partly because Word does not produce good results when compared to typesetting programs like LaTeX, which evolved in and of a more open scientific spirit. LaTeX is Open Source and constitutes a DIY effort created as part of the hobbyist DIY community that also built GNU Linux. In this sense, the very way this chapter itself was written embodies the ("white hat") hacktivist ethos (Milberry and Anderson 2009).

Maktivism and hacktivism are not the same thing, however, in that maktivism necessarily involves materiality, or matter (i.e., that which has mass and occupies space, e.g., solids, liquids, and gases), and is therefore not limited to merely writing or modifying computer programs. In short, thoughts matter, but also matter matters. As Madonna would phrase it, "You know that we are living in a material word. And I am a material girl."

With the rise of the World Wide Web, we have increasingly been living in the post-material word, in which material thinking and materiality or physicality has given way to abstract concepts like cyberspace and cyborg space. But we have now come full circle, though, back to what I call the "post-post-material age" or "post-cyborg age," wherein we must combine the material (physical) and the immaterial (computational) worlds.

A good "motto" by which the maktivist should live, then, is "Advancing Technology for Humanity," which is also the tagline of the world's largest technical society, the Institute of Electrical and Electronics Engineers (IEEE). In slightly different words, the IEEE "stands at the forefront of technological change for the betterment of humanity" (Advancing Technology for Humanity 2013). Its 2013 International Symposium on Techology and Society is also consistent with this goal (2013 IEEE International Symposium on Technology and Society).

In this framework, maktivism is understood through praxistemology (Mann 2012b) as having three components, not unlike a tripod, which is supported on all three of the following "legs," denoted, for brevity, as Praxis (P); Existentiality (E); and Questioning/inquiry/critique/study (Q).

1. Praxis: Praxis, from the Greek word "praxis," "practice," "action," "making," or "doing," refers to the materially physical practice of action, doing, making, or the like. Specifically, praxis is the particular kind of action, doing, or making typically found in the field of engineering: "Scientists think, engineers make" (Karl et al. 2012).

Heidegger laid the foundation for thinking about the relationship between technology and materiality/matter that led to some of the projects I was involved with at MIT (e.g., "Things That Think," "Bits and Atoms"), as well as more recent variations on this theme, such as the "Internet of Things." While we were studying under Professor Stephen Benton (the inventor of white-holography) at MIT, one of my classmates, Paula Dawson, was in the midst of creating some of the world's best examples of Material Thinking, for example, holographic artworks like "To Absent Friends" (Dawson 2012). Examples of this "Material Thinking" (in the Heideggerian-sense [Bolt 2007; de Freitas 2009]) form the core of what is taught in University of Toronto's first-year Engineering Sciences courses entitled *Praxis I and Praxis II* (http://www.praxis.uoftengineering.com/). I must also emphasize here that there is something refreshingly authentic about the Material Thinking community in New Zealand in particular—their papers are all available online without the need for registration, login, or paying a fee—demonstrating the true authenticity of maktivism. This brings me to the second leg of my "tripod" model.

2. Existentiality: Existentiality embodies three important attributes: (1) existence before essence, i.e., the opposite of problem-solving (Whereas Plato first envisioned a circle in terms of a collection of points equidistant from another point, and then reduced it to practice, I believe we should also allow room for doing the opposite, to be willing to tinker, or build something, first, and then figure out what it is or what it can be useful for afterward. It is possible that some of these things may never be useful in any traditional sense. We should be willing to just tinker without having to make a plan and a Gantt Chart first.); (2) self-determination and mastery over one's own destiny, through personal commitment, involvement, and experience, including "learn-by-being," such as wearable computing as a way of learning about computers by "being" a computer; and (3) authenticity as connected with creativity, i.e., being true to one's self. An example of what I mean by authenticity is an engineer who loves engineering, rather than an engineer working for just money or from a sense of duty. As Einstein has said, "love [of a subject of study or of one's work] is a better master than duty." This also means being true (authentic) to one's self, rather than being driven by trends or fashions. The opposite of this is a "poseur," or a person who works or studies in a particular field because it is fashionable, trendy, or pays well. Praxistemology is not merely transdisciplinary, interdisciplinary, or cross-disciplinary work, but, rather, trans/inter/cross-*passionary*. To paraphrase Einstein, *passion is a better master than discipline*! Sartre and Kafka help us understand (often by way of negative examples) existence, freedom, and authenticity. Moreover, Goethe's "Faust" prompts us to ask, should we, as academics, bow to peer-review and peer-acceptance—or hold to our principles, be they LaTeX, Linux, free online publishing, or community gardening? Authenticity favors an Artistic/Academic/humanistic integrity ("A" integrity) over the Business/Bookie integrity ("B" integrity) of a mafia boss who makes deals with a handshake and always honors his word.

3. Questioning: Questioning refers to work with an epistemological or pedagogical element that asks important moral and ethical questions, that is, it embodies critique in the tradition more commonly associated with the arts than with old-school engineering. To quote James Baldwin: "The purpose of art is to lay bare the questions that have been hidden by the answers." Some notable "questioners" include the following:

Leonardo da Vinci was said to be the best engineer of his time. But he was more than just a problem solver. He was also an artist, scientist, and inventor. The journal *Leonardo* (www.leonardo.info/isast/leostory.html) honors this, and is now the leading journal for the application of contemporary science and technology to the arts.

Marvin Minsky is the father of AI (artificial intelligence) (Laplante 1996). Additionally, he also invented the confocal scanning microscope and many other useful inventions. But Minsky had an amazingly deep understanding of all aspects of the human condition. My favorite of his inventions was something that has become known as "the most useless machine ever," which he built at Bell Labs with Claude Shannon. The machine consisted of a box with an on/off switch on the outside. Whenever the switch is turned on, the box opens and a robotic hand reaches out to turn the switch off. Remarkably, the machine's sole purpose is to turn itself off!

Arthur Ganson, a sculptor with MIT's Department of Mechanical Engineering, makes artworks with existentialist themes. For lack of a better word I'd call him a "praxistentialist"—one who engages in the practice of embodied existentialism. One piece in particular which speaks to this theme is entitled "Machine with Concrete." In this piece, a motor is geared down through a series of gears, each turning more slowly (and more forcefully) than the one before it. The last gear is fixed in a block of concrete.

Albert Einstein contends that "the point is to develop the childlike inclination for play and the childlike desire for recognition and to guide the child over to important fields for society. Such a school demands from the teacher that he be a kind of artist" (Einstein 1954/1982, 63).

As such, Einstein notes further, "the pursuit of truth and beauty is a sphere of activity in which we are permitted to remain children all our lives." What separates children from many adults, then, is authenticity ("A" integrity) versus professionalism ("B" integrity). Professionalism is a necessary and important part of society in many fields like dentistry or safety certification of bridges, skyscrapers, and aircraft. But there is, or should be, room in the world for "children" like Einstein, that is, for people with "A" integrity. Engineering schools and other universities should encourage fun, frolic, and unstructured play as means for invention of new technologies, as well as new ways of looking at technology and society!

In this sense, a praxistemologist is an "inventopher" (inventor philosopher) (Mann and Janzen 2012) with a playful childlike scientific spirit like Einstein. "A" integrity is Einstein's spirit-reduced-to-practice/praxis. The inventopher combines thinking with making, thus embodying a social awareness of making, such as that fostered by organizations like the IEEE SSIT. As they note,

> "Scientists think; engineers make." Engineering is fundamentally an activity, as opposed to an intellectual discipline. The goal of science and philosophy is to know; the goal of engineering is to do something good or useful. . . . It took until the mid-20th century for engineers to develop the kind of self-awareness that leads to thinking about engineering and technology as they relate to society. Until about 1900, most engineers felt comfortable in a "chain-of-command" structure in which the boss—whether it be a military commander, a corporation, or a wealthy individual—issued orders that were to be carried out to the best of the engineer's technical ability. Fulfillment of duty was all that was expected. But as the range and depth of technological achievements grew, engineers, philosophers, and the public began to realize that we had all better take some time and effort to think about the social implications of technology. That is the purpose of the IEEE Society on Social Implications of Technology (SSIT): to provide a forum for discussion of the deeper questions about the history, connections, and future trends of engineering, technology and society. (Karl et al. 2012)

Others have also proposed the combination of thinking and making, which is known as "Material Thinking" (Bolt 2007; de Freitas 2009) or "Critical Making" (Ratto 2011), or, if it contains a political element, "Hacktivism" (Boler 2008). In some sense, maktivism, and its academic counterpart, praxistemology, can be thought of as authentic and self-involved forms of material thinking or critical making. Praxistemology is an attempt to create a(n) (un)discipline that is simultaneously both broad and deep, across design, art, sustainism/science, technology, engineering (inventing and making things), and mathematics (of which I regard music/musicology as a branch), plus in some sense a kind of "boundless boundlessness."

DASTEM: STEM is an acronym for Science, Technology, Engineering, and Mathematics. A major thrust in the agenda of public education is integrating these four subject areas. Other interdisciplinary efforts like those of MIT's Media Laboratory focus on AST (Arts+Science+Technology). I coined the term "DASTEM" to denote Design + Art + Science/Sustainism + Technology + Engineering/Environment/Enterprise + Mathematics/Music/Musicology to highlight the importance of design. I regard Sustainism as a branch of science, along the lines of organizations like Science for Peace (www.scienceforpeace.ca) that address through environmentalism, nuclear weapons, greenhouse gas, climate change, and the like. Moreover, publications like *Leonardo*, the aforementioned journal of the International Society for the Arts, Sciences and Technology (ISTAST), also combine these subjects. There is also a festival called the Festival of Art, Science, and Technology (FAST) (www.arts.mit.edu/fast).

A DASTEMist is not merely a "T-shaped" or "tee-shaped" thinker (breadth + depth in only one area), but actually what I call a "tree-shaped" thinker or a person with "tree-shaped" skill sets that have broad-reaching rhizomic roots, combined with deep-reaching roots into many fields of study, plus skyward reaching branches.

DAST could then put a "heart and soul" into the "STEM," for example, going beyond "multidisciplinary" to something I call "multipassionary" or "interpassionary" or "transpassionary," that is, passion is a better master than discipline (Albert Einstein said that "love is a better master than duty"). Passion means personal involvement ("A" integrity), like we often see in the DIY social movement, which is about personal empowerment. But that personal involvement often comes through group efforts and from being citizens rather than merely consumers (Levy and Bonomo 1999; Jenkins 2009). Thus DIY is typically really DIT, so maybe it should just be called "do it" (individually *and* collectively)!

Mens et manus: Minsky and Ganson are both associated with MIT. Many schools have a Latin motto that is often just to sound scholarly but without meaning very much. MIT's motto, however, "Mens et manus," is Latin for "Mind and hand." This is the blend of praxis and theory that I think we need to encourage and further develop.

Copyleft: In addition to MIT's blend of praxis and theory, there's a third branch: inquiry or critique. We have in the preceding examples a playful sense of awe and wonder, and an inquiry/critique. As an example of the latter, consider Richard Stallman's notion of "copyleft." Stallman's philosophy, which emphasizes open access, formed the basis for Wikipedia and Linux. As the playful reversal of "copyright," copyleft forms a critique of the power relationships of intellectual property. This is yet another example of deep thinking combined with action and, in particular, the primacy of "A" integrity over "B" integrity.

GNU/Linux: Richard Stallman (GNU) and Linus Torvalds (Linux) created one of the highest-profile success stories for DIY volunteer-driven hobbyist-driver collaboration—creating what is perhaps the world's most reliable and capable operating system.
Wikipedia: Jimmy Wales built directly upon Richard Stallman's concept of inverse copyright, or "copyleft," to create Wikipedia, the "largest and most popular general reference work on the Internet," with "23 million articles, over 4.1 million in the English Wikipedia alone . . . collaboratively [written] by volunteers around the world. Almost all of its articles can be edited by anyone with access to the site, . . . [there are] editions of Wikipedia in 285 languages. . . . having an estimated 365 million readers worldwide. In 2011, Wikipedia received an estimated 2.7 billion monthly page views from the United States alone."
Lawrence Lessig is an American professor and political activist known for advocating balanced copyright and trademark laws (Wikipedia.org) that place "A" integrity ahead of "B" integrity. This integrity informs his opinion on politics: "Politics is a rare sport where the amateur is better than the professional" (Johnson 2011).
WebCite: Gunther Eysenbach envisioned doing for recipients (scholars reading and citing information) what Wikipedia envisioned for transmitients (authors wishing to give away their writings for free). Eysenbach's initiative, WebCite, enables ephemeral online documents to be reliably cited in scholarly literature (Eysenbach 2008).
Praxistemologicality: I now express, in my own opinion, an approximate degree of Praxism, Existentiality, and 'Quiry in three of the foregoing examples.

These "ratings" (opinions) are not meant to be scientifically precise, but, rather, merely to convey, with visual simplicity, an opinion that these great achievements are all high in Praxism, somewhat high in Existentiality, and very high in inQuiry/critiQue/epistemology/pedagogy. Namely, they were each created of their creator's own volition, not to solve a problem that was presented to the creator by an employee or by social trends and fashions. In this way the work can be considered to be authentic (i.e., not the work of an employee or a poseur driven by job requirements or by trends or fashion).

Of these examples, I believe that

1. "Machine with Concrete" exhibits the strongest **P**raxis (not surprising, given that Ganson is an incredible sculptor and craftsman);
2. "Copyleft" exhibits strongest **E**xistentiality. Not only does Richard Stallman "walk the walk" of Freedom, but the concept of freedom itself has, in many ways, laid the foundation for GNU, Linux, Wikipedia, and much of

the Free World. Those familiar with Sartre and Kafka will no doubt see that Stallman has a strong sensibility and sensitivity to these issues.
3. "Useless Machine" exhibits the strongest **Q**uestion; in that it is perhaps the most pure and simple example that can be used in teaching. When I showed all three projects to my five-year-old daughter, she told me she really wants (and needs!) a Useless Machine. The epistemological power of Useless Machine for pedagogy is its universality—immediately understood—and appreciated by people of all ages or disciplines.

LBB (learn-by-being): Where the foregoing three examples could be stronger, however, was in their sense of existentiality. Existentiality speaks to authenticity and freedom, as well as to "being." "Being," in this sense, includes teaching children how to measure something, using anthropomorphic units, or measurements based on the human body, such as are inches (width of the thumb) and feet, or "hands"—the units used to measure the height of horses. The human body itself becomes the ruler! When we learn about rulers and measurement by becoming the measurement instrument, I call this "learn-by-being" (Mann and Janzen 2012).

I tell my five-year-old that when we're planting flowers in the garden, we're going to use inches and feet to determine seed spacing, but if we were building a nuclear reactor we might want to use angstroms or nanometers. A garden is a fun place to be, where a lot of learning can take place, and mistakes can be made without grave consequences.

The very inaccuracy of anthropomorphic units, especially when used across various age groups, is why "learn-by-being" is so powerful as a teaching tool. It teaches children that it is OK to make mistakes, to take guesses, and to get a rough imprecise understanding of the world around us in our own special units (e.g., our own feet, despite the fact that we all differ).

Making measurements in this way exercises all three elements of praxistemology: putting into practice a personal involvement in the epistemology of measurement.

LBB then, can be summarized by considering a chronology of learning methodologies:

Q Traditional book-learning;
P Learn-by-doing, e.g., constructionism, constructivism, PBL (project/problem-based-learning);
E Learn-by-being, existential education, existemology (existential epistemology).

The foregoing examples attempt to illustrate what is meant by praxistemology. It is instructive to also include some examples of what is not praxistemology, via the use of negative examples.

Negative example 1: An armchair critic. This is a person who is not engaged in praxis.
Negative example 2: A worker in a fast-food environment. Such a person often does the work out of a sense of duty and may be less personally involved. There is some degree of practice and craft but a lesser degree of existentiality and inquiry.

I am not saying that such practice is of lesser value than other practices—indeed, it may be quite useful to society. I am simply saying that such practice is not praxistemology.
Negative example 3: An engineering professor in it for the money. Whereas such a professor may design labs (praxis) and do teaching ('quiry), there can be a lack of authenticity and personal job-transcending involvement.
Negative example 4: Bandwagon hacktivist. Political activism and hacking have both become quite fashionable. Numerous "hacker spaces" have emerged to fill a need for people who want to enter the world of hacking. Publications like Make Magazine have begun to take on military funding and are not as "pure" in their pursuit as they once were.

Again, I am not saying all hacktivists lack authenticity—there are obviously some who do—but the numbers of followers have grown tremendously as the "hacker" or "maker" tradition has entered the mainstream, and a surface vivacity of "authenticity" (authenticity as in "handmade"—not in the deeper aforementioned sense) has become fashionable.

Praxistemology is like the tripod I previously mentioned: it cannot stand up unless all three of the legs (P, E, and Q) are sufficiently present.

In this next section, I describe examples from my own practice of inventions that I hope are authentic attempts at inquiry.

Wearable computing: During my childhood, back in the 1970s (when computers were usually massive machines that required large computer rooms) I was, as far as I know, one of only two children in our city (Hamilton, Ontario) to own a computer. It was one of the first "microcomputers." I attached it to myself as a prosthetic extension of my mind and body. For more than thirty years, I have lived my everyday life in a computer-mediated world. The pictures below document various stages of my "Augmediated Reality" work that ran from the 1970s to the present.

In the 1970s and 1980s, people thought it was a crazy idea to have a body-borne computer. But when I took these inventions and ideas to MIT in the early 1990s to start a wearable computing project, people eventually began to see the merit in wearable computing. I've been recognized as "the father of wearable computing" (Mitchell 2013), and wearable computing is now a multi-billion-dollar industry. But I was not motivated by money or by trying to solve a specific problem. Instead, my wearable computer emerged more from tinkering than from planning.[1]

License to sit: Wearable computing brought me directly in touch with a sociopolitical inquiry on intellectual property. With wearable computing, the computer becomes very much a part of the mind and body, and after more than thirty years of having a computer be part of my body, I no longer really distinguish between "thinking" and "computing" (Mann 2001b, 2006).

Moreover, in the world of computing, software is often protected by patents, copyrights, trade secrets, and the like. In the world of wearable computing these restrictions can have the effect of creating "thought crimes." For example, if I think of the square root of a number, and part of my "brain" comprises silicon chips, can my thoughts end up being illegal if they drift toward patentable subject matter? When we use computing as part of our bodies, then not only are parts of our bodies owned by licensors, but the licensors control what we can do with our bodies and also can become "thought police."

Computer programs are often protected by floating licenses, and each license is called a "seat." If you manage a large computer network, you might install a "license server" or "license manager" that allows no more than ten people to use a particular computer program on your network. It is referred to as a "ten-seat floating license." My project SeatSafe (see figure 1.2) draws attention to the social implications of these proprietary licensing limits. In the world of computing, artificial scarcity is created by preventing a computer program from working unless a "license" fee is paid. Typically in large organizations, software vendors implement "floating seat licenses." These licenses limit the total number of people or instances that can use a computer program at the same time. Allowable instances of the program are called "seats."

In the 1990s and the early 2000s, my work on wearable computing was shown in various museums such as the Smithsonian, MoMA, Stedelijk, and the Science Museum, among others. When I was asked to produce an exhibit on wearable computing for Independent Curators International, I built a chair with spikes that retract when a credit card is inserted to "download a seating license," as shown in figure 1.2.

The philosophical underpinnings of this piece have many different levels. On the surface, it speaks to the commodification of "public space" and quasi-public space. Akin to park benches with dividers to prevent people from getting too comfortable, or the box-planters with serrated sharp edges

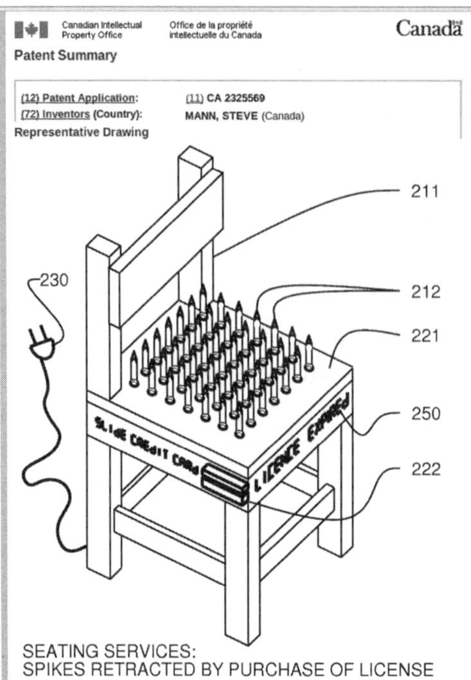

Figure 1.2
SeatSale

to prevent "vermin of the two-legged variety" from sitting down, SeatSale envisions a dystopian future where public space has been eroded and all space is controlled.

On another level, SeatSale is a reverse computing metaphor. Computing metaphors include concepts like the "trash can" on a Macintosh, or the whole concept of the "desktop metaphor." These metaphors bring objects that are familiar in the real world into the computing world. SeatSale does the opposite: it takes a concept familiar in the world of computing such as "seat license" and brings it out into the real world. For example, a software vendor might sell a "ten-seat floating license," meaning that ten people can use a program at the same time. In the world of engineering, I can remember many times when I wasn't able to run a particular program because too many other people were running it. So we'd sometimes have to track down each person and find out who was away for lunch and call them up to ask if we could shut down their program and free up a seat.

This notion of artificial scarcity—something I call "deconomics" or "sabotage economics"—is absurd in some way, and we can see that absurdity more clearly if we take the concept of the floating seat license and bring it out into the real world. With wearable computing, or smartphones, cyborg space and the real world become one and the same. So in "SeatSale: License to Sit," I asked what would happen if the real world took on aspects of the virtual world of software, like the artificially created scarcity and "deconomics/sabotage economics" used in software licensing.

Artificial scarcity becomes particularly absurd in the domain of wearable computing, for instance, where a "site license" might become a "sight license" if the computer program in a seeing aid (electric eyeglass) needs a license fee to run. Or, imagine a pacemaker that stops working because the software license for the program expires, like the license in programs like Matlab that expire at a certain point in time—the program stops running and won't work after that time period is up unless you pay more money to extend the license.

On a third level, Seatsale functioned as a series of teaching examples for teaching DIY "hacking" principles. Normally closed and secret systems like identification cards and surveillance technologies thus become opened up to inquiry. While using Seatsale as a teaching tool, I had each student obtain a surplus card reader and fingerprint scanner and taught them how to reverse engineer these products and write GNU Linux device drivers for them, etc., to think critically about the idea of licensing.

Internet of people: The I of T (Internet of Things) (VanKranenburg et al. 2011) has put sensors on the things around us. But now many of us are also putting sensors on ourselves. The sensors on people give rise to an **Internet of People, Places, and Things**, not just an Internet of Things, in that putting sensors on people will create huge strides forward in health and wellness, for individuals who choose to self-monitor. For example, an individual can now transmit live streaming (or captured) ECG (electrocardiogram), together with live first-person video, to a physician who can see what the patient is doing while examining the corresponding ECG waveforms. This can help determine the root cause of heart-related problems and identify causes of stress in the patient's environment.

Veillance: Consider, for example, a "black box" health recorder that captures information about a patient and the environment around the patient, much like the black box flight recorder on an aircraft. In the event of physical assault, murder, or accidental death, such a device might help determine the cause of injuries or death. In less-extreme examples, such a device might also help people improve the quality of their lives by helping them (and others they trust, such as their doctors or health advisers) understand the world around them.

Putting sensors on people does, however raise important privacy and copyright issues. For example, is a local capture of data for personal use considered a copy? When widely used as a vision aid, do we need to rethink open versus closed (or "clopen" to use a portmanteau coined by Vardi [2012]) access?

We already accept the I of T. And we already accept cameras on things, namely, **sur**veillance. Surveillance is a French word that means "to watch from above." Police watch citizens. Corporations watch their customers . . . But "veillance" (simply "to watch") means that sensing will occur in all directions, not just from the top down. However, protecting human life is much more important than protecting merchandise, and putting cameras on people (this is known as **sous**veillance) is a natural and direct way of achieving human security (King and Murray 2000, 2001–2002) by putting people first in a world that has previously been focused on the security of property (places and things). A transition from surveillance to veillance becomes likely—a transition in sensing (not just for security but also for quality of life and many other applications) from "things" to "persons, places, and things." The Internet of People, Places, and Things will create a more complete picture than merely the Internet of Things. For example, putting cameras on people will give rise to a veillance society rather than the surveillance society arising from putting cameras only on property (places and things). This transformation in our society is being enabled by miniaturization and mass production. Cameras that were once big and heavy gave "intelligence" to land and buildings. Now they're small enough to give that "intelligence" to people. With the growing population of the elderly, and as all of us age and our eyesight gets worse, we will look to Digital Eye Glass to help us see better. Our eyeglass prescriptions will be adaptive, automatically updating and adapting to whatever activity we're engaged in.

Giving people the ability to see is more important—and less privacy-invasive—than giving property the ability to see. The existential nature of Glass (i.e., the everyday use of it, as if it were a part of the mind and body) brings it beyond the borders of a research lab and out into the real world.

Sousveillance: Surveillance has, associated with it, an implicit politics. Even those who allege to be politically unbiased (e.g., those who merely study surveillance) are, by their very focus on surveillance and their exclusion of sousveillance, strongly biased and strongly political despite their allegedly neutral stance. The logical reciprocal to surveillance is "sousveillance" or "undersight," to describe "watching from below" (from the French word "sous," which means "from below").

I became fascinated with the otherwise hidden sociopolitical machinery that became very evident to me, as viewed through Glass (see figure 1.3) that nobody else could see. One interesting discovery was the reactions of those engaged in surveillance. It turned out that peer acceptance was not so much the issue as acceptance by authorities such as security guards and facility owners—the very people architecting and maintaining the "surveillance super highway." For example, of all the people in a department store or office building, it seemed as if the security staff in particular was the most upset with the use of a camera-based seeing aid in its establishment. These persons, in particular, objected to Glass out of fear of cameras, even though the Glass originally did not record anything (images were merely processed and passed through to the output side of the Glass).

Sur/Sousveillance: There are now hundreds or thousands of books, papers, conferences, and projects on sousveillance. Whereas surveillance is dominated by governments, corporations, and organizations, sousveillance

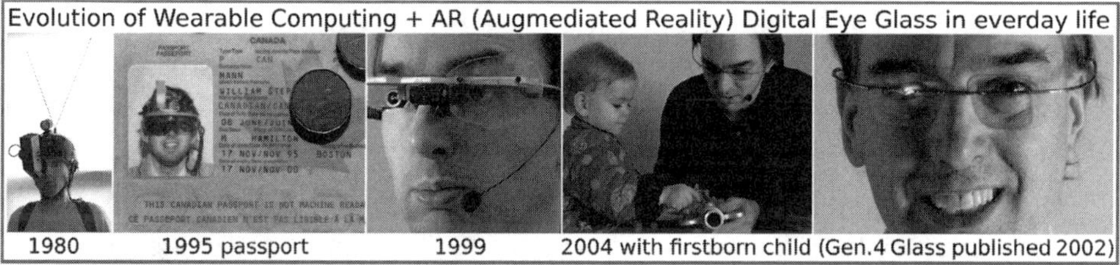

"Through the Glass, Lightly," IEEE Technology and Society, Vol. 31, Number 3, Fall 2012, p.10–14

Mann was recognized as "Father of AR" and the "Father of Wearable Computing" (IEEE ISSCC 2000)

Figure 1.3
DIY Glass

tends to be the work of individual people, in a DIY tradition that also includes tracking not only the information itself but also when large organizations choose to destroy or hide information (negative sousveillance) (Reynolds 2011).

In addition to publishing this work in scholarly research journals, work on sousveillance also often appears in the mainstream media, because it has a direct effect on society, particularly in the case of QR codes, or the two-dimensional barcodes often found on supermarket shelves, which advise consumers to use their smartphones to obtain pre-purchase information. For example, the signage on a box of watermelon advises shoppers to use their smartphones to see a sales pitch on the product to help them make a purchase decision. But many of these retail establishments which use QR codes also have signs saying "NO CELLPHONE IN STORE" and "NO CAMERAS/VIDEO." So participants are simultaneously required to use a camera, and forbidden from doing so, in order to see this content. Additionally, customers are frequently harassed by store security staff while trying to experience a little bit of augmediated reality.

Whereas Glass helps people see better, without *necessarily* recording video, I've also been working on other cameras that do the opposite: lifelong video recording without *necessarily* trying to help people see better. This project originally took the form of a camera necklace that mimics the appearance of the typical surveillance domes yet is instead a fully functional Wearable Wireless Webcam for life logging (lifelong cyborg logging), also known as life logging, moblogging (mobile logging), or the like. In 1998 I built a series of neck-worn domes, some with built-in augmented reality and gesture recognition (Mann 2000).

Although there are no laws against taking photographs of private buildings from public spaces (e.g., public roads and sidewalks), there have been numerous cases of security guards harassing photographers. Palmer and Whyte (2010) have noted a "simultaneous increase in state surveillance and the restriction of the right to take photographs in public . . . monopolize the decision as to who constitutes the citizenry of photography, . . . [and raise] questions about artistic and political responses to surveillance and photography restrictions" (177).

Meanwhile, police around the world are installing surveillance cameras throughout entire cities. Computer vision is being applied to surveillance, as well as to energy management. Just as there is a camera in most cell phones, soon there will be a camera in most light fixtures, including streetlights, for both occupancy sensing (see http://www.lsgc.com/pixelview/) and security (see http://intellistreets.com/). In 2007, the city of Liverpool made plans of this nature. "THOUSANDS of old-fashioned street lights in Mersey side [were] set to be dismantled and replaced with hi-tech CCTV-equipped lamps. The £32.7m scheme would see about 14,000 lamp posts across Knowsley modernized" (Coligan 2007).

Total surveillance has crept into most facets of our lives, including surveillance cameras in washrooms, changing rooms, and locker rooms. A 2007 *CBC News* headline indicates that Alberta's privacy commissioner is in favor of locker room surveillance cameras: "Cameras can stay in Talisman's locker room, says commissioner" (CBC News 2007). And modern automatic flush toilets, faucets, and sensor-operated showers are starting to use more sophisticated camera-based computer-vision technologies (e.g., US Patent 5828793). I call this "liquid surveillance"—surveillance (or Internet) of uncountable "stuff" like water, not just surveillance (or Internet) of countable "things" like bottles of water. More completely, "fluid surveillance" covers liquids like water, as well as surveillance of air, as can be attained by applying computer vision beyond lighting + HVAC to AWL (air, water, and light) to achieve total (sur)veillance of persons, places, things, AND stuff (Mann 2001a).

Conversely, when citizens point their cameras at the architects of the "surveillance superhighway," or simply when photographers take pictures of bridges, buildings, or surveillance cameras, they often come under attack, especially as police have placed photographers under suspicion. Police advertising campaigns promote surveillance but also ask people to report anyone taking photos and making notes about security to the police. Thus, a professor or student simply studying surveillance is likely to be harassed, investigated, and possibly harmed.

This reaction, moreover, comes at a time when innocent suspects have been roughed up by police. Some have even been killed as a result of heightened suspicion and cases of mistaken identity. For example, Jean Charles de Menezes, a Brazilian electrician, was shot to death in 2005 by police in a London subway, erroneously identified as a bombing suspect. Police seized the closed-circuit television (CCTV) recordings of the event and claimed they were blank! Menezes was shot in a crowded subway car where lots of people could have recorded the incident, but police and security guards have made people afraid to record what they see. *NBC News* and the *Miami Herald* reported on another case, that "On Memorial Day 2011, Narces Benoit witnessed and filmed a group of Miami police officers shooting and killing a suspect . . . He was then confronted by officers who handcuffed him and smashed his cellphone, but Benoit was able to sneakily preserve the video . . . he discreetly removed the [memory] card and placed it in his mouth" (Choney 2011).

It is noteworthy to consider some of the spaces in which I have been (and many others will be, as the technology becomes widespread) forbidden from entering, or where problems were encountered.[2] Of these locations, changing rooms and movie theaters emerged as the most inaccessible to the "silicon mind" and "Glass eye" that many of us will soon embrace.

Accessibility requirements will force changing rooms and washrooms to become "universal" (i.e., family-oriented with individual compartments), as washrooms are a basic need that cannot be denied to those of us who happen to have computer chips on or in our bodies. But movie theaters will remain as the central locus of contention between the "cyborg" and his or her environment, as per the Criminal Code of Canada, which states,

> (1) A person who, without the consent of the theatre manager, records in a movie theatre a performance of a cinematographic work within the meaning of section 2 of the Copyright Act or its soundtrack (a) is guilty of an indictable offence and liable to imprisonment.

Interpreted most broadly, the human brain is a recording device, and remembering a portion of a "cinematographic work" would constitute a criminal offense. But such a law is likely to be applied in a discriminatory way that criminalizes cyborgs as "existential contraband" (those of us who *are* cameras are, by our mere existence, contraband). As more people use electric eyeglasses, augmented reality, lifelong video capture devices, life gloggers, Personal Safety Devices, and so on, a large percentage of the population could be criminalized for mere memory even if they never disseminated any of their memories! Thus we can see a number of problems as the interests (some legitimate and some excessive) of copyright clash with the interests of personal use.

Veillance studies: Although there are a number of studies on the topic of surveillance, we need to look beyond surveillance to understand these problems. More generally, consider surveillance as an axis from left to right, in that we can have varying amounts of surveillance. Privacy activists might wish us to move toward or remain at the origin, whereas security activists might wish us to move further toward the right. A separate axis is sousveillance (e.g., body-worn or handheld cameras). The amount of surveillance and the amount of sousveillance can vary independently. Veillance is the total of surveillance and sousveillance. What I call "McVeillance" is defined as proliferation of surveillance while opposing sousveillance. (More generally, McVeillance is defined as the ratio [geometrically, or difference, arithmetically] of surveillance to sousveillance [Mann 2012a]).

It should be noted that both those in favor of surveillance and those opposed to it are viewing the world on a one-dimensional axis. Even those who claim to be neutral (i.e., to merely study surveillance without professing a "for" or "against" bias) are seeing the situation from a one-sided, or highly-biased, "surveillance-only" viewpoint. Thus I propose "veillance studies" (Mann 2012c) as a more neutral and unbiased framework than "surveillance studies" (Lyon 2007), which necessarily favors surveillance over other directions of veillance. By analogy, imagine replacing "political studies" with "conservative studies," when you live in a country that has both a conservative and a liberal party. You could claim that you're neither for nor against conservatives—you just study—in an ostensibly objective fashion. By omitting liberals from the discussion, your bias has been demonstrated.

La potence de la veillance: The French word for "the gallows" is "la potence." This word derives from the Latin word for power, "potential," from potens, meaning "powerful." Potence, accordingly, represents the coercive physical and/or ideological enforcement informed by surveillance. Foucault's book *Surveiller et Punir* outlines how surveillance is inextricably intertwined with punishment and power relationships.

A typical courthouse, historically, would have often had large gallows erected out in front of it. Gallows and gibbets were often placed at prominent locations in a city, such as the famous Tyburn Tree in London (a massive triple-branch gallows that could hang twenty-four convicts at the same time) and Le Gibet de Mont Faucon, high on a hill in France.

In this vein, young artist Stephanie Mann (age 5) built a conceptual art sculpture entitled "La Potence de la Veillance" that touches on this theme. The piece is comprised of a wooden camera post, in the form of a gallows frame from which a surveillance camera hangs.

Conclusion: This chapter contributes examples of praxistemology, a praxis of existential inquiry, presented as playful, childlike ways (pace Albert Einstein) of doing basic research that can solve many of the world's problems without necessarily being solution- or problem-driven.

To promote "learning-by-being," we can encourage people to engage in unstructured and free-spirited approaches, promoting lateral thinking rather than vertical problem solving. In particular, teaching and encouraging praxistemology and maktivism amplifies the processes central to critical making and DIY/DIT citizenship.

Notes

1. For the history of the MIT wearable computing project, see MIT Media Lab Director Nicholas Negroponte's account at http://wearcam.org/nn.htm. For an overview of wearable computing, see Mann 1996, Mann 1997, and http://www.interaction-design.org/encyclopedia/wearable-computing.html.

2. For more photographic documentation of sousveillance activities see http://glogger.mobi/s/tnt and also http://eyetap.blogspot.ca/.

References

2013 IEEE International Symposium on Technology and Society. Announced and site live on Oct. 27, 2012. *IEEE SSIT*. http://veillance.me (archived at http://www.webcitation.org/6CbygwUgA).

Advancing technology for humanity. 2013. *IEEE*. http://ieee.org/about/tagline/html (archived at http://www.webcitation.org/6CbyMhzn6).

Boler, M. 2010. *Digital Media and Democracy: Tactics in Hard Times*. Cambridge, MA: MIT Press.

Bolt, B. 2007. Material thinking and the agency of matter. *Studies in Material Thinking* 1 (1): 1–4.

Bricmont, J., and A. Sokal. 1998. *Fashionable Nonsense: Postmodern Intellectual Abuse of Science*. New York: Picador.

CBC News. 2007. Cameras can stay in Talisman's locker room, says Commissioner. *CBC News*, March 22. http://www.cbc.ca/news/canada/calgary/story/2007/03/22/talisman-privacy.html (accessed July 2, 2013).

Choney, Suzanne. 2013. Memory card in mouth saves police shooting video. *NBC News*, June 8. http://www.nbcnews.com/technology/memory-card-mouth-saves-police-shooting-video-122903 (accessed July 3, 2013).

Coligan, Nick. 2007. Massive CCTV scheme for Knowsley. *The Liverpool Echo*, Nov. 29. http://www.liverpoolecho.co.uk/news/liverpool-news/massive-cctv-scheme-for-knowsley-3500250 (accessed July 3, 2013).

Dawson, P. 2012. Holographic materiality. *Studies in Material Thinking* 8:1–20.

de Freitas, N. 2009. Editorial: Material Thinking as Document. *Studies in Material Thinking* 3: 1–4. http://materialthinking.org/papers/18.

Eysenbach, G. 2008. Preserving the scholarly record with webcite (www.webcitation.org): An archiving system for long-term digital preservation of cited webpages. *Proceedings ELPUB 2008 Conference on Electronic Publishing-Toronto*, 278–289, Canada, June.

Horkheimer, M. 1982. *Critical Theory*. New York: Seabury Press.

Jenkins, H. 2009. *Confronting the Challenges of Participatory Culture: Media Education for the Twenty-First Century*. Cambridge, MA: MIT Press.

Johnson, David V. 2011. Reclaiming the Republic: An Interview with Lawrence Lessig. *Boston Review*, Nov. 11. http://www.bostonreview.net/lawrence-lessig-republic-lost-campaign-finance-reform-rootstrikers (accessed July 2, 2013).

Karl, D. Stephan, Katina Michael, M. G. Michael, Laura Jacob, and Emily P. Anesta. 2012. Social implications of technology: The past, the present, and the future. *Proceedings of the IEEE* 100:1752–1781. http://ieeexplore.ieee.org/stamp/stamp.jsp?arnumber=06187687&tag=1.

King, G., and C. J. L. Murray. 2001–2002. Rethinking human security. *Political Science Quarterly* 116 (4): 585–610.

King, G., and C. Murray. 2000. Rethinking human security. Human Development Reports, May 4. http://hdr.undp.org/en/reports/global/hdr1994/chapters/.

Laplante, Phillip. 1996. Steps toward artificial intelligence. In *Great Papers on Computer Science*, ed. Marvin Minsky, 541–579. Minneapolis/St Paul: West Publishing Company.

Levy, P., and R. Bonomo. 1999. *Collective Intelligence: Mankind's Emerging World in Cyberspace*. New York: Perseus Publishing.

Lyon, David. 2007. *Surveillance Studies: An Overview*. Boston: Polity Press.

Mann, S. 2012a. McVeillance: How McDonaldized surveillance creates a monopoly on sight that chills AR and smartphone development. http://wearcam.org/mcveillance.pdf. (archived by WebCite at http://www.webcitation.org/6Cb7y7KRb), 1–13.

Mann, S. 2012b. Praxistemology: The practice of authentic inquiry for technology and society. http://wearcam.org/peq.pdf archived and time-stamped on http://www.webcitation.org/6CS6B7Zut, 1–13.

Mann, S. 2012c. *The Surveillance Scenarios*. Presented at "Identity, Privacy and Security by ReDesign," Identity, Privacy and Security Institute, University of Toronto. http://www.ipsi.utoronto.ca/events.html (archived as PDF and further time-stamped at http://www.webcitation.org/6CbxqQU49).

Mann, Steve. 1996. 'Smart clothing': Wearable multimedia and 'personal imaging' to restore the balance between people and their intelligent environments. *Proceedings, ACM Multimedia 96*; Nov. 18–22, Boston, Mass., 163–174, http://wearcam.org/acm-mm96.htm.

Mann, Steve. 1997. Wearable computing: A first step toward personal imaging. *IEEE Computer* 30 (2): 25–32. http://wearcam.org/ieeecomputer/r2025.htm.

Mann, Steve. 2000. Telepointer: Hands-free completely self-contained wearable visual augmented reality without headwear and without any infrastructural reliance.

Proceedings of the IEEE International Symposium Wearable Computing 2000 (ISWC2000), 177–178, Oct. 16–17. Additional figures appear in http://www.eyetap.org/docs/telepointer.pdf.

Mann, Steve. 2001a. Vitrionic sensors: Computer vision for an intelligent touchless water faucet and intelligent plumbing systems, *CVPR*, 1–2, Dec. 11–13. http://nguyendangbinh.org/proceedings/cvpr/2001/cd2/demos/demos/pdf.

Mann, Steve. 2001b. *Intelligent Image Processing*. New York: John Wiley and Sons.

Mann, Steve. 2001c. *Seatsale: License to Sit*. San Francisco Art Institute. http://wearcam.org/seatsale/ (accessed July 2, 2013).

Mann, Steve. 2006. Learning by being: Thirty years of cyborg existemology. In *The International Handbook of Virtual Learning Environments*, ed. J. Weiss, J. Nolan, J. Hunsinger, and P. Trifonas, vol. 14, 1571–1592.

Mann, Steve, and Ryan Janzen. 2012. The xyolin, a 10-octave continuous-pitch xylophone, and other existemological instruments. In *Proceedings of the International Computer Music Conference 2012*, 451–458.

Milberry, K. 2012. We are big brother: Is social media surveillance a threat to our sense of community? In *Communication in Question: Competing Perspectives on Controversial Issues in Communication Studies*, second ed., ed. Joshua Greenberg and Charlene Elliott, 181–189. Scarborough: Nelson Education.

Milberry, K., and S. Anderson. 2009. Open sourcing our way to an online commons contesting corporate impermeability in the new media ecology. *Journal of Communication Inquiry* 33 (4): 393–412.

Mitchell, Marit. 2013. Meet Steve Mann, the Father of Wearable Computing. *U of T News*, Mar. 13. www.news.utoronto.ca/meet-steve-mann-father-wearable-computing (accessed July 3, 2013).

Palmer, D., and J. Whyte. 2010. No Credible Photographic Interest: Photography restrictions and surveillance in a time of terror. *Philosophy of Photography* 1 (2): 177–195.

Ratto, M. 2011. Critical making: Conceptual and material studies in technology and social life. *Information Society* 27 (4): 252–260.

Reynolds, C. 2011. Negative sousveillance. *First International Conference of the International Association for Computing and Philosophy (IACAP11)*, 306–309, July 4–6, Aarhus, Denmark.

VanKranenburg, R., E. Anzelmo, A. Bassi, D. Caprio, S. Dodson, and M. Ratto. 2011. The internet of things: A critique of ambient technology and the all-seeing network of RFID. *Network Notebooks*, 2.

Vardi, Moshe Y. 2012. Open, closed, or clopen access. *Communications of the ACM* 52 (7): 5.

Wade, L., W. Weimar, and J. Davis. 2004. Effects of personal protective eyewear on postural stability. *Ergonomics* 47 (15): 1614–1623.

2 (Re)making the Internet: Free Software and the Social Factory Hack

Kate Milberry

With the emergence of global justice movement(s) in the mid-1990s, tech activists began remaking the Internet in the image of the just society they pursue. Using free and open source software (FOSS), tech activists continue to build the digital infrastructure of the "newest social movements," developing *technologies of resistance* to support activists online. The newest social movements are contemporary, broadly anti-capitalist social movements that organize loosely around anarchist politics, informed by emancipatory theory (Day 2005). By designing values into technology that are consonant with movement goals, tech activists engage in prefigurative politics. This self-reflexivity invokes the spirit of critical making as both an activity and a site for deepening a transformative sociotechnical praxis. In deploying FOSS across an increasingly commercialized and privatized web, tech activists enact their politics at both a technological and social level. Drawn from the free software and global justice movements, these values—including freedom, decentralization, heterarchy, autonomy, self-determination, collaboration, collectivism, and mutual aid—challenge capitalist norms that dominate the social factory both online and offline. This chapter considers the transformative potential of critical making as emancipated labor when it is manifest in tech activism. It locates critical making in the tradition of emancipatory theory and explores how tech activists hack the social factory, reconnecting society and technology by remaking the Internet into a more humane and democratic communication medium.

Tech Activism as Critical Making

Tech activists are hackers, coders, and self-described geeks who subscribe to the politics of the Free Software movement yet are committed to the goals of the newest social movements. These goals include gender and racial equality, economic justice, environmental sustainability, and labor and human rights, all of which they believe contribute to a freer, more just society. Tech activists build the online communication systems and software that support the broader movements to which they belong. Their prefigurative politics manifest as critical making when tech activists infuse unmet user needs, such as participatory democracy, consensus-based decision making, and security culture into the software design and development process. They further enact the values and skills necessary for deepening democracy offline through the FOSS mode of production, which relies on a set of social relations that challenge capitalist norms (Dunbar-Hester, chapter 4, this volume). Thus tech activists both anticipate and actualize the values they build into their technologies. This brand of critical making is therefore a means to an end, as well as an end in itself. It is also intentional: tech activists understand the political nature of technology as well as the sociality of its production. In producing technology that embeds new social relations, ones not founded on exploitation, exclusivity, scarcity, and profit, tech activists are remaking the Internet after the image of the better world they seek. Emancipatory theory and critical making come together in the work of tech activists as they intervene in the digital infrastructure, reconceptualizing the Internet as a contested terrain as well as a space and a tool of social critique, engagement, and change.

Species-Being, Hacking, and Emancipated Labor

The current strain of tech activism is the third wave of an historical trajectory that has its roots in hacking, which first emerged in the 1960s as a digital counterculture. Hacking in its original manifestation evokes the spirit of "species being"—that distinctively human capacity for self-determined activity that is realized in the productive or creative work of human beings. Species-being is fulfilled through emancipated labor, which Marx (1964) distinguishes from labor under capitalism. This he called "wage slavery" or estranged labor: the sale of one's physical capacities for the minimum amount required to survive. Emancipated labor is rather a "process of genuine activity" in which a person develops him- or herself. Here work is not only a means to an end "but an end in itself, the meaningful expression of human energy; hence work is enjoyable" (Fromm 1961, 41).

First-generation computer hackers were graduate students building the early Internet at MIT's Artificial Intelligence Lab. They were distinguished by their spirit of adventure, exploration, and play; they were fans who appreciated "the options, fun, excitement and fiendish fascination of computers" (Nelson 1987, 5). These early hackers "were permeated with the values of individual freedom, of independent thinking, and of sharing and co-operation" that also characterized the radical student movement of the day (Castells 2001, 24). They developed the habit of sharing source code based upon a firm belief that information should be free (Stallman 2002). Freedom is at the core of the hacker ethic (Levy 1984), which would become the philosophical and practical foundation of free and open source software.

Hacking and the FOSS mode of software development offer a contemporary example of Marx's emancipated labor. For Marx, labor is not merely the production of a commodity, or the reproduction of the physical existence of workers. Rather labor is something much more important: it is the means by which people fulfill their humanity, their species-being: "The nature of individuals . . . depends on the material conditions determining their production" (Marx and Engels 1970, 42). Thus the production and reproduction of the technical infrastructure are inextricably and dialectically bound to social life. As a genuine activity that expresses one's self, the FOSS mode of production engenders social relations that contradict the property relations that underpin modern capitalism. As a means of fulfilling one's human potential, the FOSS mode of production fosters relations of freedom, which are incorporated into the labor process at the same time as they are embedded in the outcome of that process: free and open source software. Hacking, the foundational activity of FOSS production, is commonly referred to as joyful (Himanen 2001), fun (Raymond 2001), playful (Levy 1984; Torvalds 2001) and humorous (Stallman 2002). It is often done for free, and always freely shared. FOSS as a labor process, therefore, belongs to a "much broader undercurrent revolting against . . . commodified labour and needs satisfaction" (Soderberg 2008, 44).

Emancipatory Theory and the Radical Potential of Critical Making

The possibilities for critical making as a strategy for social change appear when it is rooted in the emancipatory theory. Critical theory of technology, or critical constructivism, considers technology as a terrain of contestation and intervention by users, rather than a mysterious black box, the exclusive territory of designers (Feenberg 1991). It builds from critical theory, which provides the analytic and normative bases for social inquiry intended to reduce domination and increase freedom, "to liberate human beings from the circumstances that enslave them" (Horkheimer 1982, 244). Critical constructivism questions the social fixity of technology and looks for human interventions into the technical infrastructure of capitalism, and for the subsequent subversion (or affirmation) of dominant social values and interests that congeal there. The result of such interventions is a critical (re)making of the material world. Critical constructivism helps us understand how free and open source software increases user freedom and satisfies unfulfilled needs through hacking computer code. The FOSS mode of production inculcates a new set of social relations that challenges the capitalist mode of production upon which contemporary society is founded. In doing so, it offers a transformative vision of the future.

In critical theory's long tradition of social engagement, Feenberg (2002) calls for the creation of a politics of technological transformation that will rebuild society from its material base. In reclaiming technology from ownership and control by the technocapitalist class, the citizenry will, in dialectic fashion, become conscious of technology as both means of oppression *and* democratization. From here, the objective is to generalize the democratic tendencies of "technology for the people" to the political and economic structures of domination. The Internet as a technology-in-the-making, and the technological hack of writing free code as a constitutive part of this process, uncovers just such a possibility: that of translating critical making from the technical base to the sociopolitical realm, thereby transforming a technological practice into a social praxis of liberation. This recalls the "caring for" aspect of critical making necessary for the reconnection of society and technology (Ratto 2009), and for the humanization of technology in order to reduce human want, misery, cruelty, and violence.

Technologies of Resistance

Tech activists have heeded the call for a politics of technological transformation in building *technologies of resistance* intended to support grassroots struggle online, remaking the Internet as a more democratic and humane communication medium in the process. Such a transformation is possible because the Internet remains a flexible technology that has yet to reach closure; rather it is daily being made and remade by users and developers, as well as corporations and governments. How, then, will it concretize? What technical affordances will be baked into the architecture of the Internet; what social constraints will be laid over the top of the network? This is a social as well as a technological contest, one in which tech activists have been central. "Activist designers, software developers and digital artists have leveraged the malleability of IT and the openness of network protocols to develop utilities that are expressive of particular political commitments" (Howe and Nissenbaum 2009, 431).

Since the development of Active, the open publishing platform for Indymedia in 1999, tech activists have been rebuilding the application layer of the Internet. Concurrently, the forces of corporate and state enclosure have sought ever greater control of the Internet through cyber-surveillance on the one hand and legislation on the other (Milberry and Clement, forthcoming). Based entirely on FOSS, technologies of resistance are imbued with a prefigurative politics of emancipation. They seek to assist activists in their social justice work by providing secure communications and enhancing privacy and anonymity online. For example, email encryption is necessary for activists, who are often under surveillance by the state (Leistert 2012). The cryptographic software, *GNU Privacy Guard* (GnuPG), is a free implementation of PGP (Pretty Good Privacy), the original email encryption protocol developed by American antinuclear activist Philip Zimmerman. PGP employs public key encryption, where users have a secret key that matches a public key. Use of these keys protects the authenticity, confidentiality, and integrity of a message by creating a digital signature with the private key, which can then be verified by the public key. Zimmerman published his public key encryption software package for free on the Internet, believing it "would be of most use to dissidents, rebels and others who faced serious risks as a consequence of their beliefs" (Lucas 2006, 3).

CryptoSMS, developed by a tech activist in Germany, responds to activists' need for secure digital communication by encrypting text messages. *TextSecure* is a drop-in replacement for the Android text messaging application that encrypts messages stored on mobile phones and provides end-to-end message encryption when texting with someone else who is also using the app. It was developed by an anarchist FOSS coder, who also created *RedPhone*, another Android app that enables encrypted voice communication between RedPhone users. Encrypted mobile communication is increasingly critical with the proliferation of cell phones and the continued criminalization of dissent experienced by social movement organizers. The Anarchist Tech Support (ATS) collective advises activists to be diligent about encrypting their digital communications because these "are likely to be subject to more scrutiny" (ATS 2010). Indeed, while Deibert et al. (2008, 2010) document how totalitarian regimes around the world monitor the digital communications of human rights activists and political dissidents, Western democracies are not exempt from government spying schemes. Most notorious of these domestic surveillance programs is the "warrantless wiretapping" conducted in the United States by the National Security Agency and aided by major telecommunications carriers, including AT&T (Bamford 2008). Canada recently deployed the largest known domestic spying scheme in its history against activists opposed to the Toronto G20 Summit in 2010.

TXTMob is a text messaging system designed by tech activists to allow rapid, anonymous communication during protests. TXTMob was released as free software by the Institute for Applied Autonomy, an art and engineering collective that creates technologies for political dissent, as part of its "inverse surveillance" efforts. Activists using TXTMob on their cell phones communicate real-time information with each other about police movements, direct actions and calls for medical and legal support, helping them to remain organized during chaotic street actions. Although TXTMob has been superseded by the meteoric rise of Twitter, it is worth noting that the popular microblogging service was modeled on TXTMob (Henshaw-Plath 2008).

Psiphon is a web browser proxy created by tech activists at the University of Toronto's Citizen Lab to enable censorship circumvention. By allowing users to securely bypass content-filtering systems, Psiphon enables human rights activists, political dissidents, and pro-democracy advocates in totalitarian regimes to access the web through allies in countries without Internet censorship. Psiphon is free software, and it uses the encrypted HTTPS protocol to transfer data, enabling users to securely send requests for information to a trusted computer located in another country and receive encrypted information in return. It also allows news organizations, such as the British Broadcasting Corporation, to deliver their content in censored countries.

TrackMeNot uses obfuscation rather than encryption, anonymity, or circumvention to defend against government surveillance and corporate data mining. Developed by tech activists at New York University, TrackMeNot (2001) is a web browser extension that hides web searches in a "stream of decoy queries" (Howe and Nissenbaum 2009). Like other technologies of resistance, TrackMeNot self-consciously integrates values into its design. Such values include "transparency in interface, function, code, and strategy; personal autonomy, where users need not rely on third parties; social protection of privacy with distributed/community-oriented action; minimal resource consumption . . . and usability" (Howe and Nissenbaum 2009, 421). TrackMeNot thus builds on the critical constructivist tradition that regards technology as a site of political contestation. A good example of critical making, TrackMeNot belongs to a "class of technical tools" that helps amplify "social resistance or political voice" (421).

Crabgrass is a technology of resistance that takes a more global view: it is a platform rather than a single-issue software that enables a range of secure online communications. A project of the anarchist tech collective Riseup, Crabgrass facilitates group and network organizing "tailored to the needs of the global justice movement" (About Crabgrass n.d.). Its goal is to provide the activist community with the technical tools needed to create "active, confederal, and directly democratic social change networks" (ibid.). Crabgrass represents a different user experience than commercial social networking, one geared toward community rather than the individual. "We're trying to build tools that reflect more closely our real world experience with how people democratically organize, instead of relying on social networks or on online collaboration tools that . . . actually encode logics that are contrary to the democratic impulse we're trying to foster," explains lead developer Sparrow in a 2008 interview.

Crabgrass's emphasis on secure and democratic communication is inherent in the technical encoding of both the needs and values of activists in the newest social movements. More broadly, Crabgrass seeks to "promote social ownership and democratic control over information, ideas, technology, and the means of communication; empower organizations and individuals to use technology in struggles for liberation [and] to offer support in overcoming the systemic oppression embedded in the use and development of technology" (About Crabgrass n.d.). In this way it invokes the "caring for" practice of reconnecting society and technology inherent in critical making.

Hacking the Social Factory

The need for technologies of resistance seems out of place against the tendency to conceive of the Internet as inherently democratic. This brand of cyber-optimism belies the Internet's origins in the military-industrial complex. It further ignores the Internet's central role in informational capitalism as a locus of social control, as a means of extending capitalist social relations from the material to the immaterial realm. The associated idea that immaterial labor, with its affective, cooperative, and intellectual characteristics, is a potential site of freedom from capitalism rather than its conduit, is attractive. Certainly, this seems to be true of the emancipated labor that typifies FOSS development. Yet the concept of immaterial labor draws from a rich body of theory in the autonomous Marxist tradition, which develops "a subversive counter-interpretation of the information revolution" (Dyer-Witheford 1999, 64). On this view, the Internet, as the central terrain of immaterial labor, is not necessarily or exclusively the "material and ideological heart of informated capital" (Terranova 2000, 39). Both the Internet and immaterial labor are ambivalent; both are spheres of contestation rather than merely accessories to the global project of capital.

Immaterial labor of the sort facilitated by networked computing and the growing importance of information to capitalism gives rise to the social factory. Control of the capitalist labor process as codified in Taylorism, the scientific management of work, is generalized to all of human relations in the form of the social factory. In the bricks-and-mortar factory of Marx's day, labor ceased to be a self-determined activity of species-being and was instead "subsumed under the total process of the machinery itself, as itself only a link of the system, whose unity exists not in the living workers, but rather in the living (active) machinery" (Marx 1973, 693). In the social factory thesis, the dehumanizing machinic relations of the factory not only impose upon society but absorb it fully. Tronti calls this the "process of internal colonization" wherein "the whole of society exists as a function of the factory and the factory extends its exclusive domination over the whole of society" (Tronti, cited in Wright 2002, 37).

It is hackers, according to Wark (2004), who contest the social relations that underwrite capitalism as it has evolved in the age of information. Wark's definition of hacker is expansive, not limited to the world of computing: "Whatever code we hack, be it programming language, poetic language, math or music, curves or colourings, we create the possibility of new things entering the world" (n.p.). It is hackers who are capable of transgressing the alienation of capitalist labor and opposing, through their joyful, creative, collective and subversive labor, the social factory. FOSS as a mode of production inaugurates a new labor process—one based on voluntaristic cooperation, self-determination, and the fulfillment of species-being. It opens up new terrain for a critical remaking of the Internet following a community rather than corporate model (Feenberg and Bakardjieva 2004). At the very least, the FOSS labor process suggests a politics of technological transformation that could reinvent the Internet; at most, it offers an alternative mode of social organization founded on an altogether new set of social relations.

Conclusion: Running Servers for Revolution

Technologies of resistance embody the values inherent in the global justice and Free Software movements and actualize these values in their uptake and use. They belong to the broader tech activist project that is building the digital infrastructure of the global justice movement(s) and, in the process, critically remaking the Internet. This digital infrastructure comprises web applications and platforms that are autonomous and secure, that defend against corporate and state surveillance, and that are designed with the intention of promoting the new social relations of another, better world. In this way, tech activism goes beyond simply using Internet technology toward particular ends to include the appropriation, modification, and transformation of technology itself. "As radical techies, anar(cho)geeks, hacklab members, keyboard squatters, tech-aware activists, autonomous administrators," writes one tech activist, "we've often directly participated in that evolution, advocating subversive uses of new technologies, hacking free software and sharing knowledge with passion, running servers for revolution."[1] Activist-designed and built technologies are therefore disruptive tools that destabilize trends toward a closed, privatized, economically striated, and commercially oriented Internet. By designing software that meets their practical needs and social justice goals, tech activists contribute to the democratization of the Internet. As a "practical means of resistance," this kind of critical making can be deployed in the blind spots inherent in systems of surveillance and social control, where there is always "space to manoeuvre" (Marx 2003, 372). Produced by the free and open source method, their value lies in the reconnection of the social and the technical, offering a challenge and alternative to the alienated social relations of the social factory.

Note

1. This is taken from the invitation to participate in the People's Global Action Digital Struggles meeting to discuss issues facing radical activists using and developing Internet technology. It is archived at https://lists.aktivix.org/pipermail/aktivix-discuss/2006-June/000941.html.

References

About Crabgrass. n.d. https://we.riseup.net/crabgrass/about.

Anarchist Tech Support (ATS). 2010. *A Short Guide to Setting Up Encrypted Online Communications*. Pamphlet.

Bamford, James. 2008. *The Shadow Factory: The Ultra-Secret NSA from 9/11 to the Eavesdropping on America*. New York: Doubleday.

Castells, Manuel. 2001. The Internet Galaxy: Reflections on the Internet, Business, and Society. New York: Oxford University Press.

Day, R. J. 2005. *Gramsci Is Dead: Anarchist Currents in the Newest Social Movements*. Toronto, ON: Between the Lines.

Deibert, Ron, John Palfrey, Rafal Rohozinski, and Jonathan Zittrain, eds. 2008. *Access Denied. The Practice and Policy of Global Internet Filtering*. Cambridge, MA: MIT Press.

Deibert, Ron, John Palfrey, Rafal Rohozinski, and Jonathan Zittrain, eds. 2010. *Access Controlled: The Shaping of Power, Rights and Rule in Cyberspace*. Cambridge, MA: MIT Press.

Dyer-Witheford, Nick. 1999. *Cyber-Marx: Cycles and Circuits of Struggle in High Technology Capitalism*. Urbana: University of Illinois Press.

Einstein, Albert. 1954/1982. *Ideas and Opinions*. New York: Crown Publishing.

Feenberg, Andrew. 1991. *Critical Theory of Technology*. New York: Oxford University Press.

Feenberg, Andrew. 2002. *Transforming Technology*. Oxford; New York: Oxford University Press.

Feenberg, Andrew, and Maria Bakardjieva. 2004. Consumers or Citizens? The Online Community Debate. In *Community in the Digital Age: Philosophy and Practice*, ed. Andrew Feenberg and Darrin Barney, 1–28. Lanham, MD: Rowman & Littlefield.

Fromm, Erik. 1961. *Marx's Concept of Man*. New York: Continuum.

Henshaw-Plath, Evan. 2008. *TXTMob Gets Subpoenaed: Data Retention in the Surveillance Era*. http://anarchogeek.com/?s=TXtmob.

Himanen, Pekka. 2001. *The Hacker Ethic*. New York: Random House.

Horkheimer, Max. 1982. *Critical Theory: Selected Essays*. New York: Continuum.

Howe, Daniel C., and Helen Nissenbaum. 2009. Resisting Surveillance in Web Search. In *Lessons from the Identity Trail: Anonymity, Privacy and Identity in a Networked Society*, ed. Ian Kerr, Valerie Steeves, and Carole Lucock, 417–436. New York: Oxford University Press.

Leistert, O. 2012. Resistance against Cyber-Surveillance Within Social Movements and How Surveillance Adapts. *Surveillance & Society* 9 (4): 441–456.

Levy, Steven. 1984. *Hackers: Heroes of the Computer Revolution*. New York: Penguin Books.

Lucas, Michael W. 2006. *PGP and GPG: Email for the Practical Paranoid*. San Francisco: No Starch Press.

Marx, Gary T. 2003. A Tack in the Shoe: Neutralizing and Resisting the New Surveillance. *Journal of Social Issues* 59 (2): 369–390.

Marx, Karl. 1964. *Economic and Philosophic Manuscripts of 1844*. Ed. Dirk J. Struik. Trans Martin Milligan. New York: International Publishers.

Marx, Karl. 1973. *Grundrisse*. Trans. Martin Nicolaus. New York; London: Penguin Books.

Marx, Karl, and Fredrick Engels. 1970. *The German Ideology*. London: Lawrence & Wishart.

Milberry, K., and A. Clement. Forthcoming. Policing as Spectacle and the Politics of Surveillance at the Toronto G20. In *The State on Trial: Policing Protest*, ed. Margaret E. Beare and Nathalie Des Rosiers. Vancouver, BC: UBC Press.

Nelson, T. H. 1987. *Computer Lib: Dream Machines*. Redmond, WA: Tempus Books.

Ratto, Matt. 2009. Critical Making: Conceptual and Material Studies in Technology and Social Life. *Information Society* 27 (4): 252–260.

Raymond, Eric S. 2001. *How to Become a Hacker*. http://www.catb.org/~esr/faqs/hacker-howto.html (accessed November 4, 2009).

Soderberg, J. 2008. *Hacking Capitalism*. New York; London: Routledge.

Sparrow (lead developer, Crabgrass). 2008. Discussion with the author.

Stallman, Richard. 2002. *Free Software, Free Society: Selected Essays of Richard M. Stallman*. Boston, MA: Free Software Foundation.

Terranova, Tiziana. 2000. Free Labor: Producing Culture for the Digital Economy. *Social Text* 18 (2): 33–58.

Torvalds, Linus. 2001. What Makes a Hacker Tick? a.k.a. Linus's Law. In Pekka Himanen, *The Hacker Ethic*, n.p. New York: Random House.

TrackMeNot. 2001. http://cs.nyu.edu/trackmenot/ (accessed December 4, 2012).

Wark, McKenzie. 2004. *A Hacker Manifesto*. Cambridge, MA: Harvard University Press.

Wright, Steve. 2002. *Storming Heaving: Class Composition and Struggle in Italian Autonomist Marxism*. London: Pluto Press.

3 Fan Activism as Participatory Politics: The Case of the Harry Potter Alliance

Henry Jenkins

In a white paper released by the MacArthur Youth and Participatory Politics research network, Cathy J. Cohen and Joseph Kahne define participatory politics as "interactive, peer-based acts through which individuals and groups seek to exert both voice and influence on issues of public concern" (Cohen and Kahne 2012, vi). Participatory politics offers a more welcoming space for diverse kinds of participants than traditional politics, enables greater creativity and voice in expressing one's views, and provides a gateway to more traditional political activities, such as voting or petitioning. Citing data from a survey of more than 4,000 respondents ages 15–25, they found that those who engaged in participatory politics (roughly 40–45 percent across all racial categories) were almost twice as likely to vote as those who did not. Their research has been especially invested in understanding the role that interest-driven networks (such as those around fandom or gaming) might play in helping to bridge between cultural and political participation.

This chapter represents a study of one increasingly common form of participatory politics—fan activism. For the purposes of this discussion, "fan activism" refers to forms of civic engagement and political participation that emerge from within fan culture itself, often in response to the shared interests of fans, often conducted through the infrastructure of existing fan practices and relationships, and often framed with metaphors drawn from popular and participatory culture. (See also Brough and Shresthova 2012 and Kligler-Vilenchik et al. 2012.) Fan cultures have long been cited as textbook examples of the larger phenomenon of DIY media production, and fan activism represents an exemplar of the ways that such creative communities might evolve their own models of political and civic participation.[1]

This chapter will explore the Harry Potter Alliance (HPA), a sustained effort to mobilize a network of fans of J. K. Rowling's fantasy books around an array of different issues and concerns, ranging from human rights in

Africa to equal marriage rights, from labor rights to media concentration and net neutrality. While the Harry Potter Alliance is open to members of all ages, the group has focused its energies on attracting young people who have grown up reading the books and on helping them find a path toward political engagement. According to HPA chapter coordinator Sara Denver (pers. comm., July 2011), of the organization's 98 chapters, 24 are hosted by high schools and 33 by colleges and universities, suggesting strong student representation in the group.

The HPA embraces a politics of "cultural acupuncture," mapping fictional content worlds onto real-world concerns. A content world is the network of characters, settings, situations, and values that forms the basis for the generation of a range of stories, in the hands of either a commercial producer or a grassroots community. So the content world around Harry Potter includes characters such as Snape and Dumbledore, settings such as Hogwarts, situations such as sorting students into houses using the Sorting Hat, and values such as friendship and maternal love, any or all of which can be used to generate new narratives or to tap into the meanings associated with the original stories. The HPA works by deploying elements of the Harry Potter content world (and their accumulated meanings) as metaphors for making sense of contemporary issues.[2]

Historically, fans have often entered civic discourse when they assert their collective rights as the most active and engaged segments of the media audience. While many other forms of DIY culture have sought to establish autonomy from mainstream culture, fandom exists at the intersection of grassroots and commercial media. Given this unstable positioning, the fan identity is often an embattled one, and efforts to save shows from cancellation or to rally support for a film project have helped cement social ties between fans, define their shared interests, and shape their public status. By the time these fan groups had defined an issue, identified decision makers, developed tactics, and educated and mobilized supporters, they had completed all of the steps required for activism.

Those who participated in such efforts had built the infrastructure and acquired the personal and organizational skills to take meaningful action. In *Entertaining the Citizen*, Liesbet van Zoonen concludes that fan practices embody, "in abstract terms, the customs that have been laid out as essential for democratic politics: information, discussion, and activism" (van Zoonen 2005, 63). In a study of another fan activist group, Racebending.com, Lori Kido Lopez reaches a similar conclusion: "Some of the organization's strongest and most effective tactics rely on the skills developed as members of the fan community: honing their arguments through community discussions, producing and editing multimedia creations, educating themselves about every facet of their issue, and relying on their trusted networks to provide a database of information" (Lopez 2011, 2).

Started by Andrew Slack, a twentysomething trained community organizer who has a background in working with troubled youth, the Harry Potter Alliance is fan activism on a previously unimagined scale. The group currently has more than 100,000 members in more than seventy active chapters across the world, organized and mobilized by Slack and his forty-person staff, both volunteer and paid. When the HPA takes action, the results can be staggering: for instance, it raised $123,000 to fund five cargo planes to transport medical supplies to Haiti after the 2010 earthquake. Its Accio Books! Campaign has collected over 55,000 books for communities around the world. HPA members called 3,597 residents of Maine in just one day, encouraging them to vote against Proposition 9, which would deny equal marriage rights to gay and lesbian couples.

Running the HPA from his living room in Somerville, Massachusetts, Slack is a charismatic leader who inspires his volunteer army and part-time paid staff, but also embraces more dispersed and decentralized power structures that allow members a greater voice in the organization's decisions. Local chapters participate in national campaigns but also initiate their own activities, which reflect their own agendas (veterans' rights, say), and solicit participation by other chapters. Unlike most activist groups and charities, the HPA is not defined around a single mission: rather, it embraces a flexible framework inspired by Rowling's content world and by her own previous experience working for Amnesty International, enabling it to respond quickly to any crisis and to mobilize its dispersed members.

From the start, Slack worked within the structures of fandom, using such things as the House Cup competition. Hogwarts is organized around four houses, Gryffindor, Slytherin, Ravenclaw, and Hufflepuff, each of which embodies different ideals and virtues.[3] Harry Potter fans deploy many different "sorting" mechanisms to place members into appropriate houses, and many feel a strong sense of identification and affiliation with their house. The HPA recruits high-profile heads for each house who encourage members to take action for the cause. For example, Wrock4Equality was a House Cup competition, where members earned points for each person they contacted in the effort to rally voters against Maine's Proposition 9.

The HPA materials are not always as polished as those of some other activist groups, who work with professional media makers and consultants. Rather, the HPA embraces fandom's own DIY ethos, lowering barriers to participation by respecting the work of novices and amateurs. Many of the HPA's most effective videos simply depict students, in their bedrooms, speaking directly into the camera. The HPA has formed a strong partnership with the video blog community Nerdfighters, whose capacity to mobilize its members was a key factor in the HPA's success in a 2010 Chase Manhattan Bank online competition.

Stephen Duncombe has described a range of contemporary activist movements that embrace "a politics that understands desire and speaks to the irrational; a politics that employs symbols and associations; a politics that tells good stories" (Duncombe 2007, 9). Whereas Mark Dery (1993) described 1990s cultural and political movements as "jamming" dominant culture, Duncombe alternatively suggests that activists surf the popular imagination, hitching themselves to Hollywood's publicity to reach a larger public.

Slack describes this new form of activism as "cultural acupuncture." Recognizing that the news media was more apt to cover the launch of the next Harry Potter film than the genocide in Darfur, Slack saw the HPA as a way to identify key cultural pressure points, thus redirecting energy toward real-world problems.[4] Pinning political and social causes to Harry Potter works because this content world has a large following, is familiar to an even larger number of people, has its own built-in mechanisms for generating publicity, and is apt to attract many subsequent waves of media interest. Harry Potter constitutes a form of cultural currency that can carry the group's messages to many who would not otherwise hear them and that can channel our emotional investments. Here, again, this form of DIY citizenship speaks both within the subculture of fandom and beyond it, seeking ways to tap the power of mass media to reach a lager public.

Cultural acupuncture inspires civic participation by mapping content worlds onto real-world problems. Against a backdrop of Death Eater terrorists, bungling or manipulative government officials, a deceptive press, and repressive school authorities, Rowling tells how one young man organized his classmates into Dumbledore's Army, a loosely organized activist group, to go out and fight evil—sometimes working alone, sometimes collaborating with adult groups such as the Order of the Phoenix, but always carrying much of the burden of confronting Voldemort and his minions (Slack 2010). The HPA similarly offers its participants roles within larger-than-life campaigns. The HPA's playful deployment of terms like "Voldemedia" and "WaldeMart" maps the personalized embodiment of evil in the content world to an expanding understanding of real-world harms. Consequently, the HPA allows its young members to know who they are as activists, what they are fighting against, and what they are fighting for, all key steps toward sustaining social change.

For the HPA, overcoming the "Muggle mind-set" (Slack 2007) and releasing the power of fantasy represent vital first steps in becoming an activist. When many Harry Potter fans think of Muggles, they think first of the narrow-minded Dursley family, who keep Harry locked away in the cupboard under the stairs out of fear of and embarrassment about his magical capacities. Building on Rowling's depiction, the HPA uses the elastic concept of the "Muggle mind-set" as an all-purpose signifier for those forces that resist social justice, including many that are the targets of other kinds of activism, such as conformity, commercialization, authoritarianism, and the politics of terror. The term Muggle mind-set is as loose and as encompassing as, say, "neoliberalism" or "dominant ideology," and, like them, it links structures of belief, power, and action.

In their final struggles with Voldemort, Harry, Hermione, Ron, and their classmates had to seek out and destroy seven Horcruxes, magic objects of supreme evil containing hidden fragments of the Dark Lord's soul. In the months leading up to the release of the final movie, the HPA launched an ambitious campaign identifying and directing its collective energy against seven real-world Horcruxes. Some, such as the Starvation Wages Horcrux, called attention to global human rights issues; HPA members pursuing this Horcrux sought to get Warner Brothers to commit to license Harry Potter candies only to fair trade companies. Others represented concerns in young people's lives. For the Dementor Horcrux, the HPA partnered with Reachout.com, an online support group for teens considering suicide. The Body Bind Horcrux helped members push back against distorted body images, while for the Bullying Horcrux the HPA joined forces with the Gay-Straight Alliance to battle homophobia in schools. Its efforts against bullying included both collecting signatures for the Make It Better Oath and making phone calls to voters in Rhode Island to urge them to support an equal marriage initiative there. While critics might see such short, focused efforts as token gestures, the overall Horcrux campaign was designed to help participants understand the links between campaigns for social justice and the internalized fears and anxieties that block many from taking meaningful action. The Starvation Wages Horcrux evolved into a more sustained "Not in Harry's Name" campaign designed to pressure Warner Brothers to shift its chocolate contracts to fair trade companies, a campaign waged in the name of fans but directed against the commercial rights holder of their favorite franchise.

In starting with a fantasy about youth empowerment, the HPA addresses many prevailing concerns about young people and civic engagement. Current scholarship (Gibson 2003; Bennett 2008; Wattenberg 2008; Buckingham

2000; Levine 2007) suggests that young people are rarely addressed as political agents, that they are not invited into the political process, and that they are not consulted in the political decision-making process, whether local, state, national, or global. Existing literature suggests that young people are most apt to become politically involved if they come from families with a history of citizen participation and political activism; if they encounter teachers, especially in the civics classroom, who encourage them to reflect on and respond to current events; if they attend schools where they are allowed a voice in core decisions; and if they participate in extracurricular activities and volunteerism that give back to their community. Most forms of activism reach the same core group of participants, who already are politically engaged, and redirect them toward new issues. But, the HPA is targeting young people who are engaged culturally, who may already be producing and sharing fan culture, and it helps them extend their engagement into politics, often deploying existing skills and capacities in new ways.

As researchers such as David Buckingham (2000) have long argued, young people often feel excluded from the language and processes of adult politics. In most cases, they are not invited to participate, their issues are often not addressed, and the debates are framed in a language that assumes familiarity with debates and policies. By contrast, the HPA's cultural acupuncture approach is imaginative and playful, offering an alternative set of metaphors and analogies that are already part of young people's lives. The HPA embraces grassroots appropriation as a way of generating a new vocabulary for talking about political change.

In *The Future of Democracy*, Peter Levine argues, "There are limits to what adults and institutions can accomplish, given the opacity of youth culture and young people's resistance to being manipulated. Therefore, it is important that young people themselves have the skills and values they need to make their own sphere as constructive as possible" (Levine 2007, 76). In some ways, fan activism flies in the face of Levine's claims: fandom has historically been a space where youth and adults work together, outside of the hierarchies that shape relations at school or home, because of their shared interests and mutual passions. In contrast to traditional political organizations which often deploy youth as envelope stuffers for adult-led activities, the HPA places much of the responsibility for core decisions impacting the mission and tactics of the organization into the hands of its young participants, empowering them to make a difference in the world.

Cohen and Kahne (2012) concluded their study of young people and participatory politics with a caution: "The knowledge, skills, resources, and networks that will enable youth to be listened to by those with the power to advance their priorities may not be adequately or equitably distributed. Promoting broad and equitable access to the support, training, and infrastructure needed to move from voice to influence will be important in order for participatory politics to reach its full potential" (38). One of the hallmarks of the Harry Potter Alliance has been its capacity to broker connections between the fan activists and a range of other more established NGOs, charities, and traditional political organizations (such as Doctors for Health, Mass Equity, Free Press, The Gay-Straight Alliance, Ox-Fam, and Wal-Mart Watch) with which they partner in conducting their campaigns. In July 2007, for example, the HPA and the Leaky Cauldron, one of the most popular fan news sites, organized house parties around the country focused on increasing awareness of the Sudanese genocide. Participants listened to and discussed a podcast that featured real-world political experts such as Joseph C. Wilson, former US ambassador to Gabon, and John Prendergast, senior advisor to the International Crisis Group, alongside performances by Wizard Rock groups.

The Harry Potter Alliance is only one of a range of case studies being developed by the graduate students and researchers affiliated with the University of Southern California's Civic Paths project. Other case studies include considerations of Invisible Children and the *Kony 2012* campaign, undocumented youth and their supporters who mobilized around the DREAM act, the Students for Liberty campaign, Nerdfighters, and American Muslim youth who are struggling with the post-9/11 climate of Islamophobia. Each of these groups deploys some of the techniques of cultural production, circulation, and participation that Cohen and Kahne (2012) have identified here as "participatory politics" or that are discussed in this book as "DIY citizenship." Each deploys a range of new media tools, platforms, and practices, often in association with more traditional kinds of on-the-ground mobilization, in order to recruit and train young activists behind their cause. Most of them appropriate and remix elements borrowed from popular culture in order to frame their issues in a language that makes sense to younger participants. Each creates scaffolding that allows youth to move from forms of cultural participation we associate with the age of YouTube and Facebook into forms of political participation, hoping to translate "voice" into "influence."

Acknowledgments

This chapter was informed by the ongoing conversations of the Civic Paths Research Group in the Annenberg School of Communications and Journalism, University of Southern California, and by the MacArthur Network on Youth and Participatory Politics. My research on fan activism has been funded by the Spencer and MacArthur Foundations. This chapter is adapted from "'Culture Acupuncture': Fan Activism and the Harry Potter Alliance," originally published in *Transformative Works and Cultures* 10 (2012).

Notes

1. For example, fandom has a strong tradition of zine and online publishing that closely parallel those forms of peer-to-peer mentorship and collaborative production described by Red Chidgey (chapter 6, this volume). Harry Potter fans have applied similar logics to the development of distinctive forms of digital production, including vidding, podcasts, blogs, and MP3 musical recordings, and the HPA tapped into this infrastructure as a means of reaching out to a broader base of fans.

2. Given the fantastical setting associated with the Harry Potter books and films, these fans needed to engage in a much more active process of translation to map the content world onto real-world concerns than would be required by the fans of comedy news programs, such as *The Daily Show* and *The Colbert Report*, discussed by Catherine Burwell and Megan Boler (chapter 7, this volume).

3. Such structures provide for shared values, common identities, collective goals, and a strong sense of sociability that might allow such groups to work past other kinds of ideological differences, paralleling the functions served by the Pricescope community as described by Lana Swartz and Kevin Driscoll (chapter 22, this volume). Swartz and Driscoll, along with Joshua McVeigh-Schultz (chapter 23, this volume), are part of my Civic Paths Research Group at the University of Southern California.

4. This acupunctural model represents a formulation of the kinds of "politics of attention" that have motivated other contemporary forms of activism, ranging from Invisible Children's *Kony 2012* efforts to the Yes Men's political pranks (see Reilly, chapter 8, this volume).

References

Bennett, W. Lance. 2008. *Civic Life Online: Learning How Digital Media Can Engage Youth.* Cambridge, MA: MIT Press.

Brough, Melissa M., and Sangita Shresthova. 2012. Fandom Meets Activism: Rethinking Civic and Political Participation. In "Transformative Works and Fan Activism," ed. Henry Jenkins and Sangita Shresthova, special issue of *Transformative Works and Cultures* 10. doi:10.3983/twc.2012.0303.

Buckingham, David. 2000. *The Making of Citizens: Young People, News and Politics.* London: Routledge.

Cohen, Cathy J., and Joseph Kahne. 2012. *Participatory Politics: New Media and Youth Political Action*. Oakland, CA: The Youth and Participatory Politics Network.

Dery, Mark. 1993. *Culture Jamming: Hacking, Slashing and Sniping in the Empire of the Signs*. *Open Magazine* pamphlet series. http://markdery.com/?page_id=154.

Duncombe, Stephen. 2007. *Dream: Re-imagining Progressive Politics in an Age of Fantasy*. New York: New Press.

Gibson, Cynthia. 2003. *The Civic Mission of Schools*. Report from Carnegie Foundation and CIRCLE: The Center for Information and Research on Civic Learning and Engagement. http://www.civicmissionofschools.org/the-campaign/civic-mission-of-schools-report.

Kligler-Vilenchik, Neta, Joshua McVeigh-Schultz, Christine Weitbrecht, and Chris Tokuhama. 2012. Experiencing Fan Activism: Understanding the Power of Fan Activist Organizations through Members' Narratives. In "Transformative Works and Fan Activism," ed. Henry Jenkins and Sangita Shresthova, special issue of *Transformative Works and Cultures* 10. doi:10.3983/twc.2012.0322.

Levine, Peter. 2007. *The Future of Democracy: Developing the Next Generation of American Citizens*. Medford, MA: Tufts University Press.

Lopez, Lori Kido. 2011. Fan Activists and the Politics of Race in *The Last Airbender*. *International Journal of Cultural Studies*. doi:10.1177/1367877911422862.

Slack, Andrew. 2007. "Harry Potter and the Muggle Activists." *In These Times*, October 26. http://www.inthesetimes.com/article/3365/harry_potter_and_the_muggle_activists/.

Slack, Andrew. 2010. "Cultural Acupuncture and a Future for Social Change." *Huffington Post*, July 2. http://www.huffingtonpost.com/andrew-slack/cultural-acupuncture-and_b_633824.html.

Wattenberg, Martin P. 2008. *Is Voting for Young People?* New York: Pearson Longman.

van Zoonen, Liesbet. 2005. *Entertaining the Citizen: When Politics and Popular Culture Converge*. Lanham, MD: Rowman and Littlefield.

4 Radical Inclusion? Locating Accountability in Technical DIY

Christina Dunbar-Hester

Introduction

This chapter examines DIY (do-it-yourself) politics in the realm of practice. To do this, it follows the work of a group of media activists whose work foregrounded engagement with communication technologies. Working in a self-consciously collaborative mode, the activists promoted hands-on work with radio and Internet hardware as a means to enact DIY politics. This practice was understood to be in service of a broader goal of facilitating technical and political engagement through "demystification" of technology.

Specifically, the media activists sought to cultivate a particular mode of "maker" identity. They presented technical engagement as a strategy for leveling expertise and increasing political participation. In this, they recognized that tinkering is as much a form of cultural production as a technical one;[1] the activists sought to produce not just technical artifacts but egalitarian social relations by eroding boundaries between experts and laypeople. Activists suggested that demystification of technology through widespread hands-on making could provide an alternative to prevalent technical cultures in which authority is not distributed but resides exclusively with experts. By emphasizing technical *participation*, these activists distinguished themselves from and mounted a challenge to volunteer projects where technical *virtuosity* is paramount (notably, free and open source software projects, for example). This enabled them to focus on the deliberate cultivation of a radically participatory technical identity, enacting DIY as a mode of technical and political decision making that rests on technical empowerment, where the notion of active political and technological agency is key. (It should be noted that "technology" is largely an actors' category: the activists understood "technical" to refer to audio, computer, and radio transmission hardware, and to software related to the production of community media. I do not mean to imply that other forms of interacting with artifacts or techniques are not "technical," but for the argument presented in this chapter, I restrict technical to hardware related to media production and transmission.)

However, in practice the media activists encountered challenges in their promotion of the technical maker identity. In particular, by asking people to become identified as makers of such technologies as radio hardware and directional wi-fi antennas—to affectively take up the mantle of agency associated with making—the activists struggled with inscribed historical patterns of inclusion and exclusion, as electronics tinkering has long been associated with white masculinity. Rather than dismissing the technical maker identity as a foundation for transformative projects and social change, I argue that this episode points to the need for a reflective and evolving understanding of the potentials of DIY technical empowerment.[2]

Background

The activists whose work I present in this chapter came together in the mid-1990s as a pirate radio collective in Philadelphia, PA. After they were raided and shut down by the Federal Communications Commission in 1997, they then turned away from broadcasting and toward advocacy on the one hand and building radio stations on the other. Expanding access to low-power FM radio (LPFM) was their main issue, but in the early 2000s, they considered whether and how to expand their mission to "free the airwaves" to include not only radio but Internet-based technologies, especially community wi-fi.[3] They espoused radical left politics and considered their work to occur against the backdrop of a social movement for media democracy and a wide social change agenda. (However, groups across the political spectrum have weighed in on media issues, especially to oppose media consolidation; it would be misleading to represent all groups engaged in amateur making or tinkering, even those linking it to politics, as leaning to the political left.) The data in this chapter are drawn from a much larger ethnographic project, including participant-observation and around thirty semi-structured interviews, conducted from 2003 to 2007, and I use pseudonyms to refer to the group, Pandora Radio Project, as well as to other sites.

The group's activities encompassed both advocacy to change policy (not discussed in this chapter) and assisting citizens[4] and community groups in hands-on work with technology, including building new radio stations. Technical engagement held a special symbolic value within a diverse repertoire of activist practice. The activists convened weekly tinkering groups to build or repair electronics hardware, and they also conducted radio station "barnraisings," events where participants put a new radio station on the air over the course of a weekend.

Theorizing Technical Media Activism

Situated between manufacturers and users of technology, and between policymakers and community members, these activists occupy a mediating role. A more refined label might be "propagators" of technology, because they seek to diffuse technological artifacts related to media production, as well as to designate their appropriate uses; this relates to propagation as having to do with reproduction and replication. Specifically, the radio activists drew a connection between "maker agency" attained through tinkering or putting one's hands on an artifact, and a political identity that inclines the "maker" to not only technical but political participation. The activists presented maker agency as accessible to all; in their view, the "universal" demystification of technology would level uneven distributions of technical and political forms of capital and agency. This could combat the hoarding of technical knowledge and power by experts, and undermine elite forms of technocratic decision making more generally. The activists envisioned "everyone" as a potential "maker," and thus DIY citizenship as accessible to all.

As much as the presentation of a politics of distributed and catholic expertise is appealing in its radically egalitarian intent, this chapter argues that the activists' DIY strategy was paradoxically least effective when its universalist impulse was strongest. In other words, in spite of their explicit commitment to the universality of DIY, the activists' focus on tying political participation to technical participation may have had the puzzling consequence of unintentionally appealing to a limited range of social identities. To understand these occurrences, I draw on feminist social studies of technology. Donna Haraway insists on replacing universalist "ways of being nowhere while claiming to see comprehensively" with "views from somewhere."[5] Haraway's intervention helps explain the contradiction the radio activists experienced between their commitment to universality and egalitarianism and the fact that technical cultures always come from *somewhere,* which resulted in practical difficulties as they promoted DIY maker agency. In taking up DIY as a comprehensive "way of seeing," media activists risked "[losing] track of the social mediations of technical production."[6] An alternative to universalist DIY is what Lucy Suchman calls "located accountability,"[7] in which activists actively grapple with issues of social structure and identity that have formed around ICTs, as well as the consequences of their own position as propagators of technology.

Activism and Geek/Maker Identity

Relationships with machines have long served as sites of identity construction. In his ethnography of Xerox technicians, Julian Orr eloquently argues that the identity of technicians is defined by the ability to do things to a machine.[8] Historians Susan Douglas and Kristen Haring have shown that personal identity, especially masculinity, grew up around electronics tinkering earlier in the twentieth century.[9] These accounts of technical identity provide a useful starting point for considering the radio activists.

While the radio activists did manifest a salient technical or geek identity, they attached a distinct activist politics to technical practice.[10] In essence, they promoted a version of technical identity that connected political agency to technical work. In this way, "maker" was a way of being in the world, with distinct political implications. They emphasized *making* as a form of empowerment because of its potential to undermine a social order in which technology is esoteric and intelligible only to experts; thus critical making was linked to a general notion of social participation. However, it is important to note that in their conception of the agency of makers, technical *identity* was not necessarily quite the same as technical *skill*. This is partly because this group constructed technical identity in a somewhat unusual way, valorizing technical *participation* and demystification, as opposed to celebrating virtuosic expertise. Thus amateurs' and novices' affective relationships with technology were not straightforwardly about technical skill in itself. An important part of the radio activists' DIY politics of technology was that people with relatively less expertise could identify relatively strongly as makers of technology; indeed, the point was for nonexperts to experience maker agency.

These beliefs come into sharp focus at the site of radio station barnraisings. Approximately twice per year, volunteers and activists joined together over a weekend to build a new radio station, which was an extremely important part of the activists' practice. The activists' stated ideal was that "no one is allowed to do what they already know how to do" at a barnraising; expert engineers and activists were supposed to guide novice volunteers through the assembly of the new radio station, handing tools off to other people to learn new skills. This was seen as an exercise in community empowerment, and the technical practices were explicitly linked to political engagement. A staff activist reflected on this, invoking DIY: "[A] big part of the barnraisings [is that] it is a demystification, and making people feel like . . . oh, if I just did this enough, I could do this just as well . . . as this engineer."[11] Whether the activists' ideals were matched by the social reality (and arguably they were not), the symbolic importance of the barn-raising for the activists was that by "getting their hands dirty," volunteers and activists forged a sense of engagement in a common technological and political project, and people who did not regularly participate in technical pursuits would feel empowered as "makers."

For example, soldering a radio transmitter board is a good opportunity for novices to participate. It is relatively simple, as the board comes with instructions and can be assembled in a "paint-by-numbers" fashion, as long as the instructions and schematic are closely followed. It takes several hours of work and is a social activity; each small board can accommodate

Figure 4.1
A young woman learning to solder a transmitter board under the instruction of a radio activist during a radio station barnraising, Tanzania, 2005

a couple of people soldering and at least a few more observing or guiding at a time. The parts are differentiated enough from each other to allow the instructor(s) to point to each and converse in general terms about the role of the component and about integrated circuits; for example, "See the components that look like lentils? Anyone know what they are? Capacitors? What do they do in the circuit?" There is a small switch that is used to set the frequency. There are parts that light up when the power is switched on (diodes). And when the board is complete, if it has been assembled correctly, the instructor and volunteers can enjoy the fruits of the labor by testing the board and hearing that it works, using the transmitter, a portable receiver, a power source, and an audio source. Implicitly, the maker-empowerment form of technical identity that the radio activists cultivated at barnraisings was intended as a radical opportunity for groups who have traditionally been excluded from technical expertise.

Social Identities Confront DIY Technical Practice: Exclusion and Inclusion

Now that I have outlined the radio activists' vision for the transformative power of maker identity, I turn to two brief empirical examples of how the ideal of universal accessibility played out in the radio activists' practice.

The first case pertains to race[12] and technology. Historian Rayvon Fouché has written of the tension for African Americans in technology adoption. He notes that there are historical reasons why African Americans may in some cases have a vexed relationship with technology, citing the value of futurism on the one hand versus an uneasiness about new technology, especially that introduced by whites.[13] Ron Eglash has also explored the limitations of "geek" or technical identity as a social identity, especially in terms of its being bound to whiteness and masculinity.[14] As both Fouché and Eglash's analyses foreshadow, groups attempting even self-consciously anti-paternalist work with technology across racial identity lines may face unanticipated challenges. The promotion of a sphere in which "universal" technical (or civic) participation occurs may require bracketing inequalities of access and status, which obviously fails to reflect a social reality where certain groups enjoy privilege and dominance relative to other groups.

Since their introduction in 2000, LPFM licenses have been essentially impossible to obtain in urban areas.[15] Partly due to their desire to not exclude cities, Pandora became interested in the relevance and "appropriateness" of community wi-fi networks to their organizing mission. In 2005–2006, Pandora consulted on a project with Chicago nonprofit Neighbors for Access to Technology (NAT), that wished to turn a small network their organization had implemented as a prototype in Larch Park, an economically disadvantaged, largely African American neighborhood, into a larger network. NAT hoped to draw on Pandora's expertise leading hands-on workshops, potentially even holding a "wi-fi barnraising." A Pandora activist remarked, "As a white[16] activist group, we're in solidarity—they can use the [wi-fi network] to do it themselves, we're really privileged to do the work we do and have the impact we do."[17] Here he drew a subtle distinction between the notion of a paternalist "provision" of technology to "other," less privileged groups and Pandora's project of propagating technology through DIY—the activist was careful to indicate that the groups with whom Pandora held barnraisings were "doing it themselves" rather than exhibiting dependence on more privileged groups.

However, after arriving in Chicago for meetings, the Pandora activists felt uneasy. Many neighborhood residents were interested in attaining Internet connectivity; one person who worked closely with the community members said, "This is a chance [for the residents of Larch Park] to not just keep up with society, but to advance beyond it, people want to use this to start businesses and for education";[18] this echoes Fouché's argument that the relationship between African Americans and technological "progress" is complex. However, some residents also had a (legitimate) concern about the intentions of a group of (largely white) people from elsewhere to "improve" the neighborhood; NAT was not based in Larch Park, and Pandora was not even from Chicago. A NAT staff member picked up on this tension and said, "There will never be a time when it will be okay for hundreds of people who don't live in [Larch Park] to come volunteer there."[19] This made Larch Park a troublesome site to plan a wi-fi barnraising; a Pandora intern referred to the discrepancy among community members' expectations for Internet connectivity, the activists' goals for cultivating maker agency, and the potential for missteps having to do with perceptions of outsider, nongovernmental organization paternalism as a "liberal clusterfuck."[20] Ultimately Pandora activists decided Larch Park was not an appropriate site to strongly pursue Pandora's wi-fi interests.[21] This raises interesting questions about the limits of supposedly egalitarian collaboration across differentially privileged groups, as well as the limits of "universalist" civic or technical engagement.

The radio activists also saw gendered challenges to their implementation of DIY politics. As Douglas and Haring demonstrate, a culture of masculinity grew up around electronics (radio) tinkering earlier in the twentieth century. Ruth Oldenziel and Tine Kleif and Wendy Faulkner argue that men's masculinity and the pleasure some men attain in technical domains are mutually reinforcing projects of technical and gender construction.[22] Extending these analyses to the radio activists' interest in hands-on technical work and tinkering, it is evident that social structure has contributed to differences in familiarity and comfort with electronics hardware between women and men.[23] However, as noted earlier, the radio activists presented maker identity as an opportunity for inclusion, intending to bring excluded groups into technical practice and maker identity through DIY politics.

In an interview, one activist described Pandora's strategy to "open up" technical practice. Though Pandora was committed to DIY and egalitarianism, the group constantly struggled with diversity and inclusion in practice. One activist commented: "It's so easy to find white guys to do this stuff. Look at me, I'm a white guy. I'm not in any unique situation, I'm one of millions of white dudes who went to engineering school, I just happen to have more of a lefty attitude than most of them. That is the biggest challenge, finding people who are going to implicitly understand why it's important for people to have their hands on this technology . . . Part of [the barnraising model] is really challenging the engineers themselves to make the change."[24] Thus, he acknowledged that to make DIY work the way the activists envisioned, they needed to in some way address the fact that technical expertise was likely to be unevenly distributed in members of their community, and that overcoming this disparity meant actively attending to what Lucy Suchman might call the "social mediations of technical production." Pandora tried to address this by bringing "nontraditional" engineers and teachers (including women and people of color) to barnraisings to embody and promote a widely accessible politics of DIY and maker agency.

A skilled volunteer on whom Pandora leaned at barnraisings, a woman, also shared her impressions: "I've been sensitive to [Pandora]'s sensitivity. [They] make no bones about saying 'It's a dudefest. We need more women.' [But] . . . I feel an odd responsibility. I definitely feel like I'm extra visible and like I should be extra visible. I understand what I have to contribute . . . Chicks with Ethernet cables, there's a certain inherent value in that, even in just seeing that, especially for people who aren't used to seeing it."[25] For this volunteer, her technical skills made her feel extra-visible in the barnraising setting, as if she were part of Pandora's display of its activist vision, as someone who clearly displayed a feminine identity coupled with maker agency and technical competence. She also felt that, at least among the media activists themselves, the fact that more "makers" were men was not primarily due to sexism or exclusionary behavior on the part of the men, but to a shortage of women willing to take up maker identity and learn and display technical skills. She said: "The framework is there, ready for women like me to jump in—this community is ready for women with good tech skills, and they are who I most get along with. Unfortunately I keep finding kick-ass men."[26] Like the Pandora activist, she felt that part of the problem for the activists was a shortage of women who had the range of expertise and comfort with technology; she felt that the feminist men's attempts to be inclusive toward women were genuine and mostly adequate.[27] As a woman who was not intimidated by technology and who already possessed a high degree of technical expertise, she may have felt differently than neophytes (both women and men), who are potentially derailed by competitive, "stand-offish," or masculine displays as they try to engage with technology.[28]

Conclusions

Taken in isolation, these examples might seem too idiosyncratic to matter. However, I argue that to the contrary, these brief empirical vignettes represent a pattern of difficulties the radio activists immediately encountered when they promoted DIY technical empowerment. Even though the radio activists cherished DIY because they viewed it as accessible to all, sedimented patterns of familiarity and comfort formed around electronics

Figure 4.2
The symbolic value of hands-on "making" of community-scale technology can be seen in this artistic rendition of a group of people (men, in this case) struggling to erect a radio tower. Courtesy PRP

technologies and practices affected the activists' ability to promote maker identity. Thus an unforeseen and unintended consequence of maker identity as an activist strategy was the persistence of social structure and identity categories that have historically limited access to technical artifacts and expertise: the proposition that technical participation can be a route to social or civic egalitarianism tends to elide a history in which the codes of masculinity and whiteness have been codified around dominance, over both technology and other social groups. Specifically, some women and people of color might encounter barriers to sharing in the same affective pleasure in technical making experienced by many white men. This represents not only difficulty for egalitarian technical projects, but points to the limits of "universalist" discourse more generally: universalism all but depends on glossing over differences in power, access, and status among different groups.

In the first example, proffering the notion of the barnraising—maker identity coupled with electronics tinkering—was perceived as an ineffective challenge to the differences between the stations of Larch Park residents, NAT staff, and Pandora activists. Pandora's vision of universal DIY politics was not sufficient to overcome issues of trust or insider-outsider positionality, some of which were generated by the relationship between race and historical patterns of technological exclusion. In the second, through vigilant commitment to confronting unequally distributed "makerhood," Pandora found an ideal embodiment of "nontraditional" (i.e., woman) techie in their volunteer. The volunteer was self-conscious about her visibility but willing to play the part desired by the activists. She and the staff activist both acknowledged that as a woman who was technically skilled, comfortable displaying a technical maker identity, and at ease teaching, she was unusual in this activist technical community.

I argue that these episodes—and the patterns they represent—point to a need to reflect critically on the origin and politics of this particular technical maker culture. Engineering is one thread here, which has long been cast as a culture of exclusion;[29] amateur electronics tinkering is a related and overlapping heritage.[30] The Appropriate Technology movement is another site to which contemporary radio activism is indebted, and Carroll Pursell and Fred Turner have detailed its projects as exemplifying such tropes as American individualism, transcendentalist relationships with land, and, often, neo-traditional gender roles and racial exclusion.[31] The radio activists are not precise duplicators or direct descendents of any of these prior cultural formations, of course, but I argue that their practice has a heritage that includes all of these strands.

Thus, antecedent technical cultures play a largely unacknowledged role in the contemporary formation of technical media activism. In the example of the activists seeking out the woman "techie" to lead and be visible at barnraisings, Pandora readily recognized that it had to make an effort to combat the exclusive culture of engineering and to locate a person who was less associated with the white masculinity traditionally connected with that culture. This was an uphill struggle for the activists, but one they were willing to take on.

However, even as they tried to confront the ways in which engineering culture challenged the propagation of technology they worked toward, the activists failed to consider DIY itself. DIY itself has traditionally not been for just "anyone," and an especially technical strand of DIY may have been particularly saddled with this legacy. As illustrated in the Larch Park case, DIY was simply not enough to bridge a gap between historically disenfranchised African American neighborhood residents who wished to "keep up with society" and activists who wished to promote a much broader vision of technology as it related to maker agency. Indeed, construing DIY to be the universalist antidote to hierarchical engineering culture was ironically reproducing some of the very problems the activists sought to evade; the activists dealt better with issues of inclusion/exclusion when they painstakingly and iteratively attended to the standings and positions of members of different groups. These episodes illustrate that activists concerned with not losing sight of the "social mediations of technical production" may wish to attend more closely to where technical cultures come from—and in particular the ways in which technical DIY may import some values they do not share—as this could prove beneficial in building a desirable and egalitarian politics of technology.

This is not to reject outright DIY or the strategy of promoting technical maker identity. Instead, I turn back to Suchman's notion of "located accountability." Propagators of technology who seek to turn "everyone" into a "maker" would do well to heed that activist solutions also embody a vision from somewhere. One way out of the problem of presenting universalist projects is to recognize the partial perspectives and limited power of would-be propagators of technology; a self-consciously embodied and partial perspective can be used to make one personally responsible for one's position within the matrix of sociotechnical production. It is especially important that activists—and also scholars—be wary of advancing a romanticized notion of voluntarism or participation that celebrates the agency of peers or the centrality of technology, without seeking to understand the difficult and elusive work of building and maintaining structures of participation, especially egalitarian participation. DIY may hold promise for building new structures and identities, but DIY itself may also need to be critically and reflectively rebuilt.

Notes

1. See Carolyn Marvin, *When Old Technologies Were New* (New York: Oxford University Press, 1988), 7.

2. DIY itself has at least two points of origin: first, as a project of masculine home improvement that carved out a masculine domestic domain in an otherwise feminized one and, second, within punk and hardcore music subcultures that called for resistance to the "appropriative and controlling" impulses of the commercial music industry. See Steven Gelber, "Do-It-Yourself: Constructing, Repairing, and Maintaining Domestic Masculinity," *American Quarterly* 49, no. 1 (1997): 66–112; Steve Waksman, "California Noise: Tinkering with Hardcore and Heavy Metal in Southern California," *Social Studies of Science* 34, no. 5 (October 2004): 675–702. Mimi Nguyen discusses politics of race and gender in punk rock in "Tales of an Asiatic Geek Girl: *Slant* from Paper to Pixels," in *Appropriating Technology: Vernacular Science and Social Power*, ed. Ron Eglash, Jennifer L. Croissant, Giovanna Di Chiro, and Rayvon Fouché (Minneapolis: University of Minnesota Press, 2004), 177–190.

3. Christina Dunbar-Hester, "'Free the Spectrum!' Activist Encounters with Old and New Media Technology," *New Media & Society* 11, nos. 1 & 2 (2009): 221–240; Christina Dunbar-Hester, "Beyond 'Dudecore'? Challenging Gendered and 'Raced' Technologies through Media Activism," *Journal of Broadcasting and Electronic Media* 54, no. 1 (2010): 121–135.

4. Of course "citizen" is rightly a contentious concept for some. In my use of the term, I wish to signal activity around civic or communal participation, not to marginalize those without full legal status as citizens. (This is important as many media activists have a wider social justice orientation, including immigration rights. Several low-power radio stations Pandora built were with migrant farmworkers' groups, as well.) Though I do not have space to interrogate "citizenship" here, using it to stand in for a mode of engagement open to "everyone" may present problems.

5. Donna Haraway, "Situated Visions," in *Simians, Cyborgs, and Women* (New York: Routledge, 1991), 191.

6. Ibid., 5.

7. Lucy Suchman, "Located Accountabilities in Technology Production," Centre for Science Studies, Lancaster University, Lancaster, UK, 2003, http://www.lancs.ac.uk/fass/sociology/research/publications/papers/suchman-located-accountabilities.pdf. Suchman writes of overcoming the dichotomy between designers and users, but her insights are quite generative for thinking about technological activism as well.

8. Julian Orr, *Talking about Machines: An Ethnography of a Modern Job* (Ithaca, NY: Cornell University Press, 1996).

9. Susan Douglas, *Inventing American Broadcasting* (Baltimore, MD: Johns Hopkins University Press, 1987); Kristen Haring, *Ham Radio's Technical Culture* (Cambridge, MA: MIT Press, 2006).

10. Christina Dunbar-Hester, "Geeks, Meta-geeks, and Gender Trouble: Activism, Identity, and Low-Power FM Radio," *Social Studies of Science* 38, no. 2 (2008): 201–232.

11. Interview, July 5, 2006.

12. Theorists of critical race theory assert the following: "Race and races are products of social thought and relations. Not objective, inherent, or fixed, they correspond to no biological nor genetic reality; rather, races are categories that society invents, manipulates, or retires when convenient" (Richard Delgado and Jean Stefancic, *Critical Race Theory* [New York: NYU Press, 2001], 7). This chapter anchors the categories of race and gender to the insights of poststructuralist theorists of social identity who seek alternative explanations for the persistence of categorization and inequality, rejecting the notion of fixity or inherence in social identities.

13. Rayvon Fouché, "Say It Loud, I'm Black and I'm Proud: African Americans, Artifactual Culture, and Black Vernacular Technological Creativity," *American Quarterly* 58, no. 3 (2006): 639–661.

14. Ron Eglash, "Race, Sex, and Nerds: From Black Geeks to Asian American Hipsters," *Social Tex*, 20, no. 2 (2002): 49–64.

15. For more on this history, see Martin Spinelli, "Interference and the Public Service: The History and Impact of Low-Power FM," *Social Policy* 31 (2000): 16–25. Legislation passed in 2011 that expanded the possibilities for new LPFMs in more densely populated areas, but the largest urban markets were still likely to be excluded.

16. The activists' use of racial categories should also be read as being in dialogue with the contributions of critical whiteness/antiracism. For this group of activists, the need for media activism to ally itself with antiracism is not an afterthought; many people who are drawn to media activism began activist work on other social justice causes, but then identified media justice as the linchpin of their advocacy. Thus, much media activism can be seen as a means to an end in a larger struggle against inequality. That said, media activism is not immune to the problems faced in other social movements, which struggle with inclusion, representation, and differences in privilege and positionality between members of the movement. See, for example, bell hooks, *Talking Back: Thinking Feminist, Thinking Black* (Cambridge, MA: South End Press, 1989) on the adverse effects of racism on the women's movement.

17. Interview, February 16, 2006.

18. Field notes, March 1, 2005.

19. Ibid.

20. Field notes, March 2005.

21. Dunbar-Hester, "Beyond 'Dudecore'?"

22. Ruth Oldenziel, "Boys and Their Toys: The Fisher Body Craftsman's Guild, 1930–1968, and the Making of a Male Technical Domain," *Technology and Culture* 38, no. 1 (January 1997): 60–96; Tine Klief and Wendy Faulkner, "'I'm No Athlete [but] I Can Make This Thing Dance!'—Men's Pleasures in Technology," *Science, Technology, & Human Values* 28, no. 2 (Spring 2003): 296–325.

23. Dunbar-Hester, "Geeks, Meta-geeks"; Dunbar-Hester, "Beyond 'Dudecore'?"

24. Interview, July 5, 2006.

25. Interview, June 27, 2006.

26. Ibid.

27. Tom Digby, *Men Doing Feminism (Thinking Gender)* (New York: Routledge, 1998).

28. Dunbar-Hester, "Geeks, Meta-geeks," 218.

29. Sally Hacker, *Pleasure, Power and Technology: Some Tales of Gender, Engineering, and the Cooperative Workplace* (Boston, MA: Unwin Hyman, 1989); Marvin, *When Old Technologies Were New.*

30. Douglas, *Inventing American Broadcasting*; Haring, *Ham Radio's Technical Culture.*

31. Carroll Pursell, "The Rise and Fall of the Appropriate Technology Movement in the United States, 1965–1985," *Technology & Culture* 34 (1993): 629–637; Fred Turner, *From Counterculture to Cyberculture* (Chicago: University of Chicago, 2006).

5 Proportionate ID Cards: Prototyping for Privacy and Accountability

Brenda McPhail, Andrew Clement, Karen Louise Smith, Jennette Weber, Joseph Ferenbok, and Alex Tichine

Introduction

"ID please!"

This apparently straightforward request is an increasingly taken for granted aspect of everyday transactions in informationally mediated societies. A citizen or customer typically responds by unquestioningly providing a plastic photo ID card for inspection. Without the "right" card, a transaction can stop in its tracks. In these transactions, the ID cards we routinely present define who we are and what we can do. In aggregate, these cards enable and delimit how we participate in society—in short, they shape our citizenship.

We often think of citizenship in terms of rights and responsibilities accorded to us by virtue of belonging within the state; typically, these are circumscribed by law and custom.[1] DIY citizenship as we practice it takes seriously the concept of responsibility—not just the responsibility to follow the rules and accept legitimately imposed limits on our participation in society, but the responsibility to hold our governments accountable for making rules to reflect the kind of society in which we want to live. DIY citizenship as we approach it in our research about identification and identification documents is active, engaged, and sometimes critical citizenship. It has the potential to reveal and push the kinds of societal limits that we often take for granted.

Our approach to DIY identification is about citizen empowerment through information and tools to permit thoughtful engagement with government and other ID-requiring organizations. One of our ongoing goals as academics and advocates is to find ways to make ID infrastructure issues vivid and concrete, to make tangible artifacts that people can interact with, modify, and use and that open up the typically "black-boxed" technologies, organizational practices, and built in assumptions that are hidden within contemporary identification practices. By "hacking" ID cards and other ID infrastructures, in Milberry's use of the term,[2] we seek to challenge the social/political assumptions built in to the technologies as well as offer more democratic alternatives. The issues we hope to highlight include privacy, individual control over personal information, and the potential for changing relationships between citizen and state as identification processes go digital.

Simply showing ID cards usually poses little risk to privacy or control of personal information. In many bars, liquor stores, post offices, retail outlets, and similar establishments, an employee typically takes a quick glance to see if the photo matches the customer and that the card is authentic before proceeding with the transaction. However, when information is recorded, privacy issues do arise—especially if more information is captured than is needed for the transaction.[3] Does a bar patron showing her ID to prove her age want the bouncer to know where she lives? Does a store need to know a customer's birthdate to process a return? Inspection of identity credentials is increasingly being automated, and hence the potential for misuse of personal information escalates substantially. With the recent introduction of radio-frequency identification (RFID) chips in conventional plastic cards for "contactless" transactions, and the burgeoning adoption of smartphones with near field communication (NFC) capabilities, the privacy risks from ID transactions increase. If the current show-all approach to ID inspection continues to prevail in these automated settings, in-person transactions will come to resemble web-based transactions, where excessive collection and misuse of personal information is rampant and controversial. At the same time that smartphones are being viewed as personal data capture devices by hungry marketers, undermining individual control of personal information, they can also be designed to protect personal data and help hold data gatherers to account. To draw attention to the privacy risks of everyday ID transactions and lay the basis for citizen-centric, privacy-promoting alternatives in automated transactions, we embarked on a project of ID prototyping. While our long-term aim is to develop privacy protective digital ID wallets, our more immediate goal was to experiment with existing government-issued ID cards. The focus of this chapter is the development of transparent ID card covers that strategically reveal only what is needed for specific transactions.

This account of developing "proportionate ID" begins by articulating the rationale behind the project and its relation to prevailing privacy protection regimes. We then review the research foundations for our participatory design/DIY technology probe approach, sketch our iterative prototyping process, and describe our attempts to use ID cards with overlays in everyday situations.

Data Minimization and Citizen-Centric Design

Many jurisdictions around the world, including Canada, the United States, and Europe, have enacted privacy legislation to protect personal data when organizations collect it from individuals. While the laws vary, they are all based on well-established fair information practice principles. These foundational principles include the right of the individual to be informed about what information is being collected, for what purpose, and how it will be stored, accessed, and protected. They also oblige the organization to handle the personal information in specific ways. In particular, the "data minimization principle" requires organizations to collect no more information than is needed for the transaction. Collecting more than is necessary is a violation of this principle.[4] In Canada, our research context, the Personal Information Protection and Electronic Documents Act (PIPEDA) governs how information should be collected and used during commercial transactions and embodies data minimization as a principle.[5]

In keeping with this principle of data minimization, we have developed what we call "proportionate identification" or "prop-ID" tools to allow citizens to provide their information only in exact proportion to what is required for specific transactions when presenting a government-issued ID. Through a workshop and field-based prototyping process, we used simple materials such as vinyl overlays, ink, and existing ID cards to provide citizens with a DIY method of minimizing the organization's data view. Rather than relying solely on organizations collecting information to abide by the data minimization principle, we see the potential for citizens themselves to minimize the information that is circulated about them, putting the onus on the organization to be explicit about what information it needs and why. Using these overlays disrupts the routine (and hence often invisible) process of identification during everyday transactions; they are a visible indication of what information the user is willing to provide during the transaction based on their assessment of what is needed. If an organizational representative questions the overlay's use, this provides an opportunity to engage in a conversation with those who require IDs about their needs, practices, and processes.

This exemplifies one possibility for DIY citizenship, where the prop-ID tools encourage people to reflect on whether the personal information they are being asked to provide makes sense in the context, and to allow them to try to exercise more control when dealing with ID-requiring organizations. This approach is similar to that of other authors in this volume who encourage engagement in activities to provoke critical reflections on technology design and the political and cultural assumptions that are imbedded within them (e.g., see Kafai and Peppler, chapter 12, this volume, and McVeigh-Schultz, chapter 23, this volume). When designing our tools, while we embrace the critical making goal of using "material forms of engagement with technologies to supplement and extend critical reflection,"[6] we more explicitly base our approach on the use of technology probes.[7] We create evocative objects that *in use* provoke critique, discussion, and exploration. We are also guided in our approach to prototyping by the tenets of participatory design, which is deeply concerned with bringing democratic ideals into technology design.[8]

Key precepts that informed our design activities were as follows:

1. Information revealed in a transaction should be "proportionate" to the actual requirements of the transaction.
2. Both institutional agents and the holders of ID cards can work to minimize what personal information is collected during a transaction.
3. The process and development of alternatives should be participatory, in the sense that identity subjects should have an effective voice in the development process and influence the actual use of the new forms of ID.

We hope that these do-it-yourself and citizen-centric possibilities can be incorporated into ID schemes as they are being developed using emerging technologies, and that the concept of proportionality, so fundamental in privacy frameworks, can become a central feature of identification practices.

DIY Prototyping for "Proportionate ID"

Our research team sought means to reveal only the necessary information on ID cards during transactions. The overlay concept offered a customizable way to do this for different cards, using commercially available vinyl cling film and an ink-jet photo printer. The overlays serve the practical function of protecting unneeded personal information, but they also serve as a concrete manifestation of the proportionality principle. The overlays are probes, tools to provoke discussion and reflection on ID situations at the moment of use. The creation of the card overlays began with an analysis of the different parts of the government-issued identification cards that people use most often for ID in Ontario: the Ontario driver's license and the Ontario health card. Figure 5.1 shows the information contained on these commonly used cards.

We worked iteratively to develop an overlay that would be easy for people to create and use; we wanted a "low barrier to entry"[9] for potential users. A series of workshops brought together people interested in identification

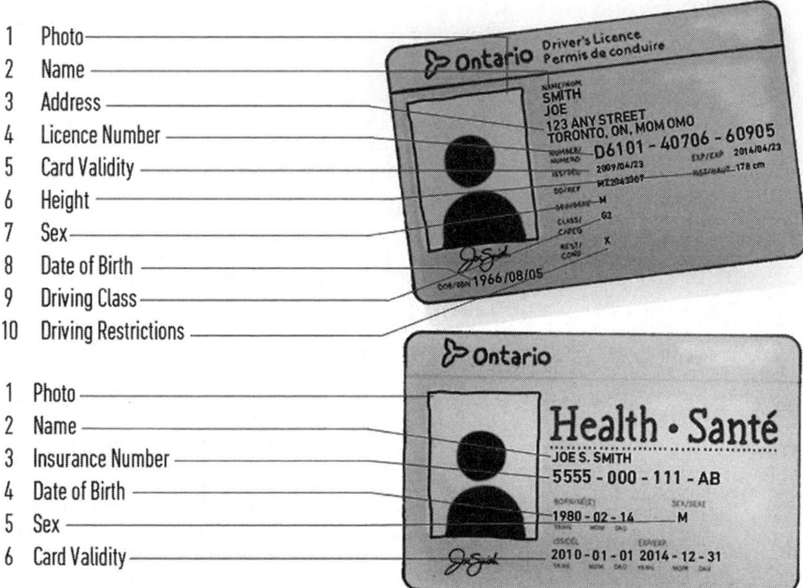

Figure 5.1
Widely issued Ontario government ID cards

and privacy issues to solicit feedback about the concept of DIY privacy-protective ID, to discuss what that ID might look like, and as prototypes were developed to talk about the features of each one. Discussions ranged from the aesthetics of the overlays (such as the graphic appearances and the wording of text), the pragmatics (such as how adaptable they were to wallets and the ease with which the overlay could be removed or changed), and the user experience (such as the confidence citizens had to use these overlays in day-to-day activity and the comfort organizations had in accepting these overlays with minimal suspicion).

Prototypes

We conducted five design iterations of the ID card overlays that changed in response to workshop feedback, researcher inspiration, and, in the final stage, organizational feedback during real-world transactions. The first iteration (prototype 1) was a customized wallet insert composed of a series of double-sided plastic sleeves. Each sleeve contained an explanation of what the ID cover was for (e.g., drinking or voting) and some information about the project and the minimum disclosure principal, including a reference to the relevant section of PIPEDA. Different sleeves were developed for transactions, with bold black bars covering unnecessary information. The sleeves were convenient for inserting and removing ID cards; however, a major drawback was that the sleeves would not fit into the card slot of a wallet.

The second iteration of our prototype tried to solve the concern people raised about having to carry multiple sleeves. We developed a single sleeve with multiple tabbed inserts, where each insert was for a different transaction. This still made the cards easy to remove but actually increased the difficulty of using the sleeve, since the correct insert had to be chosen and aligned over the card in a process that required a bit of "fiddling around" in order to get it correctly positioned.

The third iteration was a compromise in that it used single sleeves as opposed to the bulky set of sleeves, but it still had one for each kind of card and transaction in a trade-off of ease of use over multifunction convenience. Feedback from users of this variant encouraged us to adopt a form factor that fit in a standard wallet pocket for cards. In response, our fourth and fifth prototypes were a removable vinyl cling film overlay placed directly on the card.

Making Them Work: Exploring Prop-ID Card Overlays in Use Situations

For citizens to use the overlays routinely, they need to be (at least potentially) accepted by businesses that require identification. Based on participant preference from our workshop sessions, we chose single sleeves (prototype 3) and stick-on overlays (prototype 4) to test in the kinds of everyday situations that require ID. In addition to asking interested participants to try the overlays, we sent a fieldwork team out to see if we could use prop-IDs easily, or where we might encounter resistance. We also used the overlays to elicit concrete details about ID practices; when they were accepted, we asked how they met the organizations' policy requirements, and where they were rejected, we asked why, and what we could do to make them acceptable. We asked organization members questions about what information items they were looking at on the card, whether they collected or stored any information, and what different kinds of ID documents were acceptable for their organizations.

The fieldwork team identified a number of sites to visit and multiple locations of each site in different neighborhoods within Toronto, Ontario. Sites included convenience stores, The Beer Store, the Liquor Control Board of Ontario (LCBO), pubs and bars, retail stores, and polling stations. We visited at least three locations of each type of field site, using one of two approaches. In the first iteration, field-workers attempted to conduct a transaction and provided an Ontario driver's license covered with a prop-ID overlay or inside a prop-ID sleeve when asked for ID, then initiated a discussion about its acceptance or rejection based on a research script. In the second iteration, to avoid the anxiety some frontline workers exhibited when faced with the prop-ID, particularly in an alcohol-purchase situation, field-workers chose a quiet time in the business setting to approach a frontline worker or manager, show the prop-ID, and ask questions as to its potential acceptance without attempting a purchase. Before we went out into the field, we researched the ID policies of the organizations we were going to visit, but we were curious to know how those policies actually played out when frontline staff asked for IDs. There was no evaluative aspect to our approach in terms of staff behavior or the degree to which written policies were or were not followed; rather, we wanted some insight into the actual as well as ideal processes in different kinds of ID-collecting organizations.

Virtually everyone who tried to use the overlay in recent Ontario (provincial) and federal elections had it accepted with little comment or difficulty. It did occasion some curiosity at polling stations: one person who tried it told us that she noticed that one of the poll workers "was looking at it while the other [poll worker] was crossing my name off of the list; I think more out of curiosity than anything. However, neither one of them made any comment, and I was able to vote with no difficulty."

In many business settings, particularly those selling alcohol, prop-IDs were seldom accepted without comment or hesitation, and in some cases were flatly refused. There was, encouragingly, quite a high degree of sympathy for the idea of ID that would keep personal information private unless it was needed, even from workers who said they couldn't accept the overlays. All but one of the individuals interviewed told us that even though technically the items of personal information needed to verify the customer's eligibility to buy alcohol were photo and birthdate, in practice, they regularly used other items of information as a sort of cross-check of identity when they were in doubt (e.g., asking a person they suspected of borrowing an ID for the postal code on the card).

Individuals who sell alcohol have particular challenges when they check ID. Frontline workers often rely heavily on the physical features of the card for authentication of the document, including the watermarks, the reflective image in the bottom right corner, and the card's texture. Fraudulent use of ID, particularly by underage people trying to buy alcohol, was a very common concern among workers in alcohol-related businesses, and many expressed a concern about the prop-ID overlays potentially covering attempts to alter ID cards. Frontline staff generally talked about their refusal to accept the prop-ID in terms of their personal and organizational responsibility to make sure the customer really was eligible to buy liquor and that the card was unaltered and genuine beneath the overlay or sleeve prototypes. Of the Ontario sites we visited, both The Beer Store and the LCBO have clear, detailed ID policies and thorough training programs for staff members. Their concern for adhering to policy, we were told, reflected both this training, and the fact that if an error was made in allowing an alcohol purchase that should have been declined, the consequences for both the individual and the organization included significant fines, job loss, potential criminal charges, and even jail time. As one LCBO manager informed us, since a recent round of mandatory ID challenge training, no one at the LCBO can even unpack a box without having been educated on the organizational ID policy. This is positioned, publicly and organizationally, as part of the LCBO's social responsibility for promoting legal, responsible alcohol use as an Ontario government agency.

Notwithstanding these challenges, we have heard from people who have successfully used prop-ID overlays to get into bars or clubs: one participant describes using it at a local Toronto club, where "it was accepted but generated a bit of discussion. The bouncers were more curious than anything else." There is a broad range of people involved in ID check transactions across organizations with widely varying policies and training practices. And, of course, the power disparity between frontline workers and their employers means that the employee may choose to deny service rather than discuss ID policy. All of these factors make it potentially difficult for citizens to challenge organizational policies that require them to show more information than it seems should be needed for a transaction. On the other hand, the prop-ID overlays did provide an opening to discuss ID policies in a wide range of places, and we have had several participants report more success in using them during ordinary daily interactions than we experienced during our fieldwork.

Based on the feedback received from frontline workers in ID-requesting organizations, our most recent prototype maintains the overlay format rather than the sleeve. To minimize the problem of the vinyl film interfering with the reflective and tactile "security" features embedded in the card, we cut down the overlay to cover as little of the physical card as possible while still protecting the information not needed for a transaction (see figure 5.2). All our prototypes are available via our project website (http://propid.ischool.utoronto.ca/) for people to use as is or alter as needed.

Providing easy access to these tools is an important component of our DIY practice, although encouraging uptake is a perpetual challenge.

Conclusions

We created the prop-ID overlays as a design probe to fulfill two primary purposes. First, for citizens, the overlays provide a concrete artifact that, through disrupting routine ID transactions, seeks to increase individual's awareness of the kinds of information that organizations ask of them, and encourages them to question organizational policies and practices. Second, for organizations, the probe attempts, by providing the minimum information required for a transaction, to hold information-collecting bodies accountable for their collection practices. If more than the minimum information is requested, the onus is on the organization to provide the rationale for the request. By accepting these overlays, organizations help protect themselves from the charge of information misuse. In accomplishing these

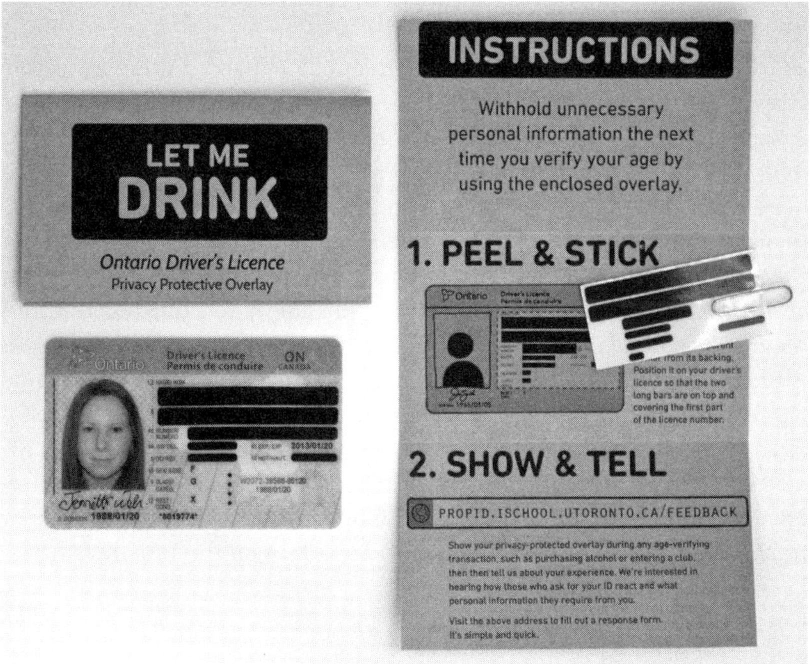

Figure 5.2
Latest prototype: Minimum size clear vinyl overlay

aims, we also laid the groundwork for the development of a smartphone-based privacy-protective digital ID wallet following the same proportionate ID principles. The Android app we are prototyping similarly reveals no more information than is actually required. This is in sharp contrast to most digital wallet apps that convey much more personal information than necessary.[10] We hope that the questioning attitudes we encourage with the physical overlays can extend into the digital realm, and that as new ID schemes are developed, citizens will apply the kinds of questions the overlays encourage—What pieces of information do you collect? Why do you need them?—to digital ID encounters. In other words, in the spirit of critical constructivism, we consider ID technology to be "a terrain of contestation and intervention by users, rather than a mysterious black box, the exclusive territory of designers."[11]

Our prop-ID overlays are attempts to contribute to the theoretical, practical, and policy contexts in which emerging technologies are being considered and deployed. Further, they are explicit attempts to engage citizens in a manner that encourages serious consideration of the ways in which ID schemes and infrastructures might affect them individually and collectively as members of our society. The ways that citizens are identified and the kinds of information collected and stored about them, who gets access to it, and what it is used for, are all highly consequential, whether collected by the state or by private organizations. Citizens have both the right and the responsibility to engage with ID policy at all levels, and we hope through the development and promotion of our DIY prop-ID tools to make the importance of this engagement obvious and the process easy. Governments and organizations, too, have a responsibility to their citizens and customers to have clear policies and the ability to explain and justify these policies; by giving people the tools to question everyday ID requests, we create interruptions in everyday practices, which we optimistically hope will encourage individual and organizational reflection on the necessity of an increasing reliance on ID provision to obtain access to services. Ultimately, in the spirit of DIY citizenship and critical making, we are interested in using technology design and implementation to explore ways of protecting citizens' rights and to help citizens take on this task themselves.

Notes

1. Turner 1997.

2. Milberry, chapter 2, this volume.

3. Bennett and Lyon 2008.

4. See, for example, Federal Trade Commission 2007 and OECD Guidelines on the Protection of Privacy and Transborder Flows of Personal Data 1980.

5. Canada 2000.

6. Ratto 2011.

7. Langdale, Kay, and Kummerfeld 2006. See also Michael and Gaver 2009.

8. Greenbaum and Kyng, 1991.

9. Reilly, chapter 8, this volume.

10. See http://propid.ischool.utoronto.ca/digital-wallet/.

11. Milberry, chapter 2, this volume.

References

Bennett, C. J., and D. Lyon, eds. 2008. *Playing the Identity Card: Surveillance, Security and Identification in Global Perspective*. New York: Routledge.

Canada. 2000. PIPEDA. http://laws-lois.justice.gc.ca/PDF/P-8.6.pdf.

Federal Trade Commission. 2007. Fair Information Practice Principles. http://www.ftc.gov/reports/privacy3/fairinfo.shtm.

Greenbaum, J., and M. Kyng. 1991. *Design at Work: Cooperative Design of Computer Systems*. Hillsdale, NJ: Lawrence Erlbaum.

Langdale, G., J. Kay, and B. Kummerfeld. 2006. "Using an Intergenerational Communications System as a 'Light-Weight' Technology Probe." Paper read at CHI '06, Montreal, Canada, April 22–27.

Michael, M., and W. Gaver. 2009. Home beyond Home: Dwelling with Threshold Devices. *Space and Culture* 12 (August): 359–370.

OECD Guidelines on the Protection of Privacy and Transborder Flows of Personal Data. 1980. Directorate for Science, Technology and Industry. http://www.oecd.org/sti/ieconomy/oecdguidelinesontheprotectionofprivacyandtransborderflowsofpersonaldata.htm.

Ratto, M. 2011. Critical Making: Conceptual and Material Studies in Technology and Social Life. *Information Society* 27 (4): 252–260.

Turner, B. S. 1997. Citizenship Studies: A General Theory. *Citizenship Studies* 1 (1): 5–18.

6 Developing Communities of Resistance? Maker Pedagogies, Do-It-Yourself Feminism, and DIY Citizenship

Red Chidgey

This xine [sic] is a little bit of everything—kiss & tell, political analysis, spy notes, diary, map of the enemy barracks, fiction, radical theory, poetry, textbook, pillow talk, autobiography, telegrams, soup cans tied together with yarn, news bulletin, how-to manual. This is one aspect to making a community of resistance. It isn't—it can't be—everything, but it's a necessary component & I want you to help me develop the others.

—Ciara Xyerra, *A Renegade's Handbook to Love & Sabotage* 3

Zines are noncommercial, amateur texts that have been picked up by various social movements as the perfect channels for communication and creativity.[1] Produced on the fringes of academia, journalism, and established art scenes, these often-photocopied publications offer a variety of voices and perspectives not usually found in the mainstream media (see figure 6.1). As art educators Kristin Congdon and Doug Blandy describe them, zines are "chaotic, disturbing, uncomfortable, sensual, complex, loud, confrontive, humorous, and often a pointed and acerbic critique of mainstream culture and contemporary life."[2] They are an intriguing form of DIY media, predominately made and read by young people.[3]

As a form of alternative media, zines inevitably create different modes of production, representation, and consumption to those found in mainstream media industries.[4] Yet they're not entirely separate entities—the skills learned through DIY media making can be brought into makers' professional lives and zinesters often appropriate and reuse materials from popular culture in their publications.[5] As social documents of lived experience and cultural ephemera, zines are increasingly finding their way out of fringe communities and into libraries, archives, publishing houses, and

Figure 6.1
Zines come in a multitude of styles, shapes, designs, and topics. Essential features include the use of a personal voice, handmade aspects, and a nonprofit ethos.

classrooms. They provide excellent sites of narration around grassroots and DIY political identities, activism, and agendas.

Drawing on zines from my personal collection and interviews with zine producers that I conducted for the research project Feminist Media Production in Europe at the University of Salzburg, this chapter begins by mapping maker identities in DIY feminist zine cultures. From considering a range of claims made about identity, power, and resistance in these networks, I then assess these statements in relation to a number of DIY citizenship discourses being currently produced within academia, popular culture, and governmental spheres. I aim to understand if there are any convergences (or indeed warning signs) over such parallel articulations. Indeed, it is my contention that several trajectories of DIY are being mobilized in the current moment—from the grassroots and participatory to the neoliberal and conservative—and that self-described DIY projects, wherever they take root, cannot necessarily guarantee liberating possibilities or outcomes by intention or declaration alone. To assess these claims, we need to understand the political, economic, and social contexts through which they take shape.

Happening Here and Now: DIY Feminism

Over the past few decades, DIY has become a strong political discourse within youth feminist movements worldwide. Emerging within North America in the early 1990s, self-declared "DIY feminisms" have since spread transnationally, with print and digital publications providing crucial sites of exchange and contact. With names like *Evolution of a Race Riot, Pretty Ugly, Clit Rocket, Fight Together, Take Back the News,* and *Reassess Your Weapons,* feminist zines are collated on a range of topics, including motherhood, rape, domestic violence, anti-deportation campaigns, environmental action, free schools, sexualities, radical histories, autonomous health, antiracism, and dis/ability. As Elke Zobl, founder of the international *Grrrl Zine Network* website, puts it, "Zines function as a space of active participation and for critical reflection—of one's self, one's community, society, and feminist activism and politics."[6]

Within these networks, there is a strong emphasis on the political role of cultural activism, community organizing, and the production of alternative spaces as part of a DIY ethos.[7] Although earlier feminist and social change movements also utilized DIY discourses and practices through their appeals to the grass roots, it is in this period of late capitalism and globalization that DIY political identities have really been brought to the fore—often in reaction to the betrayals of official politics to bring about change, and the commercialization and institutionalization of certain forms of radical politics. Subsequently, DIY feminists pitch their resistance work in the micropolitical spheres of cultural production: using zines as cheap, accessible, hands-on forms of publishing, alongside more digitally mediated forms of communication. As Jayne Armstrong observes in her ethnographic study of these networks, "DIY feminism is not united by a shared set of beliefs or a shared sense of women's oppression. DIY feminism is rather united by a shared investment in the affective, emotional, empowering and transformative potentials of independent, deprofessionalised cultural productivity. The impassioned and rallying utterance of 'produce, make, create, have fun' is key to understanding the cultural politics of DIY feminism."[8]

While pleasure and the role of the individual are accentuated in DIY feminist discourses, it is my contention that *individual action held within a collectivity* is really the basis of cultural resistance in these communities. This has led some grassroots groups, such as the Copenhagen Queer Fest, to replace the acronym DIY with DIT—"do-it-together" (see Reilly, chapter 8, this volume, for another appeal to a pluralized "do-it-yourselves" approach). As Belgian feminist Nina Nijsten discusses in her zine *Different*

Worlds, Same Heartbeats: "DIY activism could be defined as an alternative form of activism or resistance that doesn't rely on existing political power structures. By creating your own non-hierarchically organised community *together with others* and by working on alternatives . . . you can look for solutions to problems yourself and change things right here and now, independent of the current political system."[9]

DIY feminism is articulated as a present-orientated form of praxis, dedicated, in the words of Nijsten, to "daily life activism" that seeks to "cut out the middlemen" of politicians, corporations, and policy makers.[10] "Maker cultures" are seen as potential antidotes to the excesses and apathies associated with consumer capitalism. For such activists, making your own culture and politics, rather than consuming those on offer, is a political mode of engagement; a strategy further politicized by being shared. As Nijsten writes optimistically, "Taking space, making things instead of buying them, not-participating in what you think is wrong and putting your ideals into practice . . . by showing your example to others, this revolution can spread."[11] Cultural production (and boycotting) become sites for advancing one's politics and a means to establish alternative networks and economies: to form loose channels of citizenship practices, or what is affectionately referred to in zine parlance as creating "DIY democracy."[12]

Make/Shift: Maker Identities and Critical Pedagogies

Encoded within DIY feminism is a love of participatory culture (for a discussion of affective fandom, see Burwell and Boler, chapter 7, this volume). Even a cursory look at feminist zines would confirm the importance of "creating," "empowerment," "skill-sharing," "participation," and "learning" within these networks. As an article in the *Queeruption Vancouver* zine illustrates:

> DIY means learning and practicing the skills necessary to create the things we want to see, rather than relying on governments, corporations, and the media to provide for us. When we do things like grow food, sew and repair our own clothes, brew beer, build bikes, create art, films, and music, write zines, and squat buildings, we're empowering ourselves, while simultaneously taking power away from the forces that attempt to control us. Because of this, DIY is inherently political—it's the foundation on which a fully participatory and non-hierarchical society can exist.[13]

Maker cultures are seen as strategic processes through which people reclaim power in their everyday lives. This phenomena is not limited to (sub)cultural producers, however. Maker identities are in ascendance more broadly in recent times, in part led by innovations in ICTs and Web 2.0 platforms.

As the sociologist David Gauntlett suggests in his book *Making Is Connecting: The Social Meaning of Creativity, from DIY and Knitting to YouTube and Web 2.0,* five motivations underscore the *affective* lure of contemporary maker cultures, including the embodied experience of creativity; the social drive to make and share things; the psychological benefits of experiencing creativity and community; creativity as social capital; and being able to leave your mark through creating new objects and spaces of engagement.[14]

By transferring this thesis to the realm of zines, we can better understand how DIY feminists view the role of zine-making in their own lives. As members of the Lash Back collective in Ireland told me in an interview: "[Zines] are beautiful because the work, the personal effort that goes into them is so tangible. They hold potential for intimacy and learning from each other's stories . . . as well as sharing ideas and resources. We can feel connected in a way that we don't normally with glossy mainstream publications."[15] Zines are thus recognized as personally crafted artifacts and sites of activist labor and connection, becoming avenues for shared creativity and learning—important aspects for enacting "cultural citizenship" (see Reitsamer and Zobl, chapter 24, this volume) and for boosting one's reputation and esteem within the feminist zine community.

As such, DIY feminism promotes informal, peer-to-peer pedagogies and critical making practices.[16] In her book *Girl Zines: Making Media, Doing Feminism,* Alison Piepmeier sees feminist zine cultures as developing much-needed pedagogies of hope through these methods of engagement. She argues that zines are embodied social texts creating spaces and networks for the imagination, not just in terms of content, but also in the materiality of their making and distribution.[17] As the Spanish art collective Erreakzioa-Reacción also concurred in an interview with me, "We think feminist zines can both affect individual lives and promote social and political changes. They can also affect the processes, the way to do things."[18]

By affecting the ways of doing things and privileging processes over final products, zines operate as critical making tools[19] capable of fusing vernacular theorizing and material production. The US-based antiracist magazine *make/shift* makes the heritage of this practice clear, re-situating critical making tools and processes as an important legacy developed by previous feminist movements: "Part of why we make *make/shift* is to put together artistic and activist work—because *we've never believed there are clear lines separating these things,* and because one of the things feminists who preceded us gave to social-justice movements is *a politic that connects not just the personal to the political, but the critical to the creative.*"[20]

Perpetuating or Disrupting the Status Quo? Feminist Zines as Citizens' Media

With an emphasis on making, sharing, and connecting, feminist zine cultures help forge "new border spaces for critique," where young women can combine a desire to make and communicate with others with a need to avoid surveillance and adult and corporate appropriation of their cultures and politics.[21] Indeed, these zine networks proliferate at a time when youth citizenship practices are shifting in alarming ways: governments and NGOs increasingly promote discourses of personal responsibilities over secured rights, managed forms of participation over youth-led initiatives, and consumption over cultural production.[22] Citizens are thus expected to be entrepreneurial, flexible, and ultimately self-managing; the DIY imperative in these discourses shifts away from creativity, civic engagement, even fun, to the need to oversee all stages of one's life, economic position, and security, with decreasing assistance from the state.

In this vein, we also hit upon some limitations of DIY activist culture, not only in zine scenes, where participants' celebratory rhetoric of accessibility and community must be tempered by an understanding of very real instances of racism and classism within these predominately white and middle-class maker networks,[23] but also in the notion of "do-it-yourself" or even "do-it-together" possibilities. As some critics of DIY feminism have stated, "What if we can't do-it-ourselves? What if I can't? What if you can't? It is easy to assume that if we couldn't get on our modems, play in a band or be a bit wicked, then we wouldn't cut it."[24] Certain economic and cultural assumptions underpin DIY feminist rhetoric: that one has the time, resources, abilities, and support to become cultural producers (even low-entry cultural producers), and that cultural production itself is a pressing site for political engagement and resistance.

The "DIY democracy" claims of activist cultures therefore remain a point of contention for cultural scholars. For some, zines are mere flirtations with resistance, leaving mainstream codes, values, and systems intact. As Stephen Duncombe writes: "By looking for cultural and individual solutions to what are essentially structural and societal problems . . . the underground inevitably fails."[25] Other scholars have questioned the grounds on which such activism and civic engagement can be measured. Drawing on communications scholar Clemencia Rodriguez's concept of "citizens' media," Alison Piepmeier argues that zines reconfigure understandings of power, agency, and symbolic codes for their participants—in the end, it does not matter if bigger systems remain untouched because other transformations in individuals and communities are taking place, and these participatory shifts must not be underestimated or even jettisoned from understandings of what activism is and can do.[26]

Do-It-Yourself Operations? The Problems of DIY (Consumer) Citizenship

Somewhat predictably, the entrepreneurial elements of DIY politics have trickled through to popular culture, as well as governmental and academic spheres. As a quick search on an Internet bookselling site informs me, a slew of DIY-titled publications covering topics as varied as financial planning, spiritual journeys, weddings, children's craft activities, and projects for poultry farmers have emerged. Taking the "cut out the middleman" ethos to its commercial conclusion, anti-consumerist maker cultures of DIY political movements have been repositioned and reappropriated through the machinations of new commodity markets. This is DIY as depoliticized lifestyle and self-managerial branding.

Similarly, media scholar John Hartley has argued, albeit unconvincingly, that citizenship practices have expanded from civic, political, social, and cultural citizenship to what he perceives as a desirable though uneven state of mediatized, post-identity DIY citizenship: where individuals exercise their right to "semiotic self-determination" through media consumption.[27] Such a position seems to confuse media spectacle with material realities, and erases the regulatory systems of social stratifications. More worryingly, the United Kingdom has endured a wave of Tory-led "Big Society" rhetoric and measures on a governmental level.[28] Here, politicians rebrand welfare and public sector cuts as securing "greater autonomy for individuals." In this form of Orwellian double-speak, the Big Society is conjured up as a means to provide greater "self-determination" and "choice" for ordinary citizens; the reality, however, sees unpaid volunteers being recruited to replace sacked public sector workers in key services such as public libraries and police patrols.[29]

As a British journalist parodied in *The Guardian* following the public launch of the Big Society manifesto in 2010: "The scariest moment came when Andrew Lansley, the shadow health minister, said: 'You want to be your own boss, and you can with us.' What does this mean? Do-it-yourself operations? 'The procedure you want at the time you want it—all you need is a sharp knife and a mirror.'"[30] This newspaper article serves to highlight how untenable DIY discourses are when applied to existing systems (and rights) such as free national health care—the DIY impulse of the Big Society being exposed as little more than PR-spin for what Buck Clifford Rosenberg has previously referred to as the "DIYization of modern society": that is, the increasing individualization and privatization of key public spaces and services for the benefit of corporations over communities.[31]

Concluding Remarks

In this examination of DIY feminism alongside more popular, academic, and governmental interpellations of DIY citizenship, it has become apparent that the term "DIY" operates primarily as an empty signifier: a host of different meanings are inscribed onto this term and activated within widely different trajectories and contexts. In the feminist activist networks that I have looked at, DIY signifies peer education, support, and finding activist identities within a creative collectivity. As an anti-capitalist and anti-consumerist approach, DIY feminism is not the individualized, privatized, DIY of market neoliberal discourse, although elements of these discourses do seep into DIY feminist articulations and should be acknowledged as such. Limitations to DIY feminist discourses inevitably exist whenever they further a celebratory "can-do" rhetoric divorced from understandings of economic and other obstacles to participation and resource mobilization.

In principle, DIY can never behave as a regulated, top-down (or consumer-driven) practice, and, alarmingly, it should never be permitted to act as a masquerade for neoliberal, anti-welfare agendas that conspire to make the most vulnerable citizens even more so. DIY as direct action, symbolic resistance, and participatory maker cultures flourishes in decentralized, peer-led initiatives that work in small-scale projects to bring greater benefits and well-being to community members (though there is no guarantee of connection, success, or participation). As a form of DIY media, zines remain important documents for social engagement and political resistance with real, tangible effects for marginalized communities. While noting their limitations, zines shouldn't be ignored as activist tools. As Vikki Law, prison-rights activist and editor of the prisoners' zine *Tenacious*, explained to me in an interview: "Even in the age of blogs and the widespread use of the Internet, there are populations of women who are cut out of the information loop. Incarcerated women are one such population. Zines and magazines can, to some limited extent, get into the prisons and raise awareness about issues and ideas. . . . In some prisons, it's sparked discussions among women about ideas around patriarchy, sexism, [and] the necessity of speaking out."[32]

One of the continuing impacts of grassroots, exploratory zines—especially those written by or circulating within marginalized communities—is their ability to not only support maker culture, but to start new conversations. As spaces of dialogue, learning, and hope, activist zines remain important examples of radical citizens' media, holding invitations of building communities of resistance at their core. DIY media offer possibilities of engaging with social change; they also encourage readers to become participants by putting thought into action. While underground and alternative protest has a long history of appropriation by the powers that be, holding on to the distinctions between different versions of DIY, and understanding that even grassroots appeals may mask power differences and structural marginalization, is an important critical-creative position to uphold when understanding the range of DIY citizenship discourses currently being circulated in this neoliberal age.

Notes

1. As a genre, zines originated in US science-fiction writing communities in the 1930s and are commonly associated with punk music scenes in the 1970s. Yet these texts can also be positioned within a wider self-publishing heritage that includes the communication outputs of pamphleteers, suffragettes, samizdat publishers, civil rights agitators, anti-colonial struggles, and women liberationists. See Duncombe 1997; Piepmeier 2009; and Piepzna-Samarasinha 2004.

2. Congdon and Blandy 2005.

3. Zine producers act as their own writers, editors, designers, publishers, and distributors, publishing cut-and-paste documents on a photocopier or producing more sophisticated magazines through software and commercial printers. Printed in multiples of tens to a few hundred, these publications are usually sold at cost price, given away for free, or traded for a similarly valued zine or handmade artifact. See Chidgey 2009b.

4. See Atton 2002.

5. Zobl 2009.

6. Ibid., 8.

7. See Chidgey 2009a; McKay 1998; and Trapese Collective 2007.

8. Armstrong 2009, 95.

9. Nijsten 2007, 28.

10. Ibid., 29.

11. Ibid., 28–29.

12. Schenwar 2006, 78–81.

13. Queeruption Vancouver Collective 2007, n.p.

14. Gauntlett 2011.

15. Lash Back Collective 2009.

16. Zines have been used to promote creativity, self-reflection, and media and design literacies in a range of formal learning contexts. See Alexander 2002; Knobel and Lankshear 2010. There are risks to using deinstitutionalized texts within institutional settings, however. See deGravelles 2011.

17. Piepmeier 2009, 155–191.

18. Erreakzioa-Reacción 2009.

19. Ratto 2011.

20. Hoffman and Yudacufski 2009/2010, 5.

21. Harris 2004, 151–182.

22. See Harris 2004; McRobbie 2009.

23. See Piepmeier 2009, 123–154; Schilt 2005.

24. Else-Mitchell and Flutter 1998, xvi.

25. Duncombe 1997, 194.

26. Piepmeier 2009, 163.

27. Hartley 1999, 159.

28. Activists have recently argued that the "Big Society" happens, in actuality, when social movements fight oppressive states and offer alternative social visions. For example, a recent exhibition in Paris entitled The Big Society considered the role of civil disobedience and direct action in shaping contemporary Britain, such as the interventions of the suffragettes, the anti-fascist Battle of Cable Street in 1936, and the miner's strike of the 1980s. See http://workplacegallery.blogspot.com/2011/05/matt-stokes-big-society-gallerie.html. Similarly, the documentary *DIY Britain: The Real Big Society* features activists offering innovative ideas for tackling structural inequalities with regards to housing issues, alternative financial systems, and disaster relief efforts; see Prowse and Pine 2010.

29. See Cameron 2011; Travis 2010. The outsourcing of government responsibilities to unpaid citizens has, in turn, prompted new forms of public activism. Public libraries suffering forced closures have been squatted by activists and run as community initiatives—with pressure from local governments to move out so that the squatted buildings can then be sold on as capital (the implication being that "The Big Society" is only to be praised when it's government-administrated, not citizen-led).

30. Hoggart 2010.

31. Rosenberg 2005.

32. Law 2009.

References

Alexander, Jonathan. 2002. Digital Spins: The Pedagogy and Politics of Student-Centered E-zines. *Computers and Composition* 19 (4): 387–410.

Armstrong, Jayne. 2009. DIY Feminism: A Dialogical Account. PhD diss., University of East London.

Atton, Chris. 2002. *Alternative Media*. London: SAGE.

Cameron, David. 2011. "Have No Doubt, the Big Society Is on Its Way." *The Guardian*, February 12. http://www.guardian.co.uk/commentisfree/2011/feb/12/david-cameron-big-society-good (accessed February 9, 2011).

Chidgey, Red. 2009a. "DIY Feminist Networks in Europe: Personal and Collective Acts of Resistance." *Transform! European Journal of Alternative Thinking and Political Dialogue*. http://transform-network.net/journal/issue-052009/news/detail/Journal/diy-feminist-networks-in-europe-personal-and-collective-acts-of-resistance.html (accessed February 9, 2011).

Chidgey, Red. 2009b. Free|Trade: Distribution Economies in Feminist Zine Networks. *Signs: Journal of Women in Culture and Society* 35 (1): 28–37.

Congdon, Kristin, and Doug Blandy. 2005. Zines, DIY, and Critical Pedagogy. *Telemedium: The Journal of Media Literacy* 52 (1 & 2): 59–63.

deGravelles, Karin H. 2011. In the Ruins of Zine Pedagogy: A Narrative Study of Teaching with Zines. PhD diss., Louisiana State University.

Duncombe, Stephen. 1997. *Notes from Underground: Zines and the Politics of Alternative Culture*. London: Verso.

Else-Mitchell, Rosamund, and Naomi Flutter, eds. 1998. *Talking Up: Young Women's Take on Feminism*. Melbourne: Spiniflex.

Erreakzioa-Reacción. 2009. "Generating Contexts in a Fragile Scene." Interview by Red Chidgey and Elke Zobl, March 17, http://www.grassrootsfeminism.net/cms/node/159 (accessed February 9, 2011).

Gauntlett, David. 2011. *Making Is Connecting: The Social Meaning of Creativity, from DIY and Knitting to YouTube and Web 2.0*. Cambridge, UK: Polity Press.

Harris, Anita. 2004. *Future Girl: Young Women in the Twenty-First Century*. New York: Routledge.

Hartley, John. 1999. *Uses of Television*. London, New York: Routledge.

Hoffman, Jess, and Daria Yudacufski. 2009/2010. "Letters from the Editors." *make/shift* 6 (Fall/Winter): 5.

Hoggart, Simon. 2010. "DIY Government? It's Scary." *The Guardian*, April 13. http://www.guardian.co.uk/politics/2010/apr/13/conservative-manifesto-simon-hoggarts-sketch (accessed February 9, 2011).

Knobel, Michele, and Colin Lankshear, eds. 2010. *DIY Media: Creating, Sharing Learning with New Technologies*. New York: Peter Lang.

Lash Back Collective. 2009. "We Are Following an Historical Line." Interview by Red Chidgey and Elke Zobl, March 11. http://www.grassrootsfeminism.net/cms/node/380 [accessed 02.09.2011].

Law, Vikki. 2009. "Tenacious: Art and Writing from Women in Prison." Interview by Red Chidgey and Elke Zobl, January 23. http://www.grassrootsfeminism.net/cms/node/117 (accessed February 9, 2011).

McKay, George, ed. 1998. *DiY Culture: Party and Protest in Nineties Britain*. London: Verso.

McRobbie, Angela. 2009. *The Aftermath of Feminism: Gender, Culture and Social Change*. London: Sage.

Nijsten, Nina. 2007. *Different Worlds, Same Heartbeats* 1. Hasselt: Self-published.

Piepmeier, Alison. 2009. *Girl Zines: Making Media, Doing Feminism*. New York: New York University Press.

Piepzna-Samarasinha, Leah Lakshmi. 2004. Brown Star Kids: Zinemakers of Colour Shake Things Up. *Broken Pencil* 24:25–26.

Prowse, Heydon, and William Pine. 2010. *DIY Britain: The Real Big Society*. http://www.guardian.co.uk/environment/video/2010/may/11/ethical-living-diy-big-society (accessed February 9, 2011).

Queeruption Vancouver Collective. 2007. *Queeruption Vancouver*. Vancouver: Self-published.

Ratto, Matt. 2011. Critical Making: Conceptual and Material Studies in Technology and Social Life. *Information Society* 27 (4): 252–260.

Rosenberg, Buck Clifford. 2005. "Contemporary Experience and Lifestyle Scandinavian Dreams: DIY, Democratisation and IKEA." *Transformations* 11. http://www.transformationsjournal.org/journal/issue_11/article_02.shtml (accessed February 9, 2011).

Schenwar, Maya. 2006. Zines Explore Transgender Culture beyond Stereotypes. *Punk Planet* 75:78–81.

Schilt, Kristen. 2005. "The Punk White Privilege Scene": Riot Grrrl, White Privilege, and Zines. In *Different Wavelengths: Studies of the Contemporary Women's Movement*, ed. Jo Reger, 39–56. London: Routledge.

Trapese Collective, ed. 2007. *Do It Yourself: A Handbook for Changing Our World.* London: Pluto Press.

Travis, Alan. 2010."Cameron's Answer to Budget Cuts: Get Public Involved in 'DIY' Policing." *The Guardian*, July 26. http://www.guardian.co.uk/uk/2010/jul/26/cameron-budget-cuts-diy-policing (accessed February 9, 2011).

Xyerra, Ciara. 2001. *A Renegade's Handbook to Love & Sabotage 3*. Portland, OR: Self-published.

Zobl, Elke. 2009. Cultural Production, Transnational Networking and Critical Reflection in Feminist Zines. *Signs: Journal of Women in Culture and Society* 35 (1): 1–12.

7 Rethinking Media Activism through Fan Blogging: How Stewart and Colbert Fans Make a Difference

Catherine Burwell and Megan Boler

In this chapter we recount what happened when a project intended to analyze online political activism took an unexpected turn into DIY fan culture. Although we at first resisted this shift, we soon realized that an examination of digital public spheres could not overlook fans' processes of creation and community building. In fact, we found that fan practices troubled—and in doing so deepened—our conceptualizations of political engagement. As theorists intent on rethinking notions of citizenship in the context of emerging social media practices, we found that fanlike feelings and values (including interest, affinity, and sociability) intersected with and illuminated the more explicitly "political" activities we had set out to trace.

In the pages that follow, we describe our encounters with the online fan sites that have sprung up around *The Daily Show* and *The Colbert Report*. We discuss ways of theorizing the relationships among these satirical texts, fandom, and critical making, and we apply these insights to interviews with two influential female bloggers. The work of Lisa Rein (figure 7.1) and DB Ferguson demonstrates the political possibilities of DIY fan production at the same time that it reveals many of its paradoxes, including corporate media's appropriation of fan labor and creativity. Adding to the work of media theorists like Liesbet van Zoonen, John Hartley, and Noortje Marres, we argue that DIY fan culture provides significant insights into meaning production and civic engagement within mediated worlds.

"If You Want Politics, Go Away": Early Encounters with Fan Culture

In the fall of 2005 we began the first phase of inquiry on Rethinking Media, Democracy and Citizenship, a qualitative research project designed to investigate political engagement through online networks. Among the sites chosen for this investigation were online discussion boards and blogs

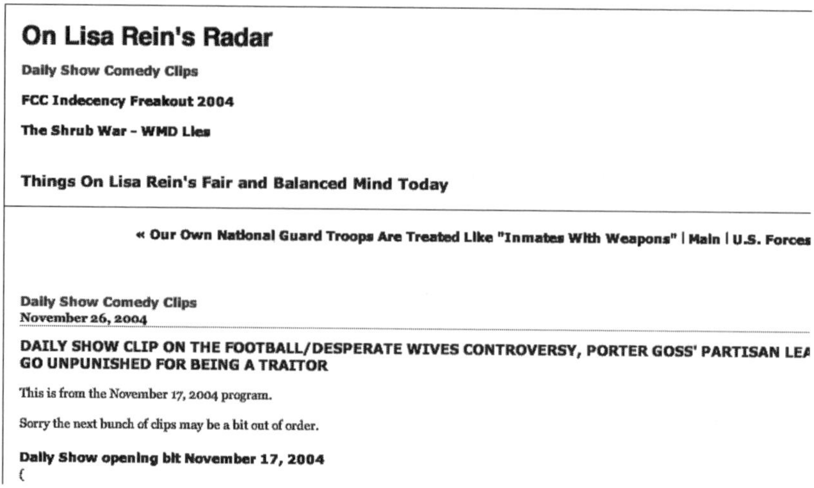

On Lisa Rein's Radar

Daily Show Comedy Clips

FCC Indecency Freakout 2004

The Shrub War - WMD Lies

Things On Lisa Rein's Fair and Balanced Mind Today

« Our Own National Guard Troops Are Treated Like "Inmates With Weapons" | Main | U.S. Forces

Daily Show Comedy Clips
November 26, 2004

DAILY SHOW CLIP ON THE FOOTBALL/DESPERATE WIVES CONTROVERSY, PORTER GOSS' PARTISAN LEA GO UNPUNISHED FOR BEING A TRAITOR

This is from the November 17, 2004 program.

Sorry the next bunch of clips may be a bit out of order.

Daily Show opening bit November 17, 2004

Figure 7.1
Screenshot from *On Lisa Rein's Radar*

devoted to *The Daily Show*. Although we had expected to find mostly "political sites"—a term we had yet to problematize—we quickly realized that much of the attention paid to the program took the form of celebrity gossip, entertainment news, and fan production. The *Jon Stewart Intelligence Agency*, for example, which billed itself as "the biggest, unofficialest, scariest, funnest Jon Stewart fan cult club on the net," included a discussion forum, a space for fans to contribute fan fiction, and a "Jon News" mailing list. On *Commentary on the Daily Show*, fans could download screen caps, read transcripts, and skim pages of quotations from past shows.

These sites presented a conundrum for us. Our project was about online spaces for civic participation and the possibility for new modes of political activism. Yet most of the sites devoted exclusively to the show demonstrated more interest in cast changes than political change. As one of *The Daily Show*'s most prolific fans, Anita, wrote succinctly in the subtitle of her blog, "If you want politics, go away." In the early stages of our research we did just that, choosing not to investigate fan production. Our oversight might be explained by the historical marginalization of fandom, for even as fan practices move into the mainstream, fans continue to be stereotyped as irrational, emotional, and peripheral to politics. Indeed, as van Zoonen has written, within modernist political discourse, fans and citizens are "constructed as involving radically different social formations and identities."[1]

Of Fans and Citizens, Affect and Activism

Our own separation of fans and citizens began to break down when our attention turned to *The Colbert Report*. Indeed, it is difficult not to connect fandom and citizenship within a program that assigns its audience the role of "Colbert Nation" and generates a flurry of fan activity that includes stuffing online ballot boxes, changing Wikipedia pages, and producing fan-made videos. These kinds of activity are not only generated by the program's producers but also initiated by fans themselves, who have started several thriving blogs dedicated to *The Colbert Report*, organized protests in support of striking writers, and devoted countless threads to discussion of the show. Indeed, the level of audience input into the show, as well as the producers' public recognition of fans, have lead both critics and fans to remark on the program's interactivity.[2] Stephen Colbert himself has noted the role fans played in generating response to his speech at the White House Correspondents' Dinner and has suggested that fans are essential to the *Report*, that they "are a character in a scene I'm playing."[3]

At the same time that fans of "fake news" were gaining visibility, our interviews with digital creators were revealing the role of affect within political expression. In 2006 and 2007, we undertook thirty-five interviews with video producers and bloggers addressing topics such as the war in Iraq, American politics, and mainstream media representations. While our questions were designed to explore the possibility of political engagement and articulations of dissent through online networks, it soon became clear that emotion, creativity, and performance were as much a part of these producers' practices and motivations as the intention to correct dominant accounts or initiate public debate. From the need to express anger at US policies to the desire to build community and create belonging, interviews with online producers pointed to the role of affect and imagination in constituting new kinds of counterpublics.

While the role of emotion in politics has long been undertheorized, perhaps because, as Brian Massumi notes, "there is no cultural-theoretical vocabulary specific to affect,"[4] a number of scholars are now filling in that gap. In *Entertaining the Citizen*, van Zoonen explores the place of emotional investment in both fan communities and political constituencies. While emotional investment has long been associated with fans' commitment to particular texts and communities, it has often been dissociated with political constituencies, where it is seen as threatening to rationality. Yet as van Zoonen argues, these distinctions between rationality and emotion are misleading. Van Zoonen argues that without "enthusiasm and anxiety, political interest and commitment would falter . . . just like fan communities would wane without the emotional input of their members."[5] In "There Is Drama in Networks," Noortje Marres makes similar claims. She writes that it is the networked *relations* among organizations and individuals that present "the most interesting site for communication, collaboration, and contestation regarding political issues."[6] Marres proposes a notion of politics that sees political activity as spread out among multiple actors, locations, and moments, and connected by the relationships and drama that make up political communication. Such a notion is echoed in John Hartley's conceptualization of citizenship not as a "static or definable condition" but as a "relational identity."[7] Within new media environments, Hartley writes, the practices of DIY citizenship that characterized the age of television are not only easier, but also increasingly mutual, enhanced by digital connectivity and social networks. This emerging understanding of politics and citizenship as relational, connected, and performative resonated with our own

Figure 7.2
Screenshot from *NoFactZone*

nascent realization that politics were in fact being enacted through fans' communities and collaborative processes of making.

Given these developments, it was no longer possible to see fan culture as peripheral to our questions about the public sphere and citizenship. Clearly there were intersections between fan DIY production and political expression that could not be overlooked. This recognition led us to broaden the scope of our investigation and include interviews with digital makers whose performances of fandom provided insight into the changing forms of political activity and digital citizenship. Lisa Rein is a cofounder of Creative Commons and the writer of the popular and eclectic blog *On Lisa Rein's Radar: Things on Lisa Rein's Fair and Balanced Mind Today*, while DB Ferguson is the creator of two Colbert-related fan sites, *NoFactZone* (figure 7.2) and *Colbert University*. Neither blogger can be identified simply as a fan or an activist; they enact the identity of both, albeit in different ways. Through our interviews with these two influential bloggers, we wanted to analyze more closely the relationship among fandom and politics, activism, and affect, and to think about how fans' practices of making might also *make politics happen*.

"People Have to See This": Building a DIY Digital Archive of *The Daily Show*

On Lisa Rein's Radar first came to our attention because of its huge archive of *The Daily Show* clips. In fact, Rein has a complete archive of the program since 2002, much of it available on her site. This archive is part of a larger and fascinating site dedicated to links and commentary on a wide range of issues, including antiwar protests, US government policy, popular culture, environmentalism, and hacktivism. Unlike DB Ferguson, whose "Colbert-centric" blogs we look at next, Rein does not identify as a fan but rather as an activist, and like many critical makers, sees her work as a form of social and political intervention. What makes Rein's practices especially interesting are the way they combine motivations associated with both fandom and political activism. Her intense emotional investment in *The Daily Show* and a desire to create communities of affinity around this text coexist easily with the intention to educate and create the conditions for political change.

Rein describes her reasons for watching *The Daily Show* in both emotional and critical terms. She explains that she began watching in the summer of 2002, when it became clear to her that Bush was planning to go to war, a development that seemed to be overlooked by mainstream media, but that was acknowledged—and critiqued—on *The Daily Show*. Rein explains that sometimes it "felt kind of like me and *The Daily Show*" were the only ones recognizing this "drumbeat to war." She describes the program as "a voice of sanity in a world gone mad," suggesting its role in alleviating a sense of alienation: "When Jon looks at the camera and just says, 'You know they're fucking insane, right?' it makes you feel better." At the same time, Rein saw the program as fulfilling the questioning role that had been abandoned by the mainstream media. "*The Daily Show* were serving the function that real news was supposed to serve and they were the only people doing it," she remarks. Rein's critical appraisal of the function of *The Daily Show*, alongside her enthusiasm for the program, supports Jonathan Gray's description of "news fans" who combine a passion for news programs and personalities with rational argument, bringing together current affairs, politics, and fandom in new combinations.[8]

Rein's own enjoyment of the show and her sense of its political significance quickly led her to want to share it with others. She explains that she first started blogging about and posting clips from *The Daily Show* when Henry Kissinger was appointed to head the 9/11 Commission:

> Nobody said anything but *The Daily Show*. They were like, "Hey who better to head up the war crimes commission than the king of war crime" . . . And I felt, God, people have to see this. I had just gotten a new camera that had analog inputs that allowed me to do my stuff. I can't get a digital signal out of the TiVo. So it's only because they have analog RCA jacks that I can put into my camera, make a tape in my camera and FireWire from my camera to my computer . . . That's how I did it. So I put that up and then you know, people cared. Two weeks later he had to step down . . . And I think a lot of it was *The Daily Show* and the Internet.

From this moment until 2005, Rein regularly posted clips from the program. She appears to have two motivations for this activity. The first was to make an archive of a program she believed provided necessary context and critique, and the second was to create a community around that archive. Concerning her decision to archive, she explains: "what I meant to happen was to put together a collection of information that could be useful for people" and "to be like a library and let everybody have access to this stuff." In fact, Rein's extensive archive *was* put to use, not only via the web but also in Dorothy Fadiman's documentary *Stealing America: Vote by Vote* (2008). Related to this desire to share important material, Rein also expresses a desire to connect with others who share a sense of alienation from mainstream news coverage. When asked whether she feels like she is part of a community through blogging, Rein replies: "That's the whole point." She elaborates by explaining that a dialogic community—formed through comments and links—developed around her archived clips, helping like-minded people find each other. "It was just nice to know that we weren't all crazy," she explains. Rein also suggests that this community may have formed around her clips in part because *The Daily Show*'s comedy provided a critical but also a playful, pleasurable space in which to engage in political discussion, gesturing toward Hartley's suggestion that "purposeful play" may model new civic potential within mediated societies in which social networks are used to create "associative relations among strangers."[9]

The sharing of materials and the creation of interpretive communities are certainly not limited to fan groups. Indeed, as van Zoonen argues, information sharing and discussion are also at the core of democratic practice. Rein's work provides an illuminating example not only of the similarities between fan and political organizing but of their intersection, in the way that a pop culture text—and shared enjoyment in that text—sits at the center of this evaluative discursive community. As Gray suggests, emotional and fanlike feelings for a text do not preclude rational responses to that text. Indeed, a response that mixes delight in the program's comic elements as well as an appreciation of its political importance within the context of shrinking public journalism not only points to the program's successful integration of comedy and news, but provides a fuller and more representative picture of emerging forms of citizenship in which participation, sociability, and affect are constitutive elements.

It is also worth noting Rein's relationship to Comedy Central and its parent company Viacom as yet another manifestation of her complex fan-activist-archivist activities. As Rein herself comments, "There was this certain sense of disbelief that I was just taking those clips and putting them up and not being challenged." The fact that Rein posted copyrighted material and was not challenged by the company later notorious among fans for its heavy-handed "YouTube purges" does indeed seem remarkable. She explains this by suggesting that she thinks Comedy Central "secretly loved what I was doing." This ties into the way that both Rein and Ferguson see their work as promoting the presence of their favorite shows. In both cases, each suspects that Comedy Central pays attention to her site, in order to gauge audience reactions and shape future content. As Rein says, echoing something they both express, "I believe that my blogging of their show brought them to a larger audience, increased their viewership . . . and got them carried in foreign countries." Rein's remarks here point us toward the complex relationship between the emerging user-producer and the mainstream media and demonstrate the ways in which fan productions, made for free, amplify the commercial presence of multinational media corporations. Indeed, as Red Chidgey demonstrates (chapter 6, this volume), DIY activities may be rather easily assimilated into corporate profit making, even as they perform important affective, communal, and political functions that may be at odds with corporate agendas.

"I Could Create It Myself": Making a Space for Fans of Fake News

Where Lisa Rein identifies herself as an activist and archivist, DB Ferguson identifies herself as an "überfan." On her "Colbert-centric" blog *NoFactZone,* she describes herself through her active consumption of popular culture and her commitment to *The Colbert Report* and its fans:

> Since a very young age, I've been what one might consider to be an überfan. I subscribed to newsletters, I wrote letters to stars, I collected, and I obsessed. . . . The Web makes it possible to be an überfan in ways that were impossible back in my teen years . . .
>
> I've been a fan of Stephen Colbert for quite some time, but after seeing the rabid fan base of Colbert come alive after the 2006 White House Correspondents' Dinner, I yearned to commune with others who had the same zeal and vigor for Mr. Colbert as I did. My quixotic charge became clear: to make a site for fans of Stephen Colbert that were as rabid as me. I could create that "ultimate" website for Colbert fans myself!

In July 2006, Ferguson began *NoFactZone,* a frequently updated blog that includes detailed episode guides, links to Colbert-related articles, a comments section, contests, and interviews. As her own description implies, part of Ferguson's motivation to create the site was her disappointment with other Colbert fan sites. Since its launch, *NoFactZone* has become one of the most visited Colbert-related sites, and has been linked to by a number of well-known sites, including *The Huffington Post* and *MediaShift.* In July 2007, Ferguson began a "sister site" called *Colbert University,* a website that houses much of the archived knowledge of *NoFactZone* under "pedagogical" categories such as "Core Curriculum," "Electives," and "Final Exam." Ferguson writes that "the goal of Colbert University is to serve as a permanent, accurate resource for those wishing to know more about the characters, terms, ideas, and world of *The Colbert Report,* and to inspire thoughtful analysis (as well as riotous enjoyment) of this groundbreaking experiment in interactive television." Just as Ferguson claims a very different identity and relationship to her chosen text than does Lisa Rein, so too do her practices, motivations, and sites provoke a different set of themes and questions.

Where Rein's passionate commitment to archiving, sharing, and discussing *The Daily Show* clips blurs the lines between fandom and political activism, Ferguson's insider knowledge of fan culture and her complex engagement with *The Colbert Report* both as a parody and as a corporately produced text raise significant questions around the politics of fandom.

Like Anita, a fan of *The Daily Show* who subtitled her blog "if you want politics, go away," Ferguson rejects what she sees as an overly politicized reading of *The Colbert Report*. She identifies *NoFactZone* as an entertainment rather than a political blog, an identity that she upholds in her decision making about the site. Shortly after the StewartColbert08 movement began, for example, she decided to remove their links from her site, feeling that they were pushing a political agenda she did not want to endorse. "On my blog I don't really talk about political stuff . . . Most of the really hardcore Stephen fans understand that he's not trying to be überliberal or überconservative or überliberal posing as conservative, he's just trying to be funny." In fact, Ferguson's view of the program as comedy first and foremost mirrors Colbert's own public representations of his work, as she notes herself when discussing Colbert's scathing White House Correspondents' Dinner speech:

> Colbert has said over and over: "I was just trying to make people laugh. You guys can read into it whatever you want. I was just trying to be funny." And I honestly kind of believe that. I think he was trying to roast [Bush] a little bit, I just don't think he realized how political the whole situation would become until after it was over.

Ferguson extends this apoliticism to Colbert's audience, remarking, "You'd be amazed at how unpolitical the Colbert fan community is." And yet for all of her rejection of political interpretations of *The Colbert Report*, her interview is nonetheless riddled with insights and questions into power and politics—the politics of fan communities, the politics of parody, and underlining both, the question of just what constitutes "the political."

Indeed, as a self-identified überfan, Ferguson is extremely savvy to the power relations and hierarchies within fandom itself. She suggests, for example, that she chose to write under the gender-neutral name "DB" because "I didn't want to lose credibility with my site by being pigeonholed as a fan girl." She similarly chooses to "write as professionally as I can" and to prohibit sexualized fan fiction, or "slash," from her site in order to keep it from being seen as a feminized and therefore denigrated space. Ferguson is also acutely aware of the circulation of power within the blogosphere. She notes with pride her site's high Google rating, its links from well-known sites, and its impressive traffic.

Ferguson's willingness to address yet another power dynamic—that which plays out between corporate media producers and user-producers like herself—is evident in her series of "Open Letters" to Comedy Central executives concerning questions of centralization and copyright. Here, Ferguson draws on an established history of fans asserting their collective rights vis-à-vis media corporations, a history Jenkins refers to earlier (chapter 3, this volume). For example, when the vice president of digital media at Comedy Central, Erik Flannigan, told the *Los Angeles Times* that the corporation wanted "to make sure if people are reacting to what's going on on the show, they're doing it in our world and on our pages,"[10] Ferguson responded by posting a letter on her site that critiqued Comedy Central's digital media strategy, and in particular its official *Colbert Nation* (figure 7.3) site, which she compares unfavorably to her own, fan-run site. Two years later, when there is news that Viacom will sue bloggers who used unauthorized clips of *The Daily Show* and *The Colbert Report*, she addresses Viacom in an open letter that reminds them that most fan bloggers do not make money from their labor, and are not only *not* redirecting profits

Figure 7.3
Screenshot from *Colbert Nation*

from broadcasters but are in fact extending their audiences. She writes that she blogs about *The Colbert Report* "simply for the love and the passion of blogging about a man and a show that I have grown to respect and admire. We're more than a news site, we're a community." Through the letters, Ferguson demonstrates how emerging forms of digitally mediated citizenship are produced through both acts of making (texts, relationships, communities) and rhetorical performances that seek to redress power imbalances built into technologically mediated societies.

Making a Difference

Visiting fan sites and talking to fan producers, activities that we initially resisted, ultimately complicated and broadened our own interpretations of political expression. It forced us to recognize the intersections between fans and citizens, and to see that citizenship might include elements of emotion, enthusiasm, participation, and sociability. By thinking about fan *practices of making* (archives, blogs, websites, networks, communities), we also came to see that fans worked to *make a difference* (to other fans, to media power differentials, to untenable political situations) and to *make sense* (of technological change, of unreliable media accounts, of a world gone mad). In a project dedicated to "rethinking" media, politics, and citizenship, the questions that fan production generated constantly pushed us to rethink fundamental building blocks of contemporary citizenship practices and what counts as "political" engagement.

Notes

1. Van Zoonen 2005, 56.

2. See Linkins 2007 and Sklar 2007.

3. Snierson 2007.

4. Massumi 2002, 27.

5. Van Zoonen 2005, 66.

6. Marres 2007, 175.

7. Hartley 2010, 234.

8. Gray 2007, 75–87.

9. Hartley 2010, 244.

10. Chmielewski 2007, C2.

References

Chmielewski, Dawn. 2007. "Building Community, Commerce for Viacom." *Los Angeles Times*, June 21.

Fadiman, Dorothy, dir. and prod. 2008. *Stealing America: Vote by Vote*. USA, Concentric Media.

Gray, Jonathan. 2007. The News: You Gotta Love It. In *Fandom: Identities and Communities in a Mediated World*, ed. Jonathan Gray, Cornel Sandvoss, and C. Lee Harrington, 75–87. New York: New York University Press.

Hartley, John. 2010. Silly Citizenship. *Critical Discourse Studies* 7 (4): 233–248.

Linkins, Jason. 2007. "Colbert: Content for It-Getters." *Huffington Post*, April 20. http://www.huffingtonpost.com/eat-the-press/2007/04/20/colbert-content-for-itg_e_46416.html.

Marres, Noortje. 2007. There Is Drama in Networks. In *Interact or Die*, ed. Joke Brouwer and Arjen Mulder, 174–188. Rotterdam: NAI.

Massumi, Brian. 2002. *Parables for the Virtual: Movement, Affect, Sensation*. Durham, NC: Duke University Press.

Sklar, Rachel. 2007. "Stephen Colbert's Web Dominance: How *The Colbert Report* Is Fast Becoming the Leader in Web-TV Integration." *Huffington Post*, August 22. www.huffingtonpost.com/eat-the-press/2006/08/22/.

Snierson, Dan. 2007. "Stephen Is King!" *EntertainmentWeekly.com*, January 4. www.ew.com/ew/article/0,20006490,00.html.

van Zoonen, Lisbet. 2005. *Entertaining the Citizen: When Politics and Popular Culture Converge*. Lanham, MD: Rowman & Littlefield.

8 Just Say Yes: DIY-ing the Yes Men

Ian Reilly

What is DIY? DIY is when you can just set out and do something, right? And you make it and there it is. You don't have to send in a job application, right? Maybe that's the definition: there's no application process.

—Andy Bichlbaum, Yes Men member

DIY-ing the Yes Men?

Google "DIY" in an images search and you will call up an eclectic library of arts and crafts, masonry, technology, architecture, transport, fashion, design, and food. You'll see images of reconstituted cardboard boxes, transistor radios, throwaway jeans, abandoned parking lots, obsolescent computers, and broken chairs. Encountering these images under the banner of online "do-it-yourself" culture creates a welcome impressionistic view that materials and objects of little to no commercial value can be repurposed and reinscribed to breathe new life into things that may otherwise be relegated to the trash bin of history. This broader practice of cultural recycling and regeneration is important not only in terms of its ability to give old objects and things a new contemporary vitality, but also because the acts of tinkering, noodling, deconstructing, and rebuilding embedded in DIY culture provide much-needed cornerstones for grappling with the contemporary world. In this chapter, I examine some of these generative facets of DIY culture through a larger exploration of the media hoaxing practices pioneered by the Yes Men. Through their countless appropriations of both corporate and state personhood, the Yes Men's brand of "identity correction"[1] serves as an excellent blueprint for thinking about how DIY activist communities can reinvent otherwise tired, worn, and static modes of political and civic engagement. To bring the Yes Men's dynamic politics to the foreground, I'll unpack the group's rich DIY ethos before turning to a more sustained discussion of its recent work with the Yes Lab for Creative Activism, a collaborative, workshop-based training ground for activists looking to replicate Yes Men-style hoaxes; in doing so, I hope to shed light on the intersections of DIY culture, civic engagement, and a promising new model of political participation.

No Application Process: Do-It-Yourselves

It's a rainy afternoon in February 2012 and Andy Bichlbaum and I are discussing, among other things, whether the Yes Men's work qualifies as DIY. As Bichlbaum would have it, "DIY is when you can just set out and do something, right?" This is a fitting description for what the Yes Men do, in large part due to the fearless resolve they've shown in pulling off some of the past decade's most memorable pranks and hoaxes, impersonating some of the most powerful corporations and institutions of our time—the World Trade Organization (WTO), Dow Chemical, Exxon, General Electric, the *New York Times*, and many others. For Bichlbaum, DIY means "there's no application process," highlighting the low barrier to entry for individuals and social groups looking to make a statement. If DIY is merely about setting out and doing something, the Yes Men have performed this role admirably since they first made headlines over twelve years ago.

As Bichlbaum argues, however, this DIY ethic is only truly effective when actions take on a cohesive collaborative bent; to pull off these labor-intensive hoaxes requires "the assistance of huge armies of individuals." We playfully noted that DIY might best be described as do-it-*yourselves* (pl.), given the often large number of group members needed to carry out a particular action. Up until very recently, doing-it-yourself for the Yes Men has meant working with/as a loose knit network of activists, technologists, artists, and community stakeholders to bring important issues to the foreground of public discourse. Despite the fact that their hoaxes have been discussed (and dissected) across various pockets of the web—YouTube videos, Twitter posts, Tumblr blogs, chat forums, Facebook newsfeeds, academic journal articles, popular press pieces—and immortalized in two documentaries, *The Yes Men* (2003) and *The Yes Men Fix the World* (2009), few (if any) Yes Men copycats have emerged. With all the publicity and critical commentary they have generated for their hoaxes, it seems probable that they would have inspired a throng of impressionable culture jammers to go out and adapt their much-lauded identity correction model. But here's the rub: just as the

Yes Men have worked tirelessly to create a culture that moves like-minded people to band together to perform similar (Yes Men–style) actions,[2] their work has actually inspired the opposite response—because their work is so funny, brave, insightful, and generally life-affirming, their admirers have all-too-often deferred to the Yes Men to do the work. "Will you please go after biotech, now?" "What about Monsanto? They would make a great target." In the pages that follow, I discuss the Yes Men's gradual shift from being expert practitioners of media hoaxing to becoming expert trainers, teachers, and facilitators of spectacle-generating modes of media activism. Through their role as facilitators, they offer already emboldened groups the opportunity (and expertise) to deploy the tools and techniques of hijacking dominant news media, all the while teaching existing activist and advocacy groups an important lesson: you can *do-it-yourselves*.

®TMark and (the Limits of) Online Collaboration and Community Building

®TMark (pronounced *art mark*) is a good point of departure for thinking about how the Yes Men imagine the power and potential of web-based activism. In simple terms, ®TMark is a clearinghouse of sorts for activists looking to participate in and contribute to a number of diverse projects and actions. Founded in 1996 by a network of artists and activists who found one another at the rise of the Internet in the mid-1990s, ®TMark emerged as an important online hub for ideas and critiques surrounding the corporate abuses of power.[3] The general idea was that interested parties could freely participate in the creation and execution of clever, funny, and ironic pranks[4] that would work toward creating greater visibility for a growing resistance movement against (the hegemony of) multinational corporations. ®TMark's impressive project listings served as a call to anonymous, interested parties on the web to donate some of their time, effort, expertise, and money toward the completion of certain actions—anything from publicizing the dangers of genetically modified foods and the need to close corporate taxation loopholes to more benign actions like changing the US motto from *E Pluribus Unum* ("Out of many, one") to *Quis Te Rogavit* ("Who asked you"). ®TMark would go on to fund about twenty activist projects in total—among them the Barbie Liberation Organization, the Yes Men's WTO impersonations, and the hugely popular Bush campaign parody site, GWBush.com—demonstrating a keen eye for augmenting what is possible under a "corporate model" and offering new dimensions for political innovation.[5] In an interesting political maneuver, ®TMark legally defined itself as a "a brokerage that benefits from 'limited liability' just like any other corporation," but unlike its multinational counterparts, "'its bottom line' is to improve culture, rather than its own pocketbook; it seeks *cultural* profit, not financial."[6] While the project's mission statement is at once insightful and noble, it remains to be seen whether the ®TMark model of collaborative, DIY activism proved a success.

For our purposes here, let's connect one of the major shortcomings of the ®TMark model with some of the more explicitly stated goals of the Yes Men. In a moment of candid reflection, Bichlbaum, an ®TMark cofounder, expresses some disappointment about the goals he had imagined for the project:

> We promoted [®TMark] as a thing that anybody could do. Anybody could participate in the system. Anybody could do subversive actions. There was nothing to it. We thought of it as promoting this sort of activism. The website had hundreds of suggestions for actions that people could do. We solicited them, people sent them in without solicitation and we posted them—any decent idea. We thought by posting them people would just do them, people would see that and go, "Oh, that's an easy thing to do. Well, I'm going to go do that." Nothing happened. None of that ever happened.

Note the DIY character of the call-to-action, the collective vision, and the inclusive nature of the project. As far as Bichlbaum was concerned, there were no significant barriers to participation and just about anyone could do "this sort of activism." In fact, one of the guiding motivations for creating ®TMark was the promise that it "would result in a profusion of thousands of actions all over the place," but the message, Bichlbaum notes, was "totally lost in translation." ®TMark's website would receive hundreds of suggestions for actions, but interest in the projects undoubtedly waned in terms of people's actual participation in these and other interventions. Again the overriding logic here is that while ®TMark seemed to have struck a chord with a small but enthusiastic online audience, it remained easier for onlookers to defer to other members of the community to bring these projects to fruition. This is not dissimilar to the words of encouragement the Yes Men receive from their admirers, goading them on to prank just about any multinational corporation with a (golden) skeleton[7] to hide. Based on these examples, it's fair to ask which strategies and tactics might best inspire others to participate in and contribute to both on- and offline activist projects. To address this question more directly, I now turn to my discussion of an emerging case study: the Yes Lab.

A New Venture: The Yes Lab for Creative Activism

The Yes Men are a group of dynamic critical makers: they make fake websites, golden phallus corporate management suits, apocalypse-themed SurvivaBalls; they create outlandish keynote presentations, absurd press releases, sensational headlines, and captivating documentaries; they also impersonate governments (Environment Canada, United States Department of Housing and Urban Development), disband powerful organizations such as the WTO, and parody America's newspaper of record (the *New York Times*). If your stated goal as media activists is to inspire others to perpetrate actions that are at once funny, absurd, ethical and moral in scope—not to mention driven by the need to advance social justice issues—but few follow in your footsteps, how do you enlist these actors into the fold? Seeking to remedy these shortcomings, the Yes Men have shifted their tactics of late to offer a more hands-on approach to training others in the art and practice of identity correction. They call this new venture the Yes Lab for Creative Activism, an organization devoted to mentoring others in their "headline-provoking methods."[8] Aside from the already inspiring body of work they have produced, this project represents the most promising outgrowth of their activism to date. Not only are they producing captivating work that challenges larger publics to think critically about corporate and state governance, they are now extending their reach into existing pockets of media activism and political advocacy to multiply the range of voices everyday citizens encounter in mainstream news media.

What Is the Yes Lab?

So what exactly is the Yes Lab? As the name suggests, the Yes Lab is a laboratory of sorts for experiments in the mobilization of activist groups and in the advancement of social justice issues. More specifically one might consider the Yes Lab as a way for "social justice organizations to take advantage of all that we Yes Men have learned—not only about our own ways of doing things, but those we've come in contact with over the decade and a half we've been doing this sort of thing."[9] To date, the Yes Lab has helped facilitate nineteen actions since October 2009—no small feat for a newly formed organization—most of which have generated modest coverage in mainstream media outlets. Actions include a US Chamber of Commerce campaign to reverse its disastrous record on climate change policies, a fake General Electric press release announcing it would donate its $3.2 billion "tax refund" to the US government, an anti-iPhone application that addresses child labor practices, factory-worker suicide, and environmental degradation, and a "self-deportation" website, among others. Much in the spirit of the Yes Men's impassioned politics, partnering groups such as Avaaz, Greenpeace, and the Occupy movement have accelerated the rate at which these and other timely critiques emerge in the public sphere. Indeed, for such groups/organizations to learn and re-deploy Yes Men–style tactics has meant a greater degree of visibility for causes and issues that don't traditionally penetrate the gatekeeping establishment and has lead to an influx of ethically motivated pranks across mainstream news media. In many ways, a Yes Lab collaboration is no different than a Yes Men action—the stunts are engineered to raise greater awareness surrounding a given issue and to raise that issue's public profile via mass media outlets—but the intent is to proliferate more actions than would be possible by the Yes Men alone. The interactions between the Yes Men and various activist organizations has undoubtedly lead to a shift in the way both groups think about their work. For example, the Yes Men's work with Occupy Wall Street (OWS) has injected some much needed laughter, play, and fun into what is otherwise a very serious movement; by the same token, the Yes Men's collaborations with OWS, Bichlbaum suggests, "has really transformed the way we do things."

Leveling the Playing Field

There are, of course, significant challenges and barriers to doing this kind of activism. Aside from what might be deemed legitimate technical barriers to participating in these kinds of actions (creating fake websites, producing multimedia content, securing online infrastructures), the work also requires modest capital investment, considerable organization and planning, knowledge, and expertise—to say nothing of the courage needed to follow through with these hoaxes. What's more, interested individuals and parties may not have the kind of social/cultural capital needed to attract a working group capable of bringing a good idea to a broader audience. Yet another hurdle worth considering is the difficulty of pairing incisive political critique and biting satire, a craft only some of the best writers and comedians ever fully master.[10] Finally, creating a bridge between comedy and activism can prove to be a controversial undertaking, especially when organizations and groups differ in their thinking regarding the value of humor in activist interventions.

Despite these and other challenges facing activists today, the Yes Lab presents a promising model for fun and engaging DIY activism that works toward reducing these barriers while emphasizing new possibilities for civic engagement. In terms of circumventing these barriers, the Yes Lab has created a thorough platform for assisting groups in the conceptualization and completion of projects. In the lead-up to a Yes Men collaboration, members of the Yes Lab

• introduce the notion of "laughtivism" (i.e., developing effective, media-friendly projects),
• brainstorm project ideas, evaluate various courses of action, and assist in choosing the best one,
• conceptualize a chosen project fully, developing a complete action plan with timelines, deadlines, and chains of responsibility,
• map out teams and determine staffing needs, and
• train groups to properly negotiate media coverage.[11]

With institutional support from New York University's Hemispheric Institute (Hemi), the Yes Lab currently enjoys the physical space and resources needed to conduct these workshop-based training sessions, preparing activists, students, and organizations to tackle work at the conceptual, technical, programmatic, and/or philosophical level. The Yes Lab's association with Hemi has not only facilitated access to physical resources, but also made possible future collaborations among New York-based artists, activists, students, and organizations.[12]

Importantly, the Yes Men's shift toward a community-centered model has not been restricted to the day-to-day operations at Hemi and is being fostered in other milieus. I myself have participated in Yes Men do-it-yourself-themed/workshop-based lectures at the University of Guelph, the Ontario College of Art and Design (OCAD), and York University. The idea behind the lectures is for the Yes Men to briefly discuss its work, explain the tactics, tools, and principles that underpin its actions, and have the audience/general public brainstorm future actions (the Yes Men's OCAD lecture was aptly billed as a "How-to Hoax Clinic"). The York University workshops were structured to assist graduate students in the elaboration of a Greenpeace campaign critiquing the Alberta Tar Sands. Within a week of the Yes Men's University of Guelph lecture (an event I helped organize), another interesting thing happened: youth vote mobs spread virally across Canada. The vote mobs were significant because they inspired a number of other flash mobs (35 in total) to materialize across the country and in the process generated a great deal of media coverage. The actions began in Guelph, caught the popular imagination via a series of cleverly produced YouTube videos,[13] and were attributed in part to the influence/direction of the Yes Men[14] (vote mob co-organizers Gracen Johnson and Yvonne Su went so far as to refer to themselves as the "Yes Women.").[15] As the Yes Lab's Mary

Notari suggests, the entire rationale for the project "is to make what the Yes Men do accessible to all," and based on the actions outlined here, there is good reason to believe this experiment is fulfilling its preliminary mandate.

Yes Men 2.0

My very first encounter with the Yes Men came in November 2005 (relatively late in the scheme of things) when university librarians organized a screening of their first film (*The Yes Men*). What was so inspiring about their high-level pranking—aside from the brazen, unapologetic way they critiqued their powerful targets—was that they made it look so natural, so seamless, so easy. If you had a basic understanding of the web, a good eye for spotting social injustices, a palpable love of mischief, and a predisposition toward weaving elaborate tales for public consumption, you could easily replicate, tailor, or adapt a Yes Men hoax. If you had friends who shared these qualities, capacities, and predispositions, so much the better. For a brief moment, I wondered if anyone would follow suit, if their actions would inspire a renewed interest in and engagement with creative and comedic modes of activism. I imagined imitators adopting and integrating the Yes Men's tactics beyond the pale of international conferences and into the realm of popular media. But I also wondered if everyday citizens could replicate the Yes Men's successes, or if figures like Andy Bichlbaum and Mike Bonanno were truly exceptional individuals who pulled off hoaxes far beyond the reach of the uninitiated. With the Yes Lab, these questions enjoy considerably less traction. In a time of real political foment, the Yes Men are now training and mentoring groups to participate in the creation of media spectacles designed to highlight social justice issues and political struggles of great civic importance. The Yes Lab offers a bridge between the media hoaxing actions of a much-revered group and DIY citizens and groups who lack the knowledge, wherewithal, or infrastructure to see these hoaxes to fruition. The effort marks an important shift in their work, demonstrating how an already successful mode of activism can be taken up to facilitate the transmission and reproducibility of inspiring work. What have the Yes Men taught me? If there's no application process to participating, we should really just do it ourselves.

Notes

1. "Identity correction" refers to the process of "exposing an entity's inner working to public scrutiny." There are, of course, multiple approaches to carrying out this

kind of project: embarrassing your target, correcting the public record regarding an issue, policy, or initiative, exposing corporate malfeasance, and reframing issues and public debates. For a nice summary, see Andy Bichlbaum's "Identity Correction," in Boyd 2012, 60–61.

2. One of the most succinct and articulate statements regarding their longstanding goals is expressed online in a larger overview of the recently created Yes Lab for Creative Activism: "The Yes Men have been doing their thing for over 12 years now. Their idea was always to inspire others to also use creative means to drive media attention to important issues, and help shape public opinion" (http://www.yeslab.org/about).

3. Thompson 2006.

4. http://www.rtmark.com/new.html.

5. For an excellent discussion of ®TMark and the Barbie Liberation Organization, see Harold 2007, 79–84.

6. http://www.rtmark.com/faq.html.

7. http://www.youtube.com/watch?v=3lxlLEb-_WM&feature=youtu.be.

8. Wells 2010.

9. http://hemisphericinstitute.org/hemi/en/yeslab.

10. *Saturday Night Live,* for example, serves as a brilliant case study for thinking about the ongoing challenges (and attendant failures) of producing relevant comedy that inspires authentic laughter. Despite the efforts of a large group of talented people, comedy, satire, and parody can often fall flat—especially where political humor is concerned.

11. http://www.yeslab.org/about.

12. At present, the Yes Lab is seeking "five activist organizations or coalitions who would like to work with the Yes Men, and with eager (and brilliant!) students, to develop and execute sexy, creative media-activism projects around their own campaign goals" (see http://yeslab.org/orgs).

13. http://www.youtube.com/watch?v=SEf34V2rmaM.

14. Immediately following the Yes Men's Guelph lecture, three of my female students approached me to tell me just how inspired they were, stating that they would soon after be participating in their own media intervention. When asked about the specifics, they merely told me that I'd be reading all about it in the days to come. As it turned out, they too were participants in the Guelph vote mobs.

15. Su 2011.

References

Boyd, Andrew, ed. 2012. *Beautiful Trouble: A Toolbox for Revolution*. New York: OR Books.

Harold, Christine. 2007. *Ourspace: Resisting the Corporate Control of Culture*. Minneapolis: University of Minnesota Press.

Su, Yvonne. 2011. "Just Voted: A Column from a 'Yes Woman.'" http://www.guelphmercury.com/print/article/516819.

Thompson, Seth. 2006. Reconfiguring the System: RTMark & Agricola de Cologne. *Afterimage* 34 (1–2): 56. http://seththompson.info/?page_id=347.

Wells, Amelia. 2010. "The Yes Men Launch the Yes Lab for Creative Activism." http://www.ameliasmagazine.com/earth/the-yes-men-launch-the-yes-lab-for-creative-activism/2010/05/28/.

II DIY and Making: Learning, Culture, Hacking, and Arts

The role of DIY in learning and artistic contexts cannot be understated. DIY practices have long been part of how various groups of people perform their connections to cultural groups and communities. Such work is seen as increasingly important in today's mediated, complex, and fluctuating social contexts, which requires citizens to engage more fully in processes of self-determination. As stated in the introduction to this volume, Hartley's notion of "DIY citizenship" emphasizes individual engagement with the processes of personal and cultural construction. Some of the chapters in this section extend Hartley's ideas, digging into the details of how individuals and groups articulate themselves through making into larger society.

For example, Orton-Johnson's contribution (chapter 9) engages directly with the idea of DIY citizenship, noting that the craft activities and communities that she studies "map directly on to Hartley's definition of the DIY citizen as a process of modern identity formation that links the private (personal) and the public (political) with mediated technologies . . . thus providing a wider lens through which to understand digitally mediated making and DIY citizenship." Her focus addresses informal contexts of craftwork, made increasingly visible through digital forms of mediation. Here, leveraging Gauntlett (2011), Orton-Johnson highlights what she terms the "intermediate or meso level of social structure that acts as an integrating element between individuals and society." She points to the need for definitions of citizenship that incorporate new ways of relating community and identity, noting that the activities she studies belie narratives noting a decline in civic and community participation—contrary to the opinion of Robert Putnam.

Bal, Nolan, and Seko (chapter 10) describe the ways a growing "maker culture" supports forms of DIY citizenship, noting: "Maker culture has the potential to represent a cultural model that encourages individual citizens to construct their own social realities, connections, and material aspects of living, to take user-generated production as a key to an individual self-determination, knowledge sharing, and community building." Of particular interest to these authors is the ways in which such a model also troubles traditional forms of formal education, requiring that associated institutions better address informal and emergent pedagogies. As they state, such changes require rethinking traditional assumptions about the state of childhood as "underdeveloped" and in need of adult guidance and protection. More important, helping children "hack" their environments through DIY sensibilities and tools can assist them in developing the autonomy and their own agency necessary for coming to terms with an uncertain future.

Similarly, Rosner and Foster's contribution (chapter 13) touches on the disconnect between formal learning institutions and informal practices, focusing on what they, following Orton-Johnson, call *digital craft* and its performance within an after-school project. Through a variety of formal and informal learning projects participants in the project engaged with hybrid textile and technological work, often using their experiences to think through and express their ideas, concerns, and anxieties about their own futures. Rosner and Foster note the creation of frictions between perceptions of what the project was intended to do and what was actually needed: "This friction between what the project required and what the Technology Lab was meant to represent—the practice of making and the aesthetics of work—unsettled the boundaries between 'clean' mass-produced technology and 'messy' DIY aesthetics." They define the term "inscribed material ecologies" to highlight the productive "manglings" of disciplines, types of work, and organizational forms they see as a key component of community-based craft practice. Importantly, their work highlights the need for "recognizing the institutional practices and politics that script the material ecology of DIY practices," seeing this as a necessary step toward more collaborative forms of education.

Kafai and Peppler (chapter 12) emphasize the need for individuals to have a more nuanced understanding of how technology works, given the ways society is increasingly technologically mediated. Their study of the workshops on e-textiles that they have organized demonstrates a number of important themes. They highlight how work with and on technology can serve to provide increasing transparency and critical perspectives. Leveraging constructivist and media literacy accounts, they note that e-textiles are particularly useful learning objects due to their boundary-crossing characteristics. Here, Kafai and Peppler point to the ways gender is constructed within their e-textile workshops, with both male and female participants seeing electronics and computer-based technologies associated with masculinity and craft and "soft textile" work associated with femininity. While pointing to the need for critical work to overcome these simplistic characterizations, they demonstrate the pernicious nature of such divides and how they work to circumscribe participation in DIY activities.

Both Rose (chapter 14) and Jenson, Dahya, and Fisher (chapter 11) study DIY documentary practices, with the former positioning such practices within a longer historical framework and the latter focusing on a specific school-based example. Rose emphasizes the importance of DIY forms historically within activist activities, noting the use of amateur filmmaking in 1968 Paris as well as in protest movements by Native Americans that same year. She provides more recent details regarding collaborative filmmaking projects as well. However, she troubles DIY as a sufficient way to understand such phenomenon, noting instead that "the concept of DIWO (do-it-with-others) is better equipped to capture the dynamics and importance of these projects."

Jenson, Dahya, and Fisher, like Rosner and Foster, highlight the need for formal public institutions to engage with the informality of DIY culture, while also noting that "DIY does not necessarily challenge or evade systemic and structural limitations that contribute to the ongoing marginalization of young media makers." Their study of the Castleguard News Network, a DIY media production club, reminds us of the complexities of such activities and how they are often dependent on the support and scaffolding of both formal and informal members of school staff. Importantly, Jenson, Dahya, and Fisher remind us to be skeptical of the "'good news' kinds of stories of children and media" noting that "our tale is much more cautionary."

Similarly, in chapter 15 de Castell explores the reciprocal processes whereby digital engagements, in particular those performed in virtual game environments, both shape and are shaped by "meat-space" engagements. She highlights problems with one of the standard claims associated with the virtual, namely that of the expansive agency virtual environments are supposed to create, Instead, she demonstrates the ways both our selves and our bodies (in the case of the Wii Fit) are "toned and disciplined through virtual game play." While acknowledging the sociality of virtual worlds, she asks the important question, "But what social identities are available to players, and within what political regimes?"

Together, the chapters in part II celebrate—and critique—DIY practices of making and learning. The authors here address and connect many of the critical questions raised in the main introduction to the book, thinking through both what it means to be a DIY citizen as well as how to educate them. If DIY citizens are a required component of modern society, they have to come from somewhere. The role of making, the liberatory (or not) nature of DIY, and the spaces and communities of DIY activities are all examined as critical components for practitioners working to productively trouble current educational institutions and to posit alternatives. Importantly, these authors do not shy away from the contradictions and the tensions involved in DIY practices and the complex trade-offs that must be navigated when engaging in technologically mediated education.

References

Gauntlett, D. 2011. *Making Is Connecting: The Social Meaning of Creativity, from DIY and Knitting to YouTube and Web 2.0.* Cambridge: Polity Press.

Hartley, J. 2004. *Creative Industries.* London: Wiley Blackwell.

9 DIY Citizenship, Critical Making, and Community

Kate Orton-Johnson

The Emergence of Digital Craft

New practices of making have shifted definitions of craft from a peripheral form of domestic production, personal enjoyment, and creative fulfillment to acts variously defined as "craftivism." Combining craft and activism, craftvism encompasses acts of radical feminism, gender subversion, political activism, and environmental advocacy as well as drawing on narratives of creativity, community, and citizenship (Minahan and Wolfram Cox 2007; Pentney 2008; Greer 2008). While craft has a long history of subversion, from political spinning bees in the 1700s to the knitted punk aesthetic of the 1970s (Turney 2009), current articulations of craftivism are focused on the intersections of personal, social, and political engagement and third-wave feminism.

In this reclaiming of domestic arts, craftivism has sought to question, disrupt, or replace dominant modes of production and consumption. Craft becomes both an expression of domestic nostalgia and "austerity chic" and a form of online entrepreneurialism, resisting mass consumption and the homogeneity of capitalist production. Common to these diverse articulations of craft is the integration of digital media with existing practices of production and consumption and a reshaping of spaces of crafting, community, and connectivity. This reshaping enables us to think of craftivism as a site for new forms of Web 2.0 production and consumption, as well as a space for DIY citizenship and critical making.

Craftivism, and the accompanying growth of digital spaces supporting and facilitating forms of making, has seen contemporary craft flourish as a technologically mediated social, economic, and cultural movement. Crafters produce and consume a broad spectrum of web content, from YouTube instructables dedicated to teaching and learning new skills, to craft blogs and craft-based social networking sites, each representing new modes of digital engagement with the material objects and activities of the craft.

Knitting in particular has enjoyed a revival in popularity in the last decade (Lewis 2011; Parkins 2004; Turney 2009), and this popularity has been accompanied by a growing presence of "crafsters"[1] on the web, with blogs, podcasts, and social networking sites connecting a global network of knitters. Communal craft-based socializing has a long history in popular culture, from quilting bees to knitting circles, and, similarly, new types of making communities have accompanied the emergence of digitally mediated crafting.

The shift of the personal practice of knitting into the sphere of public activity enables participants to express, produce, and consume "community" as part of a new form of networked leisure citizenship. This provides us with an alternative definition of participation and citizenship as a form of leisure and pleasure and as an act of collaborative connectivity, and it points to the spaces and modalities in and through which citizenship is practiced.

This chapter will conceive of DIY citizenship as an act of producing and consuming craftivism and will focus on making and community as a form of socially engaged and socially networked DIY citizenship. Drawing on qualitative interview data from knitters involved in local and global knitting networks, the ways in which a sense of self as "maker" is discursively produced through the relationships between imagined, virtual, and "real" communities of knitters is explored. Using the example of a community knitting project, I argue that, as a form of DIY citizenship, digitally mediated knitting can act as a space for the making of online and offline community; it is an activity that is a mix of the personal and the (networked) social (Rosner and Ryokai 2009).

Digitally Mediated Knitting

Contemporary knitting practices are increasingly visible as part of new offline and online landscapes of craft. Online, dedicated knitting sites have created spaces for distinct forms of knitting participation, consumption, and production. Sites such as Ravelry,[2] KnitPicks Knitting Community,[3] and DIYNetwork[4] merge Web 2.0 technologies and social networking activities allowing their members to create profiles that display their knitting and crochet projects, share resources and exchange knowledge and participate and interact in groups and forums. Like other social networking sites members connect and communicate by "friending," viewing, ranking, "liking," and "favoriting" other people's projects and activities and prosume (Toffler 1980) these environments through the management of their own profiles, projects, and relationships (Beer and Burrows 2010; Ritzer and Jurgenson

2010). Online spheres of activity enable knitters to extend their tactile knitting practices into the digital realm, to discuss projects and techniques, to blog and photograph their work, and to create and use online spaces that make (digitally) visible their often private and domestic knitting. This merges social networking, digital archiving, and lifestreaming activities with existing craft activities, enhancing and enriching the experience of knitting and the identity of creative maker (Orton-Johnson 2012).

Offline, knitting has been incorporated into a range of urban practices with DIY knitter communities participating in guerrilla knitting, knit graffiti, yarn bombing, and knit tagging.[5] Guerrilla knitting is defined as a range of practices that employ "vigorous" or "militant" knitting activity in mass demonstrations, in urban interventions, and for political causes, using knitting in controversial, unusual, or challenging ways.[6] For guerrilla knitting communities and activist groups, blogging, vlogging, and representing *material* practices in *online* spaces to a *global* audience is a vital part of the acts of citizenship and resistance that they are engaged in. In these contexts Web 2.0 technologies such as knit-specific social networking sites, alongside platforms such as Flickr, Facebook, and networks of interconnected blogs, are positioned as facilitators of local and global connectivity and political and civic engagement (Minahan and Wolfram Cox 2007; Humphreys 2008).

Online knitting community sites, such as Ravelry, have also facilitated and energized new and existing offline "stitch n bitch" groups, pub knitting circles, fiber festivals, and knit meets, providing a range of virtual and physical sites for participating in knitting as a shared, collaborative, and public activity. At both ends of this spectrum of leisure and activist knitting, technology use goes hand in hand with the craft. Knitting, alongside online articulations and representations of knitting, are seen as recursive digital/social practices, connecting material and physical activities with social networking, microblogging, and face-to-face interaction. These overlaps provide us with new ways of thinking about the construction of the creative self and the "doing" of community that orient around the identity of "maker." In turn, this "maker identity," can be conceptualized as a type of digitally mediated craftivism and, as I shall argue in this chapter, of DIY citizenship.

Making Community?

Online knitting spaces facilitate a sense of community that parallels definitions of virtual community already well documented in the research literature. These definitions emphasize a sense of identification and belonging achieved through the communicative creation of social meaning and shared experience (Baym 1998; Jones 1995, 1998; Smith and Kollock 1999; Rheingold 1993; Wellman 2001). For knitters, digital technologies fulfill many of the same functions as for other online communities, by connecting groups at local levels, by blurring online/offline boundaries and geographies, and by facilitating the organization of virtual and face-to-face events and activities. The aim here is not to recap these debates but to explore the ways in which these kinds of communities are experienced, understood, and negotiated by their members and to understand the ways in which these communities of crafters can be seen as networked DIY citizens.

This chapter draws on a series of qualitative interviews with "online" knitters and on ethnographic data and interviews with knitters involved in a project that, as part of a wider community festival in Scotland, launched an intergenerational "guerrilla knitting" art project to create an installation of yarn bombing and knit tagging in a local urban public space. Participants were recruited through local Facebook groups, through knit-specific Facebook networks, and via the groups and events functions of the knitting network site Ravelry. By the end of the first week of the project launch, over a thousand people had volunteered their time and knitting, with participants from the local community joined by global contributors sending knitted donations from South Africa, New York, Morocco, Sweden, Australia, and New Zealand. The project took place over six months in 2011 and was supported by social networking activities on Facebook and in Ravelry groups. Locally based knitters met and knitted together during dedicated project knit-a-longs and used existing knit meets or community group times to produce knitted squares. The squares were joined to become connected strips of knitted fabric that was used to tag objects in local spaces during the community festival in June 2011 (see figure 9.1).

Global groups of knitters and individual contributors also blogged about their progress and, at the end of the project, were able to view their contributions in situ via Flickr and Facebook photo albums and through postings that linked to local blogging and media coverage. During the project the participants formed a focused but geographically dislocated and temporally bounded community that used digitally mediated spaces to connect, interact, and share progress.

These local and global participants shared a sense of "community" and engagement that challenges bounded, geographically grounded definitions of involvement and citizenship. While the notion of virtual community has highlighted the irrelevance of global geography in online community formation, the collaboration of global contributors around a highly "local" project shifts the focus of this definition and raises some interesting

Figure 9.1
Knitted tagged trees during the community festival

questions about the ways in which maker identities and virtual communities interact with local/global networked craft communities. I want to argue that revisiting notions of community in the context of maker identities provides us with a new lens to think critically about the intersections, continuities, and flows between the social and the digital and between leisure practices and acts of citizenship.

The "Maker" Identity

Before revisiting notions of community and connectivity, I will outline what I am defining as the digitally mediated maker identity. Online knitting spaces extend the *boundaries* of knitting as the private leisure practice of craft becomes visible as a part of other Web 2.0 social media environments and activities. Through the processes of blogging, vlogging, and photographing their yarn and projects, knitters are extending the boundaries of their physical artifacts into the digital realm as a conscious, reflexive activity:

> I have dabbled in blogging before but now that I focus on knitting as my blogging activity it kind of makes more sense to me and it connects different parts of my life. In some ways it's quite odd that something so tactile is now translated into something, I guess you could call it almost opposite to tactile when it's online. But for me the two are bound together—I knit it, I blog it!
>
> —Jane, Ravelry member[7]

As well as an act of representation, this is also an extension of the activity of knitting to include a range of digital practices, such as photography and microblogging that, in turn, shape the meanings involved in participating in the craft. As Kuznetsov and Paulos argue, this is a form of creative storytelling: "Our participants, who create and repurpose personal objects, use online communities to broadcast self-constructed material things into the public sphere. In doing so, they symbolically project personal goals, values and practices in the digital domain. These contributions remain detached from the physical objects and states that produce them" (Kuznetsov and Paulos 2010, 8).

This digital visibility and creative storytelling contributes to the increased importance of a "creative" or "maker" identity, which may have already existed for the individual but which is made salient and is foregrounded through the digitally mediated environments of online craft culture:

> I think being part of what I see as a group of people online who take knitting seriously, and who are interested in sharing that, appeals to me and has given me a space or an idea to think of myself as someone creative and someone who can contribute to ideas about creativity instead of someone who just knits in front of the TV.
>
> —Laura, Ravelry member

This sense of self as creative maker connects with Willis's (1990) notion of symbolic creativity that he argues is a part of culture, an individual expression of creativity and an essential part of everyday life. In this context the practice of knitting, and its performative element online, can be seen as a demonstration and performance of the self, extended into and mediated by technological spaces and facilitating new networks of exchange, involvement, and engagement, transforming and extending the notion of creative maker (Willis 1990). This sense of creative identity has important implications for issues of community and connectivity, and it prompts and elicits new forms of community involvement and what I will go on in a later section to define as acts of "small citizenship."

Community as Local/Global "Involvement"

Gauntlett (2011) argues that in focusing on macrosocietal structures and microsocial interactions, we miss an intermediate or meso level of social structure that acts as an integrating element between individuals and society. Creative making and sharing activities, online and offline, are increasingly mediated through technology and virtual spaces and provide exactly the kinds of meso creative links that Gauntlett argues tie people together: the communication, exchange, and collaboration of everyday life. For knitters, participating in online communities to share and display material objects in public online spheres symbolically projects personal goals, values, and practices into the digital domain. These expressions of personal creativity simultaneously facilitate new forms of DIY citizenship and connectivity:

> When I'm putting my projects and pictures online, I'm putting a bit of myself there but I'm also saying I'm part of this group, I'm saying that I value it and am part of the wider community of knitters investing time in sharing creativity.
>
> —Sian, Ravelry member

At the level of online community involvement, this shared sense of experience, belonging, and identity is of course nothing new. However, these forms of materiality and connectivity enable community members to present their identity as "maker" and to express their creativity in ways that provide a sense of meaning and value *through* and *in* craft-specific online communities, again connecting the identity of creative maker with wider community networks of DIY citizenship:

> It's kind of like I can "out" myself as a knitter and have something that was private become something that is more meaningful and something that makes me feel that being creative is something valuable that connects me with other people.
>
> —Lisa, Ravelry member

These kinds of online communities and expressions of identity resonate with the global reach and connectivity of other types of online community. They also point to the importance of the local and global meso links that are enabled by involvement in digitally mediated craft. Perhaps what is most interesting is the seeming irrelevance of not only geographic but also temporal boundaries in the construction and experience of community and connectivity:

> I've never really had the time or inclination to do some of the things I know I should do or get involved in some of the things I think are worthwhile, but projects, through these kinds of online groups, connect me with my knitting and with a general interest in the online stuff and this means that I can be involved on a level that makes me feel like I'm contributing while still, selfishly, enjoying the things I enjoy in my life. I'm contributing to a local project but it doesn't matter to me where or what that local is or how long it lasts.
>
> —Helen, contributor to community art project

> I guess it's kind of odd but often you're contributing to projects that are based in a place or about a cause that is unrelated to you but it doesn't matter where in the world they are, that's not the point. The point is about the mix of being an online part of this group or place and then sending the knitted thing to actually be there for you while it happens.
>
> —Peter, contributor to community art project

These acts of contribution are valued *despite* their transience and, at a local and a global level, Web 2.0 and social media technologies are facilitating articulations of community that enable knitters to contribute to and feel a sense of involvement in "community" projects, broadly defined. This points to a need for diverse definitions of DIY activism that encapsulate the variety of ways in which citizenship and community are enacted and performed. These acts also challenge narratives of a decline in community participation and support Wellman et al. (2002) in their suggestion that we need to understand the ways in which *new* forms of communication and social organization are facilitating new types of connectivity. In the case of knitters, these new forms of connectivity involve a redefined understanding of what connection and locality entail and of how long these imagined connections and localities may meaningfully exist.

As with other online communities, online spaces for knitting connect individuals and groups at local and global levels, blur online/offline boundaries, and facilitate the organization of face-to-face and networked events that extend participants' understandings of "local" and of what involvement, citizenship, and community mean. The shift of the personal practice of knitting into the sphere of public activity enables participants to express, produce, and consume "community" as part of a new form of networked leisure citizenship. This citizenship is understood as a process and as set of practices that are about temporal participation alone/together in digitally mediated environments. This is contrary to suggestions that Internet engagement has led to the increasing *privacy* and domestication of community: "The observed decline (in traditional forms of community participation) has not led to social isolation, but to community becoming embedded in social networks rather than groups, and a movement of community relationships from easily observed public spaces to less accessible private homes" (Wellman et al. 2002, 292).

In the case of new forms of digitally mediated craft, the shift from the domestic to the public sphere instead enables exactly the kinds of communicative and collaborative exchanges that Gauntlett (2011) suggests are critical to the sense of meso involvement that citizens need to engage with the private and public institutions of contemporary life. In this sense these kinds of alone/together knitting communities provide a platform for making visible the personal and the private, for creating a space of shared meaning from fragmented and isolated activities, and for connecting networks of individuals around shared creative interests.

This focus on global/local (glocal) activities is not to suggest that the role of local connectivity is obsolete; as Haythornthwaite and Kendall (2010) imply, online interactions can have positive outcomes for place-based communities. What is of interest in this case are the ways in which the goals and identity of "creativity" and "maker" override local/global divides, pointing to a need to explore the complexities of the interactions between online and offline involvement, identity, and connectivity.

The nature and definition of "community" has a varied and contested history across the social sciences and defining "local," "community," and associated terminology is not an easy task. In the context of craft as a new participatory form of communal engagement, it is perhaps more useful to focus on conceptualizations of community as a cultural *process*: "It is necessary to start at an earlier stage by asking how cultural processes might *not* express, reflect or articulate a 'community,' but, on the contrary, how innovative and creative cultural processes might actually produce, not communities as such, but a range of complex and diverse community identities. In other words, I will suggest that as well as thinking about 'community' as such, we also need to develop cultural strategies that might produce new narratives of possible belonging" (Bromley 2010, 11).

Community is something made and experienced *through* participation. Acts of DIY citizenship are multiple and complex, transcending geographical regions as the digitalization of information and knowledge, networking, and global interactions shift individuals' sense of belonging and participation (Bromley 2010, 23). Digitally mediated craft allows for these expressions of community and connectivity, *through* activities that are meaningful and consistent with offline and online participation in making activities and though identification with the identity "crafter."

Acts of "Small Citizenship"

In addition to well-rehearsed debates about the role of the glocal in redefining community and of the ability of new social media to produce networked communities (Bromley 2010; Lee and Barton 2011; Robertson 1992), the connection and interaction between the identities of "maker" and "community member" also challenge more macro definitions of citizenship that orient around highly visible political and cultural acts. The desire of knitters to contribute to, create, and give shape to projects and environments at a glocal level represents citizenship and resistance in the same way as some of the more obviously political knitting practices of guerrilla activism. If we take the notion of DIY citizenship to encompass a more critical awareness of the role of making as part of a remediated definition of community, the importance of digitally mediated craft, and the maker identity as a valuable part of a shifting media ecology, supports Hartley's more flexible definition of citizenship and involvement based not on civic or political action but on a decontextualized "network of meanings" that situate identity as part of a mediasphere rather than the public sphere (Hartley 2004, 179).

Small-scale local projects and their accompanying online spaces enable participants to feel a sense of connection with other project contributors and events and this sense of broadly defined "community" is recognized as citizen involvement that is accessible and immediate despite being acknowledged as a small contribution:

> I've knitted for some big charities and projects and it's a bit like giving an anonymous donation to a huge charity appeal, you feel that you've contributed but it's such a small contribution it's a bit lost. I like getting involved in smaller things because you can feel like your bit is more meaningful and I think the online groups matter with these projects precisely because it gives them meaning for you through the other people, it's a very selfish way of looking at it I know!
>
> —Meg, contributor to community art project

Participants contributing to "local" and "community" projects understand their involvement as part of this kind of digital mediasphere but also as part of a subcultural form of leisure that provides a context for personal practices that are given broader meaning and significance when they become part of these networks of activity:

> I think it makes it not just me sitting around in front of the TV indulging myself with my knitting, it gets to be more about my knitting as a contribution to a bigger picture which kind of justifies my leisure time as something valuable, doing something valuable with my time.
>
> —Kay, contributor to community art project

This creates for knitters a global and mediated network that validates domestic leisure activities by framing them as part of broader contexts of community involvement and charity:

> I suppose what Ravelry groups or Facebook groups that call for contributions has done is make me think about how me and a group of friends and knitters here spread our knitting wings and can be part of our own knitting community and a wider community that shares the idea of who we are and what we are doing when we knit.
>
> —Beth, contributor to community art project

> It wasn't about living somewhere and being part of that community in, I guess, a normal way, it's about a sense of contribution to a bigger picture of community, do you know what I mean? A bit of me is somewhere else being part of something bigger.
>
> —Becky, contributor to community art project

In moving away from examples of DIY citizenship that are seen to be in some way socially interventionist or political in intention and representation, we allow for a broader definition of critical making and of the ways in which individuals might engage with more bounded articulations of citizenship and involvement. While participants may be global in nature, the intentions of contributors may be rather more mundane and less politically oriented than some literatures around craftivism might suggest (Pentney 2008). This is not to invalidate the intentions and contributions of these participants; rather it highlights the need to understand motivations that articulate around alternative definitions of participation and citizenship as a form of leisure and pleasure and as acts of collaborative connectivity:

> I know that there are lots of projects and things that are doing important stuff, water aid and charities and so on but for me, because I'm into the creative side of things I don't necessarily want it to be all about that, I might just want to be part of something that is about expressing my creativity and a contribution to a bigger act of that

expression in the way that [the project] it's doing, it's for people and making them smile at a creative act, it doesn't have to be about anything more than that for me.

—Sarah, contributor to community art project

These definitions may be disconnected from or irrelevant to a label given to a particular project and may not be perceived of as macro or political acts but are important for participants in providing a sense of small-scale, more micro and accessible acts of citizenship that are part of existing lifestyle practices and mediascapes.

Digital Making and DIY Citizenship?

Digitally mediated environments have brought together a diverse continuum of creative knitting practices that are mediated through technology and represented by technology. The continuum includes radical and political extremes of knitting practices as well as more invisible and micro day-to-day activities around knitting and craft. Each of these activities on the continuum maps onto online practices, from the creation of Ravelry groups in support of or to recruit knitters for a cause, to the use of blogs, photo sharing, and other lifestreaming activities. These kinds of social networking and Web 2.0 activities have created spaces for new forms of participation, consumption, and production in digitally mediated environments. They also represent new forms of bottom-up production and, as I have suggested, new ways of constructing the maker self, of doing community and of participating in acts of small citizenship. The visibility of the "domestic" identity as knitter, through membership of groups that come together virtually or physically to knit and to create and contribute to a wider global community, is represented and mediated online, creating a new form of materiality and connectivity.

While it is perhaps easy to see the political and radical extremes of knitting practices as examples of DIY citizenship and as sites of resistance, reaction, and subversion, it is more challenging to conceptualize what I have defined as the leisure knitter, and their acts of small citizenship, as social and cultural activists. However, local small-scale community projects, such as the one example provided here, demonstrate the importance of exploring how these acts are recognized by those participating in them and for understanding how these seemingly more mundane activities fit into wider definitions of community and new forms of cultural involvement and engagement. I argue that in fact these activities map directly onto Hartley's definition of the DIY citizen as a process of modern identity formation that links the private (personal) and the public (political) with mediated technologies. This connects new forms of consumption with the expression of social and cultural values that link individuals through voluntarist principle rather than proximity (Hartley 2004, 11), thus providing a wider lens through which to understand digitally mediated making and DIY citizenship.

Notes

1. The term *craftster* or *crafty hipster* is employed as an homage to the pioneer peer-to-peer sites Napster and Friendster. For example, www.craftster.org, is an online community for DIY craft with the motto "No tea cosies without irony."

2. A video tour of Ravelry is available via Vimeo (http://vimeo.com/23274072), and the key features of the site are outlined in a Ravelry tour (http://www.ravelry.com/tour/getting-started).

3. See http://community.knitpicks.com.

4. See http://www.diynetwork.com/topics/knitting/index.html.

5. For example, see http://knittaporfavor.wordpress.com, http://www.glittyknittykitty.co.uk, http://yarnbombing.com, and http://www.flickr.com/groups/yarnbombingukdiy/.

6. See, for example, knittivism and knitted terrorism: http://www.glittyknittykitty.co.uk/about.html.

7. Anonymized data extracts are taken from a series of qualitative interviews conducted with forty-three knitters active on online knitting sites and from twenty-seven contributors to the Scottish community art project.

References

Baym, N. K. 1998. The Emergence of On-line Community. In *Cybersociety: communication and community*, ed. S. Jones, 35–68. Newbury Park, CA: Sage.

Beer, D., and R. Burrows. 2010. Consumption, prosumption and participatory web cultures. Journal of Consumer Culture 10 (3): 3–12.

Bromley, R. 2010. Storying community: Re-imagining Regional Identities through Public Cultural Activity. *European Journal of Cultural Studies* 13 (1): 9–25.

Gauntlett, D. 2011. *Making Is Connecting: The Social Meaning of Creativity, from DIY and Knitting to YouTube and Web 2.0.* Cambridge: Polity Press.

Greer, B. 2008. *Knitting for Good! A Guide to Creating Personal, Social and Political Change Stitch by Stitch.* Boston: Roost Books.

Hartley, J. 2004. *Creative Industries*. London: Wiley Blackwell.

Haythornthwaite, C., and L. Kendall. 2010. Internet and Community. *American Behavioral Scientist* 53 (8): 1083–1094.

Humphreys, Sal. 2008. Grassroots creativity and community in new media environments: Yarn Harlot and the 4000 knitting Olympians Continuum. *Journal of Media & Cultural Studies* 22 (3): 419–433. http://www.informaworld.com/10.1080/10304310801989844.

Jones, S., ed. 1995. *Computer-Mediated Communication and Community*. London: Sage.

Jones, S., ed. 1998. *Cybersociety 2.0. Revisiting Computer-Mediated Communication and Community*. London: Sage.

Kuznetsov, S., and E. Paulos. 2010. "Rise of the Expert Amateur: DIY Projects, Communities, and Cultures." NordiCHI '10 Proceedings of the 6th Nordic Conference on Human-Computer Interaction: Extending Boundaries.

Lee, C., and D. Barton. 2011. Constructing Glocal Identities through Multilingual Writing Practices on Flickr.com®. *International Multilingual Research Journal* 5 (1): 39–59.

Lewis, P. 2011. Pride in the Wool: The Rise of Knitting. *The Guardian*, July 6.

Minahan, S., and J. Wolfram Cox. 2007. Stich'n Bitch: Cyberfeminism, a Third Place and the New Materiality. *Journal of Material Culture* 12 (1): 5–21.

Orton-Johnson, K. 2012. Knit, Purl and Upload: Digital Technologies, Digital Mediations and the Experience of Leisure. *Leisure Studies*. http://www.tandfonline.com/doi/full/10.1080/02614367.2012.723730.

Parkins, W. 2004. Celebrity Knitting and the Temporality of Postmodernity. *Fashion Theory* 8 (4): 425–442.

Pentney, B. A. 2008. Feminism, Activism and Knitting: Are the Fibre Arts a Viable Model for Feminist Political Action? *Thirdspace* 8 (1): n.p. http://www.thirdspace.ca/journal/article/view/pentney/210 (accessed August 1, 2013).

Rheingold, H. 1993. *Virtual Communities*. Reading, MA: Addison-Wesley.

Ritzer, G., and N. Jurgenson. 2010. Production, Consumption, Prosumption: The Nature of Capitalism in the Age of the Digital "Prosumer." *Journal of Consumer Culture* 10 (1): 13–36.

Robertson, R. 1992. *Globalization: Social Theory and Global Culture*. London: Sage.

Rosner, D. K., and K. Ryokai. 2009. Reflections on Craft: Probing the Creative Process of Everyday Knitters. *Proceedings of Creativity and Cognition*. http://people.ischool.berkeley.edu/~daniela/papers/reflectionsOnCraft-rosner-ryokai.pdf.

Smith, A., and P. Kollock. 1999. *Communities in Cyberspace*. London: Sage.

Toffler, A. 1980. *The Third Wave*. New York: Bantam.

Turney, J. 2009. *The Culture of Knitting*. New York: Berg.

Wellman, B. 2001. Physical Place and Cyberspace: The Rise of Personalized Networking. *International Journal of Urban and Regional Research* 25 (2): 227–252.

Wellman, B., A. Quan y Haase, J. Witte, and K. Hampton. 2002. Capitalising on the Internet: Social Contact, Civic Engagement, and Sense of Community. In *The Internet in Everyday Life*, ed. B. Wellman and C. Haythornthwaite, 291–324. Oxford, UK: Blackwell.

Willis, P. 1990. *Common Culture: Symbolic Work at Play in the Everyday Cultures of the Young*. Boulder, CO: Westview Press.

10 Mélange of Making: Bringing Children's Informal Learning Cultures to the Classroom

Alexandra Bal, Jason Nolan, and Yukari Seko

DIY Making as a Societal Shift

Thomas Kalil of the White House Office of Science and Technology Policy, in his opening remark at the 2010 National Science Foundation (NSF) workshop Innovation, Education and the Maker Movement, identified maker culture as the next phase of societal evolution. This evolution is based on individual fabrication becoming part of a powerful maker innovation ecosystem where products and services allow individuals to design, make, and sell it themselves, and where makers are also becoming successful entrepreneurs.[1] His position suggests the Obama administration's increasing support of hands-on, project-based approaches to learning, the practices crucial to prepare young people to become citizens of a new maker culture. For Kalil, "makers" who facilitate the emergent maker culture are those with DIY and "do-it-with-others" mindsets and those for whom "making" constitutes a significant element identity.[2]

The concept of making embraces diversity and fluidity, encouraging constant modification based upon the needs and wants of the practitioners. Maker culture can encompass a diversity of activities sometime at odds with each other, to the extent that it may undermine "exchange-value while simultaneously creating use-value outside of capitalism."[3] However, one should not consider the making ethos to be a new cultural phenomenon. Over the last forty years, this ethos has been congruent with academic traditions of sharing knowledge within a learning community. Open source advocates in academic institutions have long embraced the maker ethos by advocating free and open production models based on peer production and reciprocity as opposed to institutional norms.[4] Maker culture is incorporated in practices blending exchange value and use value into new industrial processes. And, with recent advancements in user-friendly making tools, maker culture is adapting to become an important and widely adopted industrial framework that will legitimize and formalize its position in mainstream society.

The DIY ethos is already central to an emerging global culture where local needs drive the development of sustainable solutions for societies at large. Peers can be individuals or part of organizations ranging from anonymous smart mobs to more rationalized self-organizing bodies such as commons.[5] Maker culture has the potential to represent a cultural model that encourages individual citizens to construct their own social realities, connections, and material aspects of living, to take user-generated production as a key to individual self-determination, knowledge sharing, and community building.

DIY Culture: Informal and Emergent DIY Learning

Although makers are from diverse backgrounds, the commonality is the use of informal learning to build communities and satisfy personal goals and needs through making. Livingstone defines informal learning as "any activity involving the pursuit of understanding, knowledge or skill which occurs outside the curricula of educational institutions."[6] Though informal learning can be any learning beyond explicit curriculum, for maker culture, it is an unauthorized, spontaneous, and practical experience that occurs outside the curriculum of formal and informal educational institutions.

The Internet offers one of the most conspicuous examples of a community of informal learners together accessing information, consulting peers, and becoming active social participants in the creation of their folk cultures.[7] Digital groups and communities are now distributing and sharing the new knowledge generated from their informal learning activities online, which has grown into a multitude of overlapping and intersecting, largely public, informal learning communities.[8] It is possible to learn how to urban farm[9] and/or microfarm;[10] access schematics for alternate sustainable living systems within peer-based innovation communities;[11] self-diagnose ailments[12] and provide first aid and/or self-medicate;[13] and de-school children using free digital libraries and portals.[14]

Mediated interactive environments—both virtual and physical—become a rich social sphere where DIY makers can build their own knowledge using experiential and multimodal forms of learning according to their own needs and learning goals. Learning in these environments is often stimulated and guided by experienced peers who become "experts" through the content creation as well as community building, and learning becomes embedded in the act of sharing. As such, digital co-learning among self-organizing agents constitutes a form of "emergent learning," a flexible, heuristic, inherently trans-disciplinary, peer-based learning, taking place within communities of interests outside formal institutions.[15]

Children are one of the segments of population that are involved with maker culture. Already some engage in digital informal learning communities and practices as primary forms of knowledge building and as a means of social acculturation. As educators, researchers, and co-learners in the maker culture, it is our task to help children prepare themselves for the future, nurturing their own autonomous learning capacity often disregarded in standardized education. To unpack what this may look like, we first explore the concept of "hacking" deeply rooted in early childhood experiences of open-ended inquiry, theory building, testing, and reflection, followed by an examination of how maker culture can foster informal and emergent learning that spurs new maker pedagogies for autonomous learning. We conclude with thoughts on how formal educational institutions can incorporate a maker culture as part of their reformation.

Children as Hackers: First Steps toward Critical Making

Contemporary education often sees children as socially vulnerable, underdeveloped beings requiring adult guidance and supervision. This assumption thwarts attempts to examine what young learners actually do and how they develop and practice their agency in media-rich societies. To question whether they can develop active citizenship in the maker culture, we view children as "hackers" challenging norms imposed by adults. It is our intention to resituate "hacking" as an understanding of autonomous, self-determining learning within early childhood.

"Hackers" are often portrayed in popular media with alarmist rhetoric, as computer criminals breaking into systems and stealing information. Tim Jordan, however, notes that the spirit of hacking should be understood as "altering a pre-existing situation to produce something new,"[16] supporting people working together, and sharing knowledge. Hacking constitutes a significant component of the maker culture that encourages collaborative creation while adhering to certain ethical values, such as privacy and equality. Hacking is not limited to fabrication of materials and circuitry or code development. It extends to the acts of social engagement and manipulation, including social engineering, life hacking as exemplified by the global hacker spaces movement,[17] fan activism, and participatory politics.[18]

Hacking is an act that produces unexpected outcomes out of what is already known or understood, or rather to make things that are known do new and unexpected things. It represents different learning processes that Kulikauskas describes as a "bottom-up, special-case, practical, nonstandard, unschooled, unexpected" approach as oppose to "the architect approach," which is "top-down, general-case, theoretical, grand vision, master plan, unlimited resources."[19] This hacking approach mirrors children's informal learning experiences that is an aspect of how children learn about the world.[20] Children spend their early years experimenting and hacking the world ordered by adults as they build languages, learn about social relationships, and explore the physical world. Children cultivate their hacking ability when they are exploring physical knowledge, building theories about the world around them, testing the theories they create, reflecting on results of their tests, and repeating the process with new variables and/or with ever increasing levels of complexity. Children experiment with physical knowledge by throwing things or dropping things, abstract knowledge by comparing things, and social knowledge in learning how to speak and how to engage people socially. Making a mess, playing with food, making noise, engaging in unstructured imaginary play are all examples of hacking, by way of which they experiment and counter parental orders and spaces, therefore cultivating personal awareness, self-esteem, and a sense of autonomy.[21] Reflective questions such as "What would happen if . . . ?" is an initial point of inquiry through which children learn how to pose problems as well as make informed and educated choices to solve them and be on the way to develop the self-awareness and self-criticism necessary to innovative and critical making.

DIY Pedagogy: Constructing Self-Determination and Autonomous Citizenship Practices

Social-constructivists have demonstrated how children construct knowledge and meaning in multiple social locations.[22] Digital media is one location where the hacking ethos is encouraged. Current education practices rarely prepare learners to move into new, often virtual, environments as primary social worlds, tending to employ educational principles that counter these new modes of mobile social engagement and emergent learning, and accentuate barriers that exist between school and a learner's social life.

Education must foster hacking if our goal is to sensitize children to the DIY and making values and processes that are stabilizing in society. As Burwell and Boler (chapter 7, this volume) report, youth and adults already blur the boundaries between popular culture and political engagement and remix cultural contexts within much more political contexts. In order to reflect societal shifts, education must begin to address critical making[23] and actively acknowledge the importance of the significant learning moments that exist outside schools, often in mobile and/or digital spaces. Educational institutions have the opportunity to build upon these experiences in the classroom by accepting personal interest as a driving force of learning as well as incorporating peer culture within more fluid institutional boundaries. This valuing of intrinsic interest, motivation, and the importance of personal, practical knowledge requires an open-ended and flexible emergent curriculum responsive to the goals of an educator-learner partnership. And this curriculum should validate situated emergent learning within communities of interests and practices where learners are socialized to engage in mixed spheres of social/learning interactions. The integration of informal and emergent learning opportunities into formal education can be achieved by transforming the institution into a learning node that fosters making and becomes part of a network of mobile learning commons, and that invites various community-based innovative makers to help children create sustainable solutions to local problems.[24]

Through everyday hacking, children set their own learning goals based on interests that grow from their own self-directed explorations. This hacking is embedded in their situational and cultural interest, curiosity, and boredom,[25] and given the right supports and tools, children can critically explore questions that are meaningful and important to them. Educators and parents can leverage emergent learning opportunities that support the development of autonomy in children as social actors in interest-driven learning communities,[26] nurturing children's natural abilities for creating/hacking the new out of the mundane.

In addition to hacking, autonomy constitutes a key component of the critical making ethos. Children naturally engage in learning activities and cultural production that lead to self-discovery and self-learning, and how they choose to engage in informal learning activities influences the development of autonomy. Historically, different pedagogies have reflected specific ideological positions that change the nature of autonomy a learner develops.[27] Depending on the ability of the individual to hack social norms, the individual develops autonomy as a self-controlled or determining individual. This autonomous individual has internalized the social norms and values of a specific social group to the extent of being able to critically self-regulate in accordance with the social metanarratives of an external authority within an heteronomous society. At the other end of the spectrum, an individual becomes capable of self-determination having challenged traditional norms and developed a self-awareness of being distinct from social groups. With this awareness, an individual can develop critical thinking skills to move beyond dominant social norms and create a personal social reality and potentially self-institute within an autonomous society framework.[28]

Through their self-organized learning, children increase their self-determination and autonomy as they experience for the first time a modest form of rebellion against parental and institutional heteronomy.[29] This small step is essential in their development as it represents a change in the nature of power dynamic that is necessary to prepare students for an unknowable future by fostering the confidence and self-assurance necessary to let go of inadequate traditions.

Instead of focusing on industrial processes that train children to standardized work flows, heteronomous social or cultural rituals, and authoritarian power hierarchies of specific industrial contexts, children need to be grounded in themselves and their communities of practice in order to be able to move into an uncertain future by becoming authoritative, adaptable, and flexible, skills essential to facing life and work situations our generation cannot foresee. By giving voice to children and learners, DIY making education can help develop processes that empower learners to participate in acts of self-determination and learn how to participate in various forms of production and governance; as such, it is one of the most powerful vehicles for changing power dynamics within Western capitalist institutions.[30] Central to this form of education is the ability to operate and negotiate within the social rules and contracts and governance structures of common property regimes based on self-management by a local community.[31]

Incorporating Informal Learning into Formal Education

A DIY capitalism framework is already in place, based on the practices of self-directed individuals and communities, supported by social relations, in fluid, informal arrangements. As work and daily life becomes a mesh of mobile, digital, and located activities, networks have become public spaces and workspaces where peers participate in the co-creation and co-production of knowledge and in co-working.[32] The ethos of DIY culture introduces the notion that innovation emerges from the cooperative and reciprocating informal activities of peers, both within and outside institutions, who are volunteering, inventing, and sharing their knowledge via networks and creating new social and economic realities.

But as Chidgey (chapter 6, this volume) notes, different meanings are inscribed onto the DIY term and activated within widely different trajectories and contexts. The DIY ethos has been absorbed by corporate culture that, through gaming and social media, can offer very attractive DIY production tools that already have a central place in children's lives. A casual look at children's engagement with digital media may lead many adults to believe that what they are seeing is a passive consumption of corporate-driven commercialized commodities. However, children are continually—albeit largely unconsciously—hacking norms, expectations, and the intentionality of these tools/spaces. They create their own social practices within digital spaces, particularly when environments attempt to block the kinds of interactions they would like to have.[33] And in many ways, children are DIYing their own culture and tools with which to engage in the world around them as Jenkins observes (chapter 3, this volume). The recognition of an emergent DIY ethos in children and in corporate cultures suggests societal shift toward a more autonomous society, and a need for educational change that fosters more autonomy and self-determination in children and supports children as critical makers. And in this process, educators must make sure that children are empowered to develop technological identities that engage them in civic action.

Already many educators possessed with a making ethos have explored and successfully implemented pedagogies centered on these principles. For instance, the Reggio Emilia–inspired[34] culture of listening to the hundred languages of childhood situates student interest as central to the educational process, thereby making the students visible and audible in the learning process. Some school initiatives have also begun exploring such student-centered pedagogies as part of formal pedagogical reform, including Gever Tully's tinkering school,[35] the edible schoolyard,[36] and the NOLA[37] project in the United States.

These emerging projects present ways of restructuring schools as centers that provide students with hitherto unavailable access to self-regulatory methodologies and research infrastructures, thereby facilitating collaboration between like-minded individuals and connecting learners to experts in the field. However, the self-determination principles implicit in DIY learning pedagogies limit their use in current schools. To capitalize on children's hacking proclivities in informal and formal learning environments, we must acknowledge children as social actors who need to develop self-determination and we must support their making choices regarding how and who they want to interact with. Thus, we must also insure that their informal social life—mobile, digital, and geographical—is considered a legitimate learning space. Such a change will be difficult to incorporate in formal education as maker self-determining culture and values are in direct conflict with dominant authoritarian values of educational institutions. By tradition, the public elementary mass education system teaches students to follow nineteenth-century, middle-class values as well as industrial working protocols, which tends to dwarf their own belief system and notion of being, both key to self-determination.

Even with the desire to change, these institutions are not structured or staffed in ways that can promote social and curricular change. The formal structures and social processes of institutions create barriers that are very difficult to overcome. Schools tend to block the potential for new value systems to be introduced in a hidden curriculum, which is embedded in the very nature of the school system, its internal social structures, and the behaviors and attitudes of its staff.[38]

Conclusion

Children are never far away from DIY learning spaces. Born in a current digital-rich era, young creators and learners are actively participating in DIY/making cultural processes. Digital learning spaces often allow children to use a larger array of learning modalities including musical, visual, social, and other knowledge that can better suit individuals whose dominant forms of intelligence are not addressed or are disadvantaged in formal learning settings.[39] Networked spaces, in the form of games or social media, are locations for experimentation with new forms of identity, community, and economic and social life based on self-determination, and they influence real life both in terms of learning possibilities as well as social and political life.[40]

We are in the midst of a redefinition of education that cannot remain impermeable to the influence and social life changes brought by maker culture and digital media. The inability of schools to adapt is becoming more problematic as mobile learning increasingly allows people to take education into their own hands. Some parents have already turned to private and online alternatives that better address their children's as well as their own needs. While some of the solutions offered come from within the traditional school system,[41] most of them are emerging from other contexts.

Children's formal learning is on the cusp of changes to the global regulatory and legal systems that have been planned for decades.[42] Such regulatory systems facilitate the acceptance of these alternate systems as part of accredited education. Already, these alternatives have a legitimate place within our society; formal midyear education has evolved to become part of a larger secondary educational ecology that mirrors existing heterogeneous educational markets. It has also opened the door to alternate autonomous maker cultures and practices as legitimate and to citizens developing the literacy necessary to become critical self-determined makers.

Notes

1. Dougherty 2010.

2. Ibid., ¶5.

3. Holtzman, Hughes, and Van Meter 2007, 45.

4. Marcin Jakubowski, "Marcin Jakubowski on the Global Village Construction Set & Open Source Ecology," *TED Talk 2011*, http://www.youtube.com/watch?v=zIsHKrP-66s.

5. Ostrom 1990.

6. Livingstone 1999, 51.

7. Nolan and Bakan 2010.

8. Nolan and Weiss 2002.

9. Such as http://www.theurbanfarmers.org and http://theurbanfarmingguys.com.

10. Such as http://agropedia.iitk.ac.in/ and http://therealknowhow.com.

11. Such as http://themakeproject.ning.com.

12. Using sites such as http://www.webmd.com/.

13. Using alternate medicine recipes available at sites such as http://www.ehow.com.

14. Such as http://www. neok12.com.

15. Williams, Karousou, and Mackness 2011.

16. Jordan 2008, 9.

17. Nolan and Levesque 2005.

18. Jenkins 2012.

19. Kulikauskas 2004, ¶4.

20. Nolan, Kate Raynes-Goldie, and Melanie McBride 2011.

21. Ibid.

22. Vygotsky 1978.

23. Ratto 2011.

24. Tulley 2007.

25. Schraw and Lehman, 2001.

26. Nolan, Raynes-Goldie, and McBride 2011.

27. Bal 2005.

28. Castoriadis 1987.

29. Nolan, Raynes-Goldie, and McBride 2011.

30. Foucault 2000.

31. Ostrom 1990.

32. Forlano 2008.

33. Grimes 2009.

34. Gandini 2008.

35. http://www.tinkeringschool.com.

36. http://edibleschoolyard.org.

37. http://www.nola.com/homegarden/index.ssf/2010/04/art_environmentalism_intertwin.html.

38. Longstreet and Shane 1993.

39. Bal, Seko, and Nolan 2011.

40. Bal 2011.

41. For instance, there are the publicly funded Avon Maitland District e-Learning Centre (http://www.amdec.ca) and Algoma District School Board (http://www.adsb.on.ca) accessible for homeschooling activities.

42. Bal 2007.

References

Bal, Alexandra. 2005. "Virtual Higher Education: A Liberalist or Humanist Socialization Tool," presented at the International Conference on Technology, Knowledge and Society, University of California, Berkeley, February 18.

Bal, Alexandra. 2007. "La délocalisation de la formation universitaire à Ryerson: Une évolution vers l'internationalisation du savoir," *Distances et Savoirs* 5, no. 3: 407–425.

Bal, Alexandra. 2011. Voices from One EDGE of New Media. *Function Magazine* 12 (May): 92–93.

Bal, Alexandra, Yukari Seko, and Jason Nolan. 2011. "Digital Space as Semi-permeable Membranes." Presentation at the Annual Conference of the Association of Internet Researchers, Seattle, October 15–17.

Castoriadis, Cornelius. 1987. *The Imaginary Institution of Society*. Cambridge, MA: MIT Press.

Dougherty, Dale. 2010. "Innovation, Education, and Makers. Thomas Kalil: What Would Education Look Like after a Maker Make-over?" *O'Reilly Radar*, October 4, http://radar.oreilly.com/2010/10/innovation-education-and-the-m.html.

Forlano, Laura. 2008. Working on the Move: The Social and Digital Ecologies of Mobile Work Places. In *Mobility and Technology in the Workplace*, ed. Donald Hislop, 28–42. London: Routledge.

Foucault, Michel. 2000. *Power*. Ed. D. James. Faubion, NY: New Press.

Gandini, Lella. 2008. Introduction to the Schools of Reggio Emilia. In *Insights and Inspirations from Reggio Emilia: Stories of Teachers and Children from North America*, ed. Lella Gandini, Susan Etheredge, and Lynn Hill, 24–28. Worcester, MA: Davis.

Grimes, Sara M. 2009. "The Hidden Playground." *The Escapist* 227, November 10, http://www.escapistmagazine.com/articles/view/issues/issue_227/6752-The-Hidden-Playground.

Holtzman, Ben, Craig Hughes, and Kevin Van Meter. 2007. "Do it Yourself . . . and the Movement Beyond Capitalism. In *Constituent Imagination: Militant Investigations, Collective Theorization*, ed. David Graeber, Stevphen Shukaitis, and Erika Biddle, 44–61. Oakland, CA, Edinburgh, UK: AK Press.

Jenkins, Henry. 2012. "Cultural Acupuncture: Fan Activism and the Harry Potter Alliance." *Transformative Works and Cultures* 10. http://journal.transformativeworks.org/index.php/twc/article/view/305 (accessed November 17, 2012).

Jordan, Tim. 2008. *Hacking: Digital Media and Technological Determinism*. Cambridge: Polity Press.

Kulikauskas, Andreas. 2004. "Social Hacking: The Need for an Ethics." *Journal of Hyper(+)drome. Manifestation* 1 (September). http://journal.hyperdrome.net/issues/issue1/kulikauskas.html (accessed October 18, 2010).

Livingstone, David W. 1999. Exploring the Icebergs of Adult Learning: Findings of the First Canadian Survey of Informal Learning Practices. *Canadian Journal for Studies of Adult Education* 13 (2): 49–72.

Longstreet, Wilma, and Harold Shane. 1993. *Curriculum for a New Millennium*. Boston: Allyn and Bacon.

Nolan, Jason, and Danny Bakan. 2010. Social Technologies for Young Children: Cultural Play with Songchild.org. In *Toronto/Montréal/Lille: Together Elsewhere*, ed. Louise Poissant and Pierre Tremblay, 279–291. Montreal: Presse de l'Université du Québec.

Nolan, Jason, and Michelle Levesque. 2005. Hacking Human: Data-Archaeology and Surveillance in Social Networks. *SIGGROUP Bulletin* 25 (2) (February): 33–37.

Nolan, Jason, Kate Raynes-Goldie, and Melanie McBride. 2011. The Stranger Danger: Exploring Surveillance, Autonomy and Privacy in Children's Use of Social Media. *Canadian Children Journal* 36 (2): 24–32.

Nolan, Jason, and Joel Weiss. 2002. Learning Cyberspace: An Educational View of Virtual Community. In *Building Virtual Communities: Learning and Change in Cyberspace*, ed. Ann K. Renninger and Wesley Shumar, 293–320. Cambridge: Cambridge University Press.

Ostrom, Elinor. 1990. *Governing the Commons: The Evolution of Institutions for Collective Action*. Cambridge: Cambridge University Press.

Ratto, Matt. 2011. Open Design and Critical Making. In *Open Design Now: Why Design Cannot Remain Exclusive*, ed. Paul Atkinson, Michael Avital, Bruce Mau, Renny Ramakers, and Carolien Hummels, 202–209. Amsterdam: BIS Publishers.

Schraw, Gregory, and Stephen Lehman. 2001. Situational Interest: A Review of the Literature and Directions for Future Research. *Educational Psychology Review* 13 (1): 23–52.

Tulley, Gever. 2007. *Five Dangerous Things You Should Let Your Kids Do*. TED talk, March. http://www.ted.com/talks/gever_tulley_on_5_dangerous_things_for_kids.html.

Vygotsky, Lev S. 1978. *Mind in Society*. Cambridge, MA: Harvard University Press.

Williams, Roy, Regina Karousou, and Jenny Mackness. 2011. Emergent Learning and Learning Ecologies in Web 2.0. *International Review of Research in Open and Distance Learning* 12 (3): 39–59.

11 Power Struggles: Knowledge Production in a DIY News Club

Jennifer Jenson, Negin Dahya, and Stephanie Fisher

Introduction and Background

This work builds on community-based extracurricular media production programs that are advocated by researchers and practitioners as educationally beneficial for children and young people, particularly those living in low socioeconomic conditions and facing forms of marginalization within and from outside their communities. Many of these programs have demonstrated how students' participation in media production can support specific curricular requirements, as well as contribute to understandings of digital and traditional literacies, critical analysis of popular media, and analyses of issues such as race, identity, gender, and power dynamics.[1] Scholars and researchers interested in exploring the relationship between visual media and multimodal literacies have also emphasized the different ways in which media production enables learners to encode and (re)produce knowledge that is relevant to their own lives.[2]

In this chapter, we consider the challenges and opportunities of engaging children in digital media production in the context of formal schooling. Digital media production practices are regarded as a powerful means of shifting children from being passive receivers of sometimes problematic media messages to active agents in the creation of multimodal forms of knowing. To begin, we identify some of the key issues that have emerged from similar DIY research projects and the significant barriers to working toward (a more) equitable education in relation to youth-created digital media production. We then discuss the changing state of knowledge production and communication in a new media world. Finally, we diverge from previous studies and present examples of how "do-it-yourself" (DIY) culture can provide a much needed, inherently critical, hands-on learning experience, while also highlighting how as a process, DIY does not necessarily challenge or evade systemic and structural limitations that contribute to the ongoing marginalization of young media makers.

Henry Jenkins argues that institutions (especially public ones like schools and libraries) can and indeed *should* address the known barriers and inequities in education related to active youth participation in a media saturated society. The structures in place limiting access to technology and complicating the implementation of adequate media literacy training for some[3] are, as many have argued, extremely slow to change.[4] According to Horst et al., media ecologies refer to factors such as the overarching and localized rules and regulations of institutions (homes, schools, etc.) that set the sociocultural context for learning through media consumption and/or production.[5] Sociocultural contexts that impact the ways in which media ecologies form include the structures of low-income urban communities in Canada, for instance, which face similar challenges in education as in the United States, including teachers' limited time, disassociation between teachers and students and/or the community, and the effects of poverty on students' ability to learn. The project discussed in this chapter makes learning opportunities available to a disenfranchised and largely at-risk school population in an effort to both skill up students who are very far from Prensky's widely-hailed claims of "digitally native" students and to see what they might have to tell us about their lives and communities through these multimodal productions.[6] We question how the culture of the school influenced group dynamics and the outcome of student-produced media, and we consider some of the unforeseen forces at play. In particular, we focus on the school as an institution with an ecology that affects (and indeed limits in this case) student production.

This look at a school-based, DIY media production club is situated within a multimodal literacies framework that recognizes the visual, audio, gestural, spatial, and tactile communicational modes, in addition to written and oral forms, through which teaching and learning can take place.[7] Researchers taking this approach explore the ways knowledge is differently encoded and represented across an array of forms, particularly through digital media.[8] Jewitt[9] ascribes the twenty-first-century turn to multimodality to postmodern influences: the increasing democratization of knowledge in the networked society has challenged modern configurations of truth and authority, querying both who "owns" knowledge and who creates it. Changes in the relative value of knowledge (what counts as knowledge and how one comes to know) are, as Lyotard[10] anticipated, a condition of postmodernity. Though these changes have been propelled by the proliferation of computer-based and screen-based technologies, what these technologies have brought about is a new understanding of what it means to know, including how it means to know multimodally. Digital texts (e.g., images, movies, podcasts, blogs, online social networking sites) encode knowledge very differently; accordingly, what is produced, how one knows, and how one comes to know when working with digital texts is thus different than in traditional print-based literacies.[11] The concept of multimodal literacies permeates the experiences of students discussed in this research, for whom learning through a DIY model is integrated with learning through the use of multiple forms of media and technology.

Valuing Production Values: The Castleguard News Network

The creation of a university-supported, extracurricular, media production club in a low-income elementary school in Toronto was intended to address and respond to the inadequate technological resources available to students (at home and at school), the myriad of social issues present in the surrounding neighborhood, and the generally low achievement levels that are touted as the norm. Following efforts in previous years to engage participants through animation, digital storytelling, and other types of audio-visual media, the Castleguard News Network (CNN) was created to focus the attention of the 11- to 13-year-old girls and boys participating in the program on locally relevant information that could be quickly turned into news media broadcasts. Some students had participated in our previously offered media production clubs, while others were inexperienced in media making. At any one time, there were ten to sixteen student reporters in CNN, supported by the teacher-librarian working with a small research team of two to four graduate students. The findings discussed in this chapter refer to documentation of the process and student products primarily through extensive researcher field notes and the news broadcasts students produced. Data was also collected through questionnaires about students' technology use, audio-video recordings of students at work, and semi-structured interviews with students about their experiences in the club and with media and technology more generally.

The news reports that were created reflected a wide range of student interests from school rules to March Break, sporting events, and book fairs. Productions that were student centered in terms of both requiring student interviews and focusing on student opinions were highly successful by way of demonstrating how students were able to plan the production of a short broadcast from background information to interviews and post-production on two- to three-week cycles. We begin this discussion in more depth with one example of students reporting on the hypocrisy of the school's policy on chewing gum—students were not allowed to chew it (it is against school rules), and yet they suggested that some of their teachers do so publicly. The two students working on this project arranged to interview one teacher who they claimed had, in a very specific example, been chewing gum in class. Prior to the interview, the students sent a survey around their class asking students if they had ever seen the teacher chew gum. This occurred outside the club and without the knowledge of the research team (i.e., the students initiated this on their own time in preparation for the club). The teacher responded to the accusation of chewing gum in class by saying, "You know how it is in class, you all team up and will say anything" (field notes, April 6, 2011) and continued to deny the accusation during the interview. In this case, although the experience modeled what surely happens in professional journalism when two parties are at odds about the truth of a matter, it provided students with an opportunity to practice maintaining a standard of professionalism when conducting an interview on a topic where they are personally affected. In the end, the teacher left the interview without fully addressing all their concerns—this was discouraging to the students, who expressed their belief that the teacher could deny what he had done *because he was a teacher*. This was not only an excellent opportunity to flex their storytelling and technical skills (the students had to take the footage and edit it into a coherent and fair representation of the issue), but it also presented a larger power dynamic at play: how seriously were students' voices being considered and what are the implications of this dynamic for students' interest in addressing similar issues in the future? How would the interview affect future encounters between the students and that teacher that took place outside of the production club? And most important, did CNN *really* give these students a means of dealing with the systematic inequities that are a part of the everyday practices of schooling, or did it simply serve to remind them of their "lesser" position within the school hierarchy? Although a CNN reporter was empowered to represent the "voice of the people" (so to speak), these students were unable to challenge the inequitable power dynamics that exist between students and teachers in this school.

In another example, a group of students wanted to produce a news segment on why school administrators had decided to cancel the grade 7 morning recess break. The complex ecology impacting students' "voice" is revealed in researcher field notes from April 27. Here, one researcher notes that the students' excitement for this topic has deflated, perceiving the situation as one where their voices are not being heard in response to one teacher's dismissive tone. The students had several reasonable and well-thought-out points to support their argument about the value of a morning recess break (e.g., fresh air and physical activity promotes mental stimulation). And while a news report about the issue is an appropriate avenue through which students could then share their opinions with others, it is significant that the students' interest in the topic wavered after this somewhat negative exchange with the teacher. In addition, when it later proved impossible to get an interview with the principal on this topic, student enthusiasm plummeted, as they perceived the involvement of the principal as essential to tackling important issues in a way that might result in changes to school policy. This group did nonetheless attempt to film a short segment on the playground voicing their own opinions; however, disagreements within the group about how to proceed without that pivotal interview with the principal meant the broadcast was not completed. This is another example of how the power dynamics between teachers, administrators, and students can impact the process of school-based media production and constrain the possible outcome.

In a third example, a different group also sought an interview with the principal about a change in policy regarding "casual days" (days when students were exempted from following the school dress code). The new regulation was to impose a cost of $1 to participate in this day. Although this fee was for the purpose of fundraising, three students had strong opinions about the ethics of this decision and wanted to question an administrator on the issue. The report was never completed because students spent weeks trying to arrange interview times with administrators or teachers to no avail. They were not satisfied to discuss the topic among themselves and eventually decided to move on to another topic. It should be noted here that students were trying to arrange these interviews during the set times of the club (lunch and after school), because this is when the cameras were available for use. Although the teacher-librarian agreed to supervise any interviews scheduled outside these hours, arranging an interview continued to be difficult for these students.

Each of these examples shows how the structure of schooling, namely the power dynamics that circulate there, can impose on and very greatly impact the kinds of stories that students are able to tell, even when these activities take place outside the classroom. From these examples we assert the need to consider the context in which any DIY project is created and acknowledge the structures that guide and sometimes limit students' work. While the administration supported our research agenda and presence in the school, there was little participation by anyone besides the teacher-librarian in the project, leaving a significant gap between the ideal circumstances for DIY production and the more practical realities that are encountered on the ground.

The support of the research team and teacher-librarian was not enough to meet the varied and sometimes intensive demands of our participants. Inexperienced media makers necessarily required more attention to learn the basic skills; however, our veteran participants would also monopolize one or more of the researchers for an entire session (often when learning a more advanced skill such as how to work with files created using other software). In addition to assisting students, organizers were responsible for checking on equipment, troubleshooting hardware and software, and offering conceptual and technical support during production. The scaffolding students needed in order to successfully complete a production from preplanning to editing requires a monumental amount of researchers' time, and at least in these kinds of projects, DIY is translated into a kind of PIY (pay-for-it-yourself), where those in affluent schools and communities with greater access to resources (human and hardware) have more opportunities to "do-it-yourself" because they can pay for it themselves. This limitation coupled with, in our case, the voices of some of those students already disenfranchised from the larger Toronto community being further marginalized within their local settings through existing hierarchical structures, bureaucratic road-blocks, and systemic inequities embedded in the school, make this type of work extremely demanding. It is our hope that in doing so the benefits to students greatly exceed the challenges they (and we) face along the way.

DIY+: Continuing Productions

We have argued that producing multimedia projects with students requires careful consideration for the dynamics at play in any institution and among people supporting the project, and ultimately takes an enormous amount of time and effort on the part of the teachers, students, and researchers involved. We contend that it is the collaborative effort of members of the school community that allow students to truly thrive when doing this type of work, in that their ability to tackle contentious topics that are important to them requires more than technical know-how. It is often the case that (some) of the final products from projects with similar research goals are shown as shining examples of the power of new media in the hands of youth, and in some cases we certainly do see great successes, though we have not documented those in this chapter. In those cases, what is *not* reported on is the labor and support that producing those examples entails, the examples that simply failed and why they failed, or the "hidden" but key factor that researchers very much *scaffold* students' productions and also have to learn to do so within the existing culture of the school. In our experience, some student productions face additional barriers to being able to engage key members of the school staff who would respond to their questions, leading to certain topics being altogether abandoned midproduction regardless of their importance to students. Here, the media ecology of the school environment shaped what possible productions come to completion, and therefore, in many ways, what stories and what "voices" are ultimately "heard." What we have attempted to do in this chapter is document not only what worked, but what did not work, as well as tell, in no uncertain terms, the realities of how we as researchers, the involvement of teachers and administrators, and the sociocultural structures at play in this school shaped the outcome of students' projects.

While we would like to engage in the "good news" kinds of stories of children and media to add to the growing body of work that sees these kinds of projects as transformational, what we want to argue is that our tale is much more cautionary. Doing this kind of work is labor- and resource-intensive (DIY = PIY); moreover, there are ongoing difficulties that are not reported on such as attrition and the one or two students who demand the most attention. While we support the efforts of educators and educational researchers doing this kind of work, we see this as a corrective to the ongoing and persistent discourse, identified almost a decade ago by de Castell, Bryson, and Jenson,[12] that positions educational researchers and their new media tools as "miracle workers" who allow students to leap over digital and socioeconomic divides. In particular, while we are certain that offering students the opportunity to learn how to produce media is valuable, there are boundaries around this work based on the structures in place by the institutions involved in the programs. This is not to suggest that school administrators and teachers necessarily intentionally deny students the opportunity to explore contentious issues—we are aware of the multitude of extraneous issues consuming teachers and administrators' time, particular in highly populated, low-income urban schools. In our continuing experience, however, these kinds of media interventionist projects necessarily involve more stumbling blocks than leaps, and demand work that is "messy" rather than miraculous.

Acknowledgments

This project was funded by the Social Sciences and Humanities Research Council of Canada. We gratefully acknowledge the work of Stephen Gilbert, who made this research possible within the school, as well as our very enthusiastic and willing student participants. An extended and much altered version of this work appears as "Valuing Production Values: A 'Do-It-Yourself' Media Production Club" in *Learning, Media and Technology* (2013), http://www.tandfonline.com/eprint/J9x6xmTXTUREUp8D7JQ6/full#.UkL-HashcY (accessed September 25, 2013).

Notes

1. Ito et al. 2010; Jenkins 2006; Jenkins et al. 2006; Lankshear and Knobel 2003; Lankshear and Knobel 2006; Lankshear and Knobel 2008; Peppler and Kafai 2007; Kafai and Peppler, chapter 12, this volume.

2. Bal, Nolan, and Seko, chapter 10, this volume; Karlsson 2001; Kress 2003; Kress 2010; Luke 2003; Marquez-Zenkov 2007.

3. Jenkins et al. 2006.

4. McLuhan 1964; Jenson, Taylor, and Fisher 2010.

5. Horst, Heather, Herr-Stephenson, and Robinson 2010.

6. Prensky 2001.

7. Cope and Kalantzis 2009a; Cope and Kalantzis 2009b; Kress 2003; Kress 2010; New London Group 1996.

8. Gee 2007; de Castell and Jenson 2003; de Castell and Jenson 2009; Kellner 2004; Lankshear and Knobel 2003; Lankshear and Knobel 2006.

9. Jewitt 2009.

10. Lyotard 1984.

11. Lankshear and Knobel 2008.

12. de Castell, Bryson, and Jenson 2002.

References

Cope, B., and M. Kalantzis. 2009a. Multiliteracies: New literacies, new learning. *Pedagogies: An International Journal* 4 (3): 164–195.

Cope, B., and M. Kalantzis. 2009b. A grammar of multimodality. *International Journal of Learning* 16 (2): 361–425.

de Castell, S., M. Bryson, and J. Jenson. 2002. Object lessons: Towards an *Educational* Theory of Technology. *First Monday* 7 (1). http://www.firstmonday.org/ojs/index.php/fm/article/view/923/845.

de Castell, S., and J. Jenson. 2003. Serious Play. *Journal of Curriculum Studies* 35 (6): 649–665.

de Castell, S., and J. Jenson. 2009. "Digital Hermeneutics." Paper presented at the National Reading Conference, 59th annual meeting, Albuquerque, New Mexico, December.

Gee, J. P. 2007. *Good Video Games and Good Learning: Collected Essays on Video Games, Learning and Literacy*. New York: Peter Lang.

Horst, H. A., B. Herr-Stephenson, and L. Robinson. 2010. Media Ecologies. In *Hanging Out, Messing Around, and Geeking Out: Kids Living and Learning with New Media,* Mizuko Ito et al., 29–78. Cambridge, MA: MIT Press.

Ito, M., S. Baumer, M. Bittanti, d. boyd, R. Cody, B. Herr-Stephenson, H. A. Horst, P. G. Lange, D. Mahendran, K. Z. Martinez, C. J. Pascoe, D. Perkel, L. Robinson, C. Sims, and L. Tripp. 2010. *Hanging Out, Messing Around, and Geeking Out: Kids Living and Learning with New Media*. Cambridge, MA: MIT Press.

Jenkins, H. 2006. *Convergence Culture: Where Old and New Media Collide*. New York, London: New York University Press.

Jenkins, H., R. Purushtoma, M. Weigel, K. Clinton, and A. J. Robison. 2006. *Confronting the Challenges to Participatory Culture: Media Education for the 21st Century*. Chicago: The John D. and Catherine T. MacArthur Foundation Reports on Digital Media and Learning.

Jenson, J., N. Taylor, and S. Fisher. 2010. Critical Review and Analysis of the Issue of "Skills, Technology and Learning." Report prepared for the Province of Ontario Ministry of Education. http://www.edu.gov.on.ca/eng/research/Jenson_ReportEng.pdf.

Jewitt, C. 2009. Introduction. In *The Routledge Handbook of Multimodal Analysis*, ed. C. Jewitt, 1–7. Abingdon, Oxon: Routledge.

Karlsson, J. 2001. Doing Visual Research with School Learners in South Africa. *Visual Studies* 16 (2): 23–37.

Kellner, D. M. 2004. Technological Revolution, Multiple Literacies and the Revisioning of Education. *E-learning* 1 (1): 9–37.

Kress, G. 2003. *Literacy in the New Media Age*. London: Routledge.

Kress, G. 2010. *Multimodality: A Social Semiotic Approach to Contemporary Communication*. London: Routledge.

Lankshear, C., and M. Knobel. 2003. *New Literacies: Changing Knowledge and Classroom Learning*. Buckingham, PA: Open University Press.

Lankshear, C., and M. Knobel. 2006. *New Literacies: Everyday Practices and Classroom Learning*. Maidenhead, Berkshire: McGraw Hill/Open University Press.

Lankshear, C., and M. Knobel, eds. 2008. *Digital Literacies: Concepts, Policies and Practices*. New York: Peter Lang.

Luke, C. 2003. Pedagogy, Connectivity, Multimodality, and Interdisciplinarity. Reading Research Quarterly 38 (2) (July–Sept.): 397.

Lyotard, J. F. 1984. *The Postmodern Condition: A Report on Knowledge*. Minneapolis: University of Minnesota Press.

Marquez-Zenkov, L. 2007. Through City Students' Eyes: Urban Students' Beliefs about School's Purposes, Supports and Impediments. *Visual Studies* 22 (2): 138–154.

McLuhan, M. 1964. *Understanding Media: The Extensions of Man*. New York: Routledge.

New London Group. 1996. A Pedagogy of Multiliteracies: Designing Social Factors. *Harvard Educational Review* 66 (1): 60–92.

Peppler, K., and Y. Kafai. 2007. From SuperGoo to Scratch: Exploring Creative Digital Media Production in Informal Learning. *Learning, Media and Technology* 32 (2): 149–166.

Prensky, M. 2001. Digital Natives, Digital Immigrants. *Horizon* 9 (5): 1–6.

12 Transparency Reconsidered: Creative, Critical, and Connected Making with E-textiles

Yasmin B. Kafai and Kylie A. Peppler

In this chapter, we consider how students' and adults' work with electronic textiles can expand our understanding of "transparency"—revealing power structures and constraints in the design and use of new media—a core idea promoted in participatory media[1] and critical design.[2] Electronic textiles (e-textiles), which include young people's design of programmable garments, accessories, and costumes, incorporate elements of embedded computing that allow for controlling the behavior of fabric artifacts, novel materials that can include conductive fibers or Velcro, sensors for light and sound, and actuators such as LEDs and speakers, in addition to traditional aspects of textile crafts. E-textiles can be considered a part of a larger DIY movement to promote personalized fabrication outside traditional manufacturing that can also extend into classrooms.[3]

We see the additional benefit in revealing insights about the production or design of technology itself and cultural assumptions that nowadays are often hidden or "invisible" to youth. Creative production with e-textiles encourages students and adults to question their current understandings of functionality and aesthetics, make explicit their gendered assumptions about crafts, and master the fundamentals of a new field by learning the visual, aural, and technological literacies necessary to inscribe one's self into the larger DIY and fashion culture.[4] All in all, what takes place during such creative production becomes a critical reflection on how technology design decisions are made, how they are interrelated with craft production and engineering functionality, and how they intersect with personal choices and cultural assumptions. We examine these ideas by first outlining the different perspectives, their historical antecedents, and relevant research in the constructionist tradition. We then present examples from our own research with youth and adults in e-textile workshops that illustrate how the visibility of production affords opportunities for critical engagement.

Finally we discuss how this type of production holds the potential to disrupt gender divides that are often ubiquitous in educational settings focused on high-tech media.

Constructionist Perspectives on Transparency

Our goal in using transparency as an aspect of criticality draws from approaches in media and critical design education. The field of media literacy posits that when learners understand how ownership in media works, they begin to see how information is produced and positioned. Media scholars[5] have explicitly included creative designs, ethical considerations, and technical skills in their exploration of youths' expressive and intellectual engagement with new media. They place an emphasis on creative production because it empowers individuals to redefine their position within established power structures and learn "to see clearly the ways that media shape perceptions of the world."[6] Along with the necessity of developing technical skills and ethics, the understanding of power structures has been seen as a key aspect of digital citizenship. Here, transparency is a goal that learners need to accomplish in order to understand media, and educators rooted in this tradition frequently use youths' *engagement with media* to illustrate issues of power in production.

More recently, scholars engaged in the examination of critical design have expanded the notion of transparency by focusing on the connections that designers develop in the process of creative production. This work picks up on the emotional connections and relationships that people form with technology and uses them as springboards for critical reflection "to turn the relationship between technology and society from a 'matter of fact' to a 'matter of concern.'" [7] This approach to critical design is aligned with the open source movement that allows users the necessary access to build more complex understandings of the way things work. Classes in which students use open source software and build artifacts provide students with critical understandings of production and programming processes. Transparency in these educational settings is afforded by students' *reflection with media*.

While proponents of both approaches agree that creative production can be a valuable pathway into a critical understanding of power structures and relationships, we offer a complementary perspective on transparency as a vehicle for learning. Most of today's technology designs intentionally make invisible what makes them work; yet, for educational purposes, visibility is more beneficial in promoting learning.[8] In e-textiles, for example, the fabrication of stitches, circuits, and codes reveals the underlying structures in tangible and observable ways. Like participatory media studies, we stress the importance of making media designs as a way to understand the world. Like critical design studies, we see programming and open source technology as a way to "look under the hood." Transparency in educational applications thus comes from learners' *building with media*.

Underpinning all of these approaches is a fundamental view that learning happens best while in the process of making shareable artifacts, which is at the heart of constructionist theory.[9] Constructionist activities afford transparency by providing opportunities for concretizing knowledge and highlight "the reconnection of two modes of engagement with the world that are usually held separate: critical thinking, traditionally understood as conceptually and linguistic based, and physical 'making', goal-based material work."[10] The constructionist paradigm, by encouraging the externalization of knowledge, promotes seeing the knowledge object as a distinct "other" with which we can come into meaningful relationship. This relationship consists of questions that makers ask themselves about how the external object connects to other bodies of knowledge.[11] New forms of creative interactions afforded by these connections are some of the main affordances of working with open technologies that do not hide relationships, but rather leave them open in addition to extending them to crafts and arts beyond the traditional science, technology, engineering, and math (or STEM) focus that has dominated most of the critical considerations of technology production.

It is how we come to build these knowledge relationships that is at the center of our work with e-textiles. As Turkle and Papert have argued, there are preferred ways of working with technologies, the hard over the soft, that value the formal over the concrete.[12] E-textiles complicate the relationships we have preestablished with technology in multiple ways. There is a historically gendered notion that sewing and fabric fall nearly exclusively in the domain of females, while engineering and programming are traditionally seen as within the domain of males. Furthermore, there are tensions between aesthetics and functionality that, in particular, bring out the personal in e-textiles design because these artifacts are often carried close by their designers and might have a purpose in everyday life. In contrast, the corresponding domain of robotics often seems to exist for the sole purpose of competition. We argue that e-textiles are domain-crossing objects that provide fertile contexts for revisiting and remaking relationships with technology.

Critical Tensions in E-textile Designs

Our observations draw from a series of workshops with e-textiles that we organized with diverse groups of youth and adults over the last two years. Our goal was to engage participants in learning crafts, circuitry, and coding while making e-textile artifacts. The *LilyPad Arduino* construction kit enables novice engineers/designers to embed electronic hardware into textiles.[13] Users sew LilyPad modules together with conductive thread and employ the popular Arduino or ModKit development environments to program the LilyPad microcontroller to manage sensor and output modules (like LEDs) employed in their designs. Since its commercial release in 2007,[14] LilyPad Arduino has been widely adopted by designers and engineers of all ages from around the world and employed in a number of universities in computer science, engineering, fine arts, and design courses.

The following examples are drawn from e-textile workshops with middle school youth and female engineers. Taken together, these examples illustrate how technology design decisions are made, how they are interrelated with craft production and engineering functionality, and how they intersect with personal choices and by extension promote critical reflection within locally situated e-textiles contexts.

In a middle school, six boys and four girls signed up for the e-textile workshop, meeting twice a week in an open atrium for one month. They gathered around tables where LEDs, switches, batteries, needles, and conductive thread as well as t-shirts, canvas bags, and various decorative materials were displayed. Before starting on their projects, the youth were shown a few pictures of e-textile projects and given a tutorial on how to sew an electronic circuit. They were immediately drawn to the creative possibilities of the LED assortment on the tables, though were more halting as they deliberated possible designs on T-shirts or bags. Over the course of the workshop, youth brought in supplementary materials, providing opportunities for further personalization (see figure 12.1). While all students initially laid out their complete and functional circuits by connecting alligator clips to batteries, switches, and LEDs, the move onto fabric inevitably brought its own challenges: the polarity of LEDs was often misaligned or thread endings were not properly knotted, revealing that the students' understanding of circuitry wasn't entirely infallible.

Yet there was a palpable unease when the project started and the boys saw the fabric and realized they had to sew. Throughout the weeks, the unfamiliarity of sewing—threading the conductive thread as well as guiding

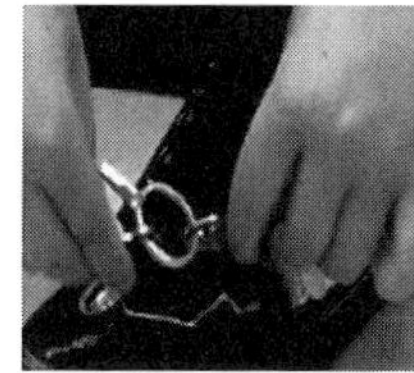
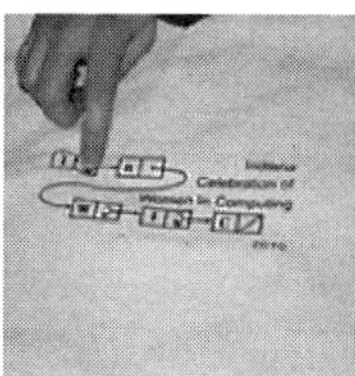
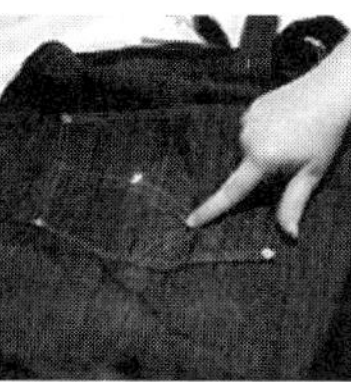

Figure 12.1
Images of completed projects from the middle-school workshop (two panels at left) and Women in Computing conference (two panels at right)

the needle through the fabric to make stitches—remained a major hurdle for all students except for one girl whose grandmother had taught her how to sew. It was also difficult for the youth to explain to others what exactly they were working on. When other students passed by the atrium, looking curiously at the tables covered with fabric and other materials, two of the participating boys immediately shouted "We're doing circuits!" while holding up their t-shirts, hinting at their identification with the more masculine aspects of the activity.

The 2011 Women in Computing conference provided a second opportunity to engage learners with the LilyPad Arduino in a less formal learning environment. Over one hundred women ranging from undergraduate students to tenured professors gathered for a three-hour e-textiles workshop. The objective of the workshop was to introduce a burgeoning field to an audience already steeped in the language of computing and engineering. After a brief presentation, the group was led through a series of steps that detailed the fundamentals of circuitry and sewing. In the process, participants utilized a simple set of e-textiles materials to create unique artifacts, including circuitry-enhanced bracelets, conference bags, gloves, and more.

And, yet, the abilities of the participants to create their projects were only slightly higher than those of the participants in our middle school workshops, despite this audience's experience with advanced programming, robotics, computer science, and engineering. Several participants worked ahead of the rest of the group, assuming that they would know what to do, only to run into hurdles down the line. Frequent mistakes included participants sewing through the circuit in one continuous thread, thus returning the power directly back to the battery source and shorting out the connection; underestimating the need for solid connections; misunderstanding polarity concepts when putting multiple lights in parallel; not even knowing how to tie basic knots, improperly tying a knot, or improperly threading a needle. Interestingly, the women who excelled in the activity were all older in age and more accustomed to the material science of working with fabric, needles, and thread. For them, the electronics were a natural extension from their prior experiences with traditional crafts.

The experiences in these workshops call two tensions to our attention. The first concerns a lack of transparency in traditional computing: the initial explorations of well-educated scholars with these materials brought their small misconceptions of circuitry concepts, such as polarity (the direction of energy), connectivity (the stability of connections), and flow (the circular path), to the fore. This was expected of middle school students but not of the more experienced engineers. However, most participants were able to connect to the wide bodies of knowledge with which they were familiar once a demonstrator made the initial parallels between the materials. The new materials thus made it more apparent that participants had understood before, but had some lingering misconceptions when transferring this understanding to a new domain—working with such a transparent medium underscores the importance of seeing how these engineering concepts apply across a range of media and conditions.

The second tension touches on a larger cultural trend concerning the role of a woman in engineering and computer science fields. The evident atrophy of a historically feminine activity (i.e., sewing) across the two youngest generations represented at the conference points to some academic females' devaluing of "women-centric" knowledge and skills. And while the vast majority of participants were drawn into the activity—especially the aura of a communal sewing circle that permeated from it—a minority of women argued that e-textiles reinforced gender stereotypes, preferring that women get involved in more male-dominated activities like robotics. This seems indicative that "women's skills" are something from which women in STEM fields continue to distance themselves. Though the causes for this tension are multifarious and deeply engrained, our hope for women's involvement in e-textiles is to return cultural capital to these largely undervalued skill sets, recognizing the potential of the unique perspectives and insights they could bring to STEM fields. Furthermore, while female engineers may have adapted the dominant epistemology of computing and frown at bringing "women's skills" into the field, girls and women just entering computer science may find comfort in the bridge between their existing gendered identities and the scientific identity they are being asked to take on.

Personal and Critical Connections in DIY Design

We are just beginning to understand how youth and adults engage with e-textiles, a relatively new addition to the DIY community but one that is becoming part of a larger personal fabrication movement. With rarely an exception, most participants approach these activities with little prior knowledge or experience in sewing, circuit design, or programming, let alone having ever used the LilyPad Arduino construction kit. While some have argued that such tangible materials can promote transparency and aesthetic engagement with technology,[15] these considerations have been articulated in regard to traditional construction kits aimed at robotics and scientific instrumentation. E-textile artifacts have similar qualities to what Turkle and Papert describe as sitting "betwixt and between the world of formal systems and physical things; it [the computer] has the ability to make abstract concrete . . . by the same time it makes it visible, almost tangible and allows a sense of direct manipulation."[16] While Turkle and Papert made this reference to objects on the computer screen, the inferences apply even more so to e-textiles. Simple misconceptions become apparent that range from not understanding what insulation does for wire, and why it's needed, to what the relationships are between an energy source and its components. While each of these represents valuable learning insights, one could easily classify them under functional understandings. What's important here is that all of this happens in a context where designers want to build something of aesthetic and personal value and within this context begin to understand the coordination of design constraints. In a paradoxical way, e-textiles make it more complicated to build with technologies while making it simpler to enter the complex relationships with technology.

Most pronounced are of course the references to the gendered nature of e-textile materials and activities that slip into conversations throughout the workshops. When middle school boys label their activities "circuit design," this is an intentional reference to engineering as a more male-appropriate and highly valued activity. These distinctions are in fact more complex since they make reference to old stereotypes that are no longer viable; most girls and women do not know how to sew, and so the seeming advantage is no longer available. Yet we also know from a recent study by Buechley and Hill[17] that examined the participation of women in the LilyPad community, that their participation is indeed much higher here than in the more engineering-centric Arduino community. While the LilyPad is a more recent technology development, it also evokes the foundations of modern computing, bringing us back to the longstanding historical connections among women, textiles, and computing: for example, Ada Lovelace's notes on the analytical engine that resulted in the first "computer program" in the nineteenth century, and the Jacquard loom (1801), which though created for weaving complex patterns in textiles, is considered the first step in the history of computing hardware.

Furthermore, more nuanced understandings of how technology works with a broader range of materials is crucial for today's DIY citizenship, as more aspects of life have moved into the digital domain. Cultivating a citizenry that understands why knowing how to build technology is important for several reasons. On a general level, it promotes understanding of the basic functionalities that underlie the designs of technology encompassing aspects such as designs of interfaces and systems. Moreover these understandings also empower citizens on a political level, providing them with resources to question decisions and designs made by others. Finally, on a personal level, the abilities to use and make technologies for expressive purposes allow for better communication and relationships. The mind-and-hand merger of the digital and physical, additionally, is brought together through creative production with e-textiles, not only bringing these aspects to the foreground but also allowing learners to externalize knowledge and reformulate their misunderstandings. E-textiles reposition youth as active creators, rather than consumers, of knowledge. These domain-crossing objects have the potential to attract marginalized youth that have been left out of the STEM pipeline in more subtle ways by capitalizing and affirming their interests in low-tech materials while simultaneously introducing STEM content. These opportunities are especially prescient as seen against the backdrop of larger economic and political changes with dual forces of massive concentrations of media ownership and profound influences from underground and urban cultures. This type of work cultivates a citizenry that understands, through transparency of technology, not only how things work, but how to make things themselves.

Acknowledgments

This work was supported by a collaborative grant (0855868/0855886) from the National Science Foundation to Yasmin Kafai, Leah Buechley, and Kylie Peppler. Any opinions, findings, and conclusions or recommendations expressed in this chapter are those of the authors and do not necessarily reflect the views of the National Science Foundation, the University of Pennsylvania, or Indiana University. We thank Diane Glosson, Quinn Burke, and Michael Moore for their help with workshop coordination; Deborah Fields and Kristin Searle for comments on an earlier version of the chapter; and Quinn Burke for his editing.

Notes

1. Henry Jenkins, Katie Clinton, Ravi Purushotma, Alice J. Robison, and Margaret Weigel, *Confronting the Challenges of Participatory Culture: Media Education for the 21st Century*. (Chicago, IL: MacArthur Foundation, 2006).

2. Matt Ratto, "Open Design and Critical Making," in *Open Design Now: Why Design Cannot Remain Exclusive*, ed. Paul Atkinson, Michael Avital, Bruce Mau, Renny Ramakers, and Carolien Hummels, 202–209 (Amsterdam: BIS Publishers, 2011); Leah Buechley, "Questioning Invisibility," *IEEE Computer* 43, no. 4 (2010): 84–86; Yasmin B. Kafai and Kylie A. Peppler, "Youth, Technology and DIY: Developing Participatory Competencies in Creative Media Production," *Review of Research in Education* 35 (2011): 89–119.

3. Buckingham, David. *Media Education: Literacy, Learning and Contemporary Culture* (Cambridge, UK: Polity Press, 2003); Barbara Guzzetti, Kate Elliot, and Diana Welsch, *DIY Media in the Classroom: New Literacies across Content Areas* (New York: Teachers College Press, 2010); Michele Knobel and Colin Lankshear, eds., *DIY Media: Sharing, Creating and Learning with New Media* (New York: Peter Lang, 2010).

4. Mark Frauenfelder, *Made by Hand: Searching for Meaning in a Throwaway World* (New York: Penguin, 2010); D. Gauntlett, *Making Is Connecting* (Cambridge, UK: Polity Press, 2011).

5. Henry Jenkins, Katie Clinton, Ravi Purushotma, Alice J. Robison, and Margaret Weigel, *Confronting the Challenges of Participatory Culture: Media Education for the 21st Century* (Chicago, IL: MacArthur Foundation, 2006).

6. Ibid., 3.

7. Ratto, "Open Design and Critical Making," 15.

8. Mike Eisenberg, Ann Eisenberg, Leah Buechley, and Nwanua Elumeze, "Invisibility Considered Harmful: Revisiting Traditional Principles of Ubiquitous Computing in the Context of Education," in *Proceedings of Fourth IEEE International Workshop on Wireless, Mobile and Ubiquitous Technology in Education (WMTE '06)*, 102–110 (New York: IEEE, 2006).

9. Seymour Papert, *Mindstorms* (New York: Basic Press, 1980).

10. Matt Ratto, "Open Design and Critical Making."

11. Uri Wilensky, "Abstract Meditations on the Concrete and Concrete Implications for Mathematics Education," in *Constructionism*, edited by Idit Harel and Seymour Papert, 193–204 (Norwood, NJ: Ablex Publishing, 1991).

12. Sherry Turkle and Seymour Papert, "Epistemological Pluralism and the Revaluation of the Concrete," *Journal of Mathematical Behavior* 11, no. 1, (1992), 3–33.

13. Leah Buechley and Mike Eisenberg. "The LilyPad Arduino: Toward Wearable Engineering for Everyone," *IEEE Pervasive* 7, no. 2 (2008): 12–15; Leah Buechley, Mike Eisenberg, Jaime Catchen, and Ali Crockett, "The LilyPad Arduino: Using Computational Textiles to Investigate Engagement, Aesthetics, and Diversity in Computer Science Education," in *Proceeding of the SIGCHI Conference on Human Factors in Computing Systems (CHI)*, 423–432 (Florence, Italy: ACM, 2008).

14. Leah Buechley and Benjamin M. Hill, "LilyPad in the Wild: How Hardware's Long Tail Is Supporting New Engineering and Design Communities," in *Proceedings of Designing Interactive Systems (DIS)*, 199–207 (Aarhus: Denmark: ACM, 2010).

15. Mitchel Resnick, Robbie Berg, and Mike Eisenberg, "Beyond Black Boxes: Bringing Transparency and Aesthetics back to Scientific Investigation," *Journal of the Learning Sciences* 9, no. 1 (2000): 7–30.

16. Turkle and Papert, "Epistemological Pluralism and the Revaluation of the Concrete," 4.

17. Buechley and Hill, "LilyPad in the Wild."

13 Woven Futures: Inscribed Material Ecologies of Critical Making

Daniela K. Rosner and Miki Foster

Introduction

Over the last few decades, a broad range of new materials and tools has entered after-school programs. Rooms have been outfitted with computer labs, computers have been connected to the Internet, and special programs have expanded to include robotics and computing workshops. Yet the nature of these transitions and their consequences for pedagogy is often difficult to distill, presenting some challenges for our theorizing of digital practice. In this chapter, we aim to better understand these shifts and their implications for critical making by discussing our experiences at an after-school club in Silicon Valley for predominantly African American and Latino youth. In particular, we discuss the conception and development of Woven Futures, a collaborative craft project that connects specific handwork activities with digital video and imagery. As a club volunteer and a technology director, we were able to observe how youth encounter and cultivate a range of interpersonal relationships and expressions as part of digital production. Building on recent work concerning collaborative education[1] and DIY maker cultures,[2] we use the clubhouse as a local context to ground an empirical exploration of critical making and what we term "inscribed material ecologies"—emergent circulations of materials conditioned by entrenched institutional and political arrangements.

Background

At the time of this work, we were a club volunteer and a technology director primarily interested in using the processes of making as a tool to consider questions of digital materiality in creative practice. Building on Ratto's critical making approach[3], we aimed to use the "act of shared construction"[4] to rethink material practices among digital tools in light of their improvisational and adaptive character, a materialist perspective most recently articulated by Barad[5] and Ingold.[6] Specifically, we sought to reflect on the ontological status of material in light of contemporary concerns for creativity, embodied skill, and collaboration in after-school education. By engaging possibilities for craft and do-it-yourself (DIY) design,[7] or what Orton-Johnson might call *digital* craft,[8] we introduced new technologies into a Northern Californian after-school clubhouse. Though this involved material outcomes, our goal was not to produce particular objects for reflection. As we will describe, our interest in the mixed material ecologies of craft and digital creative production (embroidery and digital video) had some compelling sociotechnical implications for collective learning.

The Clubhouse

The clubhouse was divided into several practical arenas: academic, technology, teen, recreation, college prep, and art. These compartments effectively consolidated the clubhouse's "disciplines" into certain times and places, thus influencing the arrangement of our present work. Miki's position as technology director entailed that she facilitate computer and video classes and individual projects in the club's Technology Lab, a room with rows of computers placed on desks lining all four walls. Prior to Woven Futures, Miki had taught three programming and electronics classes (Scratch programming, Processing programming, Arduino microcontrollers and physical computing).[9] Some youth chose to occupy the Technology Lab for the entire duration of the programming hours while others would pop in and out of the room for shorter durations. The clubhouse of the after-school program thus provided a useful setting for observing a diversity of social learning experiences among youth.

Woven Futures

The theme of this work emerged out of video interviews with participating youth and surrounding conversations. We were heavily inspired by educational technology interventions that have aimed to introduce elements of electronic textile design alongside programming skills, such as Leah Buechley's case studies with the Lilypad Arduino, a sewable microcontroller,[10] and Kafai and Peppler's corresponding e-textiles workshops, such as those discussed (chapter 12, this volume). The physical and virtual mediated learning environments discussed by Bal, Nolan, and Seko (chapter 10, this volume) support similar trans-disciplinary learning experience relevant to educational goals in math and the sciences.[11] At one level, we hoped this project would extend previous work by encouraging enthusiasm for computer science and electrical engineering among marginalized youth, drawing together familiar narrative structures with less familiar computer code. Such a project would also incorporate previous workshops' training with microcontrollers. At another level, we aimed to launch a collaborative activity that reflected the heterogeneous character of the clubhouse. To consider the diversity of experience, we chose to use the metaphor of patchwork storytelling as a springboard for engagements with material. Video interviews were conducted on Android G1 phones equipped with the Spyn, an application that uses computer vision techniques to associate digital records (images, video, text, GPS location) with locations on fabric. Originally designed for knit fabric, Spyn was adapted for use with embroidered imagery.

Early in the interviewing process, one participant asked her interviewee who the interviewee wanted to be in the future. This topic of futurity served as an entry point for examining the quality of a digital woven tapestry. As youth completed their videos, they were asked to design and embroider an associated quilt square that represented their future. As part of this process, they were also shown how to sew and embroider their square. This consideration of anticipated futures engendered longer discussion, a host of similar interviews, and, ultimately, the conceptual locus of Woven Futures.

As a technical undertaking, Woven Futures consisted of several interconnected parts: video interviews, patch design, embroidery, sewing decorative "granny" squares, sewing resistive fabric, microcontroller programming, and soldering. After patches were completed, youth and facilitators (Daniela and Miki) sewed resistive fabric to the back of each square and later soldered wires to the quilt's connection to the Arduino microcontroller. The microcontroller was equipped with custom software designed to read the specific resistance of each youth's patch and play back the patch's associated video file from a connected computer. The piece culminated in the fashioning of these parts at a Maker Faire exhibition, a demonstration of DIY projects sponsored, in part, by O'Reilly Media. Orchestration of these various pieces required scheduling flexibility (adjusting the duration and timing of the program) and resource flexibility (sharing limited resources among fluctuating numbers of participating youth). As we will see, this also became a barrier to the youth's DIY activities. Understanding DIY practices as inscribed material ecologies involves understanding both the possibilities and limits of digital practices.

Crafting Futurity: Three Cases

Emily: Distributed Material Skills

With timid enthusiasm, Emily volunteered for the Woven Futures project early in its development and saw it through until the very end.[12] Like several of her friends, she had recorded digital video many times but had never picked up a needle and thread. She created two patches illustrating her future, one in which she became a chef and the other in which she became a doctor. While she could express her thoughts fluidly in her video interview, she encountered some challenges translating her ideas to fabric: she continuously found her thread wrapped around both sides of patch, forgetting to insert the needle in and out of the same side of the fabric. While Emily was rather comfortable (and eager) to record digital video interviews, she was less sure how to convey her sentiments through fabric.

Yet Emily's discomfort with embroidery did not curtail her continued participation in the project. Discomfort became productive—pedagogically and pragmatically; it enabled her to develop a unique and personal orientation toward the design material (recorded interviews, sewing thread, and fabric). As the project continued, she developed a fondness for recording interviews with other participants, offering to retake shots and show others how to navigate the software. Her unintentionally abstract representation of food on fabric was not a deterrent. It seemed to be part of an earnest effort to demonstrate her commitment to working together.

Emily's attention was dispersed among the various material engagements: tension of the thread, the association between her patch and the digital video, and interactions with interviewees. The project did not highlight her lack of competence at embroidery per se; rather it emphasized the breadth of her interwoven social and material skills. These entangled competencies were further entrenched in relations with her friends, workspaces, and future goals. They were constitutive of both the media and her identity as a collaborative "citizen" of the clubhouse. This ecology of skill and access provided the groundwork for her inclusion in the project and her critical role in developing its creative goals. As we observe in the next example, Emily overcame her shyness to actively engage with unfamiliar club members, such as Jose.

Jose: Embracing Discomfort

During our project Jose had just entered his final year of high school and was wrestling with the question of whether to pursue a college degree in video game engineering at a nearby university. Jose was employed by the clubhouse through its teen staff program, a leadership program that gave stipends to youth for performing duties around the clubhouse. A quiet and affable character, he often helped prepare activities, arrange materials, and resolve conflicts around the clubhouse even when he wasn't working. He divided much of his time at the clubhouse between the college prep and teen rooms and the Technology Lab. Jose had also taken a few microcontroller classes at the clubhouse and was interested in computer programming.

When Woven Futures began, Jose contributed in many capacities. He wrangled youth participants into the room when the workshop was starting; he sewed resistive fabric; he conducted several video interviews. He even constructed his own patch, which read "Happy Success" in bright orange thread. In his accompanying video interview, he told Emily that he wanted these words to speak to his future. Emily and Jose had not engaged much prior, and through this interaction they learned of their respective discomforts: embroidery was new to Jose, and working with video and Arduino was new to Emily. In his role as a teen staff and elder member of the clubhouse, Jose often guided his peers and younger club members to participate in activities. However, in Woven Futures Jose took on a different role. He allowed himself to embrace a sense of awkwardness and work alongside younger more knowledgeable members. Jose's willingness to participate across age and cultural differences was facilitated by the material he created and his discomfort with the creative process.

Material Practice and Interdisciplinary Work

As Jose and Emily's experiences illustrate, creating a collaborative tapestry entailed managing material engagements among a range of social conditions. In order to allow for more convenient participation across age ranges, we adjusted the existing facilities. We left the Technology Lab doors open and focused less attention on the uninvolved youth. Project participants moved fluidly in and out of the sewing activity and the lab, whether to join a friend in another part of the clubhouse or enter into a conversation on a different topic.

This fluctuating interest in the activity was partially an effect of the participatory constraints of the clubhouse. Scheduled programs were designed to cater specifically to two or three grade levels at a time; they were meant to enable collaboration among youth within particular age ranges. Yet unenforced restrictions in addition to unexpected changes in afternoon scheduling—differences in school dismissal times, snacks, pickups, club events, and so on—led youth to frequently ignore programming constraints and move about the club freely, participating in activities they found more engaging. Participants in Woven Futures often left patches half-finished only to pick them up again two weeks later. The Technology Lab became a refuge of a sort: it offered programming that appealed to a broader spectrum of ages and unexpected interactions with material. Yet the surrounding organizational constraints ensured that this refuge was only temporary.

The diverse materials that entered the Technology Lab presented further complications. The unit director, for example, objected to the messy physical arrangement of crafting supplies in the middle of the Technology Lab. Huddled around a table, youth talked and sewed while facing away from the computers lining the walls. The ways in which youth worked together and with material made the space unidentifiable as a Technology Lab. Yet the project could not practically continue if it was divided between different technologies, digital or otherwise. Miki's position as the club's technology director further demanded that she stay in the Technology Lab during program hours, making it impossible to divide her attention between two separate rooms at different ends of the clubhouse. This friction between what the project required and what the Technology Lab was meant to represent—the practice of making and the aesthetics of work—unsettled the boundaries between "clean" mass-produced technology and "messy" DIY aesthetics. Making an electronic quilt entailed a very different set of relations than those expected in a computer lab. It disrupted our romantic vision of DIY learning to create an alternative space for realizing new projects with diverse collaborators. Woven Futures thus began to shift the balance among varied social, disciplinary, and programmatic goals.

Inscribed Material Ecologies

So far we have seen how through resistance and change, digital frameworks for creative production accommodate both possibilities and growing pains. Inside the Technology Room youth assembled a range of personal narratives, beginning with digital video explorations of futurity. The video interviews were more informal conversations than planned undertakings: youth did not prepare a statement of who and what they wanted to be but rather discussed what was important to them. They presented an idea of "future" based on their own individual experiences in the present. Some chose to focus on an activity or profession, whereas others emphasized emotional states and their relationships to family members. The designs sewn into the squares further complicated youth visions by calling for the interplay of unfamiliar social and material skills. Each patch and video was drawn into these sociomaterial arrangements: eager use of digital video software, adjustments of needles and thread, interventions by the club facilitators, family member input, and the operating rules of the clubhouse.

We then saw how the patchwork project appealed to a diversity of youth—for example, Jose, a sixteen-year-old Mexican American youth interviewing Emily, a nine-year-old youth of mixed African American and Latin American descent. The after-school club afforded the intermingling of different disciplinary activities (craft and technology, sports and photography) depending on the extent to which activities were allowed to grow and change. As we discovered, continuing Woven Futures meant resisting suggestions from the clubhouse unit director to separate the craft materials from the digital technologies. In this sense the project was integrated into conflicting club activities through its (re)inscription in the environment. Creating Woven Futures entailed negotiating a DIY space that aesthetically and affectively bridged disciplines. The project provided an opportunity for clubhouse members to collaborate and engage with each other socially despite differences in age and background. Although participation in the project prompted interactions between members and technologies that were sometimes awkward, these experiences proved to be a vital element in the DIY production of collaborative space and laid the groundwork for the more personal inscription to come.

The notion of *inscribed material ecologies* describes the interplay between the fixed and ephemeral dimensions of the practices we observed. It brings together a notion of "inscription" borrowed from science and technology scholar Madeline Akrich with the broader concept of "material ecologies," most recently articulated by Ingold.[13] Scholars of culture, information, and media have long used ecological metaphors to emphasize the evolutionary character of diverse environments. For media scholar Matthew Fuller, media ecologies stress perpetual change and fragmentation; a media ecology can be symptomatically traced by gaps in production.[14] Media practices at the clubhouse (e.g., gaming, blogging, digital video editing) were continually in a state of flux: mixing, melding, and clashing. The quilt produced by Woven Futures was a particularly vibrant site of disciplinary collision and growing pains. Keeping Woven Futures in the Technology Lab, for instance, caused some friction but allowed us to have continuity with the youth by serving as stable space for staying or leaving the project. As a result, the youth involved in Woven Futures made critical connections between the seemingly messy practice of crafting and the ostensibly streamlined interactivity of the computer. Woven Futures was a material ecology: a system of processes, flows, and interruptions.

Here we draw together the ecological metaphor with the concept of "inscription," a term Akrich[15] and Latour[16] have used to consider contexts of technical use and appropriation, for instance, where "user" activity does not meet the expectations of designers. Akrich appears interested in two features of the adoption process: first, how the composition of a technical artifact constrains action and interaction among actors, including humans and nonhumans; and, second, the degree to which actors and their interrelationships define how the object is "reshaped" and "used."[17] Among youth in the clubhouse, the material practices we highlight provided key resources for stabilizing stories and useful constraints for understanding the technologies and themselves.

We have turned to questions of inscription and ecology to illustrate the range of materials (digital or otherwise) used by participants in this project. Each stitch on fabric framed the representation of future experience, while each video traced its generative story through reflection and conversation. Just as Emily's work transitioned from an imaginative future to digital files and fabric, our orchestration of the project moved from our flexible bodies to the more secure architecture of the club. These various inscriptions were not homogenous. Some were fixed across time (the embroidered fabric), while others were stabilized across space (the digital files appearing on multiple phones). The electronic quilt carried with it the net of these processes through specific forms of inscription. We therefore identify the notion of "inscribed material ecologies" as a sensitizing concept that helps us better understand how youth make use of constraints and discomfort through DIY activities. It suggests that material practices and critical making connect and inform each other.

Upon leaving the clubhouse, we wish to highlight one last implication for the development of technology education and critical making. Well before Woven Futures, we saw that youth possessed imagination. Imagination provided courage in the face of indeterminacy by anchoring youth voices in a diversity of material inscriptions. They confounded the material logic of objects by repurposing bits and pieces of their environment on a daily basis—whether candy wrappers or YouTube videos. In this sense the creation of an electronic quilt was no exception. What makes our approach unusual is its orientation toward the material. Not only were youth encouraged to engage in new social interactions and learn new skills, they were asked to *think and feel differently* about craft: to see how diverse engagements could work together in a meaningful way, to understand how technology doesn't always come inside of a computer (or black box), and to imagine how the act of making can become more important than the object made. Through their involvement in Woven Futures, youth continued to blur the lines between various organizational standards and disciplinary trajectories and draw attention to the spaces in between. It is by recognizing the institutional practices and politics that script the material ecology of DIY practices—giving youth a voice through the messy material—that we might productively enrich collaborative education.

Conclusion

As facilitators and observers, we found that youth participants engaged in an array of material practices during the Woven Futures project. Whether embroidering individual patches or editing digital video, youth began to think differently about DIY as a response to their discomfort, familiarity, and resourcefulness. This chapter thus contributes two distinct ways of seeing and working with material. First, it approaches digital material as more than its interactional qualities, recognizing its constitution in broad range of material ecologies. Second, it suggests implications for extending the critical making methodology to consider the heterogeneity skills and practices involved in digital production. By emphasizing the physical character of digital practices, and the digital ingredients of physical activities, this perspective suggests recognizing the continued mangling of conventionally separate practical domains (e.g., art and computer science). We ultimately offer "inscribed material ecologies" as a sensitizing concept for highlighting the disruptive and affective dimensions of collaborative workspaces that promise to reshape our technological futures.

Notes

1. See, for example, studies of classroom collaboration: Buechley and Perner-Wilson 2012; Jacucci and Wagner 2003; Ratto 2011.

2. For recent accounts of critical and reflective craft and making, see Breeding 2012; Vyas, van der Veer, and Nijholt 2012; and Dawkins 2011. Also see Alleyne 2011; Kuznetsov and Paulos 2010; Gauntlett 2011; and Heyborne 2010.

3. Ratto 2011.

4. Ibid., 3.

5. Material agencies are not prefigured events but produced and enacted through their constituent entanglement, as per Barad 2007.

6. Ingold 2012.

7. Some DIY activities have emerged alongside blogs and online resources, such as IKEA hacking. See Rosner and Bean 2009.

8. See Orton-Johnson's discussion of knitting as digital craft in chapter 9, this volume, wherein new modes of digital interaction interweave with "traditional" craft artifacts and activities. Also relevant to discussions of digital craft is Sennett's reference to open source programmers as modern-day craftsmen (Sennett 2008), and McCullough's exploration of craft processes in the digital medium (McCullough 1998).

9. On Arduino, see Gibb 2010.

10. Buechley et al. 2008.

11. Rosner and Ryokai 2010.

12. This and all following names of participants are pseudonyms.

13. Ingold appears to dissolve ontological distinctions between human and material while noting their differences, which is "perpetually on the threshold of emergence." In recognizing the artisan's coupling of practices ("movements and gestures") with outcomes ("the becoming of his materials"), he moves to study what he terms "an ecology of material" (Ingold 2012, 435).

14. Fuller 2005.

15. Akrich 1992.

16. Latour 1992.

17. Ibid., 206.

References

Akrich, M. 1992. The De-scription of Technical Objects. In *Shaping Technology/Building Society*, ed. W. E. Bijker and J. Law, 205–224. Cambridge, MA: MIT Press.

Alleyne, B. 2011. "'We Are All Hackers Now': Critical Sociological Reflections on the Hacking Phenomenon." http://bit.ly/13bPGTN.

Barad, K. M. 2007. *Meeting the Universe Halfway: Quantum Physics and the Entanglement of Matter and Meaning*. Durham, NC: Duke University Press Books.

Breeding, E. H. 2012. "Crafting Resistance: The Maker Movement in the Triangle Area of North Carolina." http://repository.lib.ncsu.edu/ir/handle/1840.16/7896 (accessed December 1).

Buechley, L., M. Eisenberg, J. Catchen, and A. Crockett. 2008. "The LilyPad Arduino: Using Computational Textiles to Investigate Engagement, Aesthetics, and Diversity in Computer Science Education." In *Proceedings of the SIGCHI Conference on Human Factors in Computing Systems*, 423–432.

Buechley, L., and H. Perner-Wilson. 2012. Crafting Technology: Reimagining the Processes, Materials, and Cultures of Electronics. *ACM Transactions on Computer-Human Interaction (ToCHI)* 19 (3): 1–21.

Dawkins, N. 2011. Do-It-Yourself: The Precarious Work and Postfeminist Politics of Handmaking (in) Detroit. *Utopian Studies* 22 (2): 261–284.

Fuller, M. 2005. *Media Ecologies: Materialist Energies in Art and Technoculture*. Cambridge, MA: MIT Press.

Gauntlett, D. 2011. *Making Is Connecting*. Cambridge, UK: Polity Press.

Gibb, A. M. 2010. "New Media Art, Design, and the Arduino Microcontroller: A Malleable Tool." Pratt Institute.

Heyborne, K. 2010. Review of *Made by Hand: Searching for Meaning in a Throwaway World* by M. Frauenfelder. http://ns1.tantor.com/SellSheets/1781_MadeHand.pdf (accessed December 13, 2012).

Ingold, T. 2012. Towards an Ecology of Materials. *Annual Review of Anthropology* 41 (1): 427–442.

Jacucci, G., and I. Wagner. 2003. Supporting Collaboration Ubiquitously: An Augmented Learning Environment for Design Students. *Proceedings of ECSCW* 3:139–158.

Kuznetsov, S., and E. Paulos. 2010. "Rise of the Expert Amateur: DIY Projects, Communities, and Cultures." In *Proceedings of the 6th Nordic Conference on Human–Computer Interaction*, 295–304.

Latour, B. 1992. *Where Are the Missing Masses? The Sociology of a Few Mundane Artifacts*. Cambridge, MA: MIT Press.

McCullough, M. 1998. *Abstracting Craft: The Practiced Digital Hand*. Cambridge, MA: MIT Press.

Ratto, M. 2011. Critical Making: Conceptual and Material Studies in Technology and Social Life. *Information Society* 27 (4): 252–260.

Rosner, D. K., and J. Bean. 2009. "Learning from IKEA Hacking: I'm Not One to Decoupage a Tabletop and Call It a Day." In *Proceedings of the 27th International Conference on Human Factors in Computing Systems*, 419–422.

Rosner, D. K., and K. Ryokai. 2010. "Spyn: Augmenting the Creative and Communicative Potential of Craft." In *Proceedings of the 28th International Conference on Human Factors in Computing Systems*, 2407–2416.

Sennett, R. 2008. *The Craftsman. Allen Lane*. Penguin Books.

Vyas, D., G. van der Veer, and A. Nijholt. 2012. Creative Practices in the Design Studio Culture: Collaboration and Communication. *Cognition Technology and Work* 14 (2): 1–29.

14 Making Publics: Documentary as Do-It-with-Others Citizenship

Mandy Rose

Introduction

Documentary has its own DIY history. The story might be said to begin in Great Britain in 1935. That year Ruby Grierson, whose brother John had coined the term "documentary" a decade earlier, was working as an assistant on the film that became *Housing Problems* (1935), about living conditions in London's East End. In a legendary incident, related by Grierson in his memoirs, she invoked a do-it-yourself ethos, inviting the slum dwellers to tell their stories directly to camera. Metaphorically handing over the recording equipment, she urged them to take the opportunity to state their case: "The camera is yours. The microphone is yours. Now tell the bastards exactly what it's like to live in the slums" (Hardy 1946, 148). It did the trick, and the East Enders' direct, albeit self-conscious testimonies are still arresting and affecting today, speaking to us across the years. Lev Manovich (2001) observed the tendency of practices to move from the periphery to the center in the context of digital culture. The idea of the documentary subjects becoming agents in the making process is such a phenomenon. Ruby Grierson's intervention expressed the germ of an idea that is coming to fruition today.

For most of the twentieth century, however, documentary was a professional world in which there was little potential for do-it-yourself. Twentieth-century production and exhibition equipment was specialized, bulky, and expensive. There were film formats for amateurs—8mm, Super8, later Hi8 video. But while amateurs shot footage that they shared in private with friends and family, an exclusive cadre of documentary professionals observed and interpreted the world on our behalf, shaping footage into real-life stories that circulated in the public sphere.

At the same time, the concern of social documentary is people, and production is based on a relationship between filmmaker and human subject(s). While the dominant practice within documentary has been that the filmmaker generates the content—film, video, stills—and shapes an interpretation of the world from that material, the documentary subject has generally been afforded no agency in that process. The idea of the documentary subjects' rights has surfaced notably alongside political movements through which those excluded from systems of power have fought for their voice to be heard.

In the May '68 popular uprising in France, film was seen as a central arena of the struggle. Technicians and film resources were put at the disposal of protesters and Renault workers produced a film. Across the Atlantic in Canada that same year, a model of media access was pioneered within the Challenge for Change project, when director George Stoney agreed to a proposal by his team to hand cameras over to Native Americans who were protesting customs charges on a bridge across their land. Inspired by *You Are on Indian Land* (1969) and the Challenge for Change output that followed it, forms of access media were then developed in North America and in the United Kingdom in the 1970s. This DIY current within documentary—expressed through making tools and facilitation available so that nonprofessionals might create and present their own documentary arguments—continued through the latter years of the twentieth century, in community media and access TV, at the margins of dominant media practice.

Today, we can see not just DIY as amateur-made, participatory content within documentary, but the broader development of what we might call a DIY culture that is emerging where documentary meets the affordances of the social, semantic, and open web. In this space we find remix video, open rights frameworks, and crowd funding as a form of democratized commissioning. Here we are seeing the development of open source web documentary authoring environments (Zeega, Popcorn Maker) and nascent forms of web native production culture in which filmmakers, interaction designers, and coders approach project development through hackathons. This culture is located outside corporate and consumer relationships. It values read/write forms over passive spectatorship. It promotes new media literacies. It sees documentary as a stage for an interrogation of contemporary systems of power. Brett Gaylor's open source collaborative documentary *RiP! A Remix Manifesto* (2008) exemplifies this culture.

All these activities deserve critical attention, but there is not enough space to address them all here. In this chapter I focus instead on significant collaborative, interactive documentary practices that are emerging in the context of digital culture. In the first section, I think about these forms of collaborative documentary in relation to the concept of DIY in its original sense of amateur making. This framework can help situate these emerging practices in relation to the counterhistory within documentary in which subjects have taken on forms of agency and editorial control in the production process.

By using contemporary examples, I then suggest why the concept of DIY is problematic for documentary. Awareness that a DIY approach to documentary making is not universally available prompts a questioning of the valorization of the concept of DIY in the context of complex media production. Through the lens of cocreativity, I discuss collaborative documentaries as a strategic response to the "participation gap" (Jenkins 2006, 23).

But there is more than this at stake in these collaborative documentary practices. In my view, the concept of DIWO (do-it-with-others) is better equipped to capture the dynamics and importance of these projects. A cocreative, DIWO approach to documentary provides a progressive reworking of documentary's historic role in the public sphere, as an open space for dialogue and a stage for the performance of citizenship.

DIY or Collaborative?

The DIY current in documentary is finding expression in a growing body of North American work based on collaborative processes and involving public participation. These projects routinely incorporate the amateur, DIY media often known as user-generated or (my preference) participatory content. I begin by considering two such documentaries that provide rich material for revealing the limits of the term DIY to describe current trends.

Eighty years after *Housing Problems*, Elaine McMillion, the director of the forthcoming *Hollow: An Interactive Documentary* (2012), might be seen as Ruby Grierson's heir. Within this work-in-progress McMillion has returned to her childhood home—McDowell County, West Virginia—to create, in the words of the project website, a "hybrid community participatory project and interactive documentary" that addresses "the many stereotypes associated with the area, population loss and potential for the future." Appealing for funding on Kickstarter, McMillion describes the project's mission as "exploring the issues and future of rural America through the eyes and ideas of those living in Southern West Virginia." For McMillion and her team, representation is a central factor in the area's disenfranchisement. Story director Jason Headley writes; "Most of the thoughts and opinions of our state are formed by outside forces looking in. This project gives us the chance to do the exact opposite. To let people see West Virginia from the perspective of the people who live here."

As well as taking a conventional documentary approach—filming people talking about their lives and situations—the participatory engagement outlined for *Hollow* includes workshops to support local people in making twenty of the fifty short documentaries planned for the site. These elements will be brought together within an interactive online proposition to provide a broad audience with a picture of local life at the same time as it provides a platform for community dialogue about current and future directions. While the work is still unfinished, comments in a "What the Community Is Saying" section of the *Hollow* website suggest that the production to date has been well received locally.

A second example, *Mapping Main Street* (2010), shows how the concept of DIY plays out in another comparable collaborative project. *Mapping Main Street* (*MMS*) came about as a response to the way that politicians were invoking the idea of Main Street during the 2009 US presidential election campaign as a cipher to express their vision of America. This isn't a new tendency. Project cocreator Jesse Shapins has noted that Main Street has long been the subject of debate in America, proving "a highly contested shifting metaphor for what constitutes traditional American values and the 'average' American experience" (Shapins 2009, 2). The intention of the project, cocreator Kara Oehler explained in an interview with the author, "was really to point out the diversity and differences between all of these different places" ("Kara Oehler & Jesse Shapins on Mapping Main Street" n.d.).

The shape of the *MMS* project was then designed to mobilize a reflective and creative response to the subject of Main Street today; to catalyze multiple situated stories around this contested idea. These would take the form of stand-alone documentary shorts that could be brought together to present a grassroots view of American life. Shapins and Oehler (2010) knew from their experience of previous participatory projects that a call to action in itself would not generate a substantial, diverse response. They needed to spread the word about the project, show potential contributors what they were looking for, build partnerships, and encourage involvement.

So in May 2009 Shapins and Oehler set off on a 12,000 mile journey through the Main Streets of the United States, to gather audio stories and stills as seed content for the website. That journey generated content that became a radio series on National Public Radio (NPR), who had supported the initial project through the Makers Quest 2.0 scheme. Starting with this substantial exposure, their Collaborative Documentary Media Project has been evolving and growing ever since, with 829 streets covered at the time of writing. In what sense though is the project collaborative? In what sense might it be regarded as DIY?

Both *MMS* and *Hollow* involve forms of public participation, but inspected in closer detail, they suggest problems in the simplistic framework of DIY. For a start, there is no clear amateur/professional binary at work between content made by participants and project producers. Some contributions are by experienced media makers, while others are by journalists in the making. *MMS* has been a platform for the NPR Radio Rookies training scheme, for example. These contributions from trainees might be described as amateur but probably not as DIY, in that they are mediated by trainers, which is at odds with the idea of self-direction fundamental to the concept of do-it-yourself. Does this devalue this participatory content? The next section considers this question by asking how those taking part assess these experiences of participation.

Participation to Cocreation

How is it possible to gauge the success of these collaborative projects from the point of view of participants and therefore assess their potential impact on communities? Unfortunately there is little independent evidence to draw on. However, a reading of the "What the Community Is Saying" section of the *Hollow* website proves instructive. The statements are interesting from many points of view. There is a recurrent theme that the project has provoked something important within individual and collective self-perception:

> "I feel like I have contributed to something important and it has changed the way I see the world."

> "I'm not sure I can explain the hope and sense of community that Hollow has inspired."

> "I think it will inspire the residents of McDowell County to see the efforts of their neighbors to make changes for the better here where we all live."

There is a dynamic within which McMillion is constructed as a benefactor, almost a savior:

> "Thankful to Elaine McMillion and her team for what they have done to show McDowell County in a positive light . . . it's time the world knows that we aren't as mainstream media portrays us. We are BETTER!"

> "She has given us our county back, our voices back, and we can never thank her enough for that!"

What comes across is that people feel they have no means to represent themselves without the intervention of an outside agent. The comments are reminiscent of the tone of feedback obtained by a journalist who talked to participants about the Access TV project *Video Nation: History*, which I coproduced for the BBC in the 1990s. One said, "I had a hard upbringing. My parents forced me to give up school at sixteen. I had no qualifications, not one. Doing *Video Nation* has given me a massive lift. The BBC actually listens to me, Conrad Gorner" (France 1999). At that time, participants expressed feelings of affirmation as a result of being heard on the BBC, and gratitude to the team who facilitated that experience. This was in the pre-Internet era, when there was no other route to self-representation in the media. Almost twenty years later, the comments about *Hollow* demand to be read in the context of rhetoric of universal participation. The comparison points to the continuing lack of media participation that is still the reality for many.

Henry Jenkins (2006) has called this phenomenon the "participation gap," whereby, despite the existence and apparent accessibility of digital creative technologies, people are still excluded from taking part. Uneven participation may have less to do with the lack of access to equipment or technologies sometimes referred to as the "digital divide," and more to do with a lack of confidence in and understanding of the protocols of engagement. Participation is not open to all, Jenkins points out, but constrained and circumscribed by social context. And while the ease of use offered by Facebook and Twitter has allowed diverse new participants to post on social media platforms in recent years, there is a difference between publishing a post to communicate with friends and family and telling stories using rich media. A reading of the comments made about *Hollow* problematizes a valorization of DIY in the context of complex media making.

In this light a number of these collaborative and participatory projects—including *Mapping Main Street* and *Hollow*, but also the National Film Board of Canada's award winning *Highrise*—can be seen to be adopting a production strategy that responds to the participation gap. This can entail facilitating participation by members of marginalized communities while at the same time giving them forms of authority in the production process.

But the term "collaborative documentary" is not unique to these projects. It is also used to describe collaborations among experienced filmmakers. *99 Percent: The Occupy Wall Street Film* (2012) is one such current example. Since it is often undefined, the term "collaborative" can confuse, raising expectations of equal contribution and collective decision making.

An alternative framework is provided by the term *cocreative media*—a concept that is being refined by researchers at Queensland University of Technology in relation to digital storytelling projects and community media. "Cocreative media provides a tool for describing the ways in which participatory media are facilitated by people and organizations, not just technology" (Spurgeon 2009, 275). The term arises from a recognition of the participation gap and "complicates the idea that participatory culture is the product of an autonomous relationship between the individual creator and the magic of technology" (284). So how does this work in practice?

The Author as Cocreative Producer

In the cases of *Hollow* and *Mapping Main Street,* we can see how providing workshop-based facilitation, in the former case, and a platform that allows educators to get involved (on MMS) constitute specific ways of addressing the participation gap in the context of their respective themes. How then are we to understand the role of the producer of a collaborative and co-creative, interactive project? How does that role coexist with a devolution of editorial control and authority? In what sense is their activity different from the traditional role of a documentary producer?

Walter Benjamin's 1934 essay, "The Author as Producer" provides an apt frame of reference. Considering the options for the engaged Marxist artist, Benjamin makes a distinction between self-expression and the work of providing a platform. He proposes that the task for the committed artist is to adapt "the production apparatus" (Benjamin 1977, 94) on behalf of the workers. "This apparatus will be the better," he continues, "the more consumers it brings into contact with the production process—in short, the more readers or spectators it turns into collaborators" (98). At a very different historical moment, this model is still relevant for these cocreative documentaries being made in the context of the participation gap. The distinction between production apparatus and content is particularly resonant for these projects that involve the production of an architecture of participation and interaction as well as content itself.

What does Main Street mean for you? How does life in West Virginia look to you? The producers behind these projects pose a question but do not try to determine the answer. Their role is not a passive one, however; they work with what Benjamin calls a "mediating effectiveness" (1977, 102). They design architectures within which many responses can be gathered and presented; apparatuses for contribution, and platforms for sharing and interaction. That is not to suggest that those architectures are neutral.

Design, wording, the framing of the call to action: these present points-of-view. As the French interactive documentary producer Alexandre Brachet (2011) has said, "Interface is content."

Each project then expresses a political attitude to its theme. Participants are invited to join in a project that has an agenda, and at the same time they are provided with a platform through which they can express their own perspective and point of view. In taking part, participants become a community to interrogate a theme of shared concern. The significance of these cocreative projects is not then reducible to the presence of do-it-yourself, participatory content. It derives instead from the ways that the projects open out the range of voices that get to speak with authority and purpose within the documentary project. What's at stake is documentary as catalyst for conversations, debates, understandings among participants, communities, audiences—its role in the public sphere.

Documentary as Citizenship

Documentary has long been associated with citizenship. Grierson championed the form for its educative value, its promise to produce the informed citizen—a conception of documentary's role in the public sphere that still lingers. Michael Chanan (2000, 229) has argued for an alternative view of the work of documentary; that its "vocation" in the public sphere derives instead from its dialogic aspect. For Chanan, documentary's contribution consists in it being "internally dialogic, or double-voiced" (226). Documentary presents "a variety of individual and collective voices, and behind them, the voice of the film maker" (226). Writing in reference to linear documentary in the late 1990s, Chanan argues that this work with orchestrating multiple perspectives and subjectivities brought documentary close to a Habermasian conception of the public sphere as a space of dialogue and deliberation.

Producers are now harnessing digital technologies, platforms, and affordances in ways that amplify this dialogic character and transform the encounter between content and viewer/user. The presentation of the *Mapping Main Street* stories, for example, breaks in a significant way with the dialogic character of documentary as characterized by Chanan. Whereas a linear documentary on this theme might involve the reflection of "a variety of individual and collective voices," structured and fixed by the filmmaker within an argument, the deliberations of MMS are reflected in a diversity of perspectives and experiences that are presented without an overarching rhetorical structure. Writing about this open-ended form, Shapins (2009) has said, "There is something about collaborative and participatory processes specifically connected to documentary that foreground that dimension. . . . it's not to sort of completely relativize—there are truths that exist in the world—but I think it is to open up the possibility for having many different vantage points that can possibly help us get to different forms of understanding truth in the process."

Mapping Main Street then emphasizes the dialogic aspect that Chanan links to the public sphere. Presenting content from many people and places, it reflects but does not seek to synthesize a multiplicity of situated perspectives and knowledges. It takes advantage of cocreative production, nonlinear technology, and the database as a production tool to reflect that multiplicity, and it asks the viewer/user to engage with and consider these diverse points-of-view.

While I have argued that DIY is a problematic concept for thinking about these collaborative documentaries as *media* practices—because amateur participation is facilitated, mediated, and cocreated—the concept of DIY becomes valuable when thinking about these documentaries as *citizenship* practices. "Bottom-up, self organising, self-representing" (Hartley 2010), they take place outside conventional political forums and practices, staging purposeful dialogue among participants and with their audience. In a discussion of forms of playful ephemeral media—dance-offs, spoof videos—as "silly citizenship," John Hartley adopts the term "do-it-with-others" (DIWO) as an alternative to DIY. For Hartley, DIWO citizenship is "driven by voluntarist choices and affiliations but at the same time it has an activist and communitarian ethic where 'knowledge shared is knowledge gained.'" Mapped on to the more sober terrain of these documentary projects, this characterization chimes with their cocreative and dialogic aspects while also highlighting the ethical dimension of participation—the social and political purpose reflected in time freely given to dialogue and deliberation, as a contribution toward understanding and change.

Conclusion

A third and final documentary example serves to draw a number of these themes together and to point toward future developments for the documentary form. *Question Bridge: Black Males* (2012) is an important cocreative undertaking in which participants don't make content, though their contributions are the heart and driver of the piece. In the words of the *Question Bridge* (*QB*) website, this transmedia project, created by Chris Johnson, Hank Willis Thomas, Bayete Ross Smith, and Kamal Sinclair, "seeks to represent and redefine Black male identity in America. Through video mediated question and answer exchange, diverse members of this 'demographic' bridge economic, political, geographic, and generational divisions."

Participants are invited to offer a question that they would like to address to another black American man. Their questions—about racism, class, individual and collective responsibility—and the ensuing answers are filmed. The dialogue between participants produced through editing then makes up the work. Those taking part come together as a virtual community to interrogate their situations and challenge an oppressive, monolithic construction of their shared identity.

The filming strategy is designed to maximize the viewer's involvement. Close-up talking heads pose and answer questions directly to camera so that the viewer is positioned as the one being asked and being answered. Addressed as if she were a member of the community, she is brought into a complex affective space, called on as a peer to imagine and hear from many varied perspectives how the world looks through African American men's eyes. As an online experience, this has the intimacy of a one-to-one exchange. As an installation, this effect is created in another way—monitors are arranged so that the life-sized talking heads are at head height and the viewer is situated as part of the group. In both cases, the effect works to bring the viewer right into the dialogue, encouraging identification and disrupting the otherness that is at play in a racist construction of black male identity. Like *Hollow*, the project is designed to work on two levels. It's about a community—reflecting lived experience and complexity, and challenging preconceptions. It's also for the community—a platform through which the participants become a public, calling attention to their common concerns.

Here documentary becomes a stage for a performance of DIWO citizenship. At the same time, new forms of exhibition and interaction reframe the audience experience to bring the viewer/user into a more dynamic relationship with the content. In doing so, they highlight an aspect of documentary that is obscured by the idea of DIY—its profoundly collaborative nature, and the way that documentary meaning is made in dialogue.

References

99 Percent: The Occupy Wall Street Film. 2012. http://www.99percentfilm.com/ (accessed December 7, 2012).

Benjamin, Walter. 1977. The Author as Producer. In *Understanding Brecht*, ed. Walter Benjamin, 85–103. London, New York: New Left Books.

Brachet, Alexandre. 2011. "Strategies of collaboration in i-docs." Keynote at i-Docs Symposium, Bristol, March 25.

Chanan, Michael. 2000. Documentary and the Public Sphere. In *Grierson to the Docu-soap: Breaking the Boundaries*, ed. John Izod, Richard Kilborn, and Matthew Hibberd, 221–230. London: University of Luton Press.

France, Louise. 1999. "Two Minutes of Fame." *The Independent*, March 7. http://www.independent.co.uk/life-style/real-lives-two-minutes-of-fame-1078911.html (accessed December 7, 2012).

Hardy, Forsyth. 1946. *Grierson on Documentary*. California: Faber.

Hartley, John. 2010. "Silly Citizenship." *Critical Discourse Studies; Special Issue: Self-Mediation: New Media and Citizenship* 7 (4) (September): 233–248. http://www.tandfonline.com/doi/abs/10.1080/17405904.2010.511826 (accessed December 7, 2012).

Highrise. n.d. http://highrise.nfb.ca/ (accessed December 7, 2012).

"Hollow: An Interactive Documentary." 2012. Hollow the Film. http://www.hollowthefilm.com/ (accessed December 7, 2012).

"Hollow: An Interactive Documentary." n.d. Hollow Kickstarter page. http://www.kickstarter.com/projects/elainemcmillion/hollow-an-interactive-documentary (accessed December 7, 2012).

Housing Problems. 1935. Dir. Arthur Alton and Edgar Anstey. British Commercial Gas Association.

Jenkins, Henry. 2006. *Convergence Culture: Where Old and New Media Collide*. New York: NYU Press.

"Kara Oehler & Jesse Shapins on Mapping Main Street." n.d. CollabDocs. http://collabdocs.wordpress.com/interviews-resources/interview-4-kara-oehler-jesse-shapins-on-mapping-main-street/ (accessed May 12, 2012).

Manovich, Lev. 2001. *The Language of New Media*. Cambridge, MA: MIT Press.

"Mapping Main Street." 2010. http://www.mappingmainstreet.org/ (accessed August 3).

"Question Bridge: Black Males." 2012. Question Bridge. http://questionbridge.com/ (accessed December 7, 2012).

RiP! A Remix Manifesto. 2008. Dir. Brett Gaylor. EyeSteelFilm, National Film Board of Canada.

Shapins, Jesse. 2009."Mapping Main Street: Tracing an American Political Mythology, Urban Imaginary and Built Environment." *Writing Cities* (May).

Shapins, Jesse, and Kara Oehler. 2010. "Public Media Arts + Urban Database Documentary." Presentation at the Northeastern School of Architecture, Boston, MA, February.

Spurgeon, Christina. 2009. "Co-creative Media: Theorising Digital Storytelling as a Platform for Researching and Developing Participatory Culture." Paper presented at Australian and New Zealand Communication Association Conference, Queensland University of Technology, Brisbane, Queensland, July 8–10. http://eprints.qut.edu.au/25811/2/25811.pdf.

You Are on Indian Land. 1969. Dir. Mort Ransen. National Film Board of Canada.

15 Mirror Images: Avatar Aesthetics and Self-Representation in Digital Games

Suzanne de Castell

This chapter presents a conceptual sweep of the terrain across which a hybrid species, somewhat flesh and blood, somewhat digital, is being forged. These are spaces never discovered, because they have always and only been invented, and in these spaces, inhabitants are forged, in the dual sense of being both made and made up by human subjects who paradoxically enough discover *themselves* even as they make themselves—though the cloth with which they dress their first person singular[1] is mostly not of their own weaving, or even their own cut. To adapt from Marx, "Gamers make their own avatars, but they do not make them as they please; they do not make them under self-selected circumstances, but under circumstances existing already, given and transmitted from their game designers." This chapter draws upon several years of studying online game-based virtual worlds, and the avatars and activities players create and enact there, to discuss troubling issues of agency and accountability in the design and use of these environments, and to argue for greater attention to their real-world implications for politics, sociality, and self-formation.

Among today's most powerful DIY projects is the manufacture of digital game-based worlds whose impacts, however, are mostly overlooked by gamers who, through their own personally customized avatars, "play" in them. The reciprocal relationship between fabricated worlds and virtual subjects, and, specifically, the quality of DIY citizenship cultivated there is decidedly understudied. But as more and more of our "real lives" play out in cyberspaces not of our own design, we need to start asking what kinds of citizens we are making of ourselves there.

We best understand goodness in the individual by inquiring into the goodness of the state, argued Plato long ago, for the state is the citizen, writ large. One mirrors the other, as state and individual reciprocally require, constrain, and constitute each other. On this view, the kind of world it is within which selves are formed matters as much for self-building in virtual environments as in real ones—if indeed that distinction even makes much sense anymore.

For it has never been more true than it is today that, to quote philosopher John Austin, "Unreal wears the trousers" (Austin 1962, 7). His point, in *Sense and Sensibilia*, was that "real" gets its meaning from its opposite, so the way to understand what "real" means is to examine the various and several uses of the word "*un*real." To many who would endorse a "real/virtual" distinction, virtual worlds are unreal worlds, avatars are unreal people, virtual politics are unreal politics. There are growing respects, however, in which virtual worlds are becoming increasingly *real* worlds, populated by real people carrying out real activities in real time and within real communities, enacting *realpolitik*, albeit in very different *orders* of the real than Austin could ever have imagined. It is not simply that the virtual bleeds into the real or that the real somehow "gives substance" to the virtual, it is that the virtual *transforms* the real, materially and politically, not just semantically.

Self-formation, *selbsbildung*, is both axiomatic to, and paradigmatic of, DIY citizenship, and as techno-culturally reconfigured, it disrupts and exceeds the semantic boundaries of both "self" and "making," challenging us to devise, for the practical purposes of getting on with things, an updated understanding of fundamental ideas we can't think about a DIY movement without. With respect to our "doings" in virtual worlds, all manner of constraints on who and what we can be and do are consigned to the trash heap of history as we make for ourselves appearances, roles, and personalities far away from those we enact and inhabit "for real."

Some of the more obvious ways virtual world play has real-world impact have been well parodied in the notorious South Park "World of Warcraft" episode displaying the embodied consequences of too much time spent in "virtual space." But what needs stressing is neither that digital gameplay has physical impacts on players, nor that real players create virtual selves in any unidirectional way; rather, it is that games refashion their "real-world" players reciprocally, even as players invent and then, through transactional enactive play, discover new selves built from game-based affordances, and play new roles, both personal and political, within games' virtual spaces, which can then go on to surprise their inventors and impact the ways they come to see and be "themselves," from their personalities to their politics, in "meat space."

Avatars, though, are not enactments of a singular real-world identity (if such a thing makes sense anymore) but of particular designed dispositions, competencies, and abilities that in turn inflect and make possible different real-world selves. Not so long ago, for example, it was typical of digital games research talk for speakers to "legitimate" their authority to speak by revealing they were, for instance, a level 80 Blood Elf. Who those researchers were in the "virtual world" had thus impacted and reshaped their identities, not just in game but very much in their "real lives," rendering them serious, credible games scholars.

Similarly, in a recent paper on "Neo-immersion: Awareness and Engagement in Gameplay," Whitson et al. (2008) describe the difference made by emerging forms of haptic interface as importantly different from the pleasures derived from previous forms of digital gameplay. "In the case of *WiiFit*," they write, "our pleasure comes not from how we masterfully effect the environment though iterative gameplay, but rather how that environment effects *us* by toning and disciplining our bodies" (223). Here again is the co-constitutive "transaction" of (real) organism and (virtual) environment elucidated by John Dewey and Arthur Bentley so long ago (Dewey and Bentley 1949).

So it is by no means just Wii Fit that grants such self-formative and transformative pleasures, and it is by no means just bodies that are being toned and disciplined through virtual world play. The identificatory consequences of digital gameplay are not restricted to the virtual world of the game, but rather build up and spill over into who and what one is in what we used fondly to refer to as "the real." A player who models her decisions about relationships and even life partner choices on a self she has developed as much through game based experiences, practices, dispositions, and self understandings, as through real-world family and community social norms, values, and practices, is surely mis-described as enacting "the hybrid identity of the player in the game" (Gee 2004). This characterization no less mis-describes those players who invest considerable time, money, and pain to have their body tattooed in full color with their "larger than life" game character: can such identities really be understood as a hybridization within the game? These embodied player identities, fully and entirely "real," have migrated far indeed from screens and servers.

Interactivity in games, it's been argued, is a kind of DIY in which players have agency, taking digital gameplay beyond commodity consumption to become a new species of "2.0" production. Players design and use game modifications, for example, recoding game code. But it turns out that inordinately few players actually design or program their own game mods. And most of the mods we see players using are in effect systems and structures for in-game and meta-game accounting. It's hard to see this as productive player agency, especially when most of what is being accomplished is an archiving and continuous updating of statistics on accomplishments that reflect how well the player has followed the game's predetermined script, has played its roles correctly, and has accumulated its virtual goods.

In *World of Warcraft*, for example, it's often argued as a sign of the game's high-level cognitive demands that players must make strategic choices. But in fact, especially among accomplished players, the player works as a cog in a mechanism. As one *WoW* interviewee characterized it, you do not want to be the one messing up the "synchronized swim" of a high-level raid. Most intelligent coordination by individual players is subordinated to skillful compliance to the demands of the role, as managed by the guild leader in collaborative play.

In truth, the obsessively watched stats of high-level players don't really reflect personal accomplishments by free agents developing useful abilities.

Sociality and Politics in Virtual Worlds

Who and what you can be in a virtual world is necessarily social. But what social identities are available to players, and within what political regimes? What kinds of political and social orders are on offer in contemporary virtual worlds and how do they hail or interpellate the real-world players who create avatars that "play back" across the real-virtual divide? How agency and autonomy are regulated, how they are "reengineered" and reformed through important digital media like online games, deserves more serious consideration than it's been getting in any contemporary DIY activism agenda.

Interestingly, for example, with respect to game-based virtual worlds, "cross-world social mobility" is normatively gendered. A lot of women play with their boyfriends/partners/husbands in co-situated sessions, either in the same room and/or at the same time (and usually within the same guild), and more women than men choose to spend their time in massively multiplayer games with people they already know in the real world. Even for those who roam further from their real-life social contexts, virtual worlds like *World of Warcraft* are not necessarily highly *social* places—more like "massively single player online games." And the kinds of "selves" players make in such worlds far more typically conform to than break out of real-world stereotypes. Both males' and females' self-representations, as one female informant put it, "look like me, only a bit better." For females this means more slender bodies, and for males, bigger shoulders and more muscular legs. As we move up the experience ladder, we see more transgressive avatar design, including greater incidence of sex swapping and less direct physical resemblance. But there is only so far avatar design can take us in the virtual worlds we presently have at hand, which brings us to the question of what players are taking away from their engagements in virtual worlds.

It's long been supposed that the Internet could provide for us a "new frontier," where the baggage of inherited prejudices, deeply entrenched inequalities, traumas, insecurities of appearance, capacity, and disability could all be at long last "leveled" by the anonymity of the Internet, where "nobody knows you're a dog." But extensive study of commercial virtual world game players makes it evident that much of what players do there, when they are not simply hanging out and chatting with their friends, is more akin to work than to play, a kind of play that is prescribed and regulated, in which agency is tightly constrained and where the kinds of production and creation so enthusiastically celebrated by games and learning gurus are as rare as hen's teeth. Assuredly, virtual worlds *might* be politically innovative, gender politics *might* be entirely recast—but so far these designed environments are more regressive than progressive in both respects. Yes, players *can* design mods and add-ons, but most don't. Yes, there *can* be a wide variety of such modifications, but as a matter of fact, most people use the same small repertoire. Yes, players *do* have a vast array of multimodal affordances available to them, but most deploy very few of these. Eye-tracking studies reveal that in the visually stunning (and very expensive) rich perceptual arena of a three-dimensional world, players read numbers and charts off screens very much as if they were two-dimensional surfaces of a book. Taking real advantage of the multimodal affordances for learning through play in digital game worlds requires that we first acknowledge that what most players *are not* doing in these virtual environments is exploring, creating, producing—as evidenced by the vast wastelands, empty depopulated areas, and ghost towns that hold little interest for players once they see that no special commodities can be acquired there, no further points racked up, no particular inventory accumulated.

From their inception, mainstream massively multiplayer online games (MMOs) were destined to configure play as consumption, and if the acquisition and consumption of commodities were all there was to play, commercial game worlds would serve us well. Indeed, they *do* serve the game industry well in precisely those ways. For any other purposes, however, we had better get in the DIY activism game itself, and help *create* the kinds of ludic forms and ways of knowing differently needed to make selves and worlds worthy of inhabitation.

Attempting to encode knowledge in games and learning in play can help identify and more fully embrace the potential but rarely actualized multimodal affordances of virtual world play. Producing multimodal, ludic experiences that meaningfully engage those who play them is one serious way to reclaim so much of the joyful attention and intelligence of engagement in play. But meeting this design challenge needs people who understand how to work within an epistemology requiring serious infidelity to traditional schooling's ardor for factually correct propositions enunciated in explicit and eloquent speech or writing. Such an understanding of knowledge, of learning, of what knowledge is of most worth requires educators to surrender themselves, and their pedagogical and curricular practices, to the often unstable perils and pleasures of playful engagement with self and social formation where real and virtual worlds collide.

"Real" and "virtual," in sum, are not alternative realities but different dimensions of the same one. It's all the same space, because it's unified by time, the lived time in which we are all contained and constrained. Whether we are taken up with material or virtual engagements, we are in time and expending our time—and nothing could be more real than that simple existential fact. The presumption of a wedge between real and unreal, one that we should try to wield more effectively to pry these worlds apart, has been profoundly misleading.

We need to be asking what ethics, what agency, what accountability inhabits the borderlands conjoining real and virtual worlds, because we can see ever more clearly that there are real social and political consequences of inhabitation in these virtual borderlands.

Accountable Design

This is not without design. Contemporary reconstructions of self and sociality, ethics and public politics are not divine, or natural, and they don't just happen; there is actual planning and thinking going into the design and marketing and developing of online environments for pleasure and play and social life—people make these things. Facebook, for instance, is a designed virtual environment whose greatest achievement is connecting people—"friends." It has, though, other more sinister tendrils grafted onto its basic architecture, and it is, importantly, these appendages and not Facebook's social networking/contact tracking technology that have notable patterns of extreme harm associated with them. It's what's packed onto and into that technology, what's linked up with it and what it links up to, a corporate "structure of feeling" parasitic, by design, upon our greatest and most powerful bonds—friendship, connection, love, and community. What technology does best is connect things that otherwise wouldn't go together—they're either too far apart, or too big, or not the same kind of thing, or happen at different times. That ingenious connectivity is the essential ingredient out of which multi-participant persistent virtual worlds are built. So far, so good. But to take over and remake human sociality and to build on top of it a primitively unregulated market economy of recognition and consumption, you might have expected some effort on the designer's part to think about how users would be impacted by the way the technology's token micro-economy redefines and supports identity and relationships. In our media-savvy political world, we might have expected some intervention, even just at the "public interest" level. Or some thoughtful educational response and counteraction. But this is nowhere in sight.

Funny that we hold car companies responsible for failing brakes, and even to some degree anyway hold oil companies responsible for environmental devastation, but it's as if technology exists in a world far above our own where, without a word of criticism, without any regulation, it is free to accomplish whatever ends it can profitably be turned to. Where are the ethics of social and indeed educational technologies? Where are their politics? Teachers and parents and researchers, too, are contending with a gaping silent complicity with respect to online and virtual world technologies. And here, an aside, to just quickly note our real-world inability to deal with the impacts of the unaccountable designs we presently have and the perverse kinds of DIY that are enabled by them: first, the idea that the Clementi case[2] is really about technology at all, and, second, that it is about "invasion of privacy." At about the same time as Tyler Clementi took his own life after a webcam set up in his dorm room at Rutgers University made his private life into a public spectacle, plenty of other gay kids killed themselves, and it had nothing to do with either viral online media or invasion of privacy, but good old-fashioned homophobia. A further example—the cell phone video capture by her peers of the rape of a young woman in British Columbia, and its "viral" recirculation among and beyond them—is reported as a perverse misuse of technology, and the crime in this case is pronounced "child pornography." Our inability to conceptualize let alone deal with these all-too-familiar forms of peer-to-peer DIY communication are as much real-world incapacities as they are virtual-world deficiencies.

In neither of these cases has there been any critical address of the designs of online social media, even though we know and have known in some form or other since the earliest study of the arts of rhetoric that communication is social action for which people are responsible, and therefore how one communicates needs to be carefully chosen.

And yes, it's true that this is a world where everything, good, indifferent, horrendous, happens at the press of a button. It is a world in which the "boundary objects" (Star and Griesemer 1989) that constrain and shape and guide and give nuance to our ways of being and acting and interrelating in the world are no longer available: they have "dropped out" of our virtual lives not because anyone has forgotten to invoke them or hasn't learned how, but because they have never been created—they are not there at all.

This is an abdication of responsibility. If indeed virtual worlds open onto an untamed new frontier, why would we renounce all claims to its careful construction prior to letting children loose in a place where there are no rules or structures of accountability, no laws or ethics, no political structures, no mechanisms for reducing harms, controlling violence, prohibiting actions that are evil, stupid, or just plain thoughtless? If this were a real frontier, would anyone send his or her children into it without taking the time to build a habitable, humane world? What do we imagine we are doing consigning this unruly universe to youth and whomever else might be interested in technological possibilities in which many of us maintain no interest? The fact is there has been much money to be made and many giant careers to be built in these digital frontiers, and *this*, not educational or social or political wellbeing, has preoccupied those who have ventured forth. What needed to be done—adult inhabitation, responsible building of a humane and habitable cyberspace, making clear and accessible what government and industry are doing with new technologies in cyberspace—is *not* getting done when there is no money to be made by doing it, and the responsibility for *that* rests not at all with the children and youth now seen to be "running amok" there.

No domain is insulated or immunized from any other; all are real and all are integral to who we are making ourselves into and what kinds of worlds we are building for our necessarily limited inhabitation, and all need far more care and critical attention and serious engagement. In more and more respects, the real world/virtual world distinction produces and supports a kind of shattering into autonomous fragments that are anarchic with respect to any accountable subject. These days growing numbers of us engage in self-building and world building more online than off, so it's time for some accountable and *intelligent* design of a very different sort.

"Accountable design" is one part of the equation. The other, no less important, one is inhabitation, is world building. Time invested in the practice of forming and reforming virtual selves and online identities would be well rewarded by a shift from individualistic to societal design and production—a tremendous challenge for designers and programmers, and no less for research and player communities. What's called for is critical civic engagement with "the world that is there" to echo George Herbert Mead's (1938) catchphrase, rather than turning our backs on it. Because that works just about as well as building higher garden walls to keep out global warming. We are all affected anyway, we are all, already, inhabitants of an ethical wasteland at the hybrid horizons of a real virtual world in serious trouble, one that is crying out for our attention, a world badly and negligently built, for profits not for people, a world that needs real intervention, real engagement, and real inhabitation from us all: what we lack, what we badly need, are the means to build activist avatars, accountable virtual selves who can acknowledge, embrace, and fulfill our responsibilities as citizens in the hybrid worlds in which we live.

Notes

1. This quite lovely turn of phrase is borrowed from Illich and Sanders 1988.

2. "In 2010, gay Rutgers student Tyler Clementi committed suicide by leaping off the George Washington Bridge after learning that fellow student Dharun Ravi had used a webcam to record him kissing another man" (http://theweek.com/article/index/228243/tyler-clementi-case-is-dharun-ravis-jail-sentence-too-lenient).

References

Austin, J. 1962. *Sense and Sensibilia*. London: Oxford University Press.

Dewey, John, and A. Bentley. 1949. *Knowing and the Known*. Boston: Beacon Press.

Gee, J. P. 2004. "Video Games: Embodied Empathy for Complex Systems." *Conference Proceedings for E3*. Los Angeles.

Illich, Ivan, and Barry Sanders. 1988. *ABC: The Alphabetization of the Popular Mind*. San Francisco: North Point Press.

Mead, G. H. 1938. The Nature of Scientific Knowledge. In *The Philosophy of the Act*, ed. G. H. Mead, C. W. Morris, J. M. Brewster, A. M. Dunham, and D. Miller, 45–62. Chicago: University of Chicago Press.

Star, Susan, and James Griesemer. 1989. Institutional Ecology, "Translations" and Boundary Objects: Amateurs and Professionals in Berkeley's Museum of Vertebrate Zoology, 1907–39. *Social Studies of Science* 19 (3): 387–420.

Whitson, J., C. Eaket, B. Greenspan, M. Q. Tran, and N. King. 2008. Neo-immersion: Awareness and Engagement in Gameplay. Future Play '08. Toronto: Association for Computing Machinery.

III DIY and Design: Opening the Black Box and Repurposing Technologies

Latour famously described the need to unpack and open up the "black boxes" of technological systems (Latour 1987, 2). Borrowing the term from cybernetics, Latour used it to highlight the need to examine the practices whereby technologies and "facts" are naturalized. The chapters in part III work to unpack and reveal the often hidden work of technological naturalization, highlighting the various agencies and structures that are maintained as well as troubled by DIY experiences—or those that are claimed as "DIY." Generally, concepts of design and participatory activities are addressed and examples given that demonstrate how design practices can serve to create new publics or bring new voices into public debate.

Ratto's contribution (chapter 16) emphasizes the need for critical scholars to engage directly with the technical systems they study, calling for simultaneous material and conceptual engagements that can serve to renew a commitment to critical discourse and the materiality of technologies themselves. Leveraging his term "critical making," he connects a DIY agenda to critical scholarship and the technologies and social communities of the maker movement more generally.

DiSalvo's example of participatory "speculative" design practices (chapter 17), Light's example of the Geezers Club (chapter 19), and McSwiney and Michaud's detailed history of *Les Amis du Champ des Possibles* (chapter 20) all demonstrate how design and material engagements provide novel means for civic engagement, bringing new voices into public debate and intervention. For these authors, the importance and value of DIY is not only to be found in technological innovation or increased instrumental functionality. Instead, the value resides in the citizen empowerment instantiated by such activities. DiSalvo highlights this aspect when he notes the ways participants of his *growbots* workshops "were taking part in the endeavor of speculation: instantiating a radical imagination of the future or an alternate present." Similarly, in describing the goals of the

Democratising Technology research project, Light notes that technical literacy was not the desired outcome: "Instead, [the project] treated participants as experts on life experience, social relations, and the ethics of technology." McSwiney and Michaud's chapter provides an overview of a complex natural and human-made landscape and the DIY activities that it provides. Here, the complexity of the landscape serves as a valuable site for negotiating the equally complex needs and desires of citizens looking for a voice in the urban environment.

But it is important to recognize the preconditions and systems that many DIY practices require in order to function. Murphy, Phillips, and Pollock's contribution looks at "cloud computing" (chapter 18). Their work reminds us that many DIY activities are built upon privately owned corporate infrastructures that may actively delimit the kinds of activities seen as appropriate or even possible. The connections they draw between corporate profit and DIY production temper what is often a more overt celebratory mien. As they note, "Indeed, the underlying profit motivation of these companies' support for DIY suggests that customization—of apps, of handsets, of knowledge—will occur only insofar as it is profitable."

Continuing the theme of "infrastructure," McKim (chapter 21) and Swartz and Driscoll (chapter 22) both explore participation and social media. McKim looks at participatory forms of civil architecture, noting in particular how architecture as a field attempts to reconcile the need to embrace technological innovations often driven by experts with participatory architectural forms that are decidedly low-tech but available to the wider public. Most interestingly, he notes that participatory social forms are not being used to replace current expert knowledge but as means to connect designers and publics. Swartz and Driscoll use their analysis of online activity on a web forum to point to a number of tensions that exist between purpose-built (and often proprietary) online spaces and the ways in which users (as they constitute themselves as members and as citizens of these spaces) want to repurpose them.

These chapters all engage in novel integrations of technologies as material objects and critical social analysis, using the resultant hybridity as a way to better acknowledge the benefits and the issues associated with the DIY citizen. An important undercurrent in all these chapters involves the value of technology itself and either an explicit or implicit troubling of simplistic definitions of its social value. For these authors, not only is technology not the main space in which DIY citizenship is constituted, but technical literacy or innovation is not the primary outcome. Instead, the technical serves as a point of passage, a necessary (but problematic) infrastructure, or possibly a boundary object (Star and Griesemer 1989) around which unexpected individuals can find common cause. These chapters therefore open up some of the critical questions posed in the main introduction to this volume.

References

Latour, Bruno. 1987. *Science in Action: How to Follow Scientists and Engineers through Society*. Cambridge, MA: Harvard University Press.

Star, S. L., and J. R. Griesemer. 1989. Institutional Ecology, "Translations" and Boundary Objects: Amateurs and Professionals in Berkeley's Museum of Vertebrate Zoology, 1907–39. *Social Studies of Science* 19 (3): 387–420.

16 Textual Doppelgangers: Critical Issues in the Study of Technology

Matt Ratto

Introduction

At a conference a group builds electronics flowers, using them to explore dimensions of sharing and network technologies (Ratto and Hoekema 2009); in a city, urban agriculturalists use simple robots to explore small-scale farming and automation (DiSalvo 2012); in their workplace, designers construct an IV bag in the shape of a teddy bear and rely on the cognitive dissonance to convey affectual sensibilities about health and childhood (Dunne and Raby 2001); in a design firm, a group of designers and sales people build wearable sensors to test theories of cognitive plasticity and embodiment (Ratto 2010); at the university, a class of students uses arduinos and electronics to explore critical information issues (Ratto 2012); and in her studio, an artist clones ten trees and places them around the world as part of a material experience-experiment on nature-nuture relations (Jerimijenko 2001).

These examples, drawn from my own work and from the work of others, serve as instances of what I frame as *critical making* (Ratto and Hoekema 2009; Ratto 2011a, 2011b), materially productive, hands-on work intended to uncover and explore conceptual uncertainties, parse the world in ways that language cannot, and disseminate the results of these explorations through embodied, material forms. The use of the term "critical making," rather than related terms such as critical design (Dunne and Raby 2001), design thinking (Martin 2009), or constructionism[1] (Harel and Papert 1991), is purposeful. Rather than focusing on how more reflexive practices can improve the quality of the material world, the term critical making—like critical thinking—highlights an intention to explore how more substantial engagements with material production will improve the quality of our conceptualizations of our world. At the heart of this notion of critical making is an argument about the importance of making to understanding and intervening in the dominant modes of social life. More pragmatically, critical making frames a need to incorporate technical work alongside critical social analysis and makes a claim that doing so can both extend current scholarly critiques and direct them into society in new ways. Addressing this need demonstrates a commitment to attend to the materiality of our sociotechnical environments as has been well described in both the work of current Science, Technology, and Society (STS) scholars (e.g., Haraway 1990; Latour 1999; Shapin and Schaffer 1986) and that of past communication and media scholars (Innis 1951; McLuhan and Lapham 1994; Postman 2005).

Origins

I work at the University of Toronto in the Faculty of Information where my focus is on exploring the ways in which the materialities of our information environments matters (cf. Hayles 1993; Kirschenbaum 2008; Blanchette 2012). For the last few years I've been trying to maintain a commitment to this materiality, primarily through the study and development of research and pedagogical practices that engage directly in technical, material work, but remain motivated and connected to conceptual exploration as well. My academic work did not start out this way. Instead, my PhD research and following projects relied primarily on interviews and observational practices as well as some forms of content analysis, whether of software programs and their makers (Ratto 2005a, 2005b), loose networks of collaboration within health sciences (Ratto and Beaulieu 2007), or epistemic cultures within archeology (Ratto 2012). At some point I realized that what connected these rather diverse subjects was an emphasis on building and making things, whether operating systems, distributed health databases, or archeological models. However, I continued to struggle with a sense that observation and interview did not capture many details of highly technical material work. Further, I felt increasingly that these missing details were somehow relevant and important for understanding the complexly interwoven nature of our sociotechnical world.

I first started thinking in 2007 about the role of making as a necessary and underutilized part of critical reflection on technology and society. Until then, I had been using the more traditional forms of academic reflection, data gathering, and writing to explore questions about structure and agency and the links between technical artifacts and social organization.

However, I kept finding myself backed into reductive corners or creating ever more complicated theories about the status and role of material objects in society. At a certain point, I was reminded of the complications of the Ptolemaic system of astronomy—how ever-increasing complications of cycles and epicycles were required to keep the earth at the center of the universe as new evidence from scientific observation had to be factored in. I began to wonder if we needed a Copernican revolution in order to sweep away these wheels within wheels. I was assisted in my thinking on this by an increased attention to "materiality," to objects, and to design, a "move to the material" within STS and related fields that both excited and frustrated me. There was something quite right in this move and yet also something very wrong.

"Textual Doppelgangers"

It came to me one day while reading a fascinating (but I thought) unrelated book on art history. In his chapter addressing visuality and art, Corbett (2005) decried what he termed the use of "textual doppelgangers" within art history, claiming that most historians first replaced the art object (painting, sculpture, whatever) with a textual description and then proceeded to carry out their analysis on this replacement. Aha! Here seemed to be the "earth" in our current geocentric model of criticality and technology—too much of a dependency on textuality and language. I started to imagine a form of critical analysis that included material engagements with the domains being studied, and I soon discovered many similar forms—constructionism (à la Papert and others), various types of art and design practice, architecture, historical analyses that included the construction of material artifacts, and versions of participatory action research methods. And yet, there remained a strong disconnect between these more material forms of engagement and the conceptual work being done on technology, the built environment, and society. My sense was that creating more substantial relations between material and conceptual practices would improve the outcomes of each but that this had to be done in a way that maintained the commitments of each form of intervention—that language as a generalizing and expanding form of intervention needed to be part of the mix as did forms of technical work that allowed materiality to exceed and resist the ways in which we characterize it through language. I also quickly realized that I couldn't "think" my way to such a practice but had to actively work to "make" this form.

Failure

My initial attempt to do this failed miserably, which let me know that I was on the right track. In 2008 I was invited to give a talk at the Royal College of Art in London on the topic of distance learning and Web 2.0 technologies. My sense was that this debate had stalled with critics claiming that distance education technologies lacked the sociality of face-to-face interactions, and advocates claiming that these issues had been or would be solved by higher bandwidths, new interfaces, or other novel technological developments. These arguments fell rather neatly into the two forms of reductionism noted by Latour (2004), one group claiming an unmediated and romantic concept of the "social" and the other emphasizing a strong technological determinism.

Rather than attempt to prove or disprove these positions, I instead decided to facilitate a workshop on this topic using shared making as a way of creating joint experiences. I titled it "Taking Things Apart/Making Things Together: Critical Making and Discovery Learning" and decided to use a robot-making practice as a way to create context for the discussion. I started the ninety-minute session with a brief description and overview of the debate between advocates and denigrators of distance education, painting a conceptually clear but simplistic argument. I encouraged the participants to advocate for or against distance education and, after a brief conversation, helped the participants organize into teams. I then provided each with some small vibrating motors (typically found in pagers and cell phones), batteries, tape, glue, toothbrushes, and other craft materials. I described the notion of the "bristlebot," a type of robot that achieved its movement through the vibration of toothbrush bristles against a surface, and I pointed each team toward online resources that would help them build one. After some encouragement, the participants began to construct individual machines, referring to both the online and offline resources. Periodically, over the following forty minutes, I interrupted the teams to ask them to reflect on the kinds of help they were getting from digital resources, what help they received from their teammates and others in the room, and how the materials themselves informed their decisions. After finishing and showing off the results of their work, I proceeded to raise the topic of distance education and asked the participants to reflect on how their recent experience informed their judgment or perspective. A quick review of the participants found that few of them had changed their position and that the majority of them had trouble mapping what they had just done to the critical issues involved—though they had enjoyed the experience.

Why was this? Rather than see the event just as a failure—which in certain ways it certainly was—I saw it as a data point for a more meta-level analysis involving the relations between "making" and conceptual work. But for that analysis, I would need other data points. Luckily, soon after, I found myself planning another event, this time involving a critical analysis of the Internet as a "walled garden."

Success!

For this, I was invited to contribute to a two-day conference in Amsterdam on issues related to Web 2.0 developments (Virtueel Platform 2008). This event was organized by Virtueel Platform, an organization tasked by the Dutch government with facilitating cross-disciplinary discussions between media arts and design organizations. The main concern of the overall conference was the issue of so-called walled gardens: did closed web 2.0 network applications such as Facebook™ constitute "free riding" and the extraction of value from the network as a whole? The idea for my contribution, what I called the "Flwr Pwr" workshop, was to create a shared construction exercise that could facilitate and inform discussions around the rise of proprietary and closed "walled gardens" on the Internet and provide some common ground for thinking through the social issues involved. Using preassembled and coded components, workshop participants constructed simple electronic agents called "flwrs" that "talked" and "listened" to one another using infrared communication, and displayed the results via preset series of colored, blinking lights. By observing these lights, the makers of the flwrs could see how their flwr communicated with the others, and how the status and quality of these communications helped or hindered in the growth and maintenance of the garden as a whole. Moreover, I selected critical theories of information and exchange, such as the idea of generalized exchange and gift economies (Mauss 1990), the notion of the information commons (Benkler 2006), and a concept of information "neighborhoods" extended from the work of Jacobs (1992). I then developed specific code subroutines that metaphorically operationalized these concepts.[2]

Unlike the RCA event, the Amsterdam event was a rousing success. Participants actively engaged in the making process, using craft materials to construct personal flwrs and quickly becoming comfortable with the process for programming and customizing how their flwr behaved. Moreover, they soon began to make use of the conceptual language that accompanied the technical instructions, describing the signals sent by their flwrs as "gifts" or "commodities" (Mauss 1990), contextualizing the flwrs' relations as the result of reciprocity and "generalized exchange" (Mauss 1990), and mapping such behaviors to the open and closeness of information on the Internet. Unlike in the RCA event, the making work and the critical conceptual work seemed to meld, with one type of engagement supporting the other. Equally, this melding paid off—conversations on the idea of the Internet as a walled garden took a surprising turn when the flwrs themselves pushed back at our initially simplistic notions of open as good and closed as bad. As participants configured the flwrs with more complex rules regarding sharing, they found that in some cases, having "walls" between the flwrs helped maintain a more diverse and heterogenous network. Since the flwrs were somewhat unreliable and certainly did not constitute any kind of rigorous or authoritative source, this insight became a starting point, opening up the need for more conversation and conceptual work, rather than closing down and "proving" one particular point. Here, the flwrs served to constitute the notion of the walled garden as a "matter for concern" rather than as a "matter of fact" (Latour 2008).

Conclusion

I see the previous narratives and the practices through which they were generated as heralding the opportunity for a more sustained and material engagement with important questions regarding the relations between people and technologies. Why did the RCA bristlebot group fail to link the conceptual and the material work, whereas the Walled Garden Flwr Pwr group successfully linked these two aspects? What, in other words, allows people to bridge technical perspectives/material labor and critical social perspectives/conceptual labor? And why is this important? I end this short chapter with a few thoughts on these issues.

First, society is increasingly digitally mediated. No longer do we "go" to cyberspace—we live within it. This means the outright rejection of technology described by some past (romantic) scholars is not an option—if it ever truly was possible to live "outside" technology. Even if we choose not to own cell phones or utilize online systems and resources, as individuals and as members of a society, we are interfiliated within the flows (Castells 2000) and logics (Thrift 2011) of digitality. We must come to terms with the systems and artifacts we build and, by understanding what they do to and for us, construct them (both materially and semiotically) in more liberatory and productive ways.

Second, critical analysis of technologies is of limited usefulness if we cannot connect the results of this work to actual engagements with the technologies in question. Classic critical accounts (e.g., Ellul 1964; Heidegger

1977; Marcuse 1964) have tended to focus on technology with a capital "T," resulting in essentializing statements that are often difficult to reconcile with our lived, day-to-day experiences of digital mediation. This work remains useful and important, and the insights that emerged from it are in fact often underaddressed by current generations of technology scholars.[3] But these insights and perspectives must be concretely connected to the practices of use and design through which people and technologies are co-constituted in order for them to have any effect.

The preceding examples—bristlebots and digital flwrs—served as my initial attempts to bridge the distance between the necessary and important textual doppelgangers of critical scholarship and the objects themselves. In stating this I do not mean to claim a realist separation between the "real world" of objects and the "social world" of words and meanings. But I do want to emphasize how difficult it can be to maintain space within academic work for the materials of our material-semiotic world as well as how necessary it is to push back however slightly on scholarly logocentricism. I have continued my naive attempts to "make" such opportunities as well as to think through their ramifications.[4] Figuring out ways to bring about material engagement with the technologies we study is therefore of paramount importance—not just as a way of making better objects (though this will be an important outcome) but also so that we understand the objects that are made in a more concrete and comprehensive fashion.

Acknowledgments

I would like to thank all the participants in the critical making sessions noted in this text, as well as Bronac Ferran who invited me to participate in the RCA event, and the organizers of the Walled Garden conference. This work continues to be supported in part by the Canada Foundation for Innovation, Leader Opportunity Fund, and by the Faculty of Information, University of Toronto. Originally published as Matt Ratto, "Textual Doppelgängers: Critical Making as Pedagogy, as Research," Canadian Communications Association (CCA), proceedings of the Technologies and Media track, CCA 2012, Ottawa, Canada, May 28–30, 2012, http://www.tem.fl.ulaval.ca/en/waterloo-2012/.

Notes

1. These serve as only a few examples. Other relevant terms include adversarial design (DiSalvo 2012), critical technical practice (Agre 1997), and participatory design (Schuler and Namioka 1993).

2. For more specifics about Flwr Pwr, please see Ratto 2011a. In this article, I address in more detail what I mean here by "metaphorically" linking code and concept.

3. I would exempt from this statement the work of Andrew Feenberg and other adherents to his critical theory of technology (Feenberg 1991, 1999). This work is explicitly oriented toward bridging the divide between classic philosophy of technology's critical perspectives and more recent empirically focused technology studies scholarship. However, the relevance of this work is similarly limited by the logocentrism that I associate with other scholarship on technology.

4. I continue to document these attempts on my website, http://www.criticalmaking.com.

References

Agre, P. 1997. Towards a Critical Technical Practice: Lessons Learned in Trying to Reform AI. In *Bridging the Great Divide: Social Science, Technical Systems, and Cooperative Work*, ed. G. Bowker, L. Gasser, S. L. Star, and W. Turner, 131–157. Hillsdale, NJ: Erlbaum.

Benkler, Y. 2006. *The Wealth of Networks: How Social Production Transforms Markets and Freedom*. New Haven, CT: Yale University Press.

Blanchette, J. 2012. *Burdens of Proof: Cryptographic Culture and Evidence Law in the Age of Electronic Documents*. Cambridge, MA: MIT Press.

Castells, M. 2000. *The Rise of the Network Society* Vol. 1, *The Information Age: Economy, Society and Culture*. 2nd ed. Hoboken, NJ: Wiley-Blackwell.

Corbett, D. 2005. Visual Culture and the History of Art. In *Dealing with the Visual: Art History, Aesthetics, and Visual Culture*, ed. Caroline Van Eck and Edward Winters, 17–36. Farnham, Surrey: Ashgate Publishing.

DiSalvo, C. 2012. *Adversarial Design*. Cambridge, MA: MIT Press.

Dunne, A., and F. Raby. 2001. *Design Noir: The Secret Life of Electronic Objects*. 1st ed. Basel: Birkhäuser.

Ellul, J. 1964. *The Technological Society*. New York: Vintage Books.

Feenberg, A. 1991. *Critical Theory of Technology*. Oxford: Oxford University Press.

Feenberg, A. 1999. *Questioning Technology*. London: Routledge.

Haraway, D. J. 1990. *Simians, Cyborgs, and Women: The Reinvention of Nature*. 1st ed. London: Routledge.

Harel, I., and S. Papert. 1991. *Constructionism*. New York: Ablex Publishing.

Hayles, N. K. 1993. The Materiality of Informatics. *Configurations* 1 (1): 147–170.

Heidegger, M. 1977. *The Question Concerning Technology*. New York: Harper and Row.

Innis, H. A. 1951. *The Bias of Communication*. 1st ed. Toronto: University of Toronto Press.

Jacobs, J. 1992. *The Death and Life of Great American Cities*. New York: Vintage.

Jerimijenko, N. 2001. One Trees. http://www.nyu.edu/projects/xdesign/onetrees/.

Kirschenbaum, M. G. 2008. *Mechanisms: New Media and the Forensic Imagination*. Cambridge, MA: MIT Press.

Latour, B. 1999. *Pandora's Hope: Essays on the Reality of Science Studies*. Cambridge, MA: Harvard University Press.

Latour, B. 2004. Why Has Critique Run Out of Steam? From Matters of Fact to Matters of Concern. *Critical Inquiry* 30 (2): 225–248.

Latour, B. 2008. "A Cautious Prometheus? A Few Steps toward a Philosophy of Design (with special attention to Peter Sloterdijk)." Keynote lecture at the Networks of Design meeting of the Design History Society, Falmouth, Cornwall, September 3.

Marcuse, H. 1964. *One-Dimensional Man: Studies in the Ideology of Advanced Industrial Society*. Boston: Beacon Press.

Martin, R. L. 2009. *The Design of Business: Why Design Thinking Is the Next Competitive Advantage*. Boston: Harvard Business School Press.

Mauss, M. 1990. *The Gift: The Form and Reason for Exchange in Archaic Societies*. London: Norton.

McLuhan, M., and L. H. Lapham. 1994. *Understanding Media: The Extensions of Man*. Cambridge, MA: MIT Press.

Postman, N. 2005. *Amusing Ourselves to Death: Public Discourse in the Age of Show Business*. Rev. ed. Harmondsworth: Penguin Books.

Ratto, M. 2005a. Don't Fear the Penguins: Negotiating the Trans-local Space of Linux Development. *Current Anthropology* 46 (5): 827–834.

Ratto, M. 2005b. Embedded Technical Expression: Code and the Leveraging of Functionality. *The Information Society* 21 (3): 205–213.

Ratto, M. 2012. Critical Making Master's Course. 2012 syllabus. http://criticalmaking.com/critical-making-fi2241/.

Ratto, M. 2010. Self-Sensing and Health. http://criticalmaking.com/self-sensing-and-health-%E2%80%93-a-critical-making-experience/.

Ratto, M. 2011a. Critical Making: Conceptual and Material Studies in Technology and Social Life. *Information Society* 27 (4): 252–260.

Ratto, M. 2011b. Open Design and Critical Making. In *Open Design Now: Why Design Cannot Remain Exclusive*, ed. P. Atkinson, M. Avital, B. Mau, R. Ramakers, and C. Hummels, 202–209. Amsterdam: BIS Publishers.

Ratto, M., and A. Beaulieu. 2007. Banking on the Human Genome Project. Special issue on "Genes" and Society: Looking Back on the Future, ed. S. Z. Reuter and K. Neves-Graça, *Canadian Review of Sociology/Revue Canadienne de Sociologie* 44 (2): 175–200.

Ratto, M., and S. Hoekema. 2009. Flwr Pwr: Tending the Walled Garden. In *Walled Garden*, ed. A. Dekker and A. Wolfsberger, 51–60. Rotterdam: Virtueel Platform.

Shapin, S., and S. Schaffer. 1986. *Leviathan and the Air-Pump: Hobbes, Boyle, and the Experimental Life*. Princeton: Princeton University Press.

Schuler, D., and A. Namioka. 1993. *Participatory Design: Principles and Practices*. London: Routledge.

Thrift, N. 2011. Lifeworld Inc.—and What to Do about It. *Environment and Planning. D, Society & Space* 29 (1): 5–26. doi:10.1068/d0310.

Virtueel Platform. 2008. Walled Garden: Communities & Networks post Web 2.0. https://sites.google.com/site/walledgardenconference/.

17 The Growbot Garden Project as DIY Speculation through Design

Carl DiSalvo

Introduction

Speculative design offers the viewer compelling and provocative images for consideration, such as graphic visions of the cities-of-tomorrow or conceptual products that meld science fiction and industrial design. This kind of work has a long history in architecture, design, and art, extending back to the early twentieth-century futurists and constructivists, through to contemporary examples in the domains of critical design (Dunne and Raby 2001) and design fiction (Bleeker 2009). What is common across most forms of speculative design is that it does two things simultaneously: it instantiates a radical imagination of the future or an alternate present through design, and it challenges the status quo of design practice.

Most often, speculative design is a practice of experts, undertaken by designers who are adept in making alluring prototypes. This is not surprising because speculative design tends to work by bringing a viewer to believe that the future being proffered is plausible—despite how outrageous it might be. To achieve this requires that the images and objects presented express a realism that usually entails expertise.

But can we imagine a practice of speculation through design that is not limited to experts? How might we construct situations and environments that support participation in speculation? What might a "DIY speculation through design" be like?

These questions are among a suite of questions that motivate the Growbot Garden project: a project developed to spur dialog and explore possible futures of agricultural technology using participatory and codesign methods. Specifically, the project sought to explore the design issues of robotics and sensing technologies for small-scale agriculture—to ask how such technologies, which have been commonly designed for industrial agriculture, might be redesigned to support the practice and values of small-scale agriculture. As a research-through-design project, the answers to that question took form through prototypes and events.

In this chapter I'll discuss one instantiation of the Growbot Garden project: a set of workshops hosted at the 2010 01SJ Biennial arts festival in San Jose, California. Through this discussion I'll describe how the festival was framed as a site for public engagement with technology and describe the specifics of one of three Growbot Garden workshops. From this I'll sketch some features and possibilities of a kind of DIY speculation through design.

Speculative Design and New Forms of Public Engagement with Technology

The science museum is commonly considered to be one of the institutions through which publics come to learn about and engage with technology. Of late, speculative design has found a home in science museums as a new form of public engagement. For example, the Material Beliefs project (2007–2010) was exceptional in using speculative design to prompt and support public dialogue around social and ethical issues of emerging technologies in science museums and science centers. Such projects exemplify efforts to rethink the role of the science museum in public life and provide examples of how, through design, publics might experience science and technology in new ways. A seemingly common theme is the need to move away from the standard science museum exhibition format. In discussing how science museums might better express the controversies of contemporary science, Yaneva, Rabesandratana, and Greiner (2009) call for an "architecture of interaction" that would prompt more lively forms of communication. Notably, they draw upon the art installation as a particular form of expression to offer an alternative model of science and technology exhibition design.

At the same time as efforts are under way to rethink the role of the science museum, there are emerging practices in participatory design that are working to use design as means for critical engagement with issues, often through creative uses of technology. Pelle Ehn (2008) refers to this as "participation in design things." These design things are assemblies of human and nonhuman actors, of affordances and affects, of issues and their publics. They are in tension with the common notion of a design project, which has, or is made to have, a certain amount of fixity. For Ehn, participation in design things is about taking part in sociotechnical issues through design methods and considering how to design infrastructures or platforms to enable the open exploration of the possibilities and consequences of design things.

In developing this notion of design things, Ehn draws heavily from the work of Bruno Latour. In particular, Ehn is influenced by Latour's (2004) notions of object-oriented democracy and the shift from matters of fact to matters of concern. In his essay "Why Has Critique Run Out of Steam? From Matters of Fact to Matters of Concern," Latour asserts that what is necessary is to become what he (awkwardly) refers to as a constructivist sort of critic. More important than revealing or debunking the so-called facts are articulating the issues that motivate and mobilize publics. As he states, "The critic is not the one who debunks, but the one who assembles . . . the one who offers the participants an arena in which to gather" (246). The participation in design things that Ehn speaks of is gesture toward precisely this idea of assembling.

Our project at the 01SJ Biennial was likewise a gesture toward this idea of offering participants an arena in which to gather. It was an attempt to create a situation in which to imaginatively encounter the possibilities and issues of agricultural technologies. Rather than the science museum, however, our project was sited at an arts festival. Arguably, this allowed more opportunity to move past the facts of technology and agriculture and move toward the confluence of technology and agriculture as a matter of concern.

The Context of the 2010 01SJ Biennial

The 01SJ Biennial is one of the largest and most prestigious arts festivals in North America. To label it an arts festival, however, is a bit of a misnomer. Like the contemporary art world itself, the 01SJ Biennial extends many modes of cultural production and social action. This particular festival has its roots in technology and media arts, and this emphasis continues today. However, participants come from a range of disciplines and practices that are not limited to the common notions of art or even so-called new media. The plurality of those involved is reflected in the public positioning of the event, expressed through curatorial statements such as this:

> The 2010 01SJ Biennial is predicated on the notion that as artists, designers, engineers, architects, marketers, corporations and citizens we have the tools to (re)build the world, conceptually and actually, virtually and physically, poorly and better, aesthetically and pragmatically, in both large and small ways. 01SJ is about how powerful ideas and innovative individuals from around the world can make a difference and come together to build a unique and distributed city-wide platform for creative solutions and public engagement. (2010 01SJ Biennial 2009a)

The pluralism of participants and activities is important because it casts art as a practice and the arts festival as a context from which to engage in experimentation in effecting change, while also keeping the constitution of those actors and efforts open to being more than just the provenance of art, artists, and the art world. This is indicative of a sense of possibility for the arts, broadly construed, to proactively operate in a mode of world building. It is in this sense of possibility that we can look to art, design, and architecture as forms of inquiry and production that resonate with Latour's (2004) notion of constructivism as a practice that puts things together.

It is also worthwhile to briefly consider that this biennial frames itself as a "platform for creative solutions and public engagement" (2010 01SJ Biennial 2009a). The idea of a platform suggests that the festival is a basis for action, to be built upon. This makes it something quite different from an exhibition. If an exhibition is about display and representation, then the festival as platform is about construction and enactment. The efficacy of this platform is certainly open to question. But what is important here is less the assessment of the biennial and more the framing of its context and purposes.

There were multiple themed programs within the 2010 01SJ Biennial. The program that provided the context and purpose for the Growbot Garden project was *Out of the Garage, Into the World*. With this program, the idea of a platform was embodied in a space—an 80,000 sq. ft. hall, known as South Hall, which was reminiscent of an airplane hanger. For the festival South Hall was filled with participants exploring this notion of "(re)build[-ing] the world." As described: "*Out of the Garage, Into the World* acknowledges the blurred boundaries between garage hacking and citizen science and invites a range of such DIY laboratories and re-purposed spaces to perform in the public sphere, where the general public can observe and even participate in the process" (2010 01SJ Biennial 2009b).

Participants occupied South Hall for approximately three weeks in September. They included individuals, groups, and collectives, well known and unknown, from universities, from nonprofits, and those working independently of any formal organization. At the beginning of the month, participants arrived and began assembling their spaces within South Hall. Each was given a location determined in advance through discussion with the curators. This period of construction was open to the public, and participants were required to begin hosting workshops in their spaces almost from the start (see figure 17.1).

As tables were set up and arranged and all manner of small structures were put together, people from the surrounding blocks in downtown San Jose, a handful at a time, would wander through the space. In some cases they stopped to ask questions, but more often they just looked around, curiously. Some participants (such as ourselves) did indeed begin hosting workshops almost immediately, amid the energetic disarray of the setting.

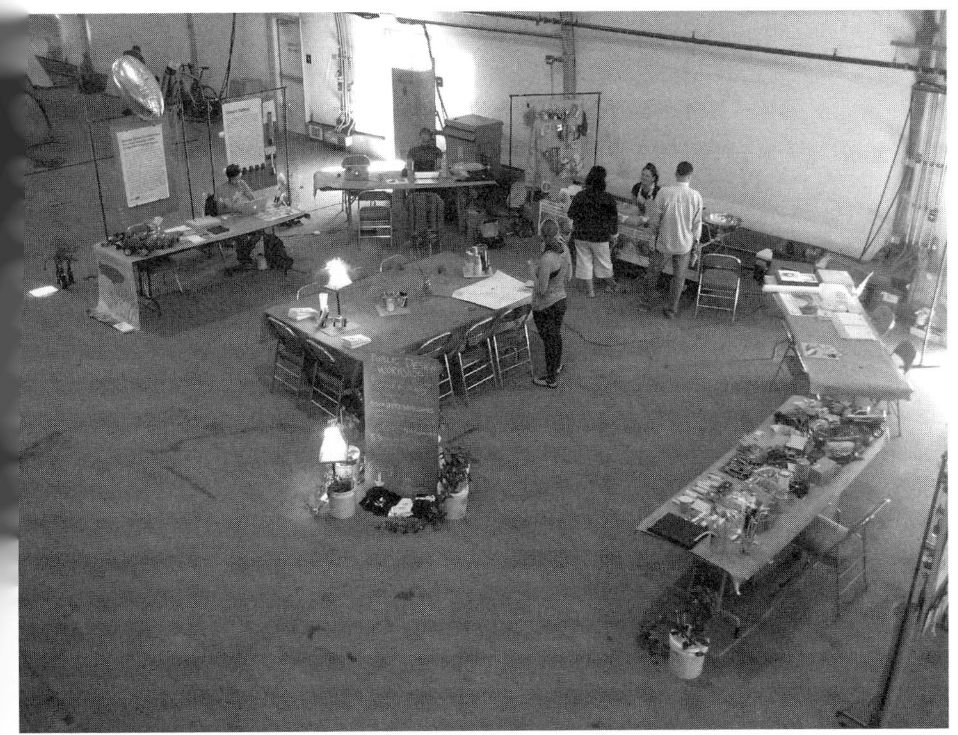

Figure 17.1
Growbot Garden project ad hoc studio space at the 2010 01SJ Biennial

Taken together, the 2010 01SJ Biennial, and in particular the *Out of the Garage, Into the World* program, and the activities and spaces of the South Hall comprise a complementary, but distinct, structure to Yaneva, Rabesandratana, and Greiner's (2009) notion of an "architecture of interaction." Here the arts are a medium for critical engagement with science and technology, but much more so on their own terms and without need for justification. In addition, the mode of art is more public art, or so-called social practice art, than installation. Indeed, the very notion of "architecture" bursts in the context of the festival—architecture is not able to metaphorically or actually contain the event.

Growbot Garden at the 01SJ Biennial

Three Growbot Garden workshops were repeated throughout the festival. Each workshop was organized around a different agricultural practice coupled with a particular technology. The workshop Sheep's Clothing paired mushroom harvesting with environmental sensors. The Food Are Here workshop paired foraging with collective digital mapping. And the workshop Municipal Systems for Autonomous Agricultural Production within Co-Opted Non-Compliant Spaces explored the design and possible uses of robotic systems for crop dispersal. This last workshop lends itself to a succinct foray into the public design of speculative events.

Municipal Systems for Autonomous Agricultural Production within Co-Opted Non-Compliant Spaces built upon the practice of seed-bombing as an interventionist tactic for reclaiming one's surroundings and as a mode of guerilla urban gardening. The term "seed-bombing" is itself playfully provocative. It refers to practices of bundling seeds and dirt together, and then throwing those bundles into spaces that are inaccessible or otherwise difficult to access for planting (e.g., a space behind a fence, or a median in roadway). It suggests a kind of confrontational or oppositional practice of surreptitious gardening. The workshop asked participants to imagine a situation in which the technologies of robotics, in particular the capacities for remote action, were put to use in support of a kind of extreme seed-bombing for those spaces even less accessible, out of reach with just an arm's throw. The workshop posed the question "What if we could access those empty spaces behind those distant fences and over those high walls, and use them for crop land?" And then it invited participants to design and experiment with technical systems that could be used for this alternate agriculture.

The awkward title was an intentional aspect of the design. It was a calculated attempt to consider how the language of robotics systems development that is so often applied to combat systems might similarly be applied to small-scale agriculture. The string of words in the title, and even their compounding and sequencing, are common within robotics research and product development, in both military and industrial contexts. But they are uncommon in regard to small-scale agriculture. In effect, then, the title was an attempt to perform a discursive appropriation and transformation of the field of robotics. It was an attempt to demonstrate the contingency of the emphasis on security and combat—that these same technical systems (as codified in language) might be put to other use.

While the title was purposefully awkward, the workshops were purposefully playful. Each workshop began with a short introduction to seed-bombing and robotics, providing just enough information for context. To make the activity accessible, vehicles for the distribution of the seed-bombs were provided as stock material, already assembled and ready to be put to use. In most cases, participants worked alone or in small groups to design and build mechanisms for seed distribution using simple prototyping materials such as cardboard, wire, miscellaneous mechanical parts, toys, and hot glue. These mechanisms were then filled with raw seed or packets of seed and soil, attached to remote-controlled weather balloons, blimps, or trucks, and tested both inside and outside of South Hall. In some cases, after testing their design, participants would tweak their mechanisms, testing them again, going through a cycle of iteration. In other cases, participants worked with mechanisms prebuilt by one of the project members. For example, the design lead for this workshop had modified a remote control truck for seed dispersal (see figure 17.2).

The truck was outfitted with cardboard container wheel mounts, such that as the wheels spun, a stream of seeds was spit from the containers. The body of the vehicle was covered in local scrub as camouflage and with the idea that this scrub itself could contain seeds that scattered or be rubbed off as it moves over the ground. As with the other vehicles, participants could test the truck and other prebuilt mechanisms both inside and outside of South Hall.

Figure 17.2
Truck adapted for remote seed dispersal

The mechanisms varied in complexity and effectiveness. The simplest mechanisms were those that used the motion of the vehicle to disperse the seeds. Examples of these included the wheel mounts for the truck (described previously) or basic platforms attached to the underside of the blimps from which seeds would fall and scatter due to the wind and inherent wobble in their flight. Other mechanisms explored the use of human effort to release the seeds, such as creating and attaching packets of seeds that could be tipped and dumped via pulling on a long string. One particularly novel mechanism design used a small toy robot found in the pile of prototyping materials as an actuating mechanism.

This toy robot vibrated back and forth to generate motion. A young participant developed an automated mechanism by attaching this toy robot to a tray of seeds, which was then suspended under a balloon, and the vibrating motion of the toy robot shook the tray just enough to scatter the seeds.

The Municipal Systems for Autonomous Agricultural Production within Co-Opted Non-Compliant Spaces workshop was conducted daily over the course of the 01SJ Biennial and brought a variety of participants ranging from people with an interest in guerilla gardening to those were who were just curious. In addition to the daily workshop sessions, attendees would regularly stop by the space. Not surprisingly, the blimps and balloons anchored in the space brought constant attention—shiny spheres floating thirty feet above the ground tend to attract interest. People would ask about the blimps and balloons, and ask to try them out, which we were happy to oblige. Although no formal count was done, it's likely that more people experienced the workshop in an ad hoc manner of dropping in to space, than that experienced it through one of the more structured workshop sessions.

Taking Part in The Endeavor of Speculation

The activities of designing, building, and experimenting with these lo-fidelity robotic systems prompted and supported a collective exploration of *what might be*. The emphasis was not on the technical specificities of robotics or the particularities of small-scale agriculture, as might be the case in a more common science museum exhibition. Rather, the emphasis was on the imaginative projection of possibilities at the intersection of robotics and small-scale agriculture. Put another way, the emphasis was not on conveying matters of fact, but on investigating matters of concern.

The form of the workshop wavered between that of a performance, an open hackspace, and a design charrette. While the objects were enticing, it was the workshop as event that was the basis of the DIY speculation through design. Different from the format of an exhibition, an event involves enactment. At the 01SJ Biennial, Growbot Garden project participants made things. They constructed mechanisms for dispersing seed, under the auspices of a different kind of agriculture. They tinkered. They tested. They took part, materially and experientially, in discovery and invention. And as they were cutting, gluing, and remote-controlling, they were also discussing, telling each other and us narratives about these seed-bombing blimps and trucks, the places they might go, and how they might work better. They were taking part in the endeavor of speculation: instantiating a radical imagination of the future or an alternate present.

In line with the work of speculative design, the Growbot Garden workshop also posed a challenge to the status quo of design practice. Most obviously, the designers were not the sole authorities in this endeavor of speculation. We, as designers, set the stage with a series of scenarios and props, but the drama itself unfolded as a collaborative affair. It was a kind of DIY speculation through design because participants were not wholly dependent upon a vision provided by experts. While the workshops relied upon conceptual and material scaffolding provided by designers, participants could bring their own desires, interests, and capabilities to the endeavor, making choices in exploring and expressing this radical imagination.

Even more than the cooperative aspects of the design event, what stands as a challenge to the status quo of design practice and foresight is the openness of the endeavor—its lack of closure. There was no product or service to be made. There was no science to be learned. There was no optimal solution to the problem of dispersing seed, no optimal mechanism or vehicle to be devised. There was simply the ongoing endeavor of speculation, seen as valuable on its own.

The appreciation of the activity of prototyping as a legitimate end in itself is a familiar topic in participatory design research. To use Ehn's language, the Growbot Garden project was more of a design thing than a design project (Ehn 2008). An open-ended process of discovery through prototyping is also a quality central to Ratto's conceptualization of critical making; as he states, "our main focus is on the act of shared construction itself as an activity and a site for enhancing and extending conceptual understandings of critical socio-technical issues" (Ratto 2011, 5). But engaging in design as a kind of inquiry that does not require resolution contrasts with much of design practice. Regardless of whether the ends are profit or social change, professional design is under pressure (often self-imposed) to assert its worth through effect.

Perhaps it's in this contrast that DIY speculation through design, or critical making, asserts its value: it provides a pause in which publics can participate in the imaginative modeling of alternative sociotechnical conditions.

Conclusion

Regardless of what terms we use—DIY citizenship, critical making, speculative design, or the participation in design things—there is a shift occurring that involves design and publics. Increasingly, efforts are being made to increase engagement with science and technology and the issues of the contemporary condition. As part of this, there is recognition that the institutions that we relied upon in the past may no longer be sufficient forums for assembly and that the practices of critique may need to be enlivened with practices of construction. And too, there is recognition that the practices of design may have much to offer in these regards. So more and more we may find alternate sites such as arts festivals providing opportunities to experiment with ways to "(re)build the world" and encounter the use of various kinds of design as modes of inquiry.

As alluring as it this is, there are nagging questions. Specifically, if DIY speculation through design provides a pause in which publics can participate in the imaginative modeling of alternative sociotechnical conditions, then what comes after that pause? Perhaps it is enough just to engage in this imaginative modeling as a creative and reflexive endeavor, the kind of which is often colloquially touted as being important to developing an informed and engaged citizenry. Or perhaps this imaginative modeling might prime some people for action, cultivating awareness and desire, and in some cases skills. Or perhaps the question of what comes after that pause is a question for others to answer. There is, after all, enough work to be done in simply creating these opportunities and scaffolding these activities.

This kind of public and participatory speculative design offers one approach for engaging publics in issues. The structure and flow of the event allows for discovery and invention in ways that are not available through a distanced consideration of an image or object. It's not that less cooperative forms of speculative design are insufficient or lack value. Rather, in the challenge to move from matters of fact to matters of concern we need more strategies and tactics. We need more sites and situations in which people can come together to collectively imagine and work toward another world, even if only momentarily and through play.

Acknowledgments

The Growbot Garden project was conceived and developed by Laura Fries, Thomas Lodato, Beth Schechter, Thomas Barnwell, and Carl DiSalvo.

References

2010 01SJ Biennial. 2009a. Curatorial Statement. http://01sj.org/ (accessed November 15, 2011).

2010 01SJ Biennial. 2009b. *Out of the Garage, Into the World* Curatorial Statement. http://01sj.org/2010/exhibitions/out-of-the-garage/ (accessed November 15, 2011).

Bleeker, Julian. 2009. "Design Fiction: A Short Essay on Design, Science, Fact and Fiction." http://drbfw5wfjlxon.cloudfront.net/writing/DesignFiction_WebEdition.pdf/ (accessed June 18, 2013).

Dunne, Anthony, and Fiona Raby. 2001. *Design Noir: The Secret Life of Objects*. Basel: Birkhauser.

Ehn, Pelle. 2008. Participation in Design Things. In *Proceedings of the Tenth Anniversary Conference on Participatory Design 2008 (PDC '08)*, 92–101. Indiana University, Indianapolis, IN.

Latour, Bruno. 2004. Why Has Critique Run Out of Steam? From Matters of Fact to Matters of Concern. *Critical Inquiry* 30 (Winter): 225–248.

Material Beliefs. 2007–2010. http://www.materialbeliefs.com/ (accessed November 15, 2011).

Ratto, Matt. 2011. Critical Making: Conceptual and Material Studies in Technology and Social Life. *Information Society* 27 (4): 1–17.

Yaneva, A., T. Rabesandratana, and B. Greiner. 2009. Staging Scientific Controversies: a Gallery Test on Science Museums' Interactivity. *Public Understanding of Science* 18 (1): 79–90.

18 Doing It in the Cloud: Google, Apple, and the Shaping of DIY Culture

Michael Murphy, David J. Phillips, and Karen Pollock

This chapter focuses on the technical and industrial organization of cloud computing, and the implications that this organization might have for DIY culture. It articulates a tension that is present throughout the collection of works featured in this section. Each of these chapters documents how a DIY ethos is cultivated across different fields (engineering, architecture, publishing, diamond appraisal). They also attend to how even DIY discourse is shaped by a combination of social, cultural, technical, and institutional forces. Joel McKim (chapter 21, this volume), for instance, looks at how the "undemocratic" field of architecture is sustained by various forces—money, accreditation, access to resources—but also how it might be challenged by others—new media technologies, new arenas of discourses, new teaching philosophies, and so on. In the end, the possibility of DIY-style engagement in architecture, as with other fields, is the result of negotiation between heterogeneous actors. This chapter directs the conversation about the possibility of DIY citizenship, with its emphasis on "bringing projects and initiatives to fruition, [on] making things happen in the world," to the subject of cloud computing. Specifically, it looks at cloud computing as an infrastructure that supports, and shapes, new ways to do-it-yourself.

The shift from the paradigm of the personal computer, in which data processing and storage occur locally, to cloud computing, where data storage and computation occurs remotely, marks a fundamental change in the way that we engage with computer technology. Where local computing requires a relatively robust and programmable terminal, cloud computing most requires access to network infrastructure (bandwidth, server farms, and so on); the terminal itself can be as basic as an Internet-enabled phone. This reliance on infrastructure forms part of a new sociotechnical system[1] that offers new possibilities and constraints for DIY citizenship. Our chapter looks at Apple and Google, two dominant industrial players in cloud computing infrastructure, to ask how user cloud computing structures and normalizes new modes of technological, political, and cultural engagement. It explains these companies' interests in certain configurations of cloud computing, and the different strategies, tactics, and resources that each uses to structure the cloud. Finally, it offers a tentative exploration of the possible ways that this pattern of closure, and its structuring of certain practices of making and participation, might affect the structure and circulation of DIY culture. In particular, it posits a problematic tension between "do-it-yourself" and "do-it-for-them."

Apple, Google, and Their Interests in the Cloud

Google and Apple offer products and services that have shifted the ways in which culture is produced and consumed. Some of these can be seen as having made cultural production more democratic. Tablets and smartphones, for example, have made software application development accessible to programmers at an individual level. Video games, productivity apps, and social networking services that reach millions of people can be produced by a single developer. This section looks at the economic interests and profit models of Google and Apple, and shows how those interests are reflected and sustained through certain configurations of hardware and software, user practice, and industrial alignments.

Apple inhabits the cloud as a retailer of hardware devices (smartphones, tablets, computers) and as a distributor of content (including apps, games, videos, and music). Financially, Apple is driven by the sale of its devices. In 2010 half of the company's $15.6 billion in third-quarter revenue came from sales of iPhones and iPads.[2] It is a culturally dominant brand: in addition to its success as a hardware company, it is also the largest music retailer in the United States.[3] Over fifteen billion iPad or iPhone applications have been downloaded from its App Store, which houses over half a million in total.[4]

Apple depends on the labors of third-party developers for the majority of its App Store content. The proliferation of independently developed apps supports Apple's interests in two ways. First, it gives users an incentive to buy the Apple hardware that the apps run on. Second, because all the apps are distributed through the App Store, Apple makes a profit on their sale. Apple has established mechanisms to encourage and facilitate app creation by relatively small-scale developers. Apple's software development kit (SDK) includes a "complete set of development tools for creating apps for iPad, iPhone, and iPod touch," a programming guide that explains the features of these devices and how they can be managed in an app, libraries of sample code and documentation, and information on how to develop applications that run universally on all Apple devices.[5] Through integration of hardware, operating system, development environment (IDE), and content distribution platform, Apple aspires to offer developers and users a seamless experience. This economic interest in the proliferation of independently developed apps suggests that the Apple ecosystem might be fertile ground for DIY making, and for the creation of varied and nonnormative forms of engagement and information exchange.

Google differs from Apple in its structural relationship to cultural production and consumption in some important ways. First, Google's profits come from advertising. It produces audiences to sell to advertisers. Google monitors individual online behavior, analyzes that behavior to infer both consumers and their desires, and sells access to those newly reified intentional consumers to advertisers, on Google's own sites (through the Adwords service), on the sites of third parties (through the Adsense service), and on mobile platforms through its various analytics and ad delivery services (Google Analytics, AdMob). The profit made from hardware and content sales is relatively insignificant. Instead, Google offers cloud-based services and applications (Search, Maps, Docs, Gmail, YouTube, the Chrome web browser). It leverages these (often free) products in the interest of attracting the largest possible base of users, developers, content providers, and advertisers to its "ecosystem."[6] These interactions can then be analyzed, and their producers commodified, and marketed and sold to advertisers as audiences. So, although the creation and maintenance of the infrastructure necessary to support all of its platforms entails enormous costs, the infrastructure itself produces the raw materials necessary to support it.

User activity within Google products is the main source of Google's revenue, but the company often relies on independent developers to create the content necessary to attract those users, and Google, like Apple, has established mechanisms to support that development. The Chrome browser and the Android smartphone operating system support independently created apps, themes, and extensions. Like Apple, Google makes the software development kit easily available. YouTube offers a platform for user-generated content and even finances amateur production of content through its Partner program. Google's mapping application programming interfaces (APIs) are open and accessible for user-created mash-ups. This approach provides Google with new sources of data related to user activity and with it the ability to create more valuable audience commodities. As Hal Varian, Google's chief economist, notes, "Anything that increases Internet use ultimately enriches Google."[7] Again, Google's economic interest in cultivating new types of users (and using) offers a wealth of potential resources for DIY making and cultural production.

Strategies of Closure

The descriptive section above offers a schematic of how and why Apple and Google make their brand and products available to DIY. Each company produces technologies as well as other "socio-cultural mechanisms" that encourage certain forms of user, and maker, engagement with their products, with technology, and with cultural production more generally. Based on the profit-making obligations of these corporations, the encouragements are structured not only toward profit, but within a particular mode of profit production. In order to satisfy economic imperatives and strategic interests, both Apple and Google attempt to close the cloud to their advantage. Each attempts to make engagement with the cloud, as a user or as a maker, easier or more useful when it is done by actions that are incorporated into their own process of profit production.

Apple: Strategy, Tactics, Resources

Apple's strategy is to create and sustain an Apple-branded experience for individuals engaging cloud computing in such a way that makes sales of hardware and content mutually supportive. Any interactivity with cloud computing facilitated by Apple devices takes place within a curated environment. Users necessarily encounter either iTunes or the App Store as an obligatory passage point, since these are portals to Apple's retail music and app sales. Developers, similarly, must use an Apple device and Apple's own Objective-C programming language to create applications, which are also subject to a thorough yet closed review process.[8] The passage points reinforce one another: because most users can only download content for their devices through iTunes or the App Store, developers have incentive to cooperate with the terms of engagement imposed by Apple in order to gain access to that potential audience. Users, similarly, are assured that anything they download from these distribution platforms is safe and functional on all Apple devices. This development of a tightly controlled, branded space has been achieved, over time, through various means—legal, technical, cultural, and of course financial.

Apple shapes use of its products technically through various hardware- and software-related restrictions incorporated in the company's devices. The iPhone can be locked to operate only on a specific carrier's network. Moreover, the operating system is configured so that each software component performs a cryptographic signature check through a "chain of trust." Applications that are not authenticated by Apple's digital signature will not pass through the chain and will not operate. Through this authentication process, Apple erects a technical barrier to "prevent iPhone owners from loading or executing applications unless they are purchased from Apple's own iTunes App Store or otherwise approved by Apple."[9] These restrictions permit Apple to exercise control over the content and types of use that are available to users of its devices. Apple vets any applications submitted for sale in the App Store based not only on technical specifications but also on its own criteria of appropriateness. Apple's developer licensing agreement reserves the company's right to reject an application for distribution "for any reason."[10]

Apple's strategy in restricting the access of its devices to approved applications has several purposes. First, it further cements the cultural and cognitive link between the handset and the content it mediates. It facilitates branding. In particular, Apple will only distribute apps that conform to its own, often puzzling, standards of decency. The Developer Program License Agreement specifically reserves the company's right to reject applications if they "contain any obscene, pornographic, offensive or defamatory content or materials of any kind (text, graphics, images, photographs, etc.), or other content or materials that in Apple's reasonable judgment may be found objectionable by iPhone or iPod touch users."[11] In an extreme instance, Apple ruled that a political cartoon application developed by Pulitzer Prize–winning satirist Mark Fiore violated this section of the agreement. For another instance, consider Grindr, a location-based mobile service designed to facilitate meetings among gay men. The subcultural reading of Grindr supposes that these meetings are primarily, or at least possibly, erotic. Yet Grindr's user agreement, to conform with Apple's distribution requirements, insists that the erotic content of Grindr profiles be assiduously eradicated.

Policing the App Store also enables Apple to enforce stringent technical standards on "making" that is done on and for Apple devices. Apple reserves several unpublished APIs for its own use and will refuse to distribute third-party apps that use those APIs. By reserving those APIs for its own use, Apple maintains a competitive advantage in writing code for its own handsets. It also can pursue a long term strategy of disintermediation of proprietary third-party application platforms, such as Adobe's Flash animation application. Although Apple eventually relented on its firm stance against Flash, the situation provides an instructive example of both how and why Apple can leverage its hardware-based market dominance to support a particular configuration of brand, technology, content, and user.

Google: Tactics, Strategies, and Resources

As mentioned earlier, Google's strategy regarding cloud computing is to ensure that, as far as possible, every use of the cloud implies a traceable interaction with Google. Such interactions are, for Google, both the raw material for knowledge production and the product to sell to advertisers. Google attempts to strengthen its position as the world's dominant Internet advertising company by making its brand and its products attractive to all types of user and developer activity. The expansion and refinement of audience that comes with increased activity and interaction within the Google "ecosystem" allows for the delivery of more numerous and also more narrowly defined audience commodities to advertisers.[12] In pursuit of this bottom line, Google makes itself accessible to a particular brand of DIY-style making.

Apple's "walled garden" of a cloud, with its tight binding of devices, carriers, users, and content, and implicit threat of exclusion, is anathema to Google's profit paradigm. Vic Gundotra, Google's senior vice-president of social business, effectively articulates this position in his presentation at Google's I/O 2010 conference. "If Google did not act," Gundotra states, users and developers would have been faced with a "draconian future, where one man, one company, one device, one carrier would be [the] only choice."[13] Google has acted in several ways, employing in each case a rhetoric of "openness."

For example, by pledging a minimum bid of $4.6 billion before the auction of wireless spectrum, Google elicited from the US Federal Communications Commission license conditions of "open access" for that spectrum, keeping it accessible to any device, application, service, or content. Google also made its Android operating system available to manufacturers of handsets and tablets free of charge and distributed a branded handset, the Nexus One, which was sold unlocked and marketed as available for use on any technically compatible network. The Android operating system also offered the possibility of a more technically radical DIY engagement: users could access root system files that Apple's operating system protects. These moves positioned Google in public opposition to Apple. The strategy persists, as Google celebrates at developer conferences the fact that Android is used by over half a million users, on hundreds of different devices, serviced by dozens of different networks. This ubiquity serves as evidence of Google openness: where Apple devices are few and costly, and restrictive in terms of their carriage by networks, Android devices are many, and their carriage is much more widely supported. Technical restrictions, therefore, do not police the ways in which users may manipulate software on an Android device.

However, Android's value in the profit chain, as with most of Google's product offerings, is as a vehicle for the production of trackable user engagement. The process of audience production includes the unique identification of the individuals whose interactions are being analyzed and whose attention is being sold. To this end, full Android functionality relies heavily on the use of a Google account. Nexus phones, for instance, require sign-in with a Google account for their purchase and activation. One must log in to the Android Market with a Google account even to see what apps are available. Contacts and calendars are by default referenced by Gmail accounts. Android "intents," which allow for fast and intuitive communication between Google products like Maps, or the Chrome web browser, and the Android device, are all mediated through a user's account.[14]

Thus, while Google positions Android as an open alternative to Apple's closed system, it also very carefully crafts the Android user's experience to engage with and amplify Google's most profitable venture (i.e., the definition of audience and its delivery to advertisers). The resources available to Android users—Android SDK, the Eclipse IDE, collaborative development platforms like Google Code—may encourage a more decentralized and "independent" form of software development, just as the availability of Google services like YouTube to amateur content producers can be seen to change the structure and dynamics of cultural production more generally. Yet this availability to DIY is structured in accordance with Google's profit orientation, just as it is with Apple's less "open" products.

Conclusion: Same as the Old Boss?

The dominance of two brands in bringing these possibilities of decentralized, nonnormative cultural production to a general population of users is cause to temper, or at least reevaluate, any celebration of a new day for "making," for social or new media-based cultural production and engagement in general. Indeed, the underlying profit motivation of these companies' support for DIY suggests that customization—of apps, of handsets, of knowledge—will occur only insofar as it is profitable. Within Apple's paradigm, this suggests a popular, culturally "safe" product that resonates with the Apple brand. Google's clients—advertisers—are interested in genres, brands, and predictable populations, not in bespoke applications or entertainments. They do not wish to capture the attention of lots of individuals, but the zeitgeist. Thus, in either case, advertisers and the culture industry will do their best to ensure that the cloud is instrumental in producing distributed, branded pop culture. Individuals will be addressed as interactive consumers, communities as fans and audiences.

There are, of course, new opportunities present within new media and new technologies for novel and nonnormative forms of cultural and political engagement. Our fear, however, is that these will remain relegated to the margins of mass culture—to those with the technological savvy to root or otherwise manipulate their devices at a basic level, to those sufficiently "connected" to find alternatives to the activities and forms of engagement sanctioned by their devices and the companies whose products and services animate them. The default means of DIY production, the easy way, will always incorporate not only "do-it-yourself" but "do-it-for-them."

Notes

1. Gillespie 2006.

2. Apple 2010b.

3. Apple 2010a.

4. Apple 2011.

5. Apple Developer 2011.

6. Iyer and Davenport 2008.

7. Levy 2009.

8. Evans 2011.

9. The Register of Copyrights 2010.

10. iPhone Developer Program License Agreement 2010, sec. 6.2, p. 7.

11. Ibid., 9.

12. Smythe 1977.

13. Google Developers 2010.

14. Ibid.

References

Apple. 2010a. iTunes store tops 10 billion songs sold. http://www.apple.com/ca/pr/library/2010/02/25iTunes-Store-Tops-10-Billion-Songs-Sold.html/.

Apple. 2010b. Apple reports third quarter results. http://www.apple.com/pr/library/2010/07/20Apple-Reports-Third-Quarter-Results.html.

Apple. 2011. Apple's App Store downloads top 15 billion. http://www.apple.com/pr/library/2011/07/07Apples-App-Store-Downloads-Top-15-Billion.html.

Apple Developer. 2011. Start developing iPad apps. https://developer.apple.com/ipad/sdk/.

Evans, J. 2011. What app developers want: Letters to Steve Jobs and Larry Page. *Tech Crunch*, April 16. http://techcrunch.com/2011/04/16/what-app-developers-want/.

Gillespie, T. 2006. Designed to "effectively frustrate": Copyright, technology and the agency of users. *New Media & Society* 8 (4): 651–669.

Google Developers. 2010. Google I/O 2010—Keynote day 2, Android demo, pt. 1. YouTube, May 20. http://youtu.be/89xc_1Vv69k.

iPhone Developer Program License Agreement. 2010. Program agreement. http://www.eff.org/files/20100302_iphone_dev_agr.pdf.

Iyer, B., and T. H. Davenport. 2008. Reverse engineering Google's Innovation Machine. *Harvard Business Review* (April): 59–68.

Levy, S. 2009. The secret of Googlenomics: Data-fueled recipe brews profitability. *Wired*. http://www.wired.com/culture/culturereviews/magazine/17-06/nep_googlenomics?currentPage=all.

The Register of Copyrights. 2010. Recommendation on the register of copyrights, June 11, 2010, p. 78. http://www.copyright.gov/1201/2010/initialed-registers-recommendation-june-11-2010.pdf .

Smythe, D. W. 1977. Communications: Blindspot of Western Marxism. *Canadian Journal of Political and Social Theory* 1 (3): 1–27.

19 Citizen Innovation: *Active*Energy and the Quest for Sustainable Design

Ann Light

Introduction

*Active*Energy is a hybrid; it represents several incarnations of a community project that is seeking social change through the high-profile design of eco-technologies by ordinary citizens with a range of engineering skills. It began as a research project, which, far from ending when the funding ran out, instead gained new adherents and new pots of money. Beyond the constant involvement of the Geezers, a group of elderly East End Londoners setting the direction of travel, and artist Loraine Leeson, providing creative leadership and facilitation, it has included work with an art gallery, a couple of charities, a secondary school, a barge-based restaurant, and a social housing association, and it has drawn in several professional engineers as well as further academics. As an example of a group of people attempting to make change in the world through designing and making, it is both typical and atypical, and, as such, characteristic of the diversity of DIY projects that reach beyond using practical skills to producing social outcomes. Its colorfulness makes it a good story, and we use it here to raise some issues that bedevil any attempt to work outside the mainstream but nonetheless impact upon it.

*Active*Energy has three ambitions: the engineering target of designing and making a turbine for use in the River Thames to generate renewable energy; the civic goal of reminding the country that there are "lost" technologies that might serve the environment well; and the social aim of showing what bored older people can do if they put their minds to it. Its roots can be traced to 2007, when a research team at the University of London, England, met a community group of older men called the Geezers, and, in the intervening years, it has become a voluntary activity, with a diverse range of adherents. (For instance, the author is still involved, principally in spotting funding opportunities and helping write applications, though no longer working in London.) Although the work is not overtly political,

*Active*Energy is interesting, both for what the Geezers have achieved by working together and for what they represent. The early days have been covered before (see Light et al. 2009; Light 2009), so this chapter includes only a brief overview of those stages before a look at recent *Active*Energy making activities as exemplary of DIY citizenship.

Early Days

Democratising Technology (DemTech; www.demtech.qmul.ac.uk) was a UK research project conceived by the author that involved a number of community groups to ask whether together we could produce a generative, open-ended form of engagement with digital technology and bring it to bear on the design of our society and tools. Led and informed by the practice of performance artist Lois Weaver, it worked with participants' values and aspirations for the future, using performance development methods as a transformational tool to produce a workshop of techniques (see Light 2011). The project ran for eighteen months from 2007 to 2008 and included a series of events, in particular an exhibition, *The Not Quite Yet*, at which several artworks based on the workshop research were shown, and a summative public symposium "On the Margins of Technology," a day of presentations and debate about the potential of technology for expanding and diversifying participation in society, with an emphasis upon participation and older people. As such, DemTech was intended to link notions of citizenship, democracy, and design. It used codesign methodologies and performance theory on changing behavior through deliberate engagement (O'Neill 1977; Boal 1979; Weaver 2007).

Running alongside Sennett's pronouncement that "making is thinking" (2008, ix) and Ratto's "Critical Making" (2011), DemTech used making as a means of engaging with and reflecting on complex issues (Weaver 2007). But it did not seek to equip older people with technical skills. Instead, it treated participants as experts on life experience, social relations, and the ethics of technology. By doing making (and participants made everything from paper objects to future personas), our purpose was stimulate an awareness of (and interest in) the designed nature of technology, and a willingness to engage in design decisions for its future, rather than create new designers or design new tools. Focal questions were person-centered: What do I want our world to be like? How might I link the things that matter to me so that I am happy, stimulated, and well-supported? In this sense, it was both a DIY citizenship and a reflective making project.

The Geezers are one of five groups of older people involved in DemTech. The Geezers meet at lunchtime on Tuesdays in a community hall in east London, part of an initiative to provide an alternative to the pub and the betting shop (Ray Gipson, pers. comm.). A fairly constant group of nine men participated at that time. The men ranged from their mid-sixties to their early eighties in age, with varied life experience, though most had left school at fourteen and spent their working days in skilled manual labor. For instance, Ted Lewis had been a boxer, then worked as a market porter most of his life; there were electricians and engineers, and several had had some involvement with the local docks. As I talked to them, it became apparent that their use of digital technology was typical for their age group (Dutton and Blank 2011): many of them were not Internet users and had little exposure to recent developments in information and communications technology (ICT). Memories of their youth were strong, coloring how they understood technology and especially what they expected the future to hold. The men told tales of saving for their first bike, machinery they had used on the docks, and their experience of the London Blitz (1940–1941). When we made up potential technologies, the men's inventions ranged from a teleporting device to magic money to a virtual holiday.

This, then, was the Geezers' first encounter with DemTech. But after they agreed to collaborate with Loraine Leeson, an artist commissioned to produce work for the project exhibition, their interest shifted to practical examples of design and a desire to make real change. The concern they had shown in the development workshops for environmental issues and their long experience of working with their hands came together in wanting to contribute a useful idea. To do so, they drew on memories of "lost" technologies. "In our living memories tidal technologies have been developed, but then set aside in favor of wind farms. Now the threat of nuclear energy is on the agenda again. We think it is time to let the Thames power London and we, the Geezers, supported by Leeson and others, intend to make it happen," read the exhibition program. They began to research water turbine design.

The first iteration of this work culminated in material for the exhibition. SPACE, a gallery in north-east London, was home to *GeezerPower* in early 2008. Leeson, the artist, projected a video of interviews with the Geezers along with her visualization of their idea for water turbines built into the Thames flood barrier. Speaking at the symposium, Lewis explained he had asked his wife to teach him to use the Internet so that he could find turbine manufacturers and their products.

Developments, Achievements . . .

Following *GeezerPower*, the Geezers became consumed by the quest to find a viable new source of power. Trips to meet turbine manufacturers and talk to engineers revealed that water turbine design had not progressed significantly in fifty years. Investigating the technology became the driver for reflecting on the politics of subsidy and the nation's research priorities. Several types of air and water turbines were sketched and discussed within the group, which, during this period, expanded to fourteen club members. But the next years were a struggle to move the project forward, keep all interested members of the community group active, and ensure that Leeson was sufficiently funded to act as a regular steward to the project.

A core group of Geezers continued their investigation into making an actual turbine. They held meetings with a range of organizations, including their local enterprise center and engineers at the University of East London. Leeson helped them to apply for grant money to continue their activities, winning £2000 from the UK's Comic Relief charity and involving engineers from the University of East London. With further funding raised by SPACE's community outreach staff, the team then developed *Active*Energy, a project that took the Geezers into nearby Bow Boys School to share ideas. Through a series of workshops led by another key player, local research engineer Toby Borland, the Geezers acted as mentors to young students and helped them evolve designs for wind turbines. One of these became the basis for a temporary public self-driven light work on the Age UK building where the Geezers regularly met, while the men tested prototypes of water turbines at the university facilities. Materials for a school education pack were conceived (but as yet are undeveloped). To quote SPACE:

> *Active*Energy took an inter-generational approach to a number of key issues facing local communities in one of London's poorest boroughs. . . . The boys were intrigued to hear about the past professional occupations of some of the senior men, especially those who worked in engineering. One of the boys thought that the Geezers were very different from other older people they knew, "because they are smarter and more expert" and because "they bother coming to speak to us." (SPACE 2010)

Leeson, reflecting on her involvement, could see value in a project that was neither solely art nor science and technology; neither wholly enterprise nor hobby:

> The artistic process retains the freedom to support and nurture the amalgamation of disparate ideas without rupturing the structure of the overarching concept. However these are also the limits of participatory art. It has the power to draw attention

to issues and mobilise public opinion—it can produce the means but not the hard outputs required for change. Art is able to identify, clarify, consolidate and celebrate, though collaboration is required with other disciplines and agencies so that shifts in ideas may be enacted. For my practice *Active*Energy represents a significant point of such convergence. (Leeson, pers. comm.)

Local press coverage grew into national coverage (Jeory 2011).

. . . and Obstacles

In 2010, an opportunity arose that would enable the Geezers to develop one of their designs for use on a restaurant barge in the river at Westminster, central London. It would power a lightwork carrying a strongly worded environmental message—a very embodied form of social media. (The barge stands just outside the UK's parliament, so the statement is potentially in breach of the legislation that keeps all demonstrations at arm's length.) It would be both a creative and a political act, with the intention of raising the profile of the technology and the need for creative thinking around energy production and consumption.

However, nothing has progressed. Funding, even for materials, specialist engineering work, and transport, has been hard to come by. Despite national and international interest in renewable energy sources and in provoking reflection on people's consumption patterns, the Geezers have not found the resources they need—either to test their approach or stir up interest in the area—after numerous applications to funding bodies. Interestingly, they continue to be best supported by arts funding as an example of socially engaged art practice, rather than as people taking initiative to improve their lives and those of the people around them.

Many paths exist to innovate commercially, but that is not a route open to the Geezers as constituted. Their status as pensioners, as amateurs and as a community group removes them from consideration for normal sources of business funding and throws them on public grants or charity. They could, for instance, apply for money to invest in solar panels with the local social housing association, but this would be to meet others' agendas not to develop their own mechanisms for generating electricity.

At present, the group occupies the space of hobbyists and fans who do their work as a pastime and expect to pay as they go. Although amateur designers are not unknown, and von Hippel (1986) documents the symbiotic relationship between lead users whose innovations fuel design evolution and the companies supplying their equipment, their existence is largely unrecognized and unsupported, or seen as a quaint inheritance from the gentleman scientists, such as Lavoisier and Darwin, who used a private income to develop their interests.[1] (Clearly, potential exists for new mechanisms to encourage other-than-commercial enterprise.)

Part of the problem is the project's hybridity. Why fund a group of unaffiliated working-class pensioners using arts to ask technological questions? The Geezers are not traditional experts, despite their increasing knowledge as laypersons of the costs and opportunities of using turbines and tidal power. They are not the stuff of "public engagement" projects, since most of these—as conceived in British research—involve bringing the public to see what scientists are doing to overcome public resistance to innovation. Public engagement is not about the practices of doing-it-yourself.

The men are charming, and they can market their novelty factor. For this reason, businesses have been approached to see if they would like to sponsor these charismatic ambassadors for social change, but that would be selling personalities rather than people conducting innovation as a legitimate social activity. It risks exploitation of people, not ideas. It encourages us to see them as something extraordinary, rather than harnessing everyday ingenuity to creative ends.

In sum, the Geezers and their supporters have explored the traditional structures through which innovation is promoted and found no obvious means to do-it-yourself as *makers* without also doing-it-yourself as funders. They can talk about innovation, and make plans and models, but, without several thousand pounds, they cannot push their activities to the level where they might have real purchase on an issue. In this way, they demonstrate the material nature of participation by exposing its material limits. This is frustrating because, unlike hobbies that fulfill in the doing of them, innovation (or even the demonstration that a space exists in which to innovate) requires an impact on some external reality, and engineering has material costs associated with it.

Who Is the DIY Citizen?

The Geezers are not overtly political; many shades of opinion can be found in their midst. At a recent get-together, Gipson and Lewis could be heard commenting, with slight irony, on the Geezers as a model for the UK's Big Society agenda (which is encouraging localism and the devolution of much civic responsibility to community level), so certainly some of them are aware of their standing with respect to current political trends.

They are also aware of themselves as having responsibilities and a *duty* to others. Gibson was a councillor in London. Others have been involved in education programs before, and the intergenerational work was motivated by the opportunity for active contribution as well as a desire to push on with design work. Their concern for the environment and to harness skills to make a difference seems motivated by disinterested citizenship. They are expressing themselves through making, through design and engineering. While this may not be "critical" making activity in the sense that *critical theory* might reference, they are taking a productively critical line with existing energy-generating activity by proposing alternative forms. They are, one might say, criticizing production by example. And, leading by example, they are nurturing awareness of sustainability issues through the vehicle of making. Both their own and others' consciousness of the need for radical energy solutions becomes embodied and developed in the act of making and seeking to make change. All this they know and see as valuable in the world around them.

The men talk of these communal values, where active citizenship is juxtaposed with consumerism and individualism, if not in these terms, then in terms with a similar implication. If we look at them as citizens, then it is very much as people of a mind to help their neighbors, take an interest in local dynamics, and solve greater-than-self crises (Crompton 2010). Such values are often attributed to their generation and their origins: people growing up during a world war in the East End of London, where poverty, migration, and ambition met in a form that suggested the way forward was to help each other. Staying, rather than moving to the suburbs, the men exhibit what is colloquially known as "East End spirit." They are also retired men who have seen their children grow and whose principal means of expression, work, is no longer available to them in its traditional form. (Indeed, when DemTech first convened, we were shocked by how disconnected our groups of older people had become from public life. We conceived of peer motivators to inspire those older people who, having left school at fourteen and been penalized by lack of choice, now sit idle, their potential unfulfilled. Are the Geezers, having been inspired, able to inspire others? And what would it take to position them in this way?)

We observe the frustration of the original group. Time is literally running out for some of the Geezers. When Leeson, Borland, and I visit, we hear news of funerals, hospital visits, and operations, as well as progress. It makes contact increasingly poignant.

As well as looking at the core group's characteristics, we must also question the role of the supporting team—artists, engineers, community developers, businessmen, researchers. Are we there because we feel kinship with the endeavor and admiration for the initiative—and are we thus part of what the men have achieved in assembling tools and knowledge? Or are we the impetus that keeps this project alive in the minds of a community group with other endeavors and Bingo on several Tuesdays a year? Both, probably. We account for the number of funding bids written and submitted. So, we have provided strong stewardship in that sense at least.

This throws attention on the skills base. Participation in the project is somewhat arbitrary, as it is with many amateur undertakings. People are not chosen to fit roles. The people in the community group are the people that joined it.

Conclusion

This book addresses two themes: DIY citizenship and creating as a critical act. The project described here began as an opportunity for codesign—to develop methods for engaging people marginalized by digital tools in discussions about the future of networked technology—and grew into a story of *citizen innovation* realized through participatory art practice, of people taking their ideas out of the speculative world of pub chat and into the minibus to do research and make concepts a reality. The work is an exemplar of citizens' creative and critical technical practice, motivated by passionate enquiry and community values, not commercial gain. Apart from any delight we can take in the initiative, this is a useful example of the hybrid space in which DIY citizenship finds itself: at once productive and resistant to dominant modes of production; involving innovation in a shape that is unsupported by traditional forms of economic infrastructure (though possibly sustainable through newer forms like crowdfunding, successor to the public subscription systems that supported libraries and other past social innovations); drawing on lay insights and potentially crossing multiple categories of societal organization—in this case, art, technology, business, energy consumption, consumer behavior, marketing, and community action.

The Geezers acted because it was more fun than sitting around as many retired people do. Their activities evolved out of the DemTech project but grew their own flavor as the men found congruent values, built their confidence, and made use of Leeson's sure-handed facilitation. DemTech sought to show there are means of engaging (older) people and involving them in complex design decisions even before plans exist. The Geezers more than proved that point.

But the story opens wider questions. If we want citizen innovation, what do the innovators need in terms of structure to sustain vision and ambition?

We saw the crucial role of good stewardship. We encountered the challenge of identifying a funding model. We still need to analyze further the social and technical ingredients of the enterprise to understand where its endurance comes from (Light et al. 2009), but the desire to do good is a striking feature. What this "good" may be is never simple. However, though community-oriented sociotechnical projects like this may struggle with the means to act, in choosing to *make* something (especially something iconic), they are able to focus their actions in a way that is both meaningful and bonding.

Acknowledgments

UK's AHRC and EPSRC for funding DemTech, and coresearchers Lois Weaver, Gini Simpson, and Pat Healey; Loraine Leeson for her creative leadership and facilitation of the *Active*Energy project; Toby Borland, Stephen Dodds, and Darryl Newport for their engineering and advice; Fiona Fieber of SPACE; and all the Geezers, especially Ray Gipson and Ted Lewis.

Note

1. The term "gentleman scientist" is clearly gendered, as reflects the main period of its use. But, although the participants discussed are male, the arguments apply, if anything more significantly, to women.

References

Boal, Agosto. 1979. *Theatre of the Oppressed*. London: Pluto Press.

Crompton, Tom. 2010. *Common Cause: The Case for Working with Our Cultural Values*. London: WWF-UK.

Dutton, William H., and G. Blank. 2011. *Next Generation Users: The Internet in Britain. Oxford Internet Survey 2011*. Oxford, UK: Oxford Internet Institute, University of Oxford.

Jeory, Ted. 2011. *The Geezers: We Won't Grow Old Gracefully. Sunday Express*, January 9. http://www.express.co.uk/posts/view/222061/The-Geezers-We-won-t-grow-old-gracefully.

Light, Ann. 2009. Democratising Technology: A Method. In *Designing for the 21st Century: Interdisciplinary Methods and Findings*, ed. Thomas Inns, 132–145. Gower, UK: Ashgate Publishing.

Light, Ann. 2011. "Democratising Technology: Inspiring Transformation with Design, Performance and Props." *Proc. CHI 2011*.

Light, Ann, Gini Simpson, Lois Weaver, and Pat Healey. 2009. Geezers, Turbines, Fantasy Personas: Making the Everyday into the Future. *Proc. Creativity and Cognition.*

O'Neill, Cecily. 1977. *Drama Structures*. Portsmouth, NH: Heinemann.

Ratto, Matt. 2011. Critical Making: Conceptual and Material Studies in Technology and Social Life. *Information Society* 27 (4): 252–260.

Sennett, Richard. 2008. *The Craftsman*. New Haven, CT: Yale University Press.

SPACE. 2010. *Active*Energy Report 2010. http://www.spacestudios.org.uk/media/uploads/2011/03/2851/activeenergy-report-2010-pdf.pdf.

von Hippel, Eric. 1986. Lead Users: A Source of Novel Product Concepts. *Management Science* 32 (7): 791–805.

Weaver, Lois. 2007. Make Something: A Manifesto for Making Performance about Making Change. In *Performing Global Feminisms*, ed. Elaine Aston and Sue-Ellen Case, 174–183. Basingstoke, UK: Palgrave Macmillan.

20 *Le Champ des Possibles*—The Field of Possibilities

Owen McSwiney and Emily Rose Michaud

Introduction

Les Amis du Champ des Possibles is a Montreal-based nonprofit group whose ambition is to preserve an urban green space as a community park and urban biodiversity reserve. The three-acre site is located in the Mile End district, which contains the smallest percentage of green space of all Montreal's Plateau-Mont-Royal districts. The city purchased the site from Canadian Pacific Railway in June 2009. The Mile End is undergoing substantial gentrification, and due to the site's proximity to the district's cultural and economic hub, it has been earmarked for development. Negotiations are currently ongoing[1] between Canadian Pacific Railway and Montreal city officials regarding the provision of a bicycle and pedestrian level crossing at the northern edge of the site. If this proposal is accepted, the site's location would assume a strategic importance as a gateway to and a first impression of the Plateau borough.

The following discussion describes the project of Le Champ des Possibles from its inception to the present. The intention is that in describing the particular intricacies of the community group's approach as well as of the field, the project may set an example and offer encouragement to other similar civic engagement initiatives.

Essentially, Les Amis reinforces the importance of the commons.[2] Active since 2007, our group promotes participatory processes, artistic practices, recreational activities, educational walks, scientific research; and public dialogue about how the space is perceived and interacted with. By engaging in concrete gestures with the space, we influence decisions regarding our neighborhood's future.

True democratic process and participatory politics can be complex—collaboration is key and compromises must be made. City officials are seldom connected to the ground-level needs of a neighborhood, and so, empowering neighborhood committees to take a lead is the first step. Significant talent, skills, knowledge, and social expertise are ready to be mobilized if city administrators are willing to engage, collaborate, and invest, thus enabling a win-win situation. Citizens can collaborate within the social landscape to create and implement the content and programming necessary for their community. By incorporating the opinions of a community, reflexive change can take place. Physical gathering is also essential to success. Face-to-face encounters, forums, and events have played a big role in the success of Les Amis du Champ des Possibles and have been instrumental in mobilizing the project.

From Freight Yard to Urban Meadow

Historical remnants play a vital role in a community's evolution. From these we learn about the past, which influences our decisions about the future. Le Champ des Possibles was the industrial heart of the Mile End district. In 1876 an additional train line was required to link Montreal's expanding port to the continent's rail network. Montreal is located on an island, and spatial constrictions between the island's edge and the central mountain informed the decision to loop the new train route—with its associated industrial fringe—around the city to enclose the Plateau borough.

In 1896 the Carmelite religious order built a convent adjacent to the train tracks. At this time, the site was relatively isolated from the city. Their presence alongside the site continues to this day. In 1910 the Saint-Louis freight yard was opened. It attracted industry as it provided a direct link between local businesses and continental markets. It stimulated the local economy and was a major factor in the district's growth. From 1950 to 1975, several giant textile factories were built and these industrial developments attracted large numbers of workers and accompanying services to the district. Therefore, the original decision to locate the freight yard in this district resulted in the Mile End developing into an urban nucleus.

Today, the site could be perceived as a microcosm of the district's evolution. Several elements in this informal open air museum testify to the site's previous industrial function. These include crumbling loading docks, buried train tracks, and buildings that curve in response to subsequently dismantled train lines. The respectful conservation of these remaining artifacts is fundamental in ensuring that the fascinating story of the evolution and life of this place is still apparent to visitors and that the district's industrial heart is appropriately acknowledged and reimagined as its present-day community heart.

Biodiversity in an Urban Setting

Since the closure of the freight yard in the mid-1980s, the field has been left to develop unhindered; it now possesses enormous biodiversity. The biodiversity present is site-specific and in dialogue with its industrial and cultural surroundings, as nature gradually reappropriates the space using whatever means it can. Seeds have train-hopped here from all over the North American continent. The wind, birds, animals, and humans have each brought seeds, and the space is now home to an astounding number of plant and animal species. This array of indigenous and introduced species is a vibrant botanical reflection of Montreal's diverse demography.

Les Amis du Champ des Possibles seeks to establish an urban biodiversity reserve and promote critical reflection on the relationship among humans, urban development, and urban biodiversity. According to Roger Latour (2012), urban botanist and founding member of Les Amis:

> An Urban Biodiversity Reserve is the ecological transformation of post-industrial or residual spaces into rich biodiversity habitats. This is achieved by the diversification of the topography (making water holes, ditches, hillocks, rock piles, etc.) and the introduction of plant species (enrichment). The choice of plant species is made according to their ecological value, human preference is not considered. The landscaping is based on what spontaneous processes have established, aesthetics being irrelevant. Such a space could be viewed as an assisted and accelerated product of a given space's biological potential.

The proposed reserve is considered in a larger geographic context as an important link along the train tracks in the city's network of biocorridors.[3] These biocorridors allow wildlife to permeate and to establish itself within the broader cityscape. "For the purpose of allowing biodiversity in the city, it is the most efficient use of the limited space available" (Latour 2012). The introduction of fruit-producing plant species would attract and sustain more bird, animal, and insect life. This in turn has the potential to create a rich playground for study—from individual visits to school field trips. Again, Latour (2012) reiterates that an urban biodiversity reserve "is a collaborative work between us, our history and spontaneous biological processes." Le Champ des Possibles is the meeting place for such collaboration.

The Roerich Garden Project

Several artists have intervened to create integrated site-specific works in the open-air studio and informal exhibition space that is the field. Some of the first documented actions that engaged with the field creatively and documented the reclamation of a public space in the face of looming development included the Roerich Garden Project and the Sprout Out Loud Guerilla Gardeners' Ensemble.

The Roerich Garden was created in 2007 as a living landmark to pay homage to this threatened green space. It drew attention to the city's plans and provoked dialogue about the many ways the community used and interacted with the field. It provided a forum to gather and to valorize the field before it was forgotten in silence. The Roerich symbol is the cultural equivalent of the Red Cross. Its three circles are said to represent art, science, and religion. Russian artist and cultural activist Nicholas Roerich developed it as an internationally recognized symbol to protect historical, cultural, and scientifically valuable monuments. Intended to prevent aerial bombing in World War II Europe, it was installed on the rooftops of museums, churches, and universities.

The gardeners' ensemble Sprout Out Loud occupied the southern section of the field from 2008 until 2010. Through their collaborative seed exchanges, planting sessions, and maintenance of the Roerich Garden, they explored concepts of public space and sought to encourage the relationship between urban dwellers and the land around them. Their goals included (1) stimulating citizen engagement and provoking dialogue regarding the importance of the commons through workshops and community events, (2) engaging with the field to document how people used and cared for the space, and (3) empowering people and inviting them to plant similar ideas in their own environments where needed.

In 2008, an initiative to document the Roerich Garden Project was launched in collaboration with Artefatica,[4] a local open publishing project. Over the span of three years, members of Les Amis and Artefatica collected stories from more than forty contributors about the space's history, uses, and potential. The result—an online book at roerichproject.artefatica—brings together texts, photos, news clippings, and archival materials, as well as examples of similar international precedents.

Les Amis du Champ des Possibles

The intention to formally protect the field as a community-appropriated space began in 2008, when the city announced the first phase of development of the Saint-Viateur East sector. Our political relationship with the borough's officials grew from several existing activities: guided botanical and historical walks, seasonal garbage cleanups, and the continued maintenance of the Roerich Garden. Over a couple of years, substantial media and political attention was garnered. One of the most notable formalized events was a citizen's forum organized by the Mile End Citizens' Committee in 2009, which was attended by over two hundred people. It featured a public lecture series centered on issues affected by development plans for the Saint-Viateur East sector. Among the topics tabled concerning the city's $9 million makeover of the neighborhood, concerns emerged around the acquisition of the field by the city and their proposed construction of a holding lot for city maintenance vehicles. Resistance to this drastic alteration concentrated the efforts of our group. The proposed redevelopment of the site provided the impetus for the community to develop an alternative proposal. In reacting to the city's redevelopment plan, community members were forced to ask themselves what they thought about the future of the site.

The Mile End Citizens' Committee mandated a subcommittee to explore alternative options that would better incorporate the local community's concerns and ideas. Le Champ des Possibles includes members from a variety of disciplines including biology, horticulture, design, architecture, urbanism, landscaping, science, art, journalism, and photography. Each background contributes to enriching the foundation of a well-grounded perspective. Civic engagement is most effective when it is most accessible to the broadest general public—an example being citizens' ideas explored through design charrettes.[5] In the fall of 2010, Les Amis became a nonprofit organization whose objective was to liaise with the borough representatives and city officials, to better communicate the local population's concerns and suggestions.

Activities and Strategies

Les Amis also facilitates knowledge exchange through educational activities. The popularity of guided visits by the local historical group, Mile End Memories, proves that the community is curious about its heritage. Keen public participation in ecologists' biodiversity tours demonstrates the educational potential of the field as a rare place for discovering biological and botanical phenomenon within an urban setting. Les Amis also organizes community cleaning days to maintain the site. The fact that the site has been adopted by people is palpable. It is a loved place, a citizen-approved place. Spontaneous declarations of affection for this place occur often through acts of creation, celebration, and memory making. However, if involvement feels like a burden, duty, or chore, it may never have lasting impact and burnout becomes inevitable. If engagement happens spontaneously and encourages genuine community participation, it will grow organically and be more likely to endure. These activities are important for other reasons too. As well as serving practical functions, the educational and cultural activities are also important as a means of countering negative perception regarding the site and issues such as fires, vandalism, broken beer bottles, strewn garbage, and graffiti. Such instances provide authorities with an excuse to assert their power. Community activities mitigate a developers' option of unfairly justifying detrimental decisions by falsely arguing that the space is unused or unsafe.

For instance, the need for vigilance was underscored by a recent event. The demolition of a building that afforded artists the opportunity to transmit public messages through graffiti could be likened to the cutting out of the community's tongue. This building was a colorful and dynamic forum whose rare curved form recalled the historic railway lines. Other means of on-site dialogue happen through the appropriation of the site's physical infrastructure. A local artistic group, Les Filles Anonymes, staged a colorful protest in their 2009 series *Actions Roses.* They highlighted the questionable illegality of pedestrians crossing the train tracks through a series of transient messages woven with fluorescent pink ribbon into the wire fence bordering the train tracks.

Reconnection

In his book *The Anesthetics of Architecture,* Neil Leach states: "The modern metropolitan individual has to develop a defense mechanism against the over stimulation of mental life in the city . . . We under react to form a defensive cocoon" (Leach 1999, 34–35). In addition to their usual functions, our senses operate as protection mechanisms in an urban setting to subconsciously filter out our immediate surroundings. This editing gradually results in a numbing of the senses, a degree of detachment as we tune out of our immediate physical environment, and a general reduction in civic engagement.

The wild space of Le Champ des Possibles provides visitors with an opportunity to reopen their senses of perception. It addresses a fundamental human need to reconnect to natural phenomena and cycles. The freedom found in wild spaces such as these plays an important role in the cultural vibrancy of a neighborhood. The project was founded on the conviction that recuperation, revitalization, and creative expression are essential to individual well-being and to the improvement of the wider urban environment.

The physical appearance of the site has come into being through a chain of aesthetically unbiased decisions and events: from its geographic origins through periods of industry and abandonment to a subsequent return to nature. Instead of aesthetics, decisions were based on the laws of science, industry, and nature. No preconceived models influence how a visitor is expected to feel or behave in this unregulated and ambiguous space. Instead, individuals create their own rules. This type of refreshingly raw and beautiful landscape is incredibly valuable to any city, whose urban design is typically determined by rules of commerce, fashion, efficiency, or prestige.

The idea of creating a nature reserve is interesting because it enables unpredictable results to flourish. As William Cronon (1995) says, "What I celebrate even more is that they (wildernesses) remind us of the wildness in our own backyards, or the nature that is all around us if only we have eyes to see it" (n.p.)

Interpretive signage could be perceived as a first step toward determining how an individual might experience and consider the space. We argue that the site's dubious *wild state* is justifiably compromised in exchange for a better overall chance of surviving the imminent threat posed by redevelopment projects. Minimal interventions, described in what follows, are proposed to encourage the public to use the space. This use may in turn lead to a strengthened sense of appreciation, so as to encourage future citizen guardianship.

Nearby is an example of another project that vindicates this strategy. The Twilight Sculpture Garden currently exhibits fifty-two metal works by sculptor Glen LeMesurier. It has undergone several transformations since 1997 due to vandalism and threats of sale. LeMesurier's garden provides an excellent example of how continued physical presence and on-site response can successfully demonstrate—to both the general public and city officials—the effectiveness of creative intervention and its role in shaping urban development.

Design Methodology and Proposal

Les Amis du Champ des Possibles proposed that the site be split into two areas: the northern section protected as an urban biodiversity reserve and the southern section zoned for public activity. The proposal addresses visitors' basic requirements, while educating them about the site. Services might include paths and lighting for safe pedestrian passage; garbage bins and composting for maintenance; and robust multifunctional furniture for rest, play, and events. To counter the paradox of development for conservation, a flexible and sustainable approach would need to be employed. Adopting the concept of community empowerment, prototypical structures would be built by voluntary semiskilled laborers, working with members of the local crafts industry. This process would discriminate in favor of indigenous skills. Using locally recycled materials would add an intrinsic quality to the project. By relying on adaptable construction systems, the community would be empowered to implement future change when deemed appropriate.

The design process involved an analysis of the physical parameters of the site that influenced a visitor's physiological senses. This resulted in a series of drawings describing a range of factors such as history, natural environment, circulation, human activity, and soil quality. A comprehensive photographic study was also undertaken. This method tested an alternative springboard for initiating a design process. It started with the emotional, the inherent, essence of the place and allowed it to inform design decisions from the bottom up. The appropriation of analytical methodologies from various disciplines was useful in establishing a wider perception of the site's context. Historical references and maps were used to imagine the landscape's various past appearances. Geographic, social, and cultural research helped to better understand the forces acting throughout the site and the complex interrelationships between these various strands. Instead of applying a generic cosmetic style to the site, our ambition was to incrementally uncover, analyze, and exhibit the accumulated remnants still present onsite. Interpretive signage would subtly inform visitors about these intricacies. Similar to a project by landscape artist Mary Miss, the counterpoint between the new elements and the existing site conditions would concentrate one's focus on particular details, while simultaneously enabling a broader comprehension of the whole environment.

A staff of local artists, botanists, and educators, supported by local volunteers, could manage care of the field and its facilities. By keeping it local, relying on the skills and resources of the immediate community, the city's budget is inevitably reduced and citizens are given a role in the shaping of their neighborhood. The city could appoint citizens as stewards of the space, or a partnership could be formed. The staff and volunteers could continue to work in an independent grassroots manner, similar to how the legendary Liz Christy Garden began in Manhattan.[6]

Conclusion

City representatives and community members form a symbiotic relationship. Ultimately elected officials are accountable to taxpayers. Decision makers need the participatory voice of citizens to express and reiterate their opinions. Citizens have a social responsibility to make their voices heard. For a vibrant cultural city, communities need the support of open-minded politicians. We must continue to bridge the gaps in our social reality, because meaningful communication across different cultures, languages, and disciplines is essential to a participatory democracy. Quality of life will improve only if we strive to efface distinctions between identities or disciplines and work toward common values.

The commons has a social value that is far-reaching. Without physical places belonging to everyone, we diminish our ability to determine our collective values. We also need urban wilderness to observe the complexities of life in their many rhythms across the seasons. We need open spaces with fresh air and open skies with a view. We need light and the freedom to encounter strangers in surprising ways. We need time to allow our senses to open wide. For fruitful hands-on participation, we need to feel effective. To feel effective, we must influence the way our environments are planned, managed, and maintained through tangible gestures. Urban landscapes need to be revived as essential places of discussion and creation. Cities contain cultural diversity, critical mass, and incredible potential for citizens to organize. For civic participation to take root, citizens need face-to-face opportunities to reimagine their environments. Les Amis du Champ des Possibles exists because it fervently believes that cities need natural, subtle, ambiguous, and generous spaces—environments where people can gather, where the rules are undefined. These spaces are vitally important as they provide an opportunity to breathe and celebrate diversity.

In April 2012, the City of Montreal announced its intention to rezone Le Champ des Possibles as a park. In May 2013, the zoning was changed from industrial to park. This decision signified a positive landmark and was greatly appreciated by the group, city and borough officials, and the wider community. Although generally welcomed, the initial draft of the city's proposal seemed generic. A municipal park is not the vision of Les Amis, as a minimal intervention is the ideal we have been pushing for. A fine balance will need to be maintained between the preservation of this wild space and an overly manicured public park. Keeping the dialogue open and transparent is imperative. The city proposal, Projet Saint-Viateur Est (2012), must pay more attention to the site's various nuances in order to respectfully integrate itself. Despite the series of meetings between city officials and Les Amis, too few of our recommendations have been included so far. This oversight concerns us, considering the fact that our submission of community-derived requests and supporting documents contained professional research and proposals. It is certainly not an ideal world, but if we are to take progressive steps toward a truly democratic process, we must act on a municipal level. Authorities must realize that sometimes locals know best, and that most often a particular set of circumstances requires a subtle, tailored approach. Apparently, ongoing negotiations with the city will be crucial in order for us to reiterate our ambitions for the site.

Le Champ des Possibles (see figure 20.1) will continue to strive toward retaining its wild character through minimal intervention, promote urban biodiversity, and develop a customized approach to respectfully acknowledge the site's particular attributes. Although such an approach requires energy, perseverance, and a willingness to do things differently, an opportunity exists to create a fantastic new type of wild place that would have a hugely positive influence on the district and act as a model on a much larger scale.

Notes

Emily Rose Michaud and Owen McSwiney are both members of the group Les Amis du Champ des Possibles.

1. As of April 2012.

2. Three of the primary aspects that define a true commons: (i) they cannot be commodified; (ii) contrary to private property, the commons is inclusive as opposed to

Figure 20.1
Bing maps

exclusive; (iii) the commons must be preserved regardless of its return on capital. *Source:* Wikipedia.

3. Also known as a wildlife or green corridor, a biocorridor is an area of habitat connecting wildlife populations separated by human activities (roads, development, logging, train tracks, etc.) (Latour 2012).

4. See book with Artefatica at roerichproject.artefati.ca.

5. A design charrette is an intensive, hands-on workshop that brings people from different disciplines and backgrounds together to explore design options for a particular area or site (Latour 2012).

6. With the help of the neighborhood, the Liz Christy Garden was one in which a garbage-strewn lot was transformed—over several decades—into a city-approved public garden, expanding across an entire block of prime real estate at the corners of Bowery and Houston in New York City.

Bibliography

Articles/Chapters/Essays

Cronon, William. 1995. The Trouble with Wilderness; or, Getting Back to the Wrong Nature. In *Uncommon Ground: Rethinking the Human Place in Nature,* ed. William Cronon, 69–90. New York: W. W. Norton & Co.

Johnstone, Lesley. 1987. "Installation: Theory and history." MA diss., University of Montreal.

Pontbriand, Chantal. 2000. "The idea of community: An exchange with Jean-Luc Nancy." *Parachute,* no. 100 (June): 14–31.

Raymond, Anita. 2000–2001. "Leçon de jardinage: Christine Maigne." *Espace Sculpture Magazine,* no. 54 (Winter): 48.

Books

Foster, Steven, and James A. Duke. 2000. *A Field Guide to Medicinal Plants and Herbs of Eastern and Central North America.* 2nd ed. New York: Houghton Mifflin Company.

Grande, John K. 2004. *Art Nature Dialogues: Interviews with Environmental Artists.* New York: State University of New York Press.

Grande, John K. 2007. *Dialogues in Diversity: Art from Marginal to Mainstream.* Grosseto, Italy: Pari Publishing.

Latour, Roger. 2009. *La Guide de la flore urbaine.* Québec: Éditions Fides.

Leach, Neil. 1999. *The Anaesthetics of Architecture.* Cambridge, MA: MIT Press.

Rocca, Alessandro. 2007. *Natural Architecture*. New York: Princeton Architectural Press.

Rogat Loeb, Paul, ed. 2004. *The Impossible Will Take a Little While: A Citizen's Guide to Hope in a Time of Fear*. New York: Basic Books.

Smith, Keri. 2007. *The Guerilla Art Kit*. New York: Princeton Architectural Press.

Stamets, Paul. 2005. *Mycelium Running: How Mushrooms Can Help Save the World*. New York: Ten Speed Press, Random House.

Tiberghien, Gilles A. 1993. *Land Art*. Paris: Éditions Carré.

Tracey, David. 2007. *Guerilla Gardening: A Manualfesto*. Gabriola Island, BC: New Society Publishers.

Wallace, Brian. 1998. *Land and Environmental Art*. Ed. Jeffrey Kastner. London: Phaidon Press Ltd.

Course Packs

Jojich, Danica, ed. 2007. Sculpture and Material Practice (SCUL 210). Montreal, QC: Eastman Systems Inc. and COPIBEC.

Exhibition Catalogues

Clément, Gilles, and Philippe Rahm. 2006. *Manières d'agir pour demain: Environ(ne) ment: Approaches for Tomorrow*, ed. Giovanna Borasi. Milan, Italy: Skira Editore. Montreal, QC: Canadian Centre for Architecture.

Franceshini, Amy. 2008. *Victory Gardens 2007+*. San Francisco: Gallery 16 Editions.

Gooding, Mel, and William Furlong. 2002. *Song of the Earth*. London: Thames & Hudson Ltd.

Spaid, Sue. 2002. *Ecovention: Current Art to Transform Ecologies*. (Copublished by Ecoartspace, Greenmuseum, and The Contemporary Arts Center). Cincinnati: Seemless Design and Printing, LLC.

Email

Roger Latour. 2012. Email message with definition of urban biodiversity reserve, to E. R. Michaud, May 11.

Web Links (accessed June 19, 2013)

Amis du Champ des Possibles. http://amisduchamp.com.

Artefatica—Roerich Project. http://roerichproject.artefati.ca.

Emily Rose Michaud. http://emilyrosemichaud.com.

Roger Latour. http://www.floraurbana.blogspot.ca.

Projet Saint-Viateur Est. 2012. http://ville.montreal.qc.ca/pls/portal/docs/PAGE/ARROND_PMR_FR/MEDIA/DOCUMENTS/SAINT_VIATEUR_PORTES_OUVERTES_PANNEAUX.PDF.

21 Distributed Design: Media Technologies and the Architecture of Participation

Joel McKim

Despite the architectural origins of the term DIY—a shorthand description for "do-it-yourself" made popular during the home improvement craze of the 1950s—there are few fields as distant from the participatory ethos of a contemporary DIY movement. Expanded public involvement is seldom the focus of a domain shaped in large part by the decidedly undemocratic forces of expert knowledge, large-scale capital investment, and unilateral decision making. This hierarchical situation is, of course, not a new one for architecture; writing in the 1960s, the Dutch architect Aldo van Eyck deplored his profession's historical allegiance with "kings, popes and tyrants."[1] And, according to the design critic Deyan Sudjik, we must now add the urban developer to van Eyck's list of autocrats dictating the conditions through which the built environment comes into being.[2] Yet notwithstanding the discipline's sometimes suspect political and economic affiliations, a current of participatory architecture can be found within its history, developing particularly within the late modern period. This brief chapter will highlight, through two examples, the emergence of this egalitarian architectural tradition and consider whether a contemporary equivalent currently exists. More specifically, the chapter will question whether social media technologies, which have widened public involvement in so many other spheres of political and social life, have had a similar impact on urban design and planning. In the introduction to this volume, Matt Ratto and Megan Boler emphasize the importance of Jacques Rancière's notion of the "redistribution of the sensible," a breaking down of established systems of representation and the traditional allocation of roles and experiences, for our conceptions of DIY politics and creative work. Although Rancière seldom mentions architecture in his discussions of our current "aesthetic regime of art," the emergence of new distributed design possibilities suggests that the traditionally hierarchical discipline may now also belong to this "age when anyone and everyone is considered to be participating in the task of 'making' history."[3]

This short genealogy of participatory architecture begins in 1959, when Aldo van Eyck, a member of the young, rebellious Team 10 delegation, presented the Congrès Internationaux d'Architecture Moderne (CIAM) with a highly democratic notion of design, one that directly challenged the norms of modern architecture established by the old guard of the organization—figures such as Le Corbusier, Siegfried Gideon, and Walter Gropius. Disillusioned with the uniformity and standardization of postwar European architecture, van Eyck had begun to champion a form of humanistic modernism that would reconcile tradition and innovation, benefiting from technological advances while also drawing from the rich repository of cultural experience. Van Eyck's vision was encapsulated in a diagram entitled the "Otterlo Circles" (named after the location of the 1959 CIAM conference), composed of two circles set side by side, beneath the caption "By Us. For Us." In the first circle, corresponding to the realm of architecture, van Eyck placed visual icons depicting the three essential design traditions he sought to combine: the classical (represented by the Parthenon and signifying "immutability and rest"), the modern (represented by an architectural sketch by the De Stijl artist Theo van Doesburgh and signifying "change and movement"), and the traditional (represented by a diagram of a New Mexican Pueblo village and signifying "the vernacular of the heart").[4] In the second circle, corresponding to the space of human relations, van Eyck placed an image of Kayapó Indians of Brazil dancing in a circle, accompanied by the text "For each man and all men."

Explaining his inclusion of indigenous people and their collective constructions in his tri-part model for architecture, van Eyck commented, "So little attention is accorded to the creative potential of the countless millions and what they made for themselves through the ages in humble multiplicity."[5] Van Eyck translated his architectural philosophy, founded on relations of equality and vernacular knowledge, into his design practices, realizing such socially engaged projects as the insertion of hundreds of playgrounds into the battered postwar landscape of Amsterdam and the establishment in 1979 of the city's Hubertus House, a hostel for single parents and children. He eschewed the top-down, tabula rasa approach of much modern architecture in favor of a design practice attuned to already existing spatial interactions and committed to incorporating the habits and desires of eventual users whenever possible.

The student protests of May 1968 and the partial redistribution of power that followed in their wake produced a second important example of participatory architecture. During this turbulent year, the Catholic University of Leuven moved its medical faculty to a campus near Brussels and revealed plans to build a student center in the same mechanistic and repetitive style as the newly constructed hospital complex. The medical students rebelled against this bureaucratic approach and insisted on enlisting the architect Lucien Kroll, already known for his democratic design approach. Using a radically collaborative method involving highly customizable floor plans and constant input by clients and inhabitants, Kroll initiated an unprecedented experiment in the organic evolution of architectural form. He explains the motivations of the Maison Médicale project as an avoidance of "every kind of authoritarian imposition" and an attempt to seek out "the greatest possible differentiation, the avoidance of repetition, and the opportunity to preserve a sense of *genius loci*."[6] Kroll's generative techniques, drawing from existing local insight, attempted to replicate the complex processes through which cities emerge over time. The end result was an exceptionally varied and fluid structure.

These two examples represent particularly salient historical precedents for contemporary models of participatory design for a number of reasons. While privileging traditional and colloquial forms of knowledge, van Eyck and Kroll were by no means opposed to technological innovation. Both architects attempted to avail themselves of modern developments in building materials and design techniques (e.g., Kroll was one of the first architects in Belgium to use the computer as a design tool). Had contemporary networking technologies been available to them at the height of their practice, it is certainly possible to imagine both designers making full use of these capabilities. Kroll and van Eyck are also notable for their success in realizing substantial projects, despite the idealism of their design philosophies. Other, perhaps even more utopian, paradigms of participatory architecture certainly exist in the form of manifestos and speculative models (Constant Nieuwenhuys's *New Babylon* proposals of the 1960s and 1970s are one important example[7]). But part of the DIY sensibility is a priority on bringing projects and initiatives to fruition, of making things happen in the world, and Kroll and van Eyck embody this action-oriented ethos. It is important to note that neither architect sought to transfer the creative process entirely onto the shoulders of the public; their goal was to join architectural and vernacular knowledge synergistically. In this sense, their approach was more "do it together" than "do it yourself" – the design skills of the architect representing a necessary resource for communities addressing complex urban problems.

Despite the now iconic status of the *Maison Médicale*, Kroll was never granted another commission in Belgium. Indeed, the subsequent decades would not be very hospitable to his ideas of radical public participation.

And in our present age of urban sprawl and commercial development projects, even architects themselves are often excluded from involvement in the design of the urban environment. Architecture critic Kenneth Frampton reminds us that 85 percent of the built production in the US is realized without the intervention of the architectural profession.[8] Mandatory public consultation processes now exist for most development projects, but as Jeremy Till argues, this mechanism is often treated as a non-binding formality or a way to achieve a passive buy-in from area residents.[9]

This recent situation is a rather bleak one, yet given the recent explosion of social networking technologies it seems, nevertheless, an appropriate moment to question whether we might be entering into a new era of participatory design culture. One indication of changing landscape is the abundance of actively followed and well-regarded architectural blogs (BLDGBLOG and A Daily Dose of Architecture to name just two) that are shifting the distribution of knowledge within the field. These and other new spaces for publication and discussion are certainly expanding what has traditionally been a very tightly regulated sphere of architectural debate. In urban development, as is the case in so many other domains, online forums are facilitating the public's ability to take involvement into their own hands. Two examples of this growth in public participation have recently surfaced in my own research. Montréal's *Quartier des spectacles* development plan, an attempt to regenerate the downtown area of the city through an emphasis on its cultural industries, met with controversy in 2009 over a proposal to raze a number of buildings on lower Saint Laurent Boulevard (a designated national historic site) in order to make room for a Hydro-Québec office building.[10] Public awareness of the proposal and the organization of a protest movement were generated largely through Internet discussion forums such as the online magazine Spacing Montréal[11] and blog sites established by performers and event-organizers associated with Café Cleopatra—a drag, cabaret and fetish show bar harkening back to the area's "red light" history, but earmarked for demolition.[12] Due in part to the visibility of this public outcry, the city has since reconsidered its plans to expropriate Café Cleopatra and is exploring more acceptable development options for this section of the *Quartier des spectacles*. This example would seem to conform to Rancière's insistence that politics "exists because those who have no right to be counted as speaking beings make themselves of some account, setting up a community by the fact of placing in common a wrong."[13]

The tumult during the summer months of 2010 over the proposed construction of the Park 51 Islamic Cultural Center in Lower Manhattan offered a warning, however, that not all forms of online engagement are necessarily productive or progressive in nature. Despite the plan's promise to provide non-denominational health and recreational facilities to the area and its enthusiastic approval by the local community board, virulently anti-Muslim blogs, such as Atlas Shrugs,[14] circulated false claims about a project they misleadingly designated the "Ground Zero Mosque." The lack of accuracy and accountability exhibited by these bloggers helped produce a national backlash against the project that was at best misinformed and at worst dangerously xenophobic. These examples illustrate both the potential and perils of the movement of architectural debate online. Yet even in the most responsible instances of web-based engagement, the staunchly "do it yourself" approach to urban planning involvement has its limitations. The need still remains for architects to find innovative means of collaborating with the public, to demystify the building process and encourage the circulation of accurate information, and to ensure that participation is not simply a matter of putting a stop to problematic projects, but also a method of envisioning and realizing new ones. The synergistic and speculative design projects described by Ann Light (chapter 19, this volume) and Carl DiSalvo (chapter 17, this volume) are two excellent examples of what can emerge from the creative collaboration between "expert" and "amateur" designers, artists, and engineers.

In the current conjunction of media technologies and architecture, the concept of participation is often replaced with the notion of interaction, a related but not entirely synonymous term. The static materiality of architectural form is, for example, increasingly animated via the infusion of media screens and lighting effects into building facades. Blocks away from the proposed location of Park 51, the podium wall of 7 World Trade Center, designed by James Carpenter, is illuminated at night by LED lights inserted between its two layers of porous stainless steel.[15] The blue and white lighting varies in response to the motion of pedestrians passing by, modifying the facade of a forty-seven-story skyscraper according to the movement of individual New Yorkers. Other experimental projects attempt to engender even more substantial interactions between architectural structures and their surrounding environments. Lars Spuybroek's D-Tower in Doetinchem, Holland, utilizes real-time information harvested from online surveys in order to reflect the changing emotional condition of the city.[16] As participants answer a series of questions designed to measure their affective state, the tower changes color according to the dominant mood of the inhabitants (love signified by red, hate by green, happiness by blue, fear by yellow). While compelling in many ways, these projects can suffer from the tendency to reduce the public to the status of data source or movement trigger. As such, these forms of interactivity could be accused of being somewhat impoverished versions of earlier participatory projects, like those of Kroll and van Eyck, that attempted to break down the organizational hierarchy of architectural production.

Perhaps as a reaction to these tendencies, current participatory architecture often employs a decidedly nontechnological methodology and aesthetic. The Bruit du Frigo (Refrigerator Noise) collective of Bordeaux-based architects, sociologists, artists, and urban planners, for instance, uses only basic materials and approaches to generate a festive atmosphere around its community-oriented projects.[17] The group's La ville, tout le monde en parle . . . Et vous? project displayed in Bordeaux's Place Camille-Jullian engaged 250 young people and other local inhabitants in a discussion about potential improvements to their city. The collective employed colorful cardboard placards and simple wood and steel structures in order to generate an unintimidating setting within the square with a deliberately DIY ambiance. The democratic spirit of Kroll and van Eyck's architecture is present in these projects (as is the speculative ethos and experimentation with the possible promoted by Carl DiSalvo [chapter 17, this volume] and Emily Rose Michaud and Owen McSwiney [chapter 20, this volume]), but their low-tech solutions can also curtail their ability to lead directly to the construction of actual architectural structures and therefore limit the extent of their impact on the built environment.

Is there any hope then of the discipline of architecture reconciling these two often-opposing design attitudes, one favoring technological innovation and the other championing grassroots community involvement? Although it still remains a relatively fledgling endeavor for the discipline, there are a few indications that architects and planners are beginning to develop ways to productively combine participatory traditions with the potential advantages of social media technologies. Urban planners have begun exploring the possibilities of web-based public consultation for the discipline, developing new approaches to existing Geographical Information Systems (GIS) that combine cartography, statistical analysis, and database technology. The SoftGIS project produced by the Aalto University in Helsinki asked residents of Järvenpää, a small city in Southern Finland, to use online applications to describe their interaction with their environment—documenting favorite locations, causes of frustration, suggestions for improvement, etc. The project allows the planners to marry "hard" GIS statistical date, such as demographic shifts and income levels, with "soft" qualitative information provided by participants using the online tools.[18] Gaming technologies have also been adapted to urban planning uses in a number of interesting ways. The Brooklyn Experimental Media Center (figure 21.1), for example, has been developing a collaborative platform called Betaville that allows users to visualize new additions to existing cityscapes. The center describes the project as "an open-source multiplayer environment for real cities, in which ideas for new works of public art, architecture, urban design, and development can be shared, discussed, tweaked, and brought to maturity in context, and with the kind of broad participation people take for granted in open source software development."[19] The development team envisions the platform being used at points in the design process when broad participation is necessary or desirable. Betaville, in other words, is not intended to replace more formal/professional design stages, but rather to compliment and enrich them.

Perhaps the most impressive usage of social media in architectural practice thus far is the Open Architecture Network—an online, open source community dedicated to improving global living conditions through the promotion of innovative and sustainable design. The network emerged out of the more established Architecture for Humanity organization as a result

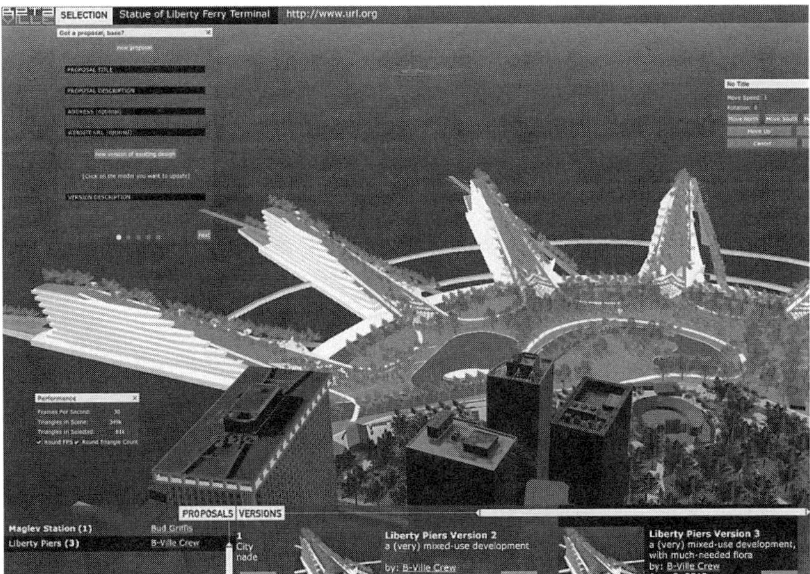

Figure 21.1
Brooklyn Experimental Media Center—Betaville (2010)

of its founder, Cameron Sinclair, winning the 2006 TED Prize. The prize allowed Architecture for Humanity to collaborate with Sun Microsystems and other technology partners to develop an online network that sponsors design competitions intended to generate the exchange of techniques and approaches applicable to projects in the developing world. One example of such a competition was the architectural brief to design a tele-medicine center, connected to worldwide network of physicians and medical databases, for Nyaya Health, an organization providing free health care services in remote areas of Nepal (figure 21.2). The submission that garnered third place in the competition was particularly notable in light of this discussion. The design proposal, submitted by Studio Wikitecture, was the collaborative effort of over forty geographically dispersed and multidisciplinary contributors.[20] Studio Wikitecture, founded by Ryan Schultz and Jon Brouchoud, builds on the virtual reality platform Second Life in order to allow multiple users to participate in an online collective design process. Among the studio's innovations is the development of a 3D design interface tool called a "Wiki-Tree" that permits users to submit, alter, and vote on new iterations of a specific project. The models of online collaboration offered by the Open Architecture Network and Studio Wikitecture, which attempt to

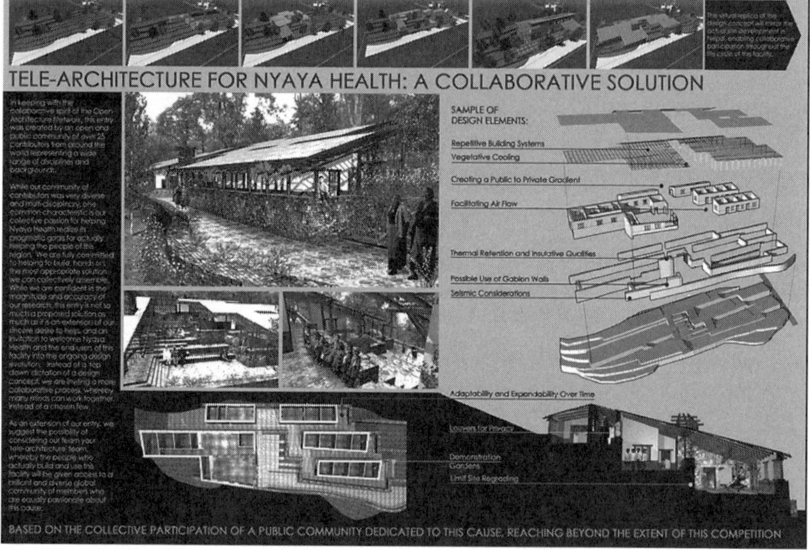

Figure 21.2
Studio Wikitecture—Nyaya Health Center (2008)

harness the creative energies of a dispersed design community with limited resources, are crucial methods of engendering a viable culture of volunteering within the discipline.

These examples confirm that new lines of communication are indeed opening up between architects and the general populace. There are still, of course, many opportunities left unexplored, but early experiments in social media use are facilitating the formation of networks composed of design professionals and members of the public working in tandem. These emerging configurations suggest ways in which meaningful and sustained interactions with actual end users or residents might potentially occur throughout the various design stages. Architects are by no means displaced in this equation, but their ability to synthesize multiple viewpoints and translate these needs and desires into material form takes precedence over any singular creative vision.

The brief (and certainly incomplete) genealogy of participatory architecture and distributed design practices offered in this chapter provides a specific perspective on the merits and shortfalls of contemporary DIY movements. In the context of architecture and urban planning, it seems clear that the desirable goal is not the promotion of a "do-it-yourself" public working independently from or in opposition to the design professions, but rather the development of effective forms of collaboration between two spheres that have too often been disconnected. And as the role of the architect becomes increasingly marginalized within finance-driven urban development, establishing inventive participatory strategies that combine expert and popular knowledge may be as essential for the designers as it is for the public. As in many other chapters in this book, a "do-it-together" model emerges as a more productive paradigm than any strict DIY formulation. The growth of social networking technologies has presented significant opportunities for the democratization of design, but the adoption of these tools has been slow within a discipline that still privileges large-scale capital investment and highly regulated organizational structures. If Rancière's notions of radical equality and the "redistribution of the sensible" are possible in the domain of architecture, they are goals that must be strived for with an awareness of the acute resource and infrastructure challenges facing any such endeavor. Experiments in participatory design of the 1960s and 1970s, such as those undertaken by van Eyck and Kroll, still serve as a reminder of what is possible to achieve within the field when vernacular intelligence, technological capacities, and design competence are brought together in creative combinations.

Notes

1. Aldo van Eyck, *The Child, the City and the Artist: An Essay on Architecture: The In-between Realm* (Amsterdam: SUN, 2008), 24.

2. Deyan Sudjic, *The 100 Mile City* (San Diego: Harcourt Brace, 1992), 33.

3. Jacques Rancière, *The Politics of Aesthetics: The Distribution of the Sensible*, trans. Gabriel Rockhill (London: Continuum, 2004), 39.

4. Francis Strauven's *Aldo van Eyck: The Shape of Relativity* (Amsterdam: Architectura & Natura, 1998) is the definitive account of the Dutch architect's resolute design philosophy.

5. Van Eyck, *The Child*, 129.

6. Lucien Kroll, *An Architecture of Complexity* (Cambridge, MA: MIT Press, 1987), 39.

7. Mark Wigley, *Constant's New Babylon: The Hyper-Architecture of Desire* (Rotterdam: 010 Uitgeverij, 1999).

8. Kenneth Frampton, "Toward an Urban Landscape," in *Center, Volume 14: On Landscape Urbanism*, ed. Dean Almy (Austin: The Center for American Architecture and Design, 2007), 115.

9. Jeremy Till, "The Negotiation of Hope," in *Architecture and Participation*, eds. Peter Blundell-Jones, Doina Petrescu, and Jeremy Till (Abingdon, UK: Spon Press, 2005), 26.

10. "Feuvert au Quadrilatère Saint-Laurent," Quartier des spectacles Montréal, http://www.quartierdesspectacles.com/2009/09/feu-vert-au-quadrilatere-saint-laurent/ (accessed November 10, 2010).

11. "Lower Main May Be Razed . . . Again," Alanah Heffez, http://spacing.ca/montreal/2009/05/07/lower-main-may-be-razedagain/ (accessed October 23, 2010).

12. "Save the Main: An Initiative to Rebuild Together," http://savethemain.com/intro.htm (accessed October 25, 2010).

13. Jacques Rancière, *Disagreement: Politics and Philosophy*, trans. Julie Rose (Minneapolis: University of Minnesota Press, 1999), 27.

14. "Ground Zero Mega Mosque Audaciously Diabolical Design: Pentagons, Crosses, Jewish Stars," Pamela Geller, http://atlasshrugs2000.typepad.com/atlas_shrugs/2010/10/ground-zero-mega-mosque-design-pentagons-and-jewish-stars.html (accessed October 5, 2020).

15. "7 World Trade Center: Podium Light Wall," James Carpenter Design Associates Inc., http://www.jcdainc.com/ (accessed on November 12, 2010).

16. "NOX D-Tower," arcspace, http://www.arcspace.com/features/nox/d-tower/ (accessed November 12, 2010).

17. "Atelier d'urbanismeutopique à Bordeaux," Bruit du Frigo, http://www.bruitdufrigo.com/index.php?id=112 (accessed May 2, 2012).

18. "SoftGIS," Centre for Urban and Regional Studies, Aalto University, http://pehmo.tkk.fi/home/ (accessed November 25, 2010).

19. "Betaville," Brooklyn Experimental Media Center, http:/betaville.net/ (accessed November 10, 2010).

20. "Opening Architecture," Studio Wikitecture, http://studiowikitecture.wordpress.com/about/ (accessed November 25, 2010).

22 "I hate your politics but I love your diamonds": Citizenship and the Off-Topic Message Board Subforum

Lana Swartz and Kevin Driscoll

I'm glad you didn't take offense to my post and glad you enjoy the interchange of opposing ideas. I do as well. By the way, I was looking at your solitaire thread a while back and it made me change my mind yet again about my ring! . . . The beauty and simplicity of your set reminded me of what I truly love. Okay, back to politics!

—A PriceScope user, November 2008

Discussion of solitaire ring design and heated political debate might seem like an unlikely juxtaposition, but for a time both could be found on the jewelry-lovers' message board PriceScope. It would not have been uncommon for two posters to argue about tax policy or abortion in one subforum while collaborating to help a third user find the perfect setting for a repoussé engagement ring setting or pink diamond accent stone in another.

On PriceScope, this culture of collaboration produces the capacity for a politics of self-determination that John Hartley describes as "DIY citizenship."[1] This in turn created the basis for more traditional forms of civic engagement, like overtly political talk and even voting. In the lead-up to the 2008 US presidential elections, the "off-topic" subforum to discuss current events became one of the most active subforums on the site. During this period, it would not have been uncommon for a shared interest in jewelry to ameliorate tension during a discussion of a divisive political issue. However, in the aftermath of the 2008 election, talk of politics seemed to eclipse talk of jewelry, undermining the basis upon which the PriceScope community had been formed.

In this chapter, we look at the everyday gender and economic politics of PriceScope's jewelry geeks. Next, we describe the rise and fall of its off-topic area as an active site of explicitly political activity. Finally, as a conclusion, we call for further study of message boards in general, which we see as an important component of a decentralized social web.

PriceScope as DIY Citizenship

PriceScope, a "consumer education" website devoted to diamonds, colored gems, and jewelry, was founded in May 2000 by a coalition of independent jewelers united in competition against chain stores. Originally, it centered on a database of diamonds available for sale. By listing their available diamonds in the database, jewelers were able to increase their geographic reach and likelihood of sale. PriceScope was not an e-commerce site in that it did not sell anything. Instead, consumers had to contact jewelers directly about diamonds found in the database.

This business model relied on a special kind of consumer: one who disdainfully dismissed overpriced, low-quality "maul" (a play on "mall") diamonds; who preferred custom-designed and hand-carved settings to mass-produced branded designs; who enjoyed a hunt for the perfect diamond more than a luxurious retail experience. It needed, as some PriceScopers have described themselves, "jewelry geeks."

Shortly after the site launched, PriceScope added a message board, and by 2002, it had displaced the diamond database as the focus of the site. The message board attracted existing jewelry geeks whose willingness to share their knowledge, in turn, created new ones. It was a place to "geek out," to "navigate esoteric domains of knowledge and practice and participate in communities that traffic in these forms of expertise."[2] In collaborative project threads, the "collective intelligence" of the community is called on to assist a single member in the design and procurement of a new piece of jewelry.[3] By 2005, some of the most active members began hitting the 10,000 post mark. By 2007, the message board had over one million posts and by 2011, there were three million.

On PriceScope, the mutual respect, shared knowledge, and time investment required for the successful realization of a jewelry project formed the context for what John Hartley describes as "DIY citizenship."[4] For Hartley, DIY citizenship "is no longer simply a matter of a social contract between state and subject, no longer even a matter of acculturation to the heritage of a given community; DIY citizenship is a choice people can make for themselves."[5] According to Hartley, DIY citizens produce their own identities through the critical selection and redeployment of material and semiotic resources plucked from the surrounding media environment.

Although DIY citizenship is realized through consumption practices, it is not as simple as selecting from the prepackaged, off-the-shelf forms of citizenship characteristic of "commodity activism."[6] For example, from a DIY citizenship perspective, a woman who bought a diamond "right hand ring" for herself as a symbol of "empowerment" should not automatically be seen as a dupe of a DeBeers-funded advertising campaign. Instead, her decision—and its personal and political dimensions—would have to be considered as part of a bespoke assemblage of values, norms, practices, and relationships.

DIY citizenship is usually not an isolated pursuit; it happens in communities. Traditionally, publics are thought to form around class, ethnic, cultural, and geographic interests. In Hartley's DIY—or "DIWO" (do-it-with-others)[7]—mode, citizenship may be enacted through affinity among strangers. This is the case for PriceScope's jewelry geeks, who enact a form of DIY citizenship in overlapping arenas of activity: the production of collaboratively self-determined ethical positions in relation to social institutions like marriage and within markets.

The DIY citizens of PriceScope produce a nuanced critique of marriage negotiated through a material symbol of the institution: the engagement ring. As one poster put it: "WE decide if and when we marry, who we marry, and how we marry. And if we want to choose the bling, we will. The ring in this century represents an understanding and commitment between two people. Not a promise from the male to the female that she'll never have to worry her pretty little head about the big bad world now that Mr. Proposal has chosen her for his very own."

Some of these women are already jewelry geeks and have worked out a "dream engagement ring" even if they are not planning to get married anytime soon. For others, the engagement ring project is an initiation into PriceScope. Through it, they become jewelry geeks and continue posting, eager to share their new knowledge with others. They also approach the jewelry market with a set of normative expectations: that technical expertise should be shared among producers and consumers; that the boundary between amateur and professional should be ambiguous; and that consumers should reject mass-produced brands in favor of artisans. Producers who meet these norms are rewarded by PriceScope consumers who view their consumption as a translocal form of the "shop independent" movement.

PriceScopers closely follow international attempts to regulate "conflict diamonds." They are more aware than casual consumers of the flaws of the current process and avoid most diamonds dubiously marketed as "ethical." Although many are concerned with the political economy of their purchases, most seem to find the ecological and human rights implications of diamonds no more objectionable than many other industrially produced goods. One member suggested that those who criticize her "blood diamonds" should be "more concerned about their own blood iPods."

Although this stance might be seen as somewhat passive or even incoherent, it is a collectively produced alternative to preset platforms of "ethical consumption," which are often nothing more than "greenwashed" attempts by corporate actors to rebrand rather than reform existing industrial practices.[8]

PriceScope and Discursive Participation

In Hartley's model, DIY citizenship is enacted outside the traditional structures, rituals, and relations of state power.[9] Unlike previous models, DIY citizenship is "post-political,"[10] in part because it claims rights not through formal politics but in "social-network markets" and in the "gift economy."[11]

To critics, this "post-political" citizenship might seem like the triumph of the market over democracy—or perhaps not even citizenship at all. For Nicholas Garnham, the DIY citizenship position is "pollyannaish," exaggerating the agency of individuals as well as the role of consumption in the formation of personal identities.[12] It offers few constructive possibilities for political action. However, for Hartley, it is this "democratization without politicization"[13] within DIY citizenship that opens up possibilities for new democratic formations. DIY citizenship, then, is the "citizenship of the future; decentralized, post-adversarial, based on self-determination not state coercion."[14] Indeed, as Elizabeth Jacka puts it, "For Hartley, it appears, democracy and politics are antagonistic concepts; perhaps he would even see politics as the enemy of democracy."[15]

Although PriceScope offers an illustration of Hartley's DIY citizenship, the theory of citizenship that seems to be in operation among users of the site is fully aligned with neither Hartley's optimism for radically reimagined formations nor his critics' fears of disengagement. Indeed, although PriceScope users use the site as a vector through which to meaningfully produce their own "DIY" identities and agencies, they also—at least for many years—used it to engage extensively in what Jacobs, Cook, and Delli Carpini call "discursive participation," that is, talking about electoral politics.[16] By tracing the persistence of both forms of citizenship on PriceScope, we can better understand their interrelation. In this case, DIY citizenship does not displace engagement in state politics. Instead, it creates the basis for a community through which more traditional, explicitly political behavior can also emerge.

Like many interest-driven message boards, PriceScope was designed with an off-topic subforum—here, titled "Around the World" or "ATW"—intended for discussion of current events or politics. The off-topic section, of which ATW is a component, is called "The PriceScope Cafe," echoing Habermas's "coffeehouse," if only incidentally.[17] Although ATW was not always one of the most active subforums, there were usually a handful of posters, mostly passionate partisans, sparring with each other. Surprisingly, debate tended to be as civil as it was animated. The collaborative practices that enabled collective intelligence activities to flourish in the on-topic project threads became deliberative norms for off-topic political talk elsewhere on the site. "I hate your politics, but I love your diamonds," one poster wrote to another, evoking the history of collaboration they shared.

Contrary to the findings of Sunstein and others who study political talk online, PriceScope was by no means an "echo chamber" of ideological homogeneity.[18] Although the vast majority of members were upper-middle-class white women, PriceScope members' political party identifications were more clearly heterogeneous. According to a poll thread created by a member in August 2008, 52 percent of the 459 members who responded were planning to vote for Barack Obama. Some 45 percent reported planning to vote for John McCain, and 3 percent reported "neither," mirroring the country's political identification: in 2008, Obama and McCain received 52.9 percent and 45.7 percent of the popular vote, respectively.[19] As Hartley notes, one of the functions of cultural citizenship is "[gathering] populations which may otherwise display few connections and . . . promoting among them a sense of common identity."[20]

Leading up to the 2008 presidential election, there was a surge of activity on ATW. As the election approached, it became one of the most active subforums on PriceScope. The political conversation became more heated, but it also became more sophisticated. There were "Debate the Debate" threads in which PriceScope users watched the debates virtually together live. In another thread, they challenged each other to prove that they could "argue the other side." One undecided member started a thread in which she asked PriceScope members to persuade her to vote and who to vote for. One user later remarked, "I don't think I would have voted if it had not been for this place and the people in it."

The experience of sustained collaboration fostered a feeling of mutual respect that mitigated the hostility that might have otherwise arisen amid a tense political debate. As one user wrote, "Whenever I think ATW is getting a bit too contentious for me, all I have to do is go over to [Show Me The Ring] or [Bride World Wide] or basically any other forum in PS and I will read message after message that are kind, supportive and helpful."

DIY citizenship, according to Hartley, creates a feeling of "cultural neighborliness"[21] that "ameliorates our manners."[22] These dynamics, developed in the PriceScope community through DIY citizenship practice, were put into the service of civil discussion of formal, state politics. This is not to suggest that electoral politics should be privileged over DIY citizenship, or that the latter is simply a platform for the former. Indeed, for PriceScopers, the two had to be kept in careful balance.

The 2008 Election: Challenges and Crises

As the election grew closer, members joked that ATW had taken over PriceScope. There were complaints about some new members posting too much about politics in the off-topic areas and not "pulling their weight" in the on-topic areas. Political discourse began to grow more heated and more personal. For too many involved in the political threads, the political debate was no longer consistently paired with collaboration around a shared interest in jewelry. Without engagement in this common passion, PriceScope members were not "a truly sovereign community" of DIY citizens, "among whom relationships, decisions and ideas are negotiated and arbitrated."[23] They were simply a group of atomized individuals arguing about politics on a message board.

A particularly tense topic was California's Proposition 8 to ban same-sex marriage, which appeared on the same ballots as the presidential election. PriceScope's terms of service had long prohibited discussions of religious beliefs, and some conservative members felt that they were unable to defend their position without being "ganged up on" for breaking the rules. But Proposition 8 was also an important issue for PriceScopers who were planning their own same-sex marriages. Near the end of a particularly divisive thread on ATW, one wrote:

> I argued head to head with Fred Phelps and the Westboro Baptist Church when I was 15! And look at me now, 21 and crying over words on the internet. ;) It was different when I didn't think I would get married and didn't even want to. I've been an activist for marriage equality since I was 12, but it wasn't until a few years ago that I thought I might want to actually get married, and not until now that I am planning to get married. Something about planning to get married and having my legal rights threatened simultaneously collided in this thread. Planning my wedding in one section of the site and having to defend my right to have it in another.

For the poster, it was disconcerting to have been met with knowledge sharing and support in the PriceScope jewelry and wedding planning forums only to discover that members of the same community were arguing against the legality of her marriage in another. Instead of diffusing conflict, the proximity of on-topic ring shopping and wedding planning to off-topic talk about Proposition 8 heightened it. After Proposition 8 passed, she posted pictures of her wedding ceremony in one forum and, not long after, in another, an open letter to the community stating that she was leaving PriceScope completely. She had been supported by PriceScope when she had used it develop the elements of "semiotic self-determination"[24] as a DIY citizen picking out an engagement ring for another woman, but she had faced an intolerable disconnect from that support in PriceScope's discussion of formal politics.

Aftermath: Clashes and Breakdowns

In the aftermath of 2008 elections, the community and collaboration enabled by the DIY citizenship of PriceScope had become fully dis-integrated from the discursive participation it had previous supported. It seemed clear that ATW had taken on a character of its own, isolated from the collaborative norms of the other PriceScope forums. The reactions to the fractious Proposition 8 threads provided the community with an opportunity to assess itself. One poster wrote: "People can argue all they want about gay marriage, but in that situation this girl was just married and then just days after, SS marriage was banned, and right now she doesn't know what will happen to her marriage. I understand that ATW is a place to debate politics, [but] what could be gained from letting this girl know that you voted against her rights (or would have if you lived in CA)?"

ATW was "a place to debate politics," but what purpose did it serve if it undermined the basis of the community that supported that very discursive participation? Political talk had become a liability to the collective intelligence activities upon which PriceScope's DIY citizenship was formed. Instead of a flow of collaborative norms from the project threads to the political threads, the destructive effects of the "bashing" that had become common on political threads began to be felt in forums beyond ATW. Moderators initially posted warnings about civility and established ground rules for political discussions—efforts that had previously been unnecessary—but they ultimately decided to prohibit political talk altogether when the situation did not improve. The regulation of political talk was justified by site moderators through a rearticulation of PriceScope as a site for sharing knowledge and expertise about jewelry and gems. A warning note posted by a moderator stated, "First and foremost, it should be duly noted that Diamond education is our first priority and always will be." ATW was described as an "extra 'recreational' area" that was a "minor part of the entire foundation of PriceScope."

Although many were disappointed, PriceScope users seemed to generally agree with the ban on political talk. Throughout the metadiscussion about whether or not PriceScope should "keep its politics," posters reminded each other of their community's shared interests, practices, and histories. One wrote, "With the founders of pricescope in mind I am somewhat ashamed that we all continue to act so poorly with this issue. . . . After all we have all come here for the love of diamonds and many of us have formed wonderful relationships."

To remind PriceScope of its former spirit, moderators encouraged members to "remember their roots" by sharing the story of what brought them to PriceScope in the first place and contributing to the new "PriceScope Community Project," which asked them to nominate diamond photography to be compiled into a book to be sold to raise money for charity. The charity project, a depoliticized form of civic engagement, was intended to repair and restructure the community upon which both the DIY citizenship and discursive participation depended.

Three years later, with the 2012 elections approaching, PriceScope had not lifted its ban on political discussion. Longtime members sometimes reminisced about ATW as the "Wild West" or, alternatively, the "good old days." One wrote, "It's a shame admin shut down such a popular forum . . . not to mention that we'd have a lot to talk about these days!" Nevertheless, discursive participation does occur subrosa, usually on subforums not as overtly coded as ATW. As long as these threads—on topics such as anti-Semitism, the BP oil leak, and the Occupy movement—do not require excessive moderation, they tend to persist. There are also threads about the everyday politics of members' personal lives—the harsh realities of having cancer in America even with insurance, salary cuts for state employees, and, yes, same-sex marriage. In most cases, because the community was able to restabilize itself after the 2008 crisis, it is able avoid destructive confrontations by appealing to shared passions and social bonds, even if it is not yet ready to call these conversations "political."

Coda: Message Boards and the Decentralized Web

Taken individually, PriceScope may appear to be a curious outlier, but its collaborative practices and deliberative norms are not unique. PriceScope's principal organizing structures—the forum, the thread, and the post—are iterations of a fundamental form of asynchronous computer-mediated communication that has been in continuous development since the late 1970s.[25] Indeed, the online message board system has served as an infrastructure for countless communities of interest—from flashlight enthusiasts to unhappy Starbucks employees, from peafowl breeders to armchair detectives, from homeowners trying to avoid foreclosure to fans of Houston hip-hop.

Recently, however, some observers have described the message board as technology in decline. Virginia Heffernan, writing for the *New York Times* online opinion page, gave message boards a "nostalgic embrace."[26] For Heffernan, the message board has become an "endangered species" as "forum villagers flee for the Facebook megalopolis."[27] She writes:

> If urban history can be applied to virtual space and the evolution of the Web, the unruly and twisted message boards are Jane Jacobs. They were built for people, and without much regard to profit. . . . By contrast, the Web 2.0 juggernauts like Facebook and YouTube are driven by metrics and supported by ads and data mining. They're networks, and super-fast—but not communities, which are inefficient, emotive and comfortable. Facebook—with its clean lines and social expressways—is Robert Moses par excellence.[28]

But, the death of the message board—for these very reasons!—may yet be greatly exaggerated. Although PriceScope members report some slowing down, many find that Facebook and other mass-scale sites are incompatible with the salient functions of "geeking out."[29] Non-niche social network sites are not designed for the development of collective intelligence and lack, for example, the ability to search an archive of past posts. Furthermore, few PriceScope users want their interest in jewelry—a "guilty pleasure" for many—to show up in their general-purpose, multi-audience feeds or even to be linked to nonpseudonymous accounts. This is especially true when seeking emotional support about the family issues that often arise through wedding planning. It might also be true for discussing politics. We expect, then, that the interest-driven message board will persist. The form will continue to evolve, even as it maintains its low profile, neither resembling nor aspiring to compete with general-purpose social network sites. People will find their way to message boards and make communities out of them.

Instead of Jane Jacobs's New York, we see the message board as the strip mall of the Internet—uniform but unique, ubiquitous, and invisible. All message boards are alike—they are produced using a handful of very similar software packages—but each is deeply particular. The key design elements that enabled PriceScope's discursive community to flourish—persistent pseudonymity, searchable archives, and an off-topic forum—are common features found among thousands of interest-driven message boards. Rather than approach each board as a wholly new site, these common infrastructural characteristics invite us to see message boards as a single highly distributed sociotechnical phenomenon, an analytic move that enables a productive comparison with monolithic social network sites like Facebook.

In addition, the message board's distributed architecture may also be essential for the sustainability of the kind of "DIY citizenship" and heterogeneous discursive political participation we describe here. Unlike messaging "platforms" provided by companies like Facebook, Twitter, or Disqus, message board software does not require the concentration of data or authority within a single institution in order to function. The highly centralized institutional architecture of the commercial services leaves them politically and economically vulnerable at a single point of failure. Should the parent company go out of business, temporarily suspend service, cancel a user's account, or be censored by a government, users are left with little recourse.[30] In contrast, it is not possible, for example, to easily censor message boards in general because each web-based message board is its own institution running on its own host. PriceScope's infrastructure will continue to function without interruption even if every other message board on the web suddenly disappears.

As the Internet is increasingly segmented into incompatible "walled gardens,"[31] scholars and activists should neither overlook communities built on decentralized infrastructures like the interest-driven message board nor surrender them to the sociotechnical scrap heap. As sites of sociality and diversity, as well as privacy, autonomy, and self-determination, they are fertile ground for citizenship formations of many kinds.

Notes

1. John Hartley, *Uses of Television* (London, UK: Routledge, 1999), 178.

2. Mizuko Ito, Heather A. Horst, Matteo Bittanti, danah boyd, Becky Herr-Stephenson, Patricia G. Lange, C. J. Pascoe, and Laura Robinson (with Sonja Baumer, Rachel Cody, Dilan Mahendran, Katynka Martínez, Dan Perkel, Christo Sims, and Lisa Tripp), *Living and Learning with New Media: Summary of Findings from the Digital Youth Project* (Cambridge: MA: MIT Press, 2008), 67.

3. Pierre Lévy, *Collective Intelligence* (New York: Basic Books, 1997).

4. Hartley, *Uses of Television.*

5. Ibid., 178.

6. See Roopali Mukherjee and Sarah Banet-Weiser, eds., *Commodity Activism: Cultural Resistance in Neoliberal Times* (New York: New York University Press, 2012).

7. John Hartley, "Silly Citizenship," *Critical Discourse Studies* 7, no. 4 (2010): 233–248.

8. See Jed Greer and Kenny Bruno, *Greenwash: The Reality behind Corporate Environmentalism* (Lanham, MD: Rowman & Littlefield Publishers, 1997).

9. Hartley, *Uses of Television*, 178.

10. Ibid., 120–121.

11. Hartley, "Silly Citizenship," 241–242.

12. Nicholas Garnham, "A Response to Elizabeth Jacka's 'Democracy as Defeat,'" *Television and New Media* 4, no. 2 (2003): 193–200.

13. Hartley, *Uses of Television,* 161.

14. Ibid., 161.

15. Elizabeth Jacka, "'Democracy as Defeat': The Impotence of Arguments for Public Service Broadcasting," *Television and New Media* 4, no. 2 (2003): 177–191.

16. Lawrence R. Jacobs, Fay Lomax Cook, and Michael X. Delli Carpini, *Talking Together: Public Deliberation and Political Participation in America* (Chicago: University of Chicago Press, 2009).

17. Jürgen Habermas, *The Structural Transformation of the Public Sphere: An Inquiry into a Category of Bourgeois Society* (Cambridge, UK: Polity, 1962; trans. 1989).

18. See Cass Sunstein, *Republic.com 2.0* (Princeton: Princeton University Press, 2007).

19. *2008 Official Presidential General Election Results*, United States Federal Elections Commission, http://www.fec.gov/pubrec/fe2008/2008presgeresults.pdf.

20. Hartley, *Uses of Television*, 158.

21. Ibid., 172.

22. Ibid., 180.

23. Ibid., 161.

24. Ibid., 157–162.

25. See Ward Christensen and Randy Suess, "The Birth of the BBS," 1989, http://chinet.com/html/cbbs.html, and *The BBS Documentary*, directed by Jason Scott (Bovine Ignition Systems, 2004).

26. Virginia Heffernan, "The Old Internet Neighborhoods." *Opinionator, The New York Times*, July 10, 2011, http://opinionator.blogs.nytimes.com/2011/07/10/remembrance-of-message-boards-past.

27. Ibid.

28. Ibid.

29. Ito et al., *Living and Learning with New Media.*

30. Erica Newland, Carolyn Nolan, Cynthia Wong, and Jillian York, *Account Deactivation and Content Removal: Guiding Principles and Practices for Companies and Users* (Cambridge, MA: The Berkman Center for Internet & Society and The Center for Democracy & Technology, 2011), http://cyber.law.harvard.edu/publications/2011/account_deactivation.

31. Jonathan Zittrain, *The Future of the Internet and How to Stop It* (New Haven, CT: Yale University Press, 2008).

IV DIY and Media: Redistributing Authority and Sources in News Media

How are social media practices reshaping landscapes of news media, public spheres, and definitions of journalism, "fairness," accuracy, and authority? Which voices/channels carry authority in the twenty-first century? *There are 5.3 billion mobile subscribers* (77 percent of the world's population). More than 250 million people access Facebook through their mobile devices. Facebook's 750 million users would constitute the world's third largest country. YouTube has 490 million unique users each month. Wikipedia authors total over 91,000 contributors, and Wikipedia hosts 17 million articles. And 50 percent of the world's population is under age thirty. How are the rapidly changing practices being used to challenge traditional media authorities, news representations, and sources of knowledge and "truths," in order to take account of massively proliferating alternative sources, documentation, accounts, and analysis? In what ways do critical making and social media practices enact forms of DIY/DIT citizenship? How and in what ways do DIY media redistribute authority? How do media ecologists understand the proliferating forms of citizen journalism and other creative DIY/DIT modes, genres, and forms of producing and circulating sensible information?

The exponential rise of "web 2.0" and participatory, interactive media has radically altered the relationship of readers and viewers to producers and broadcasters, not only in the West and North but also around the globe. While corporate-owned media arguably continue to be the news agenda-setting authorities working in close concert with government and corporate interests, the proliferation of alternative news sources that has evolved alongside information communication technologies has forever changed the relationships between media and publics. These monumental changes in the media landscape not only change how news is produced and by whom, but also reflect the significantly decreased public trust in traditional forms of "journalistic" authority. The factors that contributed to, and over time compounded, public mistrust and skepticism toward both news media and politicians (Boler 2008; Boler and Nemorin 2013) include

- diversification of sources that enables people to recognize the inherent partiality of even the most "legitimate" authorities, thus dislodging traditional assumptions about objectivity and journalism;
- traditional news sources' misinformation and willingness to serve as uncritical mouthpiece for government administrations, which compounds the existing public mistrust of politicians; for example, during the patriotic fervor in the aftermath of 9/11, and the subsequent buildup to the US preemptive invasion of Iraq that relied heavily on persuading public opinion, the traditional media broadcast and printed egregious lies and misrepresentations to justify the Bush administration's war on the basis of false accusations of Iraqi weapons of mass destruction;
- the explicit propaganda of cable news shows such as *Fox News* that unabashedly function as mouthpieces for conservative US social, economic, and political agendas;
- the surging popularity of "fake news" (*The Daily Show, The Colbert Report*), which functions as an internationally accessible, nightly source media criticism of cable and broadcast news, news pundits, and US politicians (Boler 2006; Boler with Turpin 2008).

Such factors have arguably had the effect of "demystifying" long-debated claims to journalistic objectivity as a value or even a pragmatic possibility. The magnified skepticism towards traditional news sources has also eroded the authority of corporate-owned news and its complex agendas. In an era of social media, individuals increasingly seek their news from sites like Reddit, other alternative or independent news sources, international news such as the BBC or Al Jazeera, as well as from Facebook, where the news has been chosen and filtered by "known" sources/friends.

Who are these DIY newsmakers and what are their tools and practices? As Chris Atton writes in chapter 25, "What we now term 'alternative media' . . . are about offering the means for democratic communication to people who are normally excluded from media production. They typically go beyond simply providing a platform for radical or alternative points of view: they emphasize the organization of media to enable wider social participation in their creation, production, and dissemination than is possible in the mass media." The participatory, user-friendly platforms now readily available to those with digital access increase channels of citizen journalism around the world.

Atton emphasizes the key differences between DIY media and corporate-owned media: "To distinguish alternative media from the mass media, the former must be deprofessionalized, decapitalized, and deinstitutionalized." The move to substituting the "every person"—the amateur, the soldier, the citizen, the eyewitness—for traditional icons of authority such as the national news anchor reflects the potency of the DIY shift away from professionalization. Connecting these changes to questions of social movements and change, Atton links these definitions to social movement practices: "Such media will then have the potential to more closely reflect the everyday practices of decentralized, directly democratic, self-managed, and reflexive networks of 'everyday-life solidarity' that Alberto Melucci finds at the heart of social movement activity: what he terms 'networks in the everyday.'"

Part IV highlights this book's central question of when and how "DIY citizenship" is liberatory. Should those interested in DIY celebrate this proliferation as indicative of widespread resistance, radicalism, revolution? Atton provocatively suggests: "I do not want to argue, as much cultural studies work does . . . that all popular consumption is evidence of resistance and that the fanzine writer and the personal web page owner are as transgressive as the political activist. Instead I want to argue that, in the case of the personal web page, mundanity is often all there is and that this itself is worthy of examination. Far from being a trivial observation, this is a significant one—it provides insights into the power and significance of mundane tastes, opinions, and experiences without the need for construing them as extraordinary or resistive." Detailing inspiring modes of DIT citizenship, Rosa Reitsamer and Elke Zobl (chapter 24) analyze the feminist collective production of zines and discuss how feminist alternative media producers engage in informal learning processes and networking by creating what James Paul Gee (2004) has called "affinity spaces." Within these affinity spaces, alternative feminist media producers can experiment with collective forms of participation in politics and civil society.

Bissonette's analysis of iReport as one example of "citizen journalism" embraced by corporate media (chapter 28) evidences how DIY citizenship can prove to be far from liberatory. Bissonette engages a provocative discussion of the serious tensions built into progressive visions of citizen journalism, highlighting the relationship among technologies, publics, and corporate ownership:

"If by digital democracy we think of a forum where users obtain citizenship and share power equally through presence and exercise free speech in conversation if not consensus-building, current technologies remain arguably the largest obstacle to its achievement. Technology produces a space for digital relationships, yet those who own the space threaten its arbitrary dissolution. . . . Though technology has weakened traditional intrastate controls, new, international networks of authority allow democratic forums only to the extent they coincide with market interests. The result is best described . . . as a 'commercially public medium.'. . . Citizen journalism remains tilted toward commercial gain, not democratic discourse. Nowhere is this more visible than in the medium's most popular site, iReport."

McVeigh-Schultz (chapter 23) contributes a DIY experiment in vox pop rituals, providing an intriguing illustration of how the everyday citizen, the "person in the street," can be engaged in this kind of critical making practice: "How does the role of interactive platforms complicate the concept of DIY citizenship in relation to broadcast media? And how might reimagining the rituals of public representation provoke new ways of thinking about difference and identification?" Meikle's essay (chapter 27) resonates with the questions raised by McVeigh-Schultz, as both are questioning traditional models of "one-way transmission" communication as opposed to rituals of symbolic and collective meaning making. Meikle (chapter 27) uses the failures of *Kony 2012* to address the possibilities and challenges of "*distributed citizenship*, in which individuals from across the globe were to engage in a collective project for political change—*to assume a relation within networks with one's contemporaries*; a relation not defined by or restricted to a particular geographical location or polity, but rather defined by shared meanings and collaborative creativity and action within and through networked digital media. Distributed citizenship is a political possibility of the network society in its shift from what Castells terms the space of places to the space of flows."

Ananny (chapter 26) analyzes the increased production of DIY news but pushes the question of the interconnected nature of actors and forces, challenging the idea of a "DIY news culture" unconnected from the traditional forces, outlining the significant ways in which even the most everyday, mundane "DIY" news relies on what Ananny calls "newsware." Thus despite the shifting perception of authority by readers and consumers, Ananny pushes back against the easy romanticizing of DIY news: "although the field of journalism looks significantly different than it did even five years ago and involves individuals with new types of agency, news still largely emerges from institutional forces that are beyond the meaningful influence of self-determining individuals." He goes on to pose a question that articulates the crux of questions discussed in our introduction: "The critical question for this new phase of DIY citizenship is: what does semiotic self-determination look like in the context of contemporary, networked information infrastructures that afford and constrain the conditions under which individuals can meaningfully explore identities and associations?"

Together these chapters on making and news media raise fundamental questions about meaning making, authority, and the need for new understandings of "public." As Annany (chapter 26) puts it: "It becomes critically important for those working under the rubric of DIY news to ask not 'Is this information true?' but, rather, 'What would it mean and whose experiences would be impacted if this information were considered to be true?' This kind of question places particular demands on system designers. It asks them to convene publics, not crowds—to account for those who must share consequences in addition to those who choose common interests."

The chapters in part IV offer a diverse portrait of DIY news media, questions of voice, sources, "truth," sense making, credibility and authority. With examples ranging from a vox pop experiment to feminist zines to banality of media and systems of production, we return to questions central to DIY citizenship—namely, questions about critical making, transparency, and participation at the intersections of design, platforms, publics, and news media creators.

References

Boler, M. 2006. *The Daily Show, Crossfire,* and the Will to Truth. *Scan Journal of Media Arts Culture* 3(1). http://www.scan.net.au/scan/journal/display.php?journal_id=73.

Boler, Megan, ed. 2008. *Digital Media and Democracy: Tactics in Hard Times.* Cambridge, MA: MIT Press.

Boler, Megan, with Stephen Turpin. 2008. *The Daily Show* and *Crossfire*: Satire and Sincerity as Truth to Power. In *Digital Media and Democracy: Tactics in Hard Times,* ed. Megan Boler, 383–404. Cambridge, MA: MIT Press.

Boler, Megan, and Selena Nemorin. 2013. Dissent, Truthiness, and Skepticism in the Global Media Landscape: Twenty-First-Century Propaganda in Times of War. In *The Oxford Handbook of Propaganda Studies,* ed. Russ Castronovo and Jonathan Auerbach, 390–412. New York: Oxford University Press.

Gee, James Paul. 2004. *Situated Language and Learning: A Critique of Traditional Schooling.* London: Routledge.

23 Redesigning the Vox Pop: Civic Rituals as Sites of Critical Reimagining

Joshua McVeigh-Schultz

The notion of DIY citizenship was originally framed by John Hartley as a way of accounting for the shifting cultural logic of television toward an emphasis on difference, choice, and self-determination.[1] At the same time, this framework of DIY citizenship also emphasized a movement away from values of sameness and identification with others. At the root of this argument is an embrace of a liberatory decoupling of addresser and addressee afforded by television. For Hartley writing in 1999, this decoupling is empowering for the do-it-yourself citizen, now free to appropriate meaning in ways unintended by television producers. But the same decoupling might be understood as disempowering in our contemporary media landscape, where audiences increasingly come to expect opportunities for richly mediated engagement or what Graham Meikle (chapter 27, this volume) describes in terms of "intercreativity."[2] And indeed, Hartley's later writing on the plebiscitary mechanics of vote-based reality television paints a different picture of participation, one that positions audiences as agents in an unfolding spectacle.[3]

How, then, might we rethink Hartley's original framework of DIY citizenship in light of increasing opportunities to *re*couple the link between addresser and addressee? How does the role of interactive platforms complicate the concept of DIY citizenship in relation to broadcast media? And how might reimagining the rituals of public representation provoke new ways of thinking about difference and identification?

The following chapter explores these questions through the lens of what I will refer to as civic ritual. By framing various modes of "speaking to," or "speaking for," the public in terms of civic ritual, I hope to position the architecture of address as, itself, an object of designerly attention. Aligning with Matt Ratto's notion of critical making,[4] this approach privileges the enacted experience rather than the designed object as an end in itself. Elsewhere I have described this methodology as "ritual design,"[5] taking a cue from Erving Goffman's notion of interaction ritual[6] and Julian Bleecker's adaption of this concept as a mode of design fiction.[7]

In particular, this discussion will focus on the ritual of the vox pop ("on-the-street") interview as a site of design intervention. And I will explore alternate configurations of the vox pop ritual through a project called "Synaptic Crowd: Vox Pop Experiments."[8] This work consisted of a series of interactive performances involving audience-driven interviews. The interactive component was informed by Ken Goldberg's Tele-Actor model,[9] in that online audiences used a voting mechanic to make decisions that impacted a live event. Drawing upon Marshall McLuhan's imagery of electronic media as prosthetic extensions,[10] the project explored the ways in which our projections about audiences (and by proxy, about larger social imaginaries) can be jostled by opening up interview interactions to live audience engagement. Mobile technology here figured as a catalyst for opening up new technosocial situations[11] by positioning a remote audience as a conversational partner. And I was interested in understanding how this repositioning might activate public space in ways that complicate familiar fantasies about "the street" as site of heterogeneous interaction.

The following discussion includes an examination of how the processes of identity construction embedded in the vox pop are complicated by hybrid virtual and physical interactions between performers and remote participants. I will argue that by shuffling the subject positions of the vox pop interview, the project opened up new lines of intersection between the personal and the political and suggested new strategies for activating public space. Such an approach proposes a reimagining of our civic rituals from the ground up, and in this sense attempts to address Megan Boler's appeal to trace the links between new subject formations and new theories of discursive power[12]—in particular, by locating these links within rituals of mediation and by situating live audiences as actors in the practice of place making.

Situating practices of civic design in relation to the discourse of DIY citizenship and critical making, I will argue for attention to this microsociality of mediated public life, and in particular, to a defamiliarization of the signification processes through which the public is reflected back to itself by the traditional vox pop of broadcast news. By reconfiguring the way that categories of "publics" are discursively constructed through particular forms of address, these performances engage in what DiSalvo (chapter 17, this volume) describes as "the imaginative modeling of alternative sociotechnical conditions."

Combining browser and mobile-based interfaces, the Synaptic Crowd platform enables online participants to nominate and vote on a series of questions (or statements) via a browser application while they watch a live

Figure 23.1
An intermediary holds a camera and a phone while remote audiences nominate and vote on questions (or statements) as a live vox pop interview streams online.

interview unfold in near real time. For users of the online platform, interaction proceeds according to the following flow: first, the user submits a question or statement to the public pool; second, by selecting their favorite option, the user casts a vote and increases the likelihood that this question or statement will be enunciated through the phone.

The text of a question or statement with the most votes at any given time is relayed to the phone of a remote intermediary figure located in physical space with an interviewee. This text then gets enunciated through the intermediary's phone as voice synthesized audio while online participants watch live streaming footage of the interviewee's answers.

I conducted initial performances in Santa Cruz during the spring and summer of 2009 and subsequently performed demos of the project at various conferences and exhibition spaces between 2009 and 2011.[13] In November 2010, the project was demoed at the DIY Citizenship conference's Exhibition/Hack Space.

In these performances, I was interested in understanding how allocating the responsibility of question formation to a live audience might alter parameters of social interaction in interview scenarios. In particular, I wanted to know what might happen to processes of symbolic mediation when an interviewer is no longer a stable interactional proxy for invisible audiences. What happens when live audiences can represent themselves through mediating technologies and engage directly with interviewees? How are contextual cues negotiated in such circumstances? And how might interviewees adapt to the contextual uncertainty implied by remotely distributed audiences? Would interviewees take the opportunity to turn the tables and pose questions to their collective interviewers? And how might online participants grapple with these new forms of agency? Such questions complicate the interviewer's role as mediator in a vox pop encounter and point to new opportunities for distributed audiences to intervene as actors in public space.

The Ritual of the Vox Pop

While the vox populi term predates broadcasting technology, television has nevertheless formalized the vox pop (or "on-the-street interview") form into a set of easily recognizable structures. Usually they involve a single question posed to a succession of people, then edited to emphasize inherent juxtaposition and range among the responders. Due to the way these responses are framed, vox pop sequences are not supposed to be taken as expert testimony. Instead, as Greg Myers argues, the purported news value they offer has more to do with the way that interviewees are asked to perform their opinions and account for them as signifiers of various categories of "public."[14]

Vox pop encounters usually take place in public space, but, more specifically, they take place in interstitial locations where people are in the process of doing something else (walking in the street, pumping gas, playing in a park, etc.). The "street" here functions as a fantasy of a kind of rough-and-ready Habermassian café, a physicalized antidote to Cass Sunstein's critique of digital enclaves[15]. But the reality of course is that our public spaces are rarely utilized for this kind of fluid interaction (where people from a variety of membership categories can engage with each other based solely on their co-presence in "the street"). Pedestrians don't normally accost one another in order to ask questions about topical issues of the day. But as a public ritual, the vox pop activates a fantasy about precisely this kind of world and the camera's presence (in on the street interviews) licenses a particular mode of public testimony in response.

In its edited form, the vox pop presents an imagined community made up of various prototypical categories of citizen: "the young professional," the "mom," the "construction worker," etc. And the interviewee is put in the tenuous position of having to figure out which of these stereotypical categories they are representing. Along these lines, Myers frames the vox pop as a kind of guessing game organized around the tacit negotiation of identity categories: "It is assumed that one already has an opinion . . . and the task now is to account for it, to explain why you hold it or how it came about. And this involves categorization; the question in a vox pop is not 'what do you say' but 'what does someone like you say'—and it is the interviewee's job to figure out what 'somewhat like you' means in this case.[16]

By selecting and framing these identity types, broadcast journalism reflects a particular version of the public back to itself. But in this way, traditional broadcast news also plays the role of gatekeeper by compartmentalizing the public into a set of easily digestible, inherently juxtaposed categories, with news moderators conveniently cast as neutral arbiters—an ideological stance that Nick Couldry has critiqued as the "myth of the mediated center."[17]

In my own experience asking prospective interviewees to participate in impromptu interviews, the potential interviewee typically asks the question "What is this for?" This question not only points ("in") to the here-and-now of the interview context, but also points ("out") to a there-and-then of future addressees—a mysterious audience that is both present and not-present at the same time. At stake here is the risk of recontextualization. While the question "What is this for?" can have a specific answer (e.g., "a documentary on [subject X]"), the actual process of mediation may be more complicated. A camera operator's answer to the question, then, is likely to be only half of the story. Potential interviewees must also resolve this question of context on their own by playing detective. How is the camera operator dressed? Do I trust their face? How official does the equipment look? Seizing upon these clues, the interviewee orients themselves to their nonpresent audience. In this way, the interviewee's question "What is this for?" points implicitly to another question: "To whom am I speaking?"

This implicit question is, in some ways, the flip side of Michael Warner's conception of a public as discursively constituted through address.[18] Within Warner's framework, the core question is not "To whom am I speaking?" but rather "To whom is this media addressed?" Or, alternatively, "How do *we* receive it?"—insofar as Warner's conception of "counterpublics" underscores the possibility of resistant readings. By contrast, for an interviewee in a vox pop, the interviewer's role as an interactional partner threatens to overdetermine the answer to the question "To whom am I speaking," and by extension also constrains the related question "Who am I (within this discourse)?"

Redesigning the Ritual of the Vox Pop

If the traditional vox pop of broadcast journalism invites interviewees to answer two implicit questions: "To whom am I speaking?" and "Who am I (in relation to this audience)?" then how might the vox pop be redesigned to address these questions differently, and what new modes of civic engagement—what new rituals of participation—might be possible if we change the way these questions gets answered? By enabling a live feedback loop between audience and subject, the Synaptic Crowd shuffles the agencies of the interview and enables participants to renegotiate the answers to these implicit questions in real time, presenting new intersection points between the personal and the political.

In these performative experiments, I often took on the role of the intermediary (holding the phone and initiating contact with potential interviewees). In such encounters, an atmosphere of performative play seemed to be licensed by my admission to the interviewee that I was not the originator of the question but merely the conduit for a group. This atmosphere contrasts sharply with traditional vox pop interviews I have conducted where interviewees seemed more wary about the risk that uninvited cameras can carry. By directly indexing an audience in the here-and-now, this threat seemed to be destabilized. And freed from concerns about how to address an abstract future audience, interviewees seemed remarkably comfortable in light of the novelty of the experience.

A key affordance of the platform during these performances was the ability of online participants to watch the interviewee's response as they formulated follow-ups (a feature that sets the Synaptic Crowd apart from other sorts of online question aggregation and vote-ranking tools). In this way, online audiences participate in the negotiation of context by making active decisions not only about which questions to ask, but also about when to ask a follow-up and when to introduce a new line of questioning.

Jostling Subject Positions

The structure of Synaptic Crowd encounters obstructs any smooth reconciliation between different subject positions. Instead, questions operate like pivot points that suddenly shift the remote participants' footing from one subject position to another. I have started to refer to these sorts of pivots as "inter sequitors": questions or prompts that demand an ad hoc reweaving of context, encouraging the interviewees to jump in and out of different subject positions as they grapple with an unpredictably evolving relationship to an unseen audience. We see this pivoting between different subject positions often prompted by questions that locate the interviewee in physical space. For example, an interview in which remote participants started out by asking topical questions about health care suddenly pivoted to raise questions about the interviewee's boyfriend and purpose at the beach.

Similarly, subject positions were jostled by questions that identify topical or political themes in response to interviewee answers that otherwise seemed rooted in personal experience. In one interview, for example, a seemingly benign prompt, "Describe the best day of your life," gave way to a strikingly intimate discussion of an interviewee's experience in the military. In such cases, personal topics took on political weight, but due to the way this line of questioning emerged organically from accounts of personal experience, these questions licensed interviewees to speak candidly about political or topical subjects. When the remote participants asked for this interviewee to state a position "for" or "against" the wars in Afghanistan and Iraq, for example, she pivoted again to reframe the question in terms of the *experience* of being called to duty, a discursive frame in which questions of political approval or disapproval could be treated as secondary to that of duty. Such examples stretched the boundaries between personal and political in ways we rarely see in typical on-the-street interviews.

In the design process, we decided to use a text-to-speech synthesized voice as the delivery mechanism for the utterances that the participants chose. From the perspective of the interviewee, the remote participants "speak" in one voice through the phone. This decision was made in part because we wanted the intermediary figure—the one holding the phone and initiating contact with people in public space—to hear the question or statement at the same time as the interviewee. This design decision made the process of negotiating what was appropriate much more transparent but also potentially risky.

The Role of the Intermediary

My role as intermediary required a great deal of improvised "accounting" for the remote participants' intentions, but this mode of "speaking on behalf" carried risk in that their subsequent contributions could contradict my attempts to serve as their proxy. Such risk, however, might be refreshing in the context of representative democracy where politicians and pundits are rarely called upon to account for the rhetorical strategies they use to represent others.[19]

In earlier writing on the experience, I remarked that "my role . . . as the intermediary, is to mediate these responses post facto, repairing context when necessary and giving the remote participants' speech acts a contextual wrapper so that these acts makes sense as interactional moves."[20] Interestingly, this responsibility to provide context also aligns the intermediary figure with the interviewee in a way that a typical vox pop interviewer never has to contend with. For example, in one particular exchange the remote participants actually voted for the statement "You're boring" as a way of short-circuiting the interview. Feeling as if they were attacking me as well, I got in front of the camera and retorted: "No, you're boring. Ask better questions!" In my experience, this kind of confrontational orientation to the remote participants was rare, but the fact that the agency of remote participants was so immediate, so directly implicated, meant that the interview encounters transformed the relationship between interviewee and intermediary, insofar as their shared performative risk aligned these two roles as allies with a mutual stake in responding creatively to online participants.

In many cases, the questions asked exceeded the boundaries of what I would have felt comfortable asking had I been an actual interviewer framing the questions myself. To safeguard the interviewees, I would explain at the outset that they could pass on any question that didn't suit them. However, more often then not, the interviewees were more than happy to answer questions that I would not have felt comfortable asking. Having a live audience of remote participants interact directly in this way opened up a kind of engagement that would have been impossible to achieve otherwise, raising questions about why we don't have similar expectations for live participation in other aspects of civic life.

Reconfiguring Public Speech

By positioning remote addressees as drivers of vox pop encounters, the project disrupted the typical processes through which interviewers and interviewees improvise various categories of "public" and orient themselves in relation to imagined audiences. As Warner points out, our subject positions as the imagined addressees of public speech play a crucial role in the discursive construction of publics as social imaginaries.[21] However, Warner's framework is grounded by familiar examples from broadcast and publishing models of mass media, while multidirectional platforms of communication remap the relationship among speaker, addressee, and public—and in doing so make possible new kinds of subject formations that complicate Warner's insights about the orientation of mediated public speech toward "strangerhood." For example, questions or statements that directly index the interviewee's embodied subject position (such as "I like your shirt") situate the remote participants in the role of conversational partner—a break from the kind of "address to strangers" that Warner associates with public speech.

In this way, the Synaptic Crowd shuffles the agencies of the interview and destabilizes the compartmentalizing logic of the traditional vox pop. Questions about the identity and role-inhabitance expectations of addresser and addressee can be renegotiated in real time, creating collisions between personal and political modes of address. Not only does the question "What are you doing at the beach?" invite a more intimate speech register, it also recasts any parallel talk about topical or political issues not as "merely" public, but as public performance by a situated subject who can be addressed as such.

This jostling or shuffling of subject positions also meant that different kinds of questions could be asked and different sorts of encounters and revelations were possible. Sometimes the remote participants would begin the interview flirtatiously ("You're hot!"), or at other times sought to call attention to the awkwardness of the phone's disembodied voice ("Is this interview weird?"). In such cases, the audience itself was positioned, not as a generalized other, but as a particularized interactional partner located in the here-and-now.

This configuration created opportunities for interviewees and remote participants to build trust with one another, and intimacy emerged as a collaborative achievement born out of a willingness to follow wherever the interview led. For example, an interview of a sunbathing couple that started out about exercise led to a bawdy conversation about sex and live action role-playing, and an interview about a long-distance relationship led to strikingly intimate revelations about PTSD, heartache, and nightmares. Such topics were made speakable due to the repositioning of audience as a live interlocutor. Within this context, interviewees demonstrated a willingness to explore intimate registers as a form of public speech.

Defamiliarizing the Vox Pop

By using live audience participation to drive on-the-street interviews, the project pulls back the curtain on the way that identity categories are coconstructed in the performative ritual of the vox pop. This remapping serves as a mode of defamiliarization, a term first used by Viktor Shklovsky[22] in the early twentieth century to describe literary techniques that disrupt the habituation of perception by making the familiar seem strange. This strategy is now a common feature of the methodologies of both ethnography and design.[23]

By mediating live audiences we disrupt the processes by which this coconstruction of audience and interviewee subject positions occurs. Engagement with a diverse collection of remote participants encourages the swapping of different registers, from personal to political and vice versa, and this pivoting defamiliarizes the ways that particular formations of subjecthood get constructed in relation to imagined audiences. In so doing, we reveal the masquerade behind the curation of identity types that the vox pop of broadcast media traditionally employs.

Increasingly this process of curating the public into a series of prototypical identity types has become a key feature of how TV news shows incorporate social media into their live broadcast model—using topical tweets, for example, to provide a gestalt snapshot of the public mood on a particular issue. Representing social media in this way frames the public as a series of prototypical objects of exhibition, rather than as an intelligent agent to engage.

But what happens when the public can serve as its own gatekeeper and curate its own voice? Audiences that self-organize can be threatening to the broadcast model, and we saw this in CNN's reluctance to acknowledge the #CNNFAIL meme during the initial stages of the Iranian protest movement in 2009. In such cases, broadcast news can no longer compartmentalize the public into vox pop sound bites and must instead begin to address their audience as a thinking entity capable of critique.

Conclusions

By defamiliarizing the seamlessness of our civic rituals as media spectacles, we reveal their implicit interactional rule sets and open up the possibility that they could be otherwise. In this way, strategies of critical making can be applied to rituals as well as objects, and in particular, there are opportunities to reimagine our civic rituals from the ground up by enabling audiences to intervene into public space. My approach to reconfiguring civic rituals shares with critical making an emphasis on process over product. However, rather than focusing specifically on the processes of material engagement, I emphasize the collaborative disruption, contestation, and reformulation of ritualized processes of interaction. In this sense, the approach parallels the breaching experiments of Harold Garfinkel[24] and also borrows aspects from the improvisational strategies of Augusto Boal's Theater of the Oppressed[25] as well as situationist methods of détournement.

For Ratto, critical making uses material interventions as a collaborative space for imagining alternative constructions of the relationship between society and technology,[26] and in this sense the methodology echoes Bruno Latour's interest in transforming matters of fact into matters of concern.[27] In my own work, I am similarly interested in troubling the commonsense "facthood" of civic rituals.

If remotely mediated audiences can reshape public space, we have an opportunity to defamiliarize the taken-for-granted separation between addresser and addressee that so defined twentieth-century public discourse. Along these lines, I conceive of DIY citizenship as an active engagement with, and reimagining of, the implicit performative templates that trace discursive lines between categories of "public" and everyday life. A remapping of the architecture of address, however, entails new kinds of subject positions that complicate Warner's framework of publics as discursively constituted by an imagined community of nonpresent addressees. If remote audiences can collectively "play at" the subject position of a conversational partner, then what discursive work does this new positionality imply? Drawing on Judith Butler's description of the constitutive nature of the encounter, according to which "the 'doer' is variably constructed in and through the deed,"[28] we might ask what new kinds of "doers" and what new kinds of interactional "deeds" does the concept of DIY citizenship offer? Hartley's description of plebiscitary models of audience engagement in reality television[29] provides an important clue, but there is also an opportunity to resituate this kind of plebiscitary practice as a new mode of encounter, one that leverages what Michael Hancher calls cooperative speech acts.[30]

For John Hartley, the era of DIY citizenship implies that television and popular media have the potential to proffer dreams of alternative identity formations—dreams that, while possibly unrealistic, can nevertheless serve as transformative catalysts for imagining change.[31] While self-determination in Hartley's sense is an important fantasy, one that sets the stage for the possibility of alternative identity formation, I would argue that social imaginaries like DIY citizenship have always also been about questions of "to-whom" and not just about "by-whom." In this sense, attending to the rituals that construct "the public" and mediate audiences provides a very different lens for understanding participatory culture. Using this perspective as a provocation for design research turns our attention to the structuring processes of civic rituals themselves and helps us defamiliarize their taken-for-granted facthood as a matter of concern.

Acknowledgments

Special acknowledgment goes to my collaborator Brian Alexakis who developed the Synaptic Crowd web and phone interfaces. Thanks also to my committee at UC Santa Cruz: Warren Sack, Sharon Daniel, and Irene Lusztig. Additionally, key participants in various performances included Lorenzo Estebanez (who served as cinematographer for the beach locations) as well as Natalie Loveless, Jody McVeigh-Schultz, David McVeigh-Schultz, Lyes Belhocine, Miki Foster, Laila Shereen Sakr, Annette Angus, Nick Lally, Nikolaos Hanselmann, Karl Baumann, Kathleen Kralowec, Drew Detweiler, Antoine Abou Jaoude, Kyle McKinley, Elizabeth Travelslight, Nada Miljkovic, Roopesh Sitharan, Lola Elfman, Troy Allman, Craig Hobbs, and many others. Finally, a great big thanks goes out to all the willing interview participants I encountered "on the street" who happily shared their time, energy, and open-minded spirit.

Notes

1. John Hartley, *Uses of Television* (London: Routledge, 1999). Note that Hartley's framing of DIY citizenship as marked by difference (and by a shift away from identification with others) contrasts with more contemporary observations of participatory culture that emphasize "shared content worlds" as enablers of fan cultural production.

For example, see Neta Kligler-Vilenchik et al., "Experiencing Fan Activism: Understanding the Power of Fan Activist Organizations through Members' Narratives," *Transformative Works and Cultures*, February 4, 2011, http://journal.transformativeworks.org/index.php/twc/article/view/322/273.

Similarly, Henry Jenkins (chapter 3, this volume) makes observations about how identification with a shared content world can scaffold large-scale civic engagement through a process he terms 'cultural acupuncture.'

2. Meikle here is adapting Tim Berners-Lee's concept of "intercreativity."

3. John Hartley, *Television Truths: Forms of Knowledge in Popular Culture* (Oxford: Wiley-Blackwell, 2007).

4. Matt Ratto, "Critical Making: Conceptual and Material Studies in Technology and Social Life," *Information Society* 27, no. 4 (2011): 252–260; Matt Ratto, "Open Design and Critical Making," in *Open Design Now: Why Design Cannot Remain Exclusive*, ed. P. Atkinson et al., 202–209 (Amsterdam: BIS Publishers, 2011).

5. Joshua McVeigh-Schultz, "Making Trouble: Redesigning the Rituals of Civic Life," in *ISEA* (Istanbul, 2011).

6. Erving Goffman, *Interaction Ritual—Essays on Face-to-Face Behavior* (New York: Doubleday & Company, 1967).

7. Julian Bleecker, "Design Fiction: A Short Essay on Design, Science, Fact and Fiction," *Near Future Laboratory*, 2009, http://www.nearfuturelaboratory.com/2009/03/17/design-fiction-a-short-essay-on-design-science-fact-and-fiction/.

The approach I outline here also shares ground with other reflexive or critically engaged methodologies such as "critical design," "adversarial design," "experiential scenarios," and "reflective HCI." See Anthony Dunne, *Hertzian Tales: Electronic Products, Aesthetic Experience, and Critical Design* (Cambridge, MA: MIT Press, 2008); Carl DiSalvo, *Adversarial Design* (Cambridge, MA: MIT Press, 2012); Stuart Candy, "The Futures of Everyday Life: Politics and the Design of Experiential Scenarios" (Honolulu: University of Hawaii at Manoa, 2010); Phoebe Sengers et al., "Reflective HCI: Articulating an Agenda for Critical Practice," *CHI* (2006): 1683–1686; Paul Dourish et al., "Reflective HCI: Towards a Critical Technical Practice," *CHI* (2004): 541–550.

8. The Synaptic Crowd platform was codesigned by Joshua McVeigh-Schultz and Brian Alexakis in 2008 and 2009. McVeigh-Schultz conceived of and designed early prototypes of the idea in 2008. Alexakis was hired as a collaborator to program the web and mobile application interfaces and developed the first fully functioning prototype in early 2009.

9. Ken Goldberg et al., "Collaborative Online Teleoperation with Spatial Dynamic Voting and a Human 'Tele-Actor,'" in *IEEE International Conference on Robotics and Automation* (Washington, DC, 2002).

10. Marshall McLuhan and Lewis H. Lapham, *Understanding Media: The Extensions of Man* (Cambridge, MA: MIT Press, 1994).

11. Mizuko Ito and Daisuke Okabe, "Technosocial Situations: Emergent Structuring of Mobile E-mail Use," in *Personal, Portable, Pedestrian*, ed. Mizuko Ito, Daisuke Okabe, and Misa Matsuda, 261–274 (Cambridge, MA: MIT Press, 2005).

12. Megan Boler, ed., *Digital Media and Democracy: Tactics in Hard Times* (Cambridge, MA: MIT Press, 2008).

13. Performances were conducted near the Santa Cruz Boardwalk (May 9, 2009) and at interACTIVATE, UCSC's Digital Arts and New Media MFA show (at the Santa Cruz Museum of Art and History on June 24, 2009). These events inform my writing on the project. Classroom demos employing students as remote participants and camera/phone wielding intermediaries were also conducted in various contexts between 2009 and 2011. Live demonstrations of the project were also presented at the HASTAC III conference (April 20, 2009), at the Visible Evidence XVI Conference (August 13, 2009), at the Association for Integrative Studies conference (October 8,

2009), at the International Broadcasting Convention (September 12, 2010), at the Open Video Conference (October 2, 2010), and at the DIY Citizenship conference's Exhibition/Hack Space (November 13, 2010).

14. Greg Myers, *Matters of Opinion: Talking about Public Issues* (Cambridge, UK: Cambridge University Press, 2008).

15. Cass Sunstein, "The Daily We: Is the Internet Really a Blessing for Democracy," *Boston Review*, 2001, http://bostonreview.net/BR26.3/sunstein.php.

16. Myers, *Matters of Opinion*, 209.

17. Nick Couldry, *Media Rituals: A Critical Approach* (London: Routledge, 2003).

18. Michael Warner, "Publics and Counterpublics," *Public Culture* 14, no. 1 (2002): 49–90.

19. For an extended discussion of the role of accounting in interactions between politicians and the public, see Stephen Coleman, "Direct Representation: Towards a Conversational Democracy" (London: The Institute for Public Policy Research, 2005), http://www.hcs.harvard.edu/~sjklein/direct-representation.pdf.

20. Joshua McVeigh-Schultz, "Synaptic Crowd: Vox Pop Experiments" (MFA thesis, University of California, Santa Cruz, 2009).

21. Warner, "Publics and Counterpublics."

22. Viktor Shklovsky, "Art as Technique" (1917), in *Contemporary Literary Criticism: Modernism through Poststructuralism*, ed. Robert Con Davis, 51–63 (New York, London: Longman Press, 1986).

23. Genevieve Bell, Mark Blythe, and Phoebe Sengers, "Making by Making Strange: Defamiliarization and the Design of Domestic Technologies," *ACM Transactions on Computer-Human Interaction (TOCHI)* 12, no. 2 (2005): 1–25.

24. Harold Garfinkel, *Studies in Ethnomethodology (Social and Political Theory)* (London: Polity, 1967).

25. Augusto Boal, *Theater of the Oppressed* (New York: Theater Communications Group, 1979).

26. Ratto, "Open Design and Critical Making."

27. Bruno Latour, "A Cautious Prometheus? A Few Steps Toward a Philosophy of Design (with Special Attention to Peter Sloterdijk)," in *Proceedings of the 2008 Annual International Conference of the Design History Society*, ed. Fiona Hackney, Jonathan Glynne, and Viv Minton, 2–10 (Boca Raton: Universal Publishers, 2009).

28. Judith Butler, *Gender Trouble: Feminism and the Subversion of Identity*, ed. Linda J. Nicholson, *Thinking Gender* (London: Routledge, 1990), 181.

29. Hartley, *Television Truths.*

30. Michael Hancher, "The Classification of Cooperative Illocutionary Acts," *Language in Society* 8, no. 1 (April 1, 1979): 1–14.

31. Hartley, *Uses of Television.*

24 Alternative Media Production, Feminism, and Citizenship Practices

Rosa Reitsamer and Elke Zobl

I think zines are significant on both individual levels . . . and for social movements. They . . . play important roles in DIY feminist and anti-capitalist movements. . . . Anyone can write this and in this way contribute to a kind of non-academic/non-professional but very valuable DIY political theory and herstory.

—Nina Nijsten, Belgium

Zines can function as a participatory alternative medium to give alternative views on the society that can't be found in the mainstream media. Zines also offer connections and communication between individuals and groups worldwide. These connections can be useful starting-points for further co-operation and sharing of knowledge, support and resources.

—Nina Nijsten, Belgium

Drawing on findings from our Feminist Media Production in Europe research project at the University of Salzburg (Austria),[1] this chapter demonstrates how transnational feminist alternative media—in particular, print fanzines (for a definition of zines, see Chidgey, chapter 6, this volume), blogs, and electronic fanzines (e-zines)—create spaces of civic engagement beyond consumption, and intervene in hegemonic discourses on neoliberal politics, feminism and migration. As Linda Steiner aptly puts it, alternative feminist media suggest "a model for oppositional media"[2] as they document women's attempts to improve themselves and remake the world. Chris Atton champions alternative media in general as "counterhegemonic" because they challenge hegemonic structures in society "whether on an explicit political platform, or employing the kinds of indirect challenges through experimentation and the transformation of existing roles, routines, emblems and signs."[3] What makes media "alternative" to the mainstream of corporate media conglomerates are the processes of production, the content and the interpretive strategies of its audiences.[4] As such,

Figure 24.1
Drawing 1 by Nina Nijsten (*Missy Magazine*, Germany, no. 7, 2010)

feminist alternative media offer participatory spaces, which facilitate an engagement with cultural citizenship through DIY activities. The membership in a loose community of alternative feminist media producers can be described as an essential precondition for the acquisition of citizenship in general and for cultural citizenship in particular. The efforts of alternative media to engage, produce and invest collective meaning can be described as "critical making"[5] activities providing the opportunity to reflect on and intervene in systems of power and as expressions of civic responsibility through which a competent participation in symbolic resources of society is acquired. Alternative media, we argue, can offer a space (and the means) for critical making to question national identity, reflect one's own position in society, and advance social change. This leads us to this chapter's main question: How do feminist alternative media producers acquire their knowledge for writing and (online) publishing, and how do they produce local, transnational and virtual networks through which cultural citizenship is experienced as a collective learning process?

Changing Discourses on Citizenship

In the 1950s, Thomas Marshall argued that citizenship is a justifiable ideal for the postwar Western welfare state. To Marshall, "citizenship" defines an individual's place in society as well as their relationship with their state.[6] Three main assumptions underpin Marshall's theory, all of which have influenced how youth citizenship is being theorized today. First, Marshall describes young people as "citizens in becoming" because full citizenship rights are only acquired by adults; hence, adulthood and citizenship are considered to be interconnected and interrelated. Second, citizenship is

Figure 24.2
Drawing 2 by Nina Nijsten (*ScumGrrrls*, Belgium, no. 16, 2009)

something that is bestowed on members of nation-states where 'being a member' brings with it certain kinds of benefits.[7] Third, Marshall specified social, civil, and political rights in his citizenship theory, neglecting a cultural dimension of citizenship and cultural rights.[8]

Since the 1980s, however, discourses on citizenship in general and youth citizenship in particular have undergone significant changes, shaped by deindustrialization, globalization, the retreat of the welfare state in Western societies, and a rapid growth in cultural industries. This neoliberal restructuring of society and economy is interwoven with the fragmentation of older collective forms of identification and traditional structures, as well as an increased social significance placed on individual choice and action.[9] As a result, Marshall's emphasis on social, civil, and political rights has been overtaken by a new discourse of "active citizenship" and "consumer citizenship." These paradigms emphasize duty, responsibilities, and individual effort, along with consumption and managed forms of participation (e.g., citizenship programs in schools).[10] As Anita Harris argues, "Young people are increasingly called upon to participate in the polity and in civil society, and to develop their civic knowledge, and yet this is in an environment of reduced opportunity for the mobilisation of a traditional citizenship identity and its associated activities."[11]

Social rights are thus restructured as the individual concerns of young people who should not rely on the state, but instead try to make the best choices for themselves in order to achieve economic security. At the same time, according to a neoliberal capitalistic logic, economic independence and security are no longer linked to one's capacity for production but to their capacity for consumption, as work continues to diminish in importance as a pathway through which to create an identity and a sense of belonging. Civil rights then become operational if one has the money to enter into a consumer relationship. Civic viability is thus inextricably linked with consumption and personal responsibility. In these new discourses, the language of "clients" and "consumers" has replaced that of citizenship.[12]

The concept of cultural citizenship differs from neoliberal ideals of "active citizenship" and "consumer citizenship" as well as from older liberal notions of citizenship revolving around "having" rights and responsibilities. Liberal notions of citizenship, as suggested by Marshall, neglect the cultural dimension of citizenship and thus ignore cultural rights, while neoliberal citizenship ideals introduce a new conception of citizen as self-actualizing and responsible in the context of risk. Cultural citizenship, on the contrary, can function as a crucial concept for exploring processes of cultural meaning production and participation.[13] The concept allows for an exploration of new, more individualized forms of activism and social participation at a time when young people are alienated from the political system and show less interest in such formal politics as voting, political parties, and political organizations. This concept stresses the importance of culture for participation and the articulation of identity and belonging. It shifts the focus away from membership in a polity, as suggested by Marshall, onto common experiences, discourses of empowerment, and recognition of difference.[14] Cultural citizenship "entails all those cultural practices that allow competent participation in society and includes the rights to be represented and to speak actively. Media as a particular form of cultural production is both an engine and an actor in the processes of self-making and being-made, in which people acquire their individual, group-specific and social identities."[15] Furthermore, the concept of cultural citizenship is central "for understanding the process of societal meaning production, since it intimately links cultural production, cultural products and audiences and binds them firmly together."[16] Access to the relevant symbolic resources of society is mediated through education and schooling as well as through the capacity of speaking, reading, and writing.[17] Hence, competent participation in the symbolic resources presumes the possibility to acquire cultural production in society.[18]

Alternative cultural production, DIY culture, and alternative feminist media production all prove instrumental for participating in the symbolic resources of society and for developing new, more individualized forms of activism. DIY culture, in particular, "encourages individuals to make their own culture, rather than simply consuming what is mass-produced for them by the mainstream culture industries and complaining that there are no alternatives."[19] The beginnings of DIY culture are rooted in the avant-garde art movements of the 1950s and the emerging social movements of the 1960s. In the late 1970s, punk rock media and style revolved around the DIY ethos with self-produced fanzines, independent record labels, and alternative distribution networks, the result being that DIY as an organizing principle gained a greater currency in alternative cultures. A large section of feminist alternative media producers position themselves within self-organized feminist DIY cultures.[20] However, it is important to take into consideration how this actualization is still dependent on structural conditions. Young people are affected differently by the new constructions of citizenship according to their embedded position in society, as Anita Harris has pointed out. They therefore articulate different ideas about the role and significance of feminist alternative media production and formulate different demands for enacting citizenship to bring about societal change.

Interventions into Hegemonic Discourses on Neoliberal Politics, Feminism, and Migration

One way for transnational feminist self-published print zines, blogs, and e-zines to engage in and to articulate cultural citizenship is by making interventions into hegemonic discourses on neoliberal politics, feminism, and migration. Genderblog, a German weblog founded in 2005 with a particular focus on popular culture and cultural representation informed by postmodern theories on gender and sexuality, articulates the idea of intervening into hegemonic discourses on feminism as such: "The idea for Genderblog was to offer a possibility to publish texts and to respond to questions which are of interest to us and which are discussed in the media. In recent years mainstream media often pick up feminist topics but there is a strong tendency to discredit feminism and to describe feminism negatively. With a blog, one can easily respond to these discourses because blogs are fast to produce and easy to find on the Internet and they offer a possibility to refer to other texts by setting links."[21]

The relatively fast and easy production of responses critiquing the ways in which feminist topics are negotiated in the German-speaking press enables the contributors of Genderblog, a loose group of writers, to gain some control over information and their own cultural productions. These efforts to engage, produce, and invest collective meaning can be described both as critical making activities that provide the opportunity to reflect on and intervene in systems of power as well as expressions of civic responsibility through which a competent participation in symbolic resources of society is acquired.

In this sense of "critical" making, the multilingual Austrian e-zine *Migrazine. Online Magazin von Migrantinnen für alle* (Migrazine. Online Magazine by Female Migrants for All) offers a more precise response to the hegemonic discourses on migration. Published since 2006 by MAIZ, an autonomous migrant organization in Linz, the initial idea of Migrazine was to produce a feminist alternative online media where women with migrant backgrounds are responsible for the whole process of media production. According to their website, Migrazine is "self-organised participation in the media landscape, intrusion into the dominant discourse, democratisation of information."[22] In a 2011 issue of *Migrazine*, the term "Second Generation" ("Secondo"/"Seconda") is taken up to refer to the life realities of people "who are not migrants, but are constructed as 'the Other' by members of majority societies." Several writers address the self-understanding of a "post-migrant" generation which calls traditional identity conceptions into question and introduces a new vocabulary of belonging. Hence, Migrazine can be understood as an elaborated response to the hegemonic discourses on the "First" and "Second Generation" of migrants in Western societies by demanding political rights for migrants, such as the right to vote, and by intervening in the violent stereotypical representations through which people with migrant backgrounds are constructed as "the Other." In this respect, alternative media production becomes a means for critical making to question national identity, to reflect one's own position in society, and to advance social change.

Migrazine and other like-minded publications question traditional identity constructions and national identities, especially with regards to the strict European immigration laws, and propose that one's individual identity exists at the intersection of multiple identity categories. As feminist media producers, they test collective forms of participation in civil society in order to reinvent a new notion of citizenship in the context of globalization and migration. But how do feminist alternative media producers acquire their knowledge for writing and (online) publishing, and how do they produce local, transnational, and virtual networks through which cultural citizenship is experienced as a collective learning process?

Affinity Spaces: Networks and Informal Learning Processes

The vast majority of feminist media producers acquired their knowledge of writing and (online) publishing through informal learning practices in local, transnational, and virtual networks outside of formal educational institutions. As feminist activist and Draft—Prepih blogger Tea (Slovenia) explains: "I think the zine community was my best writing school . . . just because it never forced me to fit a certain genre or style of writing . . . and you had almost guaranteed feedback. . . . It was a kind of peer review system, so it was never intimidating and it let you continue with pleasure, without any inhibitions."[23]

Trading information and skills has always been a part of (sub)cultural production, and female cultural producers often act within communities that function as DIY learning environments.[24] Feminist self-empowerment strategies and leftist critiques of capitalism converge in alternative media sites. Bottom-up processes of learning by doing, skill-sharing, and learning by cooperating with other media producers also transform creativity and cultural production into collective and collaborative processes. In this respect, critical making in the context of feminist media production comprises always various dimensions of doing-it-together.

As such, we can speak of these sites as culturally productive "affinity spaces"[25] where people are brought together by a common goal and participate through informal learning practices and networking. "Affinity spaces" are physical and/or virtual places sustained by common interests, such as challenging the hegemonic media discourses on feminism and migration and an interest in feminist cultural production in which people are allowed to participate according to their skills. In these spaces, knowledge is distributed in face-to-face interactions and through virtual networks using new information and communication technologies. These informal learning practices constitute, we argue, an enactment of citizenship because the acquisition of experience, knowledge, and participation in the symbolic resources of society are important dimensions of cultural citizenship. In this respect, we can understand cultural citizenship as a learning process.[26]

In addition, cultural citizenship, as a socially and culturally constructed model of citizenship, includes a constructive approach toward community that manifests itself in the production of local, transnational, and virtual networks. This leads to a sense of community at a time when traditional security nets are disappearing.[27] Networks are formed around alternative book fairs, feminist fanzine festivals, conferences, exhibitions, workshops, online distribution networks, mailing lists and message boards, among other things.[28] These networks support the noncommercial distribution of feminist alternative media as they place value on varied, process-related social relations and communication processes over more established standards of professionalization, expertise, and legally maintained intellectual property.[29]

The artist of Trouble X Comics (Germany) emphasizes the benefit of such virtual networking: "By publishing the comics on the Internet, I'm also making them accessible to others. . . . It is very much networking. I have an exchange with other people and get even more from the other people. It's not that I only give out content, but I also get content."[30] Blogs, MySpace, Flickr and Facebook are all used as tools of dissemination. To prevent artworks from circulating in unwanted social contexts, a Creative Commons License is issued alongside the illustrations. Yet the artist is also aware that "social networking" through Web 2.0 portals is time intensive, that virtual interactions feign social proximity, and that capitalist exploitation is not inevitably excluded: "I am very present on the Internet, and many know my stuff. That's a bit of capitalist marketing, what I'm doing."[31] This access enables networking and exchange with other feminist alternative media producers. Virtual communication and archiving platforms such as the Feminist Poster Project[32] or Grassroots Feminism also facilitate such networking among people with common interests.

Beyond online networks, media production on a local level also plays a significant role for feminist alternative media producers. For example, the Grrrl Zines A Go-Go collective in San Diego "doesn't just want to encourage zine making"[33] through the zine workshops they have offered for (and with) girls, young women, and underprivileged youth in the greater Southern California community since 2002; they also share and pass on their experiences and knowledge by publishing zines with how-to instructions for conducting zine workshops, collaborating with community groups, and getting involved in DIY zine archiving. These zine workshops offer a low-threshold, informal learning opportunity to explore self-publishing and to develop collective self-empowerment and authorial processes. Such practices have particular significance in neoliberal times as they stand in contrast to—and offer critical spaces apart from—the focus on individual effort, consumption, and managed forms of participation within the "active citizenship" and "consumer citizenship" discourses we explored earlier.

Zines, blogs, e-zines, and zine workshops can be understood as a medium for local, transnational, and virtual dialogue, as a medium for community and network building, and as an exchange of experiences and knowledge among alternative media producers. Membership in and solidarity with a loose community of alternative feminist media producers is not defined in terms of belonging to a nationality and the acquisition of formal rights. This membership in a community can be described as an essential precondition for the acquisition of citizenship in general and for cultural citizenship in particular (for an exploration of the online and offline community of knitters as a form of socially engaged and socially networked DIY citizenship, see Orton-Johnson, chapter 9, this volume).

Conclusion

While one could argue that feminist alternative media can be seen as an expression of DIY citizenship (a position taken up by the 2010 DIY Citizenship: Critical Making and Social Media conference in Toronto), when we follow the description of DIY citizenship as self-determination set out by John Hartley,[34] we see this notion of DIY citizenship as too optimistic and premature. As Joke Hermes points out:

> Like Hartley, I believe in the value of self-determination, but perhaps a little caution is needed in pronouncing fan cultures, urban youth culture, taste constituencies, consumer-sovereignty movements, and football supporters as card-carrying members of a new democracy. . . . I am slightly more pessimistic, and more influenced by Foucault's dictum that the exercise of power calls forth counterforces. All politics, whether style politics or governmental policy, involve rules and so do forms of community building. Rules involve a notion of what is and what is not acceptable, what can and cannot be accepted. Rules refer to norms and of necessity lead to inclusion and exclusion.[35]

In addition to Hermes's objection, we suggest that the concept of cultural citizenship is a more useful and applicable tool for exploring the citizenship practices of feminist alternative media producers than the concept of DIY citizenship, because cultural citizenship allows a critical discussion of the neoliberal use of the term "do-it-yourself" in the context of choice biographies. Feminist alternative media production provides a means to engage in cultural citizenship practices beyond the increasing obligation of young people to "produce, stage and cobble together their biographies themselves"[36] and to manage their careers with flexibility, self-responsibility, and personal risk management.

Feminist alternative media production thus becomes a means for a younger generation to question national identity and citizenship; to intervene in hegemonic discourses on neoliberal politics, feminism, and migration; and to invent collective forms of participation in politics and civil society by producing and maintaining affinity spaces for networking and informal learning practices. Like Hermes, we suggest that mechanisms of inclusion and exclusion and discursive and structural inequalities are essential to consider when reflecting on people's participation in the symbolic resources in society by which they express and enact (cultural) citizenship. As such an exploration goes beyond the scope of this chapter, more research in this area—for example, in relation to a critical reflection of privileges (such as white privilege), access to power, and mechanisms of exclusion—needs to be done.

Acknowledgments

The authors (Rosa Reitsamer and Elke Zobl) have contributed equally to this article. The research for this project was funded by the Austrian Science Fund (FWF): P21187.

Notes

1. The Feminist Media Production in Europe research project investigated 106 blogs and 39 e-zines published in Europe between 2009 and 2011. All quotes from feminist media producers in this article refer to interviews conducted within the project (see www.grassrootsfeminism.net/cms/). See Zobl, Reitsamer, and Grünangerl 2012. The authors have contributed equally to this chapter.

2. Steiner 2000, 1331.

3. Atton 2002, 27.

4. Atkinson 2010, 22.

5. See Ratto 2011.

6. See Marshall 1950 and Marshall 1992.

7. See also Blackman and France 2001.

8. See Stevenson 2001.

9. See Beck 1992.

10. See Harris 2004.

11. Harris 2008, 484.

12. Harris 2004, 64–70.

13. See Klaus and Lünenborg 2012.

14. See Stevenson 2001; Delanty 2002; Klaus and Lünenborg 2004a; and Klaus and Lünenborg 2004b.

15. Klaus and Lünenborg 2012, 204.

16. Ibid., 204.

17. See Rosaldo 1999.

18. Klaus and Lünenborg 2004a, 108.

19. Kearney 1998, 561.

20. Regarding Riot Grrrl and Ladyfest activism, see, e.g., Chidgey 2009, Monem 2007, and Schilt and Zobl 2008.

21. Interview with Genderblog (Germany): http://genderblog.de/.

22. Migrazine (Austria): www.migrazine.at; authors' translation.

23. Draft—Prepih blogger "Tea" (Slovenia): http://prepih.blogspot.com.

24. See Piano 2002.

25. See Gee 2004.

26. Delanty 2002.

27. See Beck 1992.

28. See Zobl 2011.

29. See Atton 2002.

30. At her/his express wish, the artist of Trouble X Comics (http://troublex.blogsport.de/).will not be mentioned by name, but will be represented in the text anonymously and ambiguously.

31. The artist of Trouble X Comics.

32. The Feminist Poster Project (Belgium): http://feministposterproject.wordpress.com/.

33. Grrrl Zines A Go-Go collective: www.gzagg.org.

34. See Hartley 1999.

35. Hermes 2005, 9.

36. Beck 1994, 13.

References

Atkinson, Joshua D. 2010. *Alternative Media and Politics of Resistance. A Communication Perspective.* New York: Peter Lang.

Atton, Chris. 2002. *Alternative Media.* London, Thousand Oaks, New Delhi: Sage.

Beck, Ulrich. 1992. *Risk Society: Towards a New Modernity.* London: Sage.

Beck, Ulrich. 1994. "The Reinvention of Politics: Towards a Theory of Reflexive Modernization." In *Reflexive Modernisation,* ed. Ulrich Beck, Anthony Giddens, and Scott Lash, 1–55. Cambridge: Polity Press.

Blackman, Shane, and Alan France. 2001. "Youth Marginality under Postmodernism." In *Culture and Citizenship,* ed. Nick Stevenson, 180–197. London: Sage.

Chidgey, Red. 2009. DIY Feminist Networks in Europe. Personal and Collective Acts of Resistance. *Transform! European Journal of Alternative Thinking and Political Dialogue* 5:159–165.

Delanty, Gerard. 2002. Two Conceptions of Cultural Citizenship: A Review of Recent Literature on Culture and Citizenship. *Global Review of Ethnopolitics* 1 (3) (March): 60–66.

Gee, James Paul. 2004. *Situated Language and Learning: A Critique of Traditional Schooling.* London: Routledge.

Harris, Anita. 2004. *Future Girl: Young Women in the Twenty-First Century.* New York, London: Routledge.

Harris, Anita. 2008. Young Women, Late Modern Politics, and the Participatory Possibilities of Online Cultures. *Journal of Youth Studies* 11 (5): 481–495.

Hartley, John. 1999. *Uses of Television.* London, New York: Routledge.

Hermes, Joke. 2005. *Re-reading Popular Culture.* Malden, Oxford: Blackwell.

Kearney, Mary Celeste. 1998. Girls, Girls, Girls: Gender and Generation in Contemporary Discourses of Female Adolescence and Youth Culture. PhD diss., University of Southern California.

Klaus, Elisabeth, and Margreth Lünenborg. 2004a. "Medienhandeln als Alltagshandeln. Über die Konstituierung gesellschaftlicher Identität durch cultural citizenship in der Mediengesellschaft." In *Mediengesellschaft: Strukturen, Merkmale, Entwicklungsdynamiken*, ed. Kurt Imhof, Heinz Bonfadelli, Roger Blum, and Otfried Jarren, 100–113. Opladen/Wiesbaden: Westdeutscher Verlag.

Klaus, Elisabeth, and Margreth Lünenborg. 2004b. Cultural Citizenship: Ein kommunikationswissenschaftliches Konzept zur Bestimmung kultureller Teilhabe in der Mediengesellschaft. *Medien & Kommunikationswissenschaft* 52 (2): 193–213.

Klaus, Elisabeth, and Margreth Lünenborg. 2012. "Cultural Citizenship: Participation by and through Media." In *Feminist Media: Participatory Spaces, Networks and Cultural Citizenship*, ed. Elke Zobl and Ricarda Drüeke, 197–212. Bielefeld: Transcript.

Marshall, Thomas H. 1950. *Citizenship and Social Class and Other Essays*. Cambridge: Cambridge University Press.

Marshall, Thomas H. 1992. *Bürgerrechte und soziale Klassen: Zur Soziologie des Wohlfahrtsstaates*. Frankfurt, New York: Campus.

Monem, Nadine, ed. 2007. *Riot Grrrl: Revolution Girl Style Now!* London: Black Dog Publishing.

Piano, Doreen. 2002. "Congregating Women: Reading 3rd Wave Feminist Practices in Subcultural Production." *rhizomes*, no. 4 (Spring). www.rhizomes.net/issue4/piano.html (accessed November 1, 2011).

Ratto, Matt. 2011. "Open Design and Critical Making." In *Open Design Now: Why Design Cannot Remain Exclusive*, ed. Paul Atkinson, Michael Avital, Bruce Mau, Renny Ramakers, and Carolien Hummels, 202–209. Amsterdam: BIS Publishers.

Rosaldo, Renato. 1999. "Cultural Citizenship, Inequality and Multiculturalism." In *Race, Identity and Citizenship: A Reader*, ed. Rodolfo D. Torres, Louis F. Mirón, and Jonathan Xavier Inda, 253–261. Malden, Oxford: Blackwell.

Schilt, Kristen, and Elke Zobl. 2008. "Connecting the Dots: Riot Grrrls, Ladyfests, and the International Grrrl Zine Network." In *Next Wave Cultures: Feminism, Subcultures, Activism*, ed. Anita Harris, 171–192. New York: Routledge.

Steiner, Linda. 2000. "MEDIA: Alternative." In *Routledge International Encyclopedia of Women*, vol. 3, ed. Cheris Kramarae and Dale Spender, 1328–1331. New York: Routledge.

Stevenson, Nick, ed. 2001. *Culture and Citizenship*. London, Thousand Oaks, New Delhi: Sage.

Zobl, Elke. 2011. "Zehn Jahre Ladyfest: Rhizomatische Netzwerke einer lokalen, transnationalen und virtuellen queer-feministischen Szene." In *They Say I'm*

Different . . . Popularmusik, Szenen und ihre AkteurInnen, ed. Rosa Reitsamer and Wolfgang Fichna, 208–227. Vienna: Löcker.

Zobl, Elke, and Rosa Reitsamer, with Stefanie Grünangerl. 2012. "Feminist Media Production in Europe: A Research Report." In *Feminist Media: Participatory Spaces, Networks and Cultural Citizenship*, ed. Elke Zobl and Ricarda Drüeke, 11–54. Bielefeld: Transcript.

25 Alternative Media, the Mundane, and "Everyday Citizenship"

Chris Atton

In his 1934 essay "The Author as Producer," Walter Benjamin argued that in order for political propaganda to be effective, it was not enough to merely reproduce the radical or revolutionary content of an argument in a publication.[1] The medium itself required transformation: the position of the work in relation to the means of production had to be critically realigned. This requires not only the radicalizing of methods of production but a rethinking of what it means to be a media producer. What we now term "alternative media" can be thought of as being organized along similar lines to Benjamin's desideratum. They are about offering the means for democratic communication to people who are normally excluded from media production. They typically go beyond simply providing a platform for radical or alternative points of view: they emphasize the organization of media to enable wider social participation in their creation, production, and dissemination than is possible in the mass media. Raymond Williams highlighted three aspects of communication as foci for this realignment: "skills, capitalization and controls."[2] In an explicit echo of Williams, James Hamilton has argued that to distinguish alternative media from the mass media the former must be deprofessionalized, decapitalized, and deinstitutionalized.[3] In short, they must be available to ordinary people without the necessity of professional training, without excessive capital outlay and they must take place in settings other than media institutions or similar systems. Such media will then have the potential to more closely reflect the everyday practices of decentralized, directly democratic, self-managed and reflexive networks of "everyday-life solidarity" that Alberto Melucci finds at the heart of social movement activity: what he terms "networks in the everyday."[4] It is at this level—the level of the mundane—that I wish to examine the creative and production practices of alternative media.

This chapter traces an increasingly "intimate" trajectory. I begin by examining the fanzine, a medium that deals with the fan's relationship with the celebrity, where the fan attempts to bridge the gulf between their two worlds through discrimination and productivity.[5] I then turn to social movement media that attempt to personalize arguments and protests against global injustices (such as environmental destruction and human rights abuses) by locating them among the everyday activities of the activists. Through this process they are also made relevant at a productive level, encouraging and enabling activists and readers to participate in the creation of the media themselves. Finally, I turn to the perzine and the personal website where the consumption of mass media products is internalized to such a degree that we seem to see only the personal world of the author, where the external world appears only as a faint stimulus.

I will argue that these movements away from (and, in some cases, the absence of) professionalism, capitalization, and institutionalization in alternative media practices are highly suggestive of a "banal media" that, lacking three significant "markers" of mainstream media, are likely to be unregarded, at least in terms of their productive capacities, if not in terms of their content. In short, they are "uninteresting" media.[6] To claim alternative media as uninteresting is to go against the grain of the critical histories of alternative media studies where such media are most often seen as extraordinary, whether as engines for radical or revolutionary social change, as the vehicles for remarkable rebels to proclaim their philosophies, or as vanguards of a new politics. I do not want to argue, as much cultural studies work does (following a position popularized by John Fiske), that all popular consumption is evidence of resistance and that the fanzine writer and the personal web page owner are as transgressive as the political activist. Instead, I want to argue that, in the case of the personal web page, mundanity is often all there is and that this itself is worthy of examination. Far from being a trivial observation, this is a significant one—it provides insights into the power and significance of mundane tastes, opinions, and experiences without the need for construing them as extraordinary or resistive.

What happens when "ordinary" people produce their own media? I want to explore some aspects of 'popular' media production and its intersection with everyday life. To do so will be to reveal congruencies with the everyday cultural production that takes place through mass production, as well as to take the notion of "everyday production" and its place in identity formation to a different place: to that of the originating producer within everyday life. Popular media production might then be considered a primary form of everyday cultural production. In this respect my chapter resonates with other interests in the present volume, in particular the chapters on zines.

Like Rosa Reitsamer and Elke Zobl's study of feminist media, much of what I present here examines creative work by individuals and argues for their significance as originators of their own culture, even when (as in the case of Jody, my final example), culture is predicated on the products of mass culture. I too am interested in the appropriation and repositioning of symbolic resources that do not require high levels of professional or technical skills. However, with the exception of my discussion of social movement media, I am wary of making claims for the status of these "DIY" media as species of activism, unless we consider activism to be practiced through the transformation of the medium alone (the publishing process and its outcomes), which would be to offer a highly attenuated version of Benjamin's position. Later in this chapter, I will engage with the notion of cultural citizenship and the possibilities it offers for thinking through the connections between my examples of "mundane media production," what Nina Nijsten terms "daily life activism" (in Red Chidgey's chapter) and citizenship in broader settings.

Fanzines

In his classic account of British subcultures, Dick Hebdige briefly applies his method to punk fanzines, finding in their graphics and typology homologies of "punk's subterranean and anarchic style."[7] He does make not this explicit, but we may read from this the extension of the everyday tactics of bricolage from the music and dress of punk (i.e., from its dominant signifying practices) to the production of "an alternative critical space media within the subculture itself."[8] Teal Triggs further emphasizes the homological and expressive values of fanzines in her survey of British fan production.[9] She also offers purchase to an understanding of the significance of the mundane in fanzine production, where she reminds us that from the earliest days fanzine producers made use of available materials, improvising their publications from what was around them. Fanzines might be handwritten, duplicated with carbon paper. As simple and accessible office technologies became available, fanzine editors would employ the hectograph, the mimeograph, the photocopy. Surplus machinery would be bought cheaply and repaired at home; the photocopy shop would become the venue of necessity during a lunch hour. If possible, production would be surreptitiously slotted into the gaps in the working day (if the editor was in work).

As a former fanzine editor myself, I well remember my own clandestine fanzine production in various work places: agitatedly printing off and collating as many copies as I could without detection on the office photocopier, print runs dependent on my freedom from surveillance that week. At other times the fanzine becomes interwoven into the domestic routine. The editorial office is in reality the spare bedroom, the collation taking place on the dining room table or the living room floor. There can be something of the ludic, even the festive in these activities. Where it involves more than one person, fanzine production is often the site for social gatherings, such as those that take place during the final stages of production: the "mail-out party" might bring together editor and writers to collate, fold, and staple copies of the publication, as well as to address and stamp envelopes. Fanzines offer the possibility of creativity within a social setting and production that is structured not as a separate occupational duty (and certainly not as a professional activity) but as part of the activities of everyday life.

We should also consider how under such mundane conditions formal and professional methods of organization, production, editing, and writing are transformed. As such activities become deprofessionalized, formal training becomes unnecessary. While some skills may be learned (such as how to operate a photocopy or a DTP software package), in other cases "skill" may be scorned or minimized, as in the case of the deliberately cut-up and disruptive collage texts that remain a feature of many punk fanzines (though such practices may come to constitute a skill of sorts, to be admired or emulated according to their own expressive criteria). Capital outlay becomes contingent: the production and distribution of the publication becomes dependent on the available resources. Self-exploited labor and petty theft from work places (whether of paper or copying facilities) help defray costs. No fanzine is immune from economic stringency, but it is one of the few forms of publishing (pamphlets and home cassette copying are other examples) where the dominant laws of the marketplace—supply and demand, economies of scale, break-even points—hardly apply. Production is emphatically deinstitutionalized: it not only takes place outside a formal organizational structure, its reliance on improvisation keeps the process of production mobile, moving between work and home, different parts of the home, inserting itself between everyday routines—even becoming everyday routines.

Social Movement Media

Other alternative media share these features, even those that enjoy stability and longevity (most fanzines remain relatively short-lived and erratic in frequency of appearance). The direct-action newsletter *SchNEWS* (www.schnews.org.uk/) appears every week across the UK and has remained a fixture within the grassroots environmental protest movement since its first appearance in 1994. *SchNEWS* disparagingly—yet celebratorily—calls itself a "disorganization," publishing weekly out of apparent chaos, out of that "hectic mayhem called, ominously, 'the office.'"[10] We should be wary of reading too much into what is surely meant (at least partly) ironically. After all, the publication, for all its brevity (it is only two sides of A4) does appear regularly every week. Though its distribution is occasionally haphazard (subscribers have complained that at times no issue appears, then the last three appear in one envelope), the concerted effort required to produce such a publication should not be ignored. However fluid the processes, however casual the editors seem to be, however random their methods might appear from their own descriptions, the work gets done. I believe that their deliberate self-effacement springs from a desire neither to be seen as autocratic decision makers, nor to be considered a clique. While their methods of working might well be chaotic at times, this emphasis on amateurism and disorganization seems to seek out readers (and activists) to participate who might otherwise be put off by a more "professional" approach. If the content of *SchNEWS* is about changing lives and defending the environment in order to better enjoy life, and its form a model for enabling others to participate in it or even produce similar media, then it is appropriate that the publication itself should be an inextricable part of living, not something bracketed off in "the office." For all the talk of "disorganization," there is a work schedule of sorts, though this takes its place as part of wider schedule of domestic work, activism and play, described in a leaflet produced by the "Justice?" collective responsible for *SchNEWS* and summarized by George McKay thus: "Monday is for gardening at the Justice? allotment; Tuesday is a day off; Wednesday is for weekly meetings ending up in the pub; Thursday is for putting *SchNEWS* together; Friday is printing and distribution day, followed by the pub; Saturday there's a street stall; Sunday is for chilling out. Actions and parties are fitted around these regular events."[11] The regular members of the collective "rely on people coming in [to the *SchNEWS* 'office'], ringing up, writing stories, passing us bits of paper in the pub, taking bits from the paper [i.e., the mainstream press], [and from] the underground press. Someone starts a story, someone else adds a bit, someone else has their say—means you can't have an ego or say 'that's my story.' Sit around on Thursday evening— people shouting out headlines" (from my interview with Warren, a member of the editorial collective).

Here we see alternative media production taking its place among the everyday routines of subsistence and leisure. For its producers *SchNEWS* appears as important as their more mundane activities. By preserving the production of the paper as an unprofessionalized and deinstitutionalized activity, its producers weave it into the quotidian fabric of their lives. We know from Althusser and Foucault that professional and institutional ideologies are also woven into our daily lives and therefore it is not simply the processes of deprofessionalization and deinstitutionalization that enable productive power to emerge in the everyday. There is though a distinction to be made: whether we are concerned with the Foucauldian microphysics of power or Althusser's ideological state apparatuses, their processes are, as Althusser has emphasized, deeply unconscious, indirectly transmitted through structures that reproduce ideologies rather than through the "consciousness" of institutions and value systems. By contrast, *SchNEWS*'s deinstitutionalizing impulses are deliberate and admitted—they operate consciously and reproduce explicitly.

The Perzine and the Personal Web Page

In his exploration of what it means to speak of a culture of everyday life, John Fiske refers to the "weaving of one's own richly textured life within the constraints of economic deprivation and experience, . . . of controlling some of the conditions of social existence [and] of constructing, and therefore exerting some control over, social identities and social relations."[12]

Fiske is interested not in people who through their actions and activities proclaim themselves to be part of a subculture nor, as in the case of *SchNEWS*, a counter-culture, but in people whose activities are not necessarily directed toward explicit social change. Their activities, while they might be culturally political, are not radically political. Fiske's cultural consumers become producers through the process of selecting, collocating, and critically incorporating media texts into their own lives. In his claims for these consumer-producers he stresses the infractory, political nature of their activities of identity building and sociality. The appropriation of capitalist resources as elements of everyday culture is considered as resistance, as the activity of "guerrillas . . . evading hegemonic capture."[13] Fiske is careful, though, to talk of such cultural activity as "progressive"; the implication of such activity in capitalism prevents it from ever being radical. As with most studies that examine the deployment of mass-produced media and cultural resources in everyday life, Fiske's interest in production focuses on how people "make do" or "improvise" cultural formations for and through themselves according to an everyday logic of bricolage. This making-do is concerned with "*ways of using* the products imposed by a dominant economic order."[14]

I want to explore some aspects of this process by focusing now on the personal rather than the collective, the interior and reflective rather than the outward and impulsive. In alternative media terms, a suitable candidate for this type of "everyday theorizing" is the perzine. The perzine can be thought of as a fanzine whose subject is the editor of the publication; that is, it deals with the editor's everyday life—their tastes, experiences, sense of humor, fads. If the fanzine offers a critical space for the amateur to write about their consuming passions, the perzine functions like a public journal of that person's life (a classic example is the American perzine *Cometbus*, each issue filled with short, first-person narratives of the picaresque doings of one "Aaron Cometbus" as he makes his way around the cultural underbelly of the United States). Perzines can be considered as instances of popular production rooted in the specificities of everyday life. Their authors represent their own quotidian experiences, producing their own lives as a work.[15] Through this work they produce difference and through that difference (as Stuart Hall reminds us) comes social identity and social relations.[16]

Production and sociality are together wrought from everyday experience through what Fiske calls the "bottom-up production of difference," created by the popular producer from the available technological resources of the dominant order.[17] The perzine (along with other types of zine) is thus able to liberate its producer(s) from the controls and limits set by the dominant order by redeploying its resources in infractory ways. In Certeau's terms, the place that is the political economy and the site of production of the mass media becomes inhabited by those people normally outside it.[18] As they practice media production within this place, they establish their own spaces: the space that is the perzine might be considered as an instance of Certeau's "practised place," an exemplar of alternative media production as a set of practices embedded in everyday life.

My last example takes us further into the mundane to where it becomes the raw material for cultural production by an "ordinary person" to a significantly greater extent than even the personal stories of Aaron Cometbus (which, in the end, have a literary flair). For this reason I make no apology for examining it in some detail. What I now focus on is a personal website that gives full flight to the banal as its subject matter. *The Big DumpTruck!* (www.bigdumptruck.com/, subtitled "Throwing Little Thought Pebbles at Your Windshield") is produced by Jody LaFerriere, a suburban office worker, mother, and resident of Massachusetts. The following give some indication of the type and style of content found on Jody's site at the time this research was undertaken (November 2000):

1. "My Favorite Xmas Music": this includes albums by The Carpenters, John Denver and The Muppets, Johnny Mathis, and *A Charlie Brown Christmas* ("These are the ones I listen to year after year."). She encourages visitors to her site to "have fun with Amazon. Enter 'Christmas' as your search term and see what you get!";
2. LaFerriere's list of "Famous People Who Have a First Name for a Last Name," which on November 1, 2000, included around 400 entries, including Woody Allen, Klaus Barbie (!), Eric Carmen, Joseph Conrad, Martin Denny, Philip K. Dick, Dean Martin, Diana Ross, and Mary Shelley;
3. More lists (LaFerriere likes lists a great deal). Others have included "What We're Giving Trick-or-Treaters This Year: Charleston Chews, 100 Grands, Baby Ruths, Twizzlers" (from http://www.bigdumptruck.com/ on November 1, 2000) and "Favorite Words that Begin with the Letter 'P': Peanut, Pumpkin, Planetary, Pithy, Perhaps";
4. "Pick of the Dump," which on October 29, 2000, was the DVD of *Toy Story 2*. "Ever since we bought this it's been playing in the DVD player. As the mom of an almost three-year-old, I can say that *Toy Story 2* is less "scary" than the first one. And the animation is better (of course)";
5. An account of her brief meeting with American TV Food Network chef Emeril Lagasse at a book signing: "He made the spinach salad with potatoes, onions and bacon from the Christmas book. I wish I had been able to taste it, because it smelled unbelievable. He didn't really pass it around to anyone, and by the time he was done he went to sign books so I didn't really see what happened to it";
6. LaFerriere's Open Letters to, among others, the ice cream man ("I pray that you will fly by before I give in to the temptation and find my wallet or raid the change jar"); Massachusetts Highway Department ("I am so tired of the Route 2 commute getting worse every year"); and the US Mint ("I just wanted to drop you a note to let you know that you can ease up on the pennies. I've got way too many of them.").

LaFerriere uses the products of capitalism to create both her own mundane cultural forms and her means of communication. The decapitalization in the handwritten or photocopied fanzine is not to be found here; personal Internet connectivity, as we know, remains largely the province of the affluent, white middle-class. In both her choice of cultural products and her choice of medium LaFerriere is resolutely suburban. Doubly then, her activities will tend to be overlooked by academics who insist on or look for resistance and infraction in everyday cultural production (as does Fiske) or who regard popular (civic) use of the Internet narrowly as a tool for political empowerment within marginalized communities. Yet, following Certeau, may we not argue that "marginality is becoming universal,"[19] at least in the sense that there is a majority of nonproducers of culture? LaFerriere is surely part of that silent majority hidden from most studies of everyday cultural production by slipping through what we might think of as the standard "grids of disempowerment" formed by the intersection of such essentializing categories as gender, age, class, and race. In part this might be because LaFerriere's activities represent an uncomfortable accommodation with capitalism. Her consumption tends to the spectacular (her site contains many images of the products she adores: CD sleeves, Emeril Lagasse book covers); LaFerriere has even had designed *Big DumpTruck!* mugs and mouse mats. Her activities force us to reassess the claims made by James Hamilton regarding deprofessionalization, decapitalization, and deinstitutionalization as imperatives of alternative media. Such practices as LaFerriere's alert us to the problematic of "purity" in alternative media practices.[20]

To see these practices of "mundanization" we need very different conceptual tools from those used in the valorization of popular (productive) consumption. The latter seek the extraordinary within the everyday, finding there resistance, infraction, and the refusal to accommodate with dominant cultural forces—that is, radical critical activity within mundane activities. Instead, we require a model that encourages us to resignify both the everyday and what we construe as "significant." Andrew J. Weigert has described the everyday as "a taken-for-granted reality which provides the unquestioned background of meaning for each person's life."[21] In LaFerriere's case it is the very everyday nature of her website that we must question—for that is all there is. It is not a background against which extraordinary actions are played out, it is the background that is itself of interest. We must not render this background as foreground; that would once again find the extraordinary in the mundane. Weigert's formulation offers us the possibility of examining the everyday (the background) as the substantive content of LaFerriere's media production while it remains unmarked, significant but not extraordinary.

If popular culture produced by consumers has any political progressiveness, however marginal, it is surely not to be found here. LaFerriere's producerly, cultural activities are concerned with the commonplace, the trite, even the dull. She creates her own texts through far more subdued means than the cultural "guerrillas" that Fiske champions: "evading hegemonic capture" could not be further from her agenda. LaFerriere is "breaking out" very differently from fanzine or perzine editors. She takes with her the desires and pleasures of the mainstream, of the unabashedly popular, simply hoping to embrace them in the virtual company of like-minded others. This is hardly radical, there is nothing infractory or antagonistic here. She enacts a selection of texts rather than an interpretation of them—her choices are closer to "top tens," there is little evidence of their being transformed into a new cultural form. What they do become, though, is communicated and they themselves are the vehicles for communication.

LaFerriere does not just want to share her tastes with others; she wants others to use them to communicate with her, to embellish them, to embroider the mundane with more mundanity (How long does a list of people with a last name for a first name have to be? Answer: as long as Jody wants it to be). What do the texts she selects signify? Do they not stand as tokens for sociality? They do not simply proclaim LaFerriere's tastes, they reach out to seek others who share her tastes and who will valorize them by contributing similarly to her website. What is at stake here is the power of these texts as socially centered signs for intersubjective communication; LaFerriere's tastes are perhaps marginal after all, at least marginal in her neighborhood. So she looks more widely for a community. The texts then become socially relevant (regardless of any qualitative value they may have to either LaFerriere or her virtual community), suggesting what Janice Radway has called "the possibility of the social."[22] Are LaFerriere's activities perhaps a "therapeutics for deteriorating social relations" in suburban life?[23]

The fanzine and the perzine in their productive contexts have the capacity to reduce cultural distance. The everyday conditions of production and the everyday experiences from which they are created break down the classic aesthetic barriers we see erected in high-art value systems between cultural activity and everyday life. High cultural capital and educational capital, along with economic capital, are not required. Further, the perzine *requires* the elision of cultural activity and everyday life: the stuff of the latter becomes the content and informs the processes of the former. Anyone can produce a zine, anyone can read one, goes the philosophy of the zinester: there are few barriers to participation at any level.

The Mundane Is Not the Trivial

Meaghan Morris has criticized two tendencies toward the banal in cultural studies, one that employs "the term 'banality' to frame a theory of media" (represented by Baudrillard), the other that seeks to find subversion in every banal instance of popular culture (she cites Fiske).[24] For Morris banality is an "irritant" (as is its cognate, triviality) that is harmful when employed as a "framing concept to discuss mass media" and popular culture.[25] Her argument rests in large part on tracing the etymological development of the term in its emerging cultural contexts through Old English and German. She highlights two related meanings: the first related to the issuing of a summons, the second to "proclaim[ing] under orders," obediently cheering the conquering hero. Together they offer an exegesis of "banality" as "a figure inscribing power in an act of *enunciation*."[26] Morris argues that academics working in popular culture or mass media will themselves become subjects of banality through their celebration of that banality, formulating edicts about how the banal must be understood at the same time as slavishly mimicking the banal in their work. Is my work culpable of this twin sin? As Morris herself is aware, a later meaning gives "banal" in medieval French to mean "communal use." Might we not recover that notion as well for our objects of study, to refer positively to the productive use of the "common" people? It is perhaps not too far-fetched to suggest reviving this remaining dimension of the obsolete complex of meanings around "banal" to refer to the productivity through which the texts created by LaFerriere signify not the worthless and the worn (the "trivial") but what we might call the "significant everyday." This is not, as I have stressed, to find in LaFerriere's website a resistive, Fiskean power of what we might call "progressive consumption." Instead we have the expression of the everyday as Weigert's "taken-for-granted reality."

The mundane choices and quotidian accounts and images that LaFerriere offers us suggest two consequences for the study of mundane behavior. First, by becoming foregrounded they remind us of the power and significance such beliefs, choices, and decisions have for ordinary people. Second, they encourage us to look at web-based communication not simply in terms of the (now overworked) "empowering" and rhizomatic models of networked, democratic opportunity (that is, as engines for social change) or simply as additional opportunities for commerce and industry, but as instances of everyday sociality—and to look at research into such communication practices as ethnomethodological, as the study of "people's methods for doing everyday life."[27] These activities are worthy of attention precisely because the production of these "banal media" is becoming so widespread. Even where popular culture is valorized and the binarism of high/low culture seems ousted once and for all, it is possible that a site such as LaFerriere's might evade our attentions or, worse, be deemed not worthy of our attention at all. The personal web page is perhaps outrunning the self-declared zine in terms of its focus on the quotidian details of its owners' lives. Though it appears to have little of the socially transformative value we might expect from other alternative or radical forms of media, compared with the increasingly professionally mediated products and processes of media culture it contains within it an "awkwardness" that we must not ignore. In our explorations of the mundane in media production, we must take note of what John Corner calls the "sheer *awkwardness* of communication by 'fairly ordinary people.'"[28]

Conclusion: Where Is the Citizenship in the Mundane?

What are we to make of these examples of mundane media production in terms of citizenship? Earlier I noted Nina Nijsten's term "daily life activism." Nijsten's argument is that feminist media producers politicize an engagement with the world not through any explicit collective action (as we might find in social movement media), but through individual projects that can be seen as contributing to communities or even producing communities. Red Chidgey (chapter 6, this volume) argues that the "maker identity" that represents the praxis of daily life activism enables cultural production to function as a site for political activity. Her argument resembles that of Clemencia Rodriguez, whose work on citizens' media Chidgey invokes. There are, I think, some valuable parallels between the strategies and practices of cultural production discussed by Chidgey (and by Reitsamer and Elke Zobl, chapter 24, this volume) and those discussed by Rodriguez, but there also limits to both approaches. I want to conclude this chapter with some observations about the deployment of the notion of citizens' media to the everyday, mundane practices of media production discussed here.

"Citizens' media" is a term that has a particular explanatory power for Rodriguez. She has shown how in rural communities in Colombia (usually local neighborhood communities or villages, but also groups of young people or women), media technologies are deployed to engage social groups in becoming "active citizens" of their own locale.[29] Through the making of films as well as radio and television programs that embody their own situations, fears, and dreams, local people who are trapped in cultures of violence can begin to realize their own methods of coping with that violence. Citizens' media can be thought of as the "lived experience of nonviolent ways to manage conflict, deal with difference, and interact with one another."[30] In short, local communities become engaged in everyday political action.

I feel very uncomfortable transferring Rodriguez's arguments about her case studies to the examples I present in this chapter; after all, the reappropriation of public spaces and the reintegration of communities Rodriguez describes are situated in regions that are best described as war zones or, at least, warlike zones. The conditions of media production, as well as conditions of social and political necessity, are so removed from the relative comfort of the cases in this chapter as to be incomparable. That said, at the heart of the notion of citizen's media is an argument about performativity that is, I think, transferable to other contexts and can help to inform our understanding of everyday cultural citizenship. Rodriguez encourages us to consider media practice in a performative sense, where individuals and groups use media to experience the world as they construct it for themselves, to shape local cultural and collective imaginaries. If the examples in this chapter (and perhaps elsewhere in this book) seem to veer toward the private, the solipsistic, and the politically occluded, we might instead see the political power of mediation as performance as the capacity of everyday culture to produce communities through the actions of individuals.

Notes

This chapter is a revised and expanded version of "The Mundane and Its Reproduction in Alternative Media," first published in the *Journal of Mundane Behavior* 2, no. 1 (February 2001), www.mundanebehavior.org.

1. Benjamin 1982.

2. Williams 1980, 54.

3. Hamilton 2000.

4. Melucci 1996.

5. Fiske 1991.

6. Brekhus 1998.

7. Hebdige 1979, 112.

8. Ibid., 111.

9. Triggs 1995.

10. *SchNEWS Reader* 1996, unpaginated.

11. McKay 1996, 177.

12. Fiske 1992, 160

13. Fiske 1991, 137.
14. Certeau 1984, xiii; emphasis in original.
15. Lefebvre 1991.
16. Hall 1990.
17. Fiske 1992, 165.
18. Certeau 1984.
19. Ibid., xvii.
20. Atton 2002.
21. Weigert 1981, 36.
22. Radway 1999.
23. Certeau 1984, xxiv.
24. Morris 1996, 147.
25. Ibid., 165.
26. Ibid., 165; emphasis in original.
27. Weigert 1981, 38.
28. Corner 1996, 174; emphasis in original.
29. Rodriguez 2011.
30. Ibid., 254.

References

Atton, Chris. 2002. *Alternative Media*. London: Sage.

Benjamin, Walter. 1982. "The Author as Producer." In *Modern Art and Modernism: a Critical Anthology*, ed. Francis Frascina and Charles Harrison, 213–216. London: Paul Chapman in association with the Open University.

Brekhus, Wayne. 1998. A Sociology of the Unmarked: Redirecting Our Focus. *Sociological Theory* 16:34–51.

Certeau, Michel de. 1984. *The Practice of Everyday Life*. Berkeley, CA: University of California Press.

Corner, John. 1996. Mediating the Ordinary: The 'Access' Idea and Television Form. In *Television Times: A Reader*, ed. John Corner and Sylvia Harvey, 165–174. London: Arnold.

Fiske, John. 1991. *Understanding Popular Culture*. London: Routledge.

Fiske, John. 1992. Cultural Studies and the Culture of Everyday Life. In *Cultural Studies*, ed. Lawrence Grossberg, Cary Nelson, and Paula A. Treichler, 154–173. New York, London: Routledge.

Hall, Stuart. 1990. Cultural Identity and Diaspora. In *Identity: Community, Culture and Distance*, ed. John Rutherford, 222–237. London: Lawrence and Wishart.

Hamilton, James F. 2000. Alternative Media: Conceptual Difficulties, Critical Possibilities. *Journal of Communication Inquiry* 24 (4): 357–378.

Hebdige, Dick. 1979. *Subculture: The Meaning of Style*. London: Routledge.

Lefebvre, Henri. 1991. *Critique of Everyday Life. Volume I: Introduction*. London: Verso.

McKay, George. 1996. *Senseless Acts of Beauty: Cultures of Resistance since the Sixties*. London: Verso.

Melucci, Alberto. 1996. *Challenging Codes: Collective Action in the Information Age*. Cambridge: Cambridge University Press.

Morris, Meaghan. 1996. Banality in Cultural Studies. In *What Is Cultural Studies? A Reader*, ed. John Storey, 147–167. London: Arnold.

Radway, Janice. 1999. "On the Importance of Readers and Reading: Points of Origin in Book History." Paper presented at the Society for the History of Authorship, Reading and Publishing's Annual Conference, Madison, WI, July 15–18.

Rodriguez, Clemencia. 2011. *Citizens' Media against Armed Conflict: Disrupting Violence in Colombia*. Minneapolis: University of Minnesota Press.

SchNEWS Reader. 1996. Brighton: SchNEWS.

Triggs, Teal. 1995. Alphabet Soup: Reading British Fanzines. *Visible Language* 29 (1): 72–87.

Weigert, Andrew J. 1981. *Sociology of Everyday Life*. New York, London: Longman.

Williams, Raymond. 1980. Means of Communication as Means of Production. In *Problems in Materialism and Culture: Selected Essays*, 50–63. London: Verso.

26 Critical News Making and the Paradox of "Do-It-Yourself News"

Mike Ananny

In his foundational study of television watching, Hartley (1999) describes do-it-yourself (DIY) citizenship as "the practice of putting together an identity from the available choices, patterns and opportunities . . . no longer simply a matter of social contract between state and subject, no longer even a matter of acculturation to the heritage of a given community, DIY citizenship is a choice people can make for themselves" (Hartley 1999, 178). Essentially, while earlier conceptualizations of citizenship were wrapped up in geographic or identity-based memberships—living somewhere, inhabiting demographics—Hartley suggests that contemporary citizenship also entails "semiotic self-determination" (179), individually navigating and experimenting with the range of associations and identities offered by increasingly networked and mediated civic spheres.

In many ways, this book is both an extension and critique of Hartley's notion of DIY citizenship. Like Hartley's television watchers, the groups described here—for example, fan communities (Jenkins's Harry Potter Alliance, or Burwell and Boler's *The Daily Show* and *The Colbert Report* fan-bloggers), feminist media creators (Chidgey's zine makers), activist networks (Reilly's Yes Men), and craft communities (Orton-Johnson's knitters, Rosner and Foster's weavers, or DiSalvo's Growbot gardeners)—develop identities and associations by engaging with media and through mediated relationships. That is, Hartley's citizen is still engaged in semiotic self-determination, but her tools, techniques, and relationships live within a new set of materials, practices, and communities (what McKim's essay, chapter 21, this volume, refers to as "architectures of participation"). The critical question for this new phase of DIY citizenship is: what does semiotic self-determination look like in the context of contemporary, networked information infrastructures that afford and constrain the conditions under which individuals can meaningfully explore identities and associations?

Situating DIY News

This tension between individual self-determination and information infrastructure has always been central to the practices and significance of the press. In many ways, the idea of citizenship as an individual, choice-based exercise in semiotic self-determination is at the heart of contemporary debates within the critical study of networked news. Specifically, what role can or should the self-determining individual—as an audience member, content creator, and information curator—play in the construction and circulation of news?

News organizations increasingly use sophisticated, algorithmic tracking techniques to analyze, predict, and prepare content for individual readers' preferences, while news consumers have unprecedented opportunities to customize and personalize their news environments and experiences (Anderson 2011; Lee, Lewis, and Powers 2012; Peters 2012; Thurman and Schifferes 2012). And although there is a thriving practice and study of "citizen journalism" (e.g., see Lewis, Kaufhold, and Lasorsa 2010 and Rosen 2008 for overviews), most people's news emerges from an *institutional* environment in which audiences concentrate around and attend to a relatively small number of sources (Pew 2012; Hindman 2008; Webster and Ksiaze, 2012). For example, news organizations often mimic each other's content and publication rhythms (Boczkowski 2010); there is a significant gap between what the press produces and what readers consume or want to consume (Boczkowski, Mitchelstein, and Walter 2010; Boczkowski and Peer 2011); readers have many opportunities to comment on and engage with news (Domingo 2011; Napoli 2011), but few opportunities to meaningfully impact the conditions under which it is produced (Himelboim and McCreery, 2012; Williams, Wardle, and Wahl-Jorgensen 2010); and even the very idea of what "valuable" news means is highly contested (Meijer 2012). Essentially, although the field of journalism looks significantly different than it did even five years ago and involves individuals with new types of agency, news still largely emerges from institutional forces that are beyond the meaningful influence of self-determining individuals.

In a sense, then, "do-it-yourself (DIY) news" is a curious and paradoxical idea. Making, filtering, or reading news *yourself* is antithetical to both the highly networked institutional conditions under which news circulates today and the normative ideal of making news a democratic and *public* product. My aim here is to explore this paradox along three dimensions.

First, for news to serve democratic functions (as opposed to simply personal or informational ones), it must pass a pragmatic test that is both social and normative. That is, information is news—and information processing is news making—because it is, in some way, significant to *publics*. It matters to people who have no choice but to share resources and consequences—to experience outcomes from which they cannot simply extract themselves as private individuals. Second, in its ideal form, news is information that self-interest, friends, markets, or algorithms alone may not reveal. Although the mainstream press often falls short of this ideal, it earns institutional and cultural legitimacy (though not necessarily its economic health) from how well it helps publics *hear*—not how well it help individuals speak. Finally, and most pragmatically, contemporary news production is inherently intertwined and networked. It is simply not possible to "do" news yourself in any meaningful way without encountering and engaging with actors who, together, define the infrastructure of networked news production—what I call "newsware."

Scholars from a wide variety of disciplines have noted the problematic nature of the word "yourself" within studies of DIY systems as they trace the inherently social-constructionist nature of imagining, realizing, using, and evaluating technological systems (Ratto 2011). Human–computer interaction, computer-supported cooperative work, participatory design, and ubiquitous computing all increasingly place sociological and ethnographic questions at the centers of their disciplines, encouraging scholars and designers alike to understand the relational and social contexts in which systems are designed, deployed, and interpreted (Dourish and Bell, 2011; Goodwin 1995; Simon 1996). Similarly, science and technology studies scholars reject accounts of human behavior that ascribe complete agency to people or technologies, or that presume the preexistence of a social sphere distinct from the actors and systems that, together, *create* social spaces (Latour 2005; Latour and Weibel 2005; Klein and Kleinman 2002). And, finally, while developmental psychologists have historically appreciated the role that social contexts, objects, and systems play in making visible individuals' understandings of various concepts and phenomena (Piaget 1954; Vygotsky 1978, 19–30), contemporary learning sciences scholars and designers have increasingly focused on creating computational systems with "digital manipulatives" (Resnick 1998) that let learners "converse with materials" (Bamberger and Schon 1983; Papert 1980) in two senses: testing and asserting understandings of the world against the affordances and constraints of materials that conceptually respond to a designer's actions, and using computational materials as starting points for conversations with others about how to instantiate ideals of the world in materials forms.

Each of these disciplines integrates social and the technological questions, rightly seeing human behavior emerging from individual agencies and social structures (Giddens 1984). But there are differences between social and political analysis—between reading sociotechnical systems for their relational features versus critiquing how they structure dependencies among people who must share consequences. That is, although some human–computer interaction scholarship rightly depicts design as a value-laden activity (Friedman, Kahn, and Borning 2006) and is beginning to see media design through the lens of public spheres (Le Dantec and DiSalvo 2013; Lindtner et al. 2011), there is still a need to understand how system design decisions structure public spheres, shape flows of power, and create the conditions under which people can discover or create shared consequences (Boler 2010; Castells 2008).

The idea of *critical* making is relevant to this need. It is, as Ratto (2011) and Latour (2005) explain, about recasting "matters of fact" (that rest upon assumptions about the world's natural or immutable state) into "matters of concern" (that highlight the inherently contestable and contingent nature of sociotechnical relationships). Critical making offers a conceptual opportunity to connect the design of public spheres with a normative model of the public sphere as a place for ongoing contestation of identities and interests (Calhoun 1998).

In this sense, *critical* news making is never a "do-it-yourself" activity. It is not only about pursuing self-interests—learning what you want to know—but also about acknowledging the social and institutional contexts of those interests, environments, and conditions in which public goods circulate and from which it is impossible to extract yourself, ignore, or *not* care about. Although networked technologies may give individuals numerous opportunities to express themselves, filter data, and share information (activities that *look* like news making), if we are interested in understanding DIY news's democratic implications we must ask: what counts as news, what can news do, and how should we make it?

A Pragmatic Test for News

The possibility or impossibility of doing news on your own lies partly in your definition of news. Some models emphasize the press's informational and transactional nature—expecting journalists "to verify what information is reliable and then order it so people can grasp it efficiently" (Kovach and Rosenstiel 2001, 19)—while others take a more expansive view, asking it to check power, convene publics, mobilize social movements, and engender empathy (Schudson 2008, 12). Indeed, this latter view recognizes the press's unique role as an institution that is, ideally, concerned with the *public's* needs (Carey 1987), not with serving as a mouthpiece for special interests, or fulfilling the information desires of individual consumers.

Out of this image of the press emerges a particular test of news.[1] Rooted in pragmatist philosophy (Dewey 1927/1954; James 1907/1981), this test is not so much concerned with whether an utterance is "true" but, rather, on what impact its truth might have—how assumptions about its truthfulness guide people to act. Critically, this test does not judge news significance according to a particular fact's objective certainty but, rather, in terms of the cultural and social processes that make news meaningful and actionable. Whether something qualifies as "news" depends upon the conversations *around* news and the shared consequences that result (Dewey 1927/1954). This is why news, as opposed to information, can never be the exclusive domain of private or personal interests, and cannot rely solely upon marketplace logics for its creation or significance. It is public—meaningful to a community of shared consequences—because it matters to those impacted by its perceived truth or falsity.

Therefore, deciding what "counts" as news is never really a choice that can be meaningfully made by any individual or self-selected group that creates, filters, or consumes information—be they professional news editors, system designers, or citizen journalists. It becomes critically important for those working under the rubric of DIY news to ask not "Is this information true?" but, rather, "What would it mean and whose experiences would be impacted if this information were considered to be true?" This kind of question places particular demands on system designers. It asks them to reflect upon what it means to convene publics, not crowds—to account for those who must share consequences in addition to those who choose interests.

News and a Public Right to Hear

In a sense, crowds assemble while publics are entailed. Crowds are "gatherings of people . . . sharing a common activity" while publics are "premised on the existence of common ground not only physically but also socially and politically" (Butsch 2008, 8–12). Crowds are often defined by their visibility: they have a presence and voice that can be observed, and they are often attended to and engaged with. In contrast, publics share consequences even when they do not speak. Although I might not attend an antiwar rally or complain about my city's air quality, I might still be drafted or suffer from asthma.

It becomes necessary, then, to see participation *alone* as insufficient evidence of a DIY news system's public value. Spaces where people choose to gather and speak are not necessarily the same as public spheres since such spaces may not account for those who are absent or invisible, for individuals who cannot or choose not to speak. In its ideal form, the press is a "listening institution" that guarantees the public's right to meaningfully encounter ideas it might not hear if it were only to listen to those who chose to (or were allowed to) speak. As free speech scholar Alexander Meiklejohn wrote, in any system of democratic expression, the "point of ultimate interest is not the words of the speakers, but the minds of the hearers . . . what is essential is not that everyone shall speak, but that everything worth saying shall be said" (1948, 25).

To be clear, I am not arguing that people should *not* speak, or that some people should be silenced. Rather, my aim is to highlight two complementary ideas. First, what is critical for robust and diverse democratic communication is the free circulation of speech and active support for speech that may not survive in marketplaces or crowdsourced valuations of self-selected speakers. The US Constitution, for example, guarantees freedom *of* speech, not freedom *to* speak. Second, there exists a category of listening-as-action sometimes dismissed as passive or suboptimal in discussions of participatory, DIY cultures. Often derisively labeled "lurkers" or, more generously, called legitimate peripheral participants (Lave and Wenger, 1991) who are "listening-in" (Rogoff et al. 2003) and have yet to move to the "center," critical makers might reexamine the act of listening (Crawford 2009; 2010), recognizing its varied and valuable dimensions. Accounting for those who leave less visible traces of participation—but who are nonetheless full and legitimate members of publics who share consequences—can help highlight the listener's role as a critical member of a collective who must be willing to thoughtfully adopt, adapt, integrate, and reject new ideas being spoken (Lacey 2011).

The free circulation of speech and the sense of plurality created through listening are both essential for an affirmative account of democratic freedom. That is, it matters not only that individuals are free from illegitimate constraints on their private desires and actions, but also that they encounter ideas that could not have originated from self-interests, chosen friends, marketplaces, or crowdsourced algorithms.

It becomes critical, then, for DIY news systems not only to pass the pragmatic test of news, but also to account for listening as a political act. DIY news must acknowledge and account for those who are attentive and implicated, if not visible and expressive. Listening may never result in measurable or observable traces, but it is just as essential to DIY citizenship as more visible forms of participation. Listening is participation, and participation requires listeners.

Newsware

Even if you disagree with these first two arguments—that DIY news is a contradiction because news must pass a socially mediated pragmatic test, and that news is ideally about ensuring a public right to hear—there is a third, more pragmatic reason that news cannot be made alone: networked boundary infrastructures I call "newsware."

By "newsware" I mean the emerging set of often invisible and relational technologies, algorithms, interfaces, practices, and norms out of which news emerges. They are embedded in—and help create—the material, social, and ideological conditions under which publics envision and listen to themselves. Newsware does not live within any single organization, professional tradition, or software system; rather, it is a "boundary infrastructure" (Star and Ruhleder 1996, 113) in which various actors come together to enact and debate what each thinks news is, or should be.

This idea of a boundary infrastructure in which various actors have differential access to—and awareness of or power over—news production is an opportunity to question the very idea of autonomy in news making. Studies of mainstream institutional presses have noted that, although reporters claim considerable autonomy in their individual reporting (Gans 1979, 101), their independence rarely extends beyond narrowly "operational" decisions (relatively minor decisions about, e.g., who to interview, what constitutes the lede, and which quotes to use) to "allocative" issues (more fundamental decisions about the conditions under which news organizations operate, e.g., what sections a newspaper should have, when stories should appear, or who should be hired or fired) (Murdock 1977).

Consider the following three examples of newsware. First, the *New York Times*, *NPR*, and the *Guardian* all offer application programming interfaces (APIs) to let those with programming skills and interests create news websites and apps that re-present news organization stories in novel formats. These software toolkits are essentially meeting places where news organization system designers, casual hackers, software entrepreneurs, and journalists come together to create novel forms of news. Together, they constitute a "programming public" that reconfigures traditional relationships between news organizations and readers, defining conditions under which readers encounter news. Several questions arise, though, that highlight the problematic nature of any single actor's claims to autonomy: how does a programmer access the news organization's API, how is this access monitored, and what contractual obligations is she under? Can programmers earn money by placing advertisements alongside news organizations' content? How often must the API-acquired content be refreshed, and who controls how often a news story is updated? No actor can fully participate in this API-driven network without encountering and relying upon others.

Second, consider Spot.us, a website through which both budding and experienced journalists can raise money to fund original reporting by earning microgrants from a community of donors interested in supporting news work. Aspiring reporters pitch an idea and a budget and rely upon the Spot.us community for the necessary funds. Not only does being successful mean having an idea that the community finds interesting and valuable; it also means relying upon the Spot.us designers to create a microgranting system with features that help projects raise money. For example, Spot.us labels projects "unfunded" or "almost funded"—which labeling system generates the most funding, and when does a project move from one category into the other? Which projects are featured on Spot.us's front page? Should Spot.us allow anonymous donations or require its funders to be named? How sufficiently different should projects be from one other in order not compete for similar pools of potential funders? Answers to these questions depend not only upon the would-be reporter's project or the amount of money requested, but also upon design decisions made by the Spot.us creators and the dynamics of the Spot.us community.

Third, consider AOL's "Seed" system, an infrastructure to connect contract reporters with AOL's algorithmically determined editorial priorities. Seed analyzes activity on the AOL network, determines which topics are popular with readers and valuable to advertisers, and generates a list of assignments and topics for Seed stringers to write about. Contract reporters write stories, gain visibility through Seed, and are paid by AOL according to a sliding scale that shifts depending on whether the story came from AOL or the reporter, what licensing terms the reporter has agreed to, and whether the story has appeared elsewhere. This type of system gives would-be reporters access to audiences they are otherwise unlikely to reach but raises other questions: what kind of algorithms and values drive Seed's web traffic analysis and story assignments? When is this algorithm changed, how transparent are these changes, and what prompts them? How much are reporters paid for generating their own stories versus writing those that Seed suggests, and how does this change reporters' incentives to write critical or seemingly unpopular stories? Although reporters may want to write a particular story, their ability to do so *and* reach a wide audience depend upon their ability to navigate AOL's concordant editorial, technological, and economic constraints.

All three examples illustrate that networked news is not something that can be done alone. If the contemporary DIY news producer's aim is to create web presences, analyze news organization data, engage in original reporting, earn revenue, and gain visibility, she is very likely going to quickly encounter newsware that both enables and constrains her work. The key to navigating this networked terrain is acknowledging the interdependent actors, making purposeful connections among them, and interrogating what they mean for public spheres.

Conclusion

The aim here has been to explore the idea of "do-it-yourself news" and its potentially paradoxical nature along three dimensions. First, unlike generic information, news must pass a social and normative pragmatic test—it must *matter* to people who must share consequences and cannot retire to private interests. Second, news is not about knowledge acquisition, self-interest, or even self-determination; rather, it is about collectively creating and sustaining public goods. To practice and study news critically means accepting the public as your unit of analysis. Finally, even putting aside these normative and conceptual aspects of news, as the infrastructure of news production and circulation—what I call "newsware"—becomes increasingly networked and dependent upon distributed actors, it is simply not possible to "do" news yourself, as an individual.

To be clear, I do not minimize the value of individuals and self-organized teams creatively reimagining the press and constructing novel systems for news work. It is vitally important for new actors to create prototypes of what networked press could be, inventing new and compelling forms of storytelling, demonstrating novel funding models, and orienting audiences to traditionally undercovered issues.

Rather, my aim here is to draw a distinction between "DIY news" and what might be called "DIY information production and dissemination" by highlighting the normative and public aspects of news. News needs to matter to people who share consequences. It must help to ensure that people hear perspectives that self-interests, markets, friends, self-selected crowds, or personalization algorithms alone may not reveal. Essentially, DIY news projects need to design for publics, not simply users or customers who opt in. Newsware is meant to be an analytical and empirical lens for tracing ideas of the public sphere through networked news production infrastructure—for critiquing the conditions under which publics are or could be made visible.

Note

1. Thanks to Theodore L. Glasser for the phrase "pragmatic test of news" and describing this idea.

References

Anderson, C. W. 2011. Between creative and quantified audiences: Web metrics and changing patterns of newswork in local U.S. newsrooms. *Journalism: Theory, Practice, Criticism* 12 (5): 550–566.

Bamberger, J., and D. A. Schon. 1983. Learning as reflective conversation with materials: Notes from work in progress. *Art Education* 36 (2): 68–73.

Boczkowski, P. 2010. *News at work: Imitation in an age of information abundance*. Chicago, IL: University of Chicago Press.

Boczkowski, P., E. Mitchelstein, and M. Walter. 2010. Convergence across divergence: Understanding the gap in the online news choices of journalists and consumers in Western Europe and Latin America. *Communication Research* 38 (3): 376–396.

Boczkowski, P., and L. Peer. 2011. The choice gap: The divergent online news preferences of journalists and consumers. *Journal of Communication* 61:857–876.

Boler, M. 2010. Introduction. In *Digital media and democracy: Tactics in hard times*, ed. M. Boler, 1–50. Cambridge, MA: MIT Press.

Butsch, Richard. 2008. *The citizen audience: Crowds, publics, and individuals*. New York: Routledge.

Calhoun, C. 1998. The public good as a social and cultural project. In *Private action and the public good*, ed. W. Powell and E. Clemens, 20–35. New Haven: Yale University Press.

Carey, J. W. 1987. The press and the public discourse. *Center Magazine* 20:4–15.

Castells, M. 2008. The new public sphere: Global civil society, communication networks, and global governance. *Annals of the American Academy of Political and Social Science* 616 (1): 78–93.

Crawford, K. 2009. Following you: Disciplines of listening in social media. *Continuum: Journal of Media & Cultural Studies* 23 (4): 525–535.

Crawford, K. 2010. News to me: Twitter and the personal networking of news. In *News online: Transformations and continuities*, ed. G. Meikle and G. Redden, 115–131. New York: Palgrave Macmillan.

Dewey, J. 1927/1954. *The public and its problems*. New York: Swallow Press.

Domingo, D. 2011. Managing audience participation: Practices, workflows and strategies. In *Participatory journalism*, ed. J. B. Singer, A. Hermida, D. Domingo, et al., 76–95. Malden, MA: Wiley-Blackwell.

Dourish, P., and G. Bell. 2011. *Divining a digital future: Mess and mythology in ubiquitous computing*. Cambridge, MA: MIT Press.

Friedman, B., P. H. Kahn, and A. Borning. 2006. Value sensitive design and information systems. In *Human-computer interaction in management information systems: Foundations*, ed. P. Zhang and D. Galletta, 348–372. London: M. E. Sharpe.

Gans, H. 1979. *Deciding what's news*. New York: Vintage.

Giddens, A. 1984. *The constitution of society: Outline of the theory of structuration*. London: Polity Press.

Goodwin, C. 1995. Seeing in depth. *Social Studies of Science* 25 (2): 237–274.

Hartley, J. 1999. *Uses of television*. London: Routledge.

Himelboim, I., and S. McCreery. 2012. New technology, old practices: Examining news websites from a professional perspective. *Convergence* 18 (4): 427–444.

Hindman, M. 2008. *The myth of digital democracy*. Princeton, NJ: Princeton University Press.

James, W. 1907/1981. *Pragmatism*. Amherst, NY: Prometheus Books.

Klein, H. K., and D. L. Kleinman. 2002. The social construction of technology: Structural considerations. *Science, Technology & Human Values* 27 (1): 28–52.

Kovach, Bill, and Tom Rosenstiel. 2001. *The elements of journalism*. New York: Three Rivers Press.

Lacey, Kate. 2011. Listening overlooked: An audit of listening as a category in the public sphere. *Javnost—The Public* 18 (4): 5–20.

Latour, B. 2005. *Reassembling the social: An introduction to actor-network-theory*. Oxford, UK: Oxford University Press.

Latour, B., and P. Weibel, eds. 2005. *Making things public: Atmospheres of democracy*. Cambridge, MA: MIT Press.

Lave, J., and E. Wenger. 1991. *Situated learning: Legitimate peripheral participation*. Cambridge, UK: Cambridge University Press.

Le Dantec, Christopher A., and Carl DiSalvo. 2013. Infrastructuring and the formation of publics in participatory design. *Social Studies of Science*. doi: 10.1177/0306312712471581.

Lee, A. M., S. C. Lewis, and M. Powers. 2012. Audience clicks and news placement: A study of time-lagged influence in online journalism. *Communication Research*. doi: 10.1177/0093650212467031.

Lewis, S. C., K. Kaufhold, and D. L. Lasorsa. 2010. Thinking about citizen journalism: The philosophical and practical challenges of user-generated content for community newspapers. *Journalism Practice* 4 (2): 163–179.

Lindtner, S., J. Chen, G. R. Hayes, and P. Dourish. 2011. Towards a framework of publics: Re-encountering media sharing and its user. *ACM Transactions on Computer-Human Interaction* 18 (2): 1–25.

Meijer, I. C. 2012. When news hurts: The promise of participatory storytelling for urban problem neighbourhoods. *Journalism Studies* 14 (1): 13–28.

Meiklejohn, A. 1948. *Free speech and its relation to self-government*. New York: Harper.

Murdock, G. 1977. *Patterns of ownership: questions of control*. Milton Keynes, UK: Open University Press.

Napoli, P. M. 2011. *Audience evolution: New technologies and the transformation of media audiences*. New York: Columbia University Press.

Papert, S. 1980. *Mindstorms: Children, computers, and powerful ideas*. New York: Basic Books.

Peters, C. 2012. Journalism to go: The changing spaces of news consumption. *Journalism Studies* 13 (5–6): 695–705.

Pew. 2012. "The state of the news media: An annual report on American journalism." http://www.stateofthemedia.org/2012 (accessed June 2013).

Piaget, J. 1954. *The child's construction of reality*. London: Routledge & Kegan Paul.

Ratto, M. 2011. Critical Making: Conceptual and material studies in technology and social life. *Information Society* 27 (4): 252–260.

Resnick, M. 1998. Technologies for lifelong kindergarten. *Educational Technology Research and Development* 46 (4): 43–55.

Rogoff, B., R. Paradise, R. M. Arauz, M. Correa-Chavez, and C. Angelillo. 2003. First-hand learning through intent participation. *Annual Review of Psychology* 54 (1): 175–203.

Rosen, J. 2008. "A most useful definition of citizen journalism." Press Think. http://archive.pressthink.org/2008/07/14/a_most_useful_d_p.html (accessed June 2013).

Schudson, M. 2008. Six or seven things news can do for democracy. *Why democracies need an unlovable press*, 11–26. Cambridge, UK: Polity Press.

Simon, H. 1996. *Sciences of the artificial*. Cambridge, MA: MIT Press.

Star, S. L., and K. Ruhleder. 1996. Steps toward an ecology of infrastructure: Design and access for large information spaces. *Information Systems Research* 7 (1): 111–134.

Thurman, N., and S. Schifferes. 2012. The paradox of personalization: The social and reflexive turn of adaptive news. In *The handbook of global online journalism*, ed. E. Siapera and A. Veglis, 373–392. Oxford, UK: Wiley-Blackwell.

Vygotsky, L. 1978. *Mind in society: The development of higher psychological processes*. Cambridge, MA: Harvard University Press.

Webster, J. G., and T. B. Ksiaze. 2012. The dynamics of audience fragmentation: Public attention in an age of digital media. *Journal of Communication* 62:39–56.

Williams, A., C. Wardle, and K. Wahl-Jorgensen. 2010. The limits of audience participation: UGC @ the BBC. *Journalists, sources, and credibility: New perspectives*, ed. B. Franklin and M. Carlson, 152–166. London: Routledge.

27 Social Media, Visibility, and Activism: The *Kony 2012* Campaign

Graham Meikle

On March 5, 2012, the thirty-minute video *Kony 2012* was uploaded to YouTube. Within its first week online, the film had been viewed 100 million times, the fastest any online video had ever reached that number, and had figured in more than 5 million tweets. A Pew survey in the days after the film's release found that almost 60 percent of young adults in the United States were aware of the video.[1] *Kony 2012* was an activist campaign film built around the affordances of social media. It was intended to mobilize support and action to stop the activities of Joseph Kony, the leader of the Lord's Resistance Army (LRA), a paramilitary organization founded in Uganda in 1987, and subsequently active throughout several other central African countries. The LRA has been charged with abducting thousands of children to take part in its armed actions and with a range of other atrocities including systematic mutilations and forcing children into sexual slavery. Its founder, Joseph Kony, was indicted by the International Criminal Court (ICC) in the Hague in July 2005 on multiple counts of crimes against humanity and war crimes.

Kony 2012 was made by Invisible Children, a US nonprofit organization founded in 2004 in opposition to the LRA. The film includes backstory on Invisible Children's earlier campaigning efforts, its lobbying in Washington, its contributions to development projects in Uganda, and its publicizing of Kony's actions across campuses throughout the United States. The film frames these through social media, with images of the growth of its Facebook presence used as a key visual indicator of the campaign's momentum, and archive footage of earlier campaign events introduced within the film by clicking on embedded video links on Invisible Children's Facebook page. *Kony 2012* states that the US government committed troops in an advisory capacity in November 2011 to help regional authorities capture Kony. This, the viewer is told, is not enough, and a global campaign of publicity is said to be necessary to ensure those troops are not withdrawn before their mission is complete.

Invisible Children's strategy was to put pressure on the US administration to continue providing military and logistical support to efforts to arrest Kony and bring him to the ICC prosecution. The tactic to achieve this strategic goal was to "make Kony famous." In a bizarre inversion of the cultural logic of media celebrity, the campaign aimed to turn Joseph Kony into a celebrity in order to maximize public awareness and, in turn, put pressure on the United States to pursue his capture. This publicity campaign was built around the affordances offered by social media for the circulation and sharing of ideas and images, of emotions and opinions.

The enormous attention drawn by the film was a "weird global media event," to use McKenzie Wark's term.[2] It was a *media* event, in that it did not take place in a physical space but rather played out through networks of digital connections. It was a *global* media event, in that it captured the news agenda around the world: from the BBC and the *Guardian* to a front-page story in the *New York Times*; to Australia, where the film was broadcast in full on a major national TV network; and across Africa, where it provoked much controversy and outrage. And it was a *weird* global media event in that its unpredictable novelty and its unexpected circulation made it resistant to normal news frames and narratives. Its weirdness was sealed, and the campaign perhaps fatally derailed, when the film's director and on-screen narrator Jason Russell performed a very public breakdown two weeks after its release, being filmed naked and pounding the streets with his fists in rush-hour traffic in San Diego—video of which also spread rapidly across the Internet. Mediated visibility, as John Thompson has observed, "is a double-edged sword."[3]

This essay does not engage with the debates around the accuracy of *Kony 2012*'s account of the current situation in Uganda, or with those around the geopolitical efficacy of its approach.[4] This essay instead focuses on what the *Kony 2012* events reveal about the uses of social media in activist campaigns; on the importance of questions of *visibility* in understanding social media; and on the centrality of collaborative making and sharing in a social media environment in which the media are no longer just what we watch, read, or listen to—the media are now what we *do*.

Social Media and Visibility

Kony 2012 begins with a ninety-second montage of images and clips, moving from shots of the Earth seen from space, to images illustrating social media: fragments of YouTube videos show a child being rescued from the Haitian earthquake, a young woman in an audiology clinic hearing her own voice for the first time, images of Twitter and Facebook from the Arab Spring, a child learning to ride a bike, grandparents and grandchildren sharing a video chat, and images of cursors clicking on "share" buttons. Director Jason Russell's voiceover begins: "Right now, there are more people on Facebook than there were on the planet two hundred years ago. Humanity's greatest desire is to belong and connect. And now we see each other, we hear each other, we share what we love, and it reminds us what we all have in common. And this connection is changing the way the world works. Governments are trying to keep up and older generations are concerned. The game has new rules."

These new rules revolve around the capacity of networked digital media to make their users visible to others in new ways. Social media are only the most recent manifestation of the fact that developments in communication always bring new kinds of visibility to new forms of public. The rise of the newspaper, for example, along with the emergence of the modern nation-state, the expansion of reading publics through formal education, the extension of the franchise, and the development of national railway networks, made possible the modern national consciousness of the "imagined community," through which the shared stories of a national culture make its common interests and concerns visible in new ways. Subsequent innovations in communication also brought changes to the visible. The emergence of the electric telegraph brought global news to light at electric speed. With photography came new forms of claim to the real, made visible and durable, and with broadcasting came the domestication of the public world, and the publicizing of the domestic sphere, each made visible to the other on-screen. Live news, made possible by satellite and cable, enabled the mediation of events that unfold before the eyes of viewers and reporters alike.[5] Media make the invisible visible.

Social media too make the invisible visible. Social media blur the distinction between public and personal communication. They manifest a convergence between the broadcast model of messages sent to nobody in particular, and personal mediated communication, as in email, phone calls, letters, texting, and online chat. A distinctive characteristic of this social media convergence is that moments of personal communication can now be made visible to new kinds of audiences and publics. We do not just create profiles and add connections, but we also *view* the connections made by others and their interactions in our online networks.[6] Flows of communication are made visible to self-selected audiences, and also to what may be larger, unpredictable, unknowable, invisible audiences as ideas and images, texts and comments, messages, gestures, and affective moments are circulated online.

In discussions of social media, this increased visibility of personal communication is usually framed around questions of privacy, and social media tools and firms are interrogated for their privacy policies and practices—who owns the data and what are they allowed to do with it? As danah boyd points out, what we do in a networked digital environment is persistent, searchable, replicable, and scalable.[7] But this usual frame of privacy is too narrow a frame through which to understand social media interactions. Much of what people share on social networks is not intended to be private in the first place—it's intended to be visible, intended to be shared. Across the convergent media environment, enhanced forms of visibility are implicated not only in surveillance imposed upon us from without, but also in dimensions of performance and display with which we choose to engage. We present and perform versions of ourselves for self-selected audiences. And there are uses of such performance to connect with others—to network, interact, and *share* with others we might never have encountered otherwise. This capacity for sharing leads to the affordances of social media for collaboration, networking, and shared creativity and communication. Social media make us visible to others and make those others visible to us in turn. This creates opportunities for collective action and collaborative creativity.

Caring and Sharing

The *Kony 2012* campaign tried to build on these affordances of mediated visibility in drawing supporters together to demonstrate and perform their support, to make Kony visible to new kinds of audience in new kinds of way, and to capitalize on networks to facilitate collaborative action by its young target viewers (compare with Henry Jenkins's discussion of the Harry Potter Alliance, chapter 3, this volume). "It's obvious that Kony should be stopped," says Russell in a voiceover. "The problem is 99 percent of the planet doesn't know who he is. If they knew, Kony would have been stopped long ago." In a crucial move, the fact that Kony is still at large is framed by the film as a problem of *visibility*—and, moreover, is presented as a problem that can be solved by using social media and their affordances of visibility.

Jason Russell's five-year-old son Gavin is used in the film as the viewer's proxy. Russell explains Invisible Children's position on Kony and the

LRA to Gavin, in order to introduce it to the viewer. Luis Moreno Ocampo, prosecutor for the International Criminal Court in the Hague, is then interviewed on camera to set Kony in an appropriate international juridical context. Kony, we are told, was the first man indicted by the ICC, in July 2005, for crimes against humanity. Both Ocampo and Gavin are then shown saying the solution is to "stop" Kony. "Here's the biggest problem," Russell tells his son. "You want to know what it is? Nobody knows who he is." Gavin demurs—he knows who Kony is; he can see him in the picture his dad gave him. Russell disagrees with him: "He's not famous. He's invisible. *Joseph Kony is invisible.*"

The solution, Russell says in voiceover, is to make Kony visible. Invisible Children plans to make Joseph Kony a household name. A rapid montage of posters, graffiti, stickers, and campaign actions is cut to electronic dance music, as Russell explains that the campaign is to target twenty celebrities (including Jay-Z, Mark Zuckerberg, Ellen DeGeneres, and Rihanna) and twelve senior US politicians (including George W. Bush, Mitt Romney, John Kerry, and Bill Clinton, but not Barack Obama or any member of his administration). George Clooney is shown telling an interviewer: "I'd like indicted war criminals to enjoy the same level of celebrity as me. That seems fair." Supporters are urged to tweet these public figures, or contact them in other ways, in order to urge them to "make Kony famous."

In order to make Kony famous, supporters had to *share* the film. The everyday act of sharing through social media, already taken for granted, is worth more attention. "In our society," observes Manuel Castells, "the protocols of communication are not based on the sharing of culture but on the culture of sharing."[8] We now share ideas, information, meanings—and noise—through networks of mediated sociality. From this perspective, mediated circulation is an unfinished process of connections, associations, and relationships, with each link, like, and share opening up different kinds of association, different possibilities for meaning, different trajectories for further circulation.[9] Each encounter establishes new relations between the viewing individuals and the project of the *Kony 2012* campaign—invisible associations and connections made visible. This is where the metaphor of the "viral" video breaks down. *Kony 2012* circulated so widely through the social media environment not because it possessed some intrinsic infective capacity that its viewers were powerless to resist, but because many different individuals in many different contexts found it meaningful and chose to make it visible—to *share* it with others. The practice of sharing is key to making the invisible visible in the networked digital environment of social media.

This sharing, and the extraordinary circulation of *Kony 2012,* was precipitated by Invisible Children's years of networking and mobilizing of youth groups on high school and college campuses across the United States. The Civic Paths research project at the University of Southern California had been tracking Invisible Children's network activity for several years before the release of the film, and found that the rapid circulation of *Kony 2012* was boosted by members of preexisting networks and groups of supporters sharing the video and the hashtag *#Kony2012* to their own networks of friends and followers in a coordinated launch.[10] Data visualization by analysts at SocialFlow also revealed the importance of leveraging existing supporters to circulate the video.[11] This matters because it demonstrates how successful social media campaigns need to be grounded in networks, both online and offline. The affordances of networked digital media do not substitute for offline connections and communities, but rather can make those connections and communities visible to others who may wish to join them.

James Carey once observed that to be a citizen "is to assume a relation in space to one's contemporaries."[12] Carey's concern was to connect the problems of establishing and maintaining a democracy on the scale of the United States with certain conceptions of communication. He drew an important distinction between what he called the *transmission* view of communication—through which messages are sent across space for the purposes of controlling territory—and a *ritual* view of communication, understood as a symbolic process of maintaining community through time. Neither approach is quite right for the social media environment, in which the centralized production and one-way distribution of the transmission model blurs with the ritual, personal communication and sharing of networked individuals. Meanings are not just *transmitted* through networks—rather, they *circulate,* with each new moment of sharing sparking a fresh association in a fresh context.

Kony 2012 tried to invoke a kind of *distributed citizenship,* in which individuals from across the globe were to engage in a collective project for political change—*to assume a relation within networks with one's contemporaries*; a relation not defined by or restricted to a particular geographical location or polity, but rather defined by shared meanings and collaborative creativity and action within and through networked digital media. Distributed citizenship is a political possibility of the network society in its shift from what Castells terms the space of places to the space of flows: "the *space of flows* is the material organization of simultaneous social interaction at a distance by networking communication, with the technological support of telecommunications, interactive communication systems, and fast transportation technologies."[13] The film's distribution, circulation, and widespread sharing across the space of flows of social media platforms highlight the possible contours of distributed citizenship: a set of potentials made possible by networked digital media, and given impetus by unprecedented global human mobility—the movements of students, migrants, tourists, refugees, businesspeople—and the altered experiences and awareness of culture, connection, and community that result.[14]

"Buy Our Action Kit!": Social Media Activism and Intercreativity

If the only goal of *Kony 2012* had been to "make Kony famous," it would have to be judged a success. However, the film also sought to mobilize its supporters into a mass action on April 20, 2012—"Cover the Night"—in which as many people as possible around the world were to coordinate and collaborate in a campaign of graffiti, posters, yard signs, and other manifestations of Kony's name and image, using designs by artist Shepard Fairey, who created Barack Obama's iconic "Hope" image. Yet despite the 100 million views, and the millions of tweets, links, likes, and shares, participation in this event fell well below expectations. Media reports from around the world told of tiny gatherings of supporters in empty public spaces. In part, this might be explained by the scrutiny to which Invisible Children left itself open with the high-profile visibility of its campaign and its resulting examination of its own agenda, finances, and earlier online presence, to say nothing of Russell's naked public meltdown. Criticisms of the project, many very telling, circulated through social media, just as endorsements of it did. But in part it also points to a basic limitation of the "Cover the Night" proposition, which did not offer supporters the logical extension of the campaign. "Cover the Night" was not a call to collaborative, shared creativity, but rather to consumption of a prepackaged campaign product.

To set this observation in context, let's consider a central concept for understanding the social media environment—*intercreativity,* defined by World Wide Web creator Tim Berners-Lee:

> We ought to be able not only to find any kind of document on the Web, but also to create any kind of document, easily. We should be able not only to follow links, but to create them between all sorts of media. We should be able not only to interact with other people, but to create with other people. *Intercreativity* is the process of making things or solving problems together. If *interactivity* is not just sitting there passively in front of a display screen, then *intercreativity* is not just sitting there in front of something "interactive."[15]

Berners-Lee identifies here the crucial element of collaborative online creativity. Intercreativity is intrinsic to social media, through their capacity to connect people who are made visible to each other through digital networks. So it ought to be central to any attempt to use social media for political or cultural activism. It is possible to identify four dimensions of such intercreative online activism. There is *textual* intercreativity, as existing media images and narratives are reimagined and reworked into entirely new texts or into hybrid subversions of their component images. There is *tactical* intercreativity, as activists develop online variations of established protest gestures and campaign tactics. There is *strategic* intercreativity, building upon the traditions and conventions of alternative media to create an open, participant-centered media space that represents a strategic alternative to the established media. And there is *network* intercreativity, as participants work to build new media network models, including those that link open source software to experimental online publishing practices.[16]

The *Kony 2012* campaign's "Cover the Night" event, viewed from a perspective of intercreativity, could have been a challenge to its supporters to create, collaborate on, and share the most novel, surprising, and powerful responses they could imagine. But instead of an appeal for supporters to create their own textual, tactical, strategic, and network approaches, the film presents a repertoire of products available for purchase—posters, stickers, yard signs, and a bracelet with a unique ID number that gives access on the campaign website to "the mission to make Kony famous." "Everything you need," explains Russell, "is in a box called the action kit." The film does not mention that this box cost $30.

This weakness of *Kony 2012* is made clearer when set in the context of critical making. In Ratto's account of critical making projects, these should have three distinct phases: a conceptual phase, in which existing literature is reviewed and ideas are formulated and combined; a separate stage for the design and building of prototypes; and a reflective, iterative phase of revision and redesign.[17] The *Kony 2012* campaign, by analogy, presented its conceptual phase in the form of the film itself and its initial design phase in the materials for the "Cover the Night" event. What the campaign lacked was an emphasis on a reflective process of collaborative redesign and revision—a third phase, to continue the analogy with Ratto's model of critical making, in which participants would have been encouraged to refine, revise, and redesign the campaign. It was not that there was anything to *prevent* anyone from initiating their own creative participation and responses to *Kony 2012*, but rather that the film and campaign were designed in a way that sought to channel participation—the preferred response presented by the film was to join the prepackaged campaign rather than create a DIY response. *Kony 2012* was less DIY citizenship than weird kind of IKEA activism, in which participation involved paying a noticeable sum of money to buy the exact same stuff as everyone else, while then having to add one's own labor on top of that.

Ratto points to a useful distinction between caring *about* and caring *for* an issue—between having an abstract understanding of a situation and having an engaged investment in it.[18] The *Kony 2012* campaign provided information and encouraged action, prompting people to care *about* the issue of LRA activity and the importance of stopping Joseph Kony's activities. But its promotion of prepackaged participation encouraged supporters to join in with someone else's idea rather than to make their own creative response and, in so doing, failed to encourage developing the degree of investment that could have enabled supporters to care *for* the issue.

Conclusion

Social media bring with them new kinds of visibility, new opportunities and requirements to monitor and be monitored, to perform and display, and to connect with others who are newly visible to us and to whom we are ourselves in turn made visible. The *Kony 2012* campaign illustrates the importance and centrality of the visible in relation to social media. It points to the possibilities, the limitations, and the dangers of a politics of enforced visibility or radical transparency. It also suggests that the use of a consumption model of social media activism is not necessarily going to translate into widespread action—"Buy our action kit!" is not a proposition that is best suited to an environment in which mediation is not something we are subject to, but also something that we *do*. A media politics, an Internet activism, of intercreativity, of collaboration and collaborative making, and of collaborative creativity and sharing, is one better suited to an environment in which public media and personal communication converge, and in which the potential of that convergence is realized by people not only sharing but creating together.

Notes

1. Lee Rainie et al., "The Viral Kony 2012 Video," *Pew Internet & American Life Project*, March 15, 2012.

2. Wark's definition of a weird global media event: "Something of significance that appears to happen in a particular place, but which actually takes place along the

vectors which connect that place to a world. The world called into being by the event is not global in the sense of universal, but rather it invokes *a* world. Its weirdness stems from some unexpected novelty in where and how it happens" (2012, 208).

3. Thompson 2005, 41.

4. For which, start with Zuckerman 2012.

5. On "imagined community" and the significance of print, see Anderson 1991. On the telegraph, see Carey 1989. On photography, see Barthes 1981 and Evans 1978. On broadcasting, see Meyrowitz 1985. On live news, see Wark 1994 and Friedland 1992.

6. This is the three-part definition of social media offered by boyd and Ellison (2007), although this definition lacks the crucial element of the convergence of public media with personal communication. For more on this dimension of convergence, see Meikle and Young 2012, 59–78.

7. boyd 2011.

8. Castells 2009, 126.

9. Sumiala 2008.

10. Jenkins 2012.

11. Lotan 2012.

12. Carey 1989, 4.

13. Castells et al. 2007, 171.

14. On the significance of human mobility here, see Appadurai 1996 and Urry 2007.

15. Berners-Lee 1999, 182–183; emphasis in original.

16. For a fuller discussion of these dimensions of activist intercreativity, see Meikle 2010, 363–377.

17. Ratto 2011a.

18. Ratto 2011b.

References

Anderson, Benedict. 1991. *Imagined Communities*. Rev. ed. London: Verso.

Appadurai, Arjun. 1996. *Modernity at Large*. Minneapolis: University of Minnesota Press.

Barthes, Roland. 1981. *Camera Lucida*. London: Vintage.

Berners-Lee, Tim. 1999. *Weaving the Web*. London: Orion Business Books.

boyd, danah. 2011. Social Network Sites as Networked Publics: Affordances, Dynamics, and Implications. In *A Networked Self: Identity, Community, and Culture on Social Network Sites*, ed. Zizi Papacharissi, 39–58. London: Routledge.

boyd, danah, and Nicole B. Ellison. 2007. Social Network Sites: Definition, History and Scholarship. *Journal of Computer-Mediated Communication* 13 (11). http://jcmc.indiana.edu/vol13/issue1/boyd.ellison.html (accessed August 7, 2012).

Carey, James. 1989. *Communication as Culture*. New York: Routledge.

Castells, Manuel. 2009. *Communication Power*. Oxford: Oxford University Press.

Castells, Manuel, Mireia Fernandez-Ardevol, and Jack Linchuan Qiu, and Araba Sey. 2007. *Mobile Communication and Society*. Cambridge, MA: MIT Press.

Evans, Harold. 1978. *Pictures on a Page*. London: Pimlico.

Friedland, Lewis A. 1992. *Covering the World*. New York: Twentieth Century Fund.

Jenkins, Henry. 2012. "Contextualizing #Kony2012: Invisible Children, Spreadable Media, and Transmedia Activism." *Confessions of an Aca/Fan*, March 12. http://henryjenkins.org/2012/03/contextualizing_kony2012_invis.html (accessed August 7, 2012).

Lotan, Gilad. 2012. "[Data Viz] KONY2012: See How Invisible Networks Helped a Campaign Capture the World's Attention." *SocialFlow*, March 14. http://blog.socialflow.com/post/7120244932/data-viz-kony2012-see-how-invisible-networks-helped-a-campaign-capture-the-worlds-attention (accessed August 7, 2012).

Meikle, Graham. 2010. Intercreativity: Mapping Online Activism. In *International Handbook of Internet Research*, ed. Jeremy Hunsinger, Lisbeth Klastrup, and Matthew Allen, 363–377. Dordrecht: Springer.

Meikle, Graham, and Sherman Young. 2012. *Media Convergence*. Basingstoke: Palgrave Macmillan.

Meyrowitz, Joshua. 1985. *No Sense of Place*. New York: Oxford University Press.

Rainie, Lee, Paul Hitlin, Mark Jurkowitz, Michael Dimock, and Shawn Neidorf. 2012. "The Viral Kony 2012 Video." *Pew Internet & American Life Project*, March 15. http://pewinternet.org/Reports/2012/Kony-2012-Video.aspx (accessed August 7, 2012).

Ratto, Matt. 2011a. Critical Making: Conceptual and Material Studies in Technology and Social Life. *Information Society* 27 (4): 252–260.

Ratto, Matt. 2011b. Open Design and Critical Making. In *Open Design Now: Why Design Cannot Remain Exclusive*, ed. P. Atkinson, M. Avital, B. Mau, R. Ramakers, and C. Hummels, 202–209. Amsterdam: BIS Publishers.

Sumiala, Johanna. 2008. Circulation. In *Keywords in Religion, Media and Culture*, ed. David Morgan, 44–55. London: Routledge.

Thompson, John B. 2005. The New Visibility. *Theory, Culture & Society* 22 (6): 31–51.

Urry, John. 2007. *Mobilities*. Cambridge: Polity.

Wark, McKenzie. 1994. *Virtual Geography*. Bloomington: Indiana University Press.

Wark, McKenzie. 2012. *Telesthesia*. Cambridge: Polity.

Zuckerman, Ethan. 2012. "Unpacking Kony 2012." *My Heart's in Accra*, March 8. http://www.ethanzuckerman.com/blog/2012/03/08/unpacking-kony-2012 (accessed August 7, 2012).

28 A Digital Democracy or Twenty-First-Century Tyranny? CNN's iReport and the Future of Citizenship in Virtual Spaces

Devan Bissonette

One of the most seductive aspects of the digital age is its potential to create a virtual democratic model of participatory cyber-citizenship. The present reality is far bleaker. Amid the cacophony of virtual discourses, the anonymity of participatory media has become a harbinger of an uncivil society. While much is said about the growing influence of social media over human connectivity, what about its impact on producing and interpreting information, the building blocks of a society's understanding of itself and the world? As professional reporters' century-long monopoly over information production declines, the forums where a new breed of citizen journalists could freely debate current events have become caught in a struggle between digital democracy and twenty-first-century tyranny.

The New Age

If, as Michael Schudson argues, the future of democracy online lies in understanding citizenship in digital spaces, we must recognize how and where its participants interact to best grasp the potential for the virtual newsroom to operate as a free, participatory forum.[1] Foremost are the citizen journalists, individuals defined not by personal status but access. They offer information, critiques, and personal experiences alongside older guardians of community standards in the production of news content.[2] Citizen journalists move fluidly among their roles as researchers, reporters, gatewatchers, and commentators, always positioned to contest meaning.[3]

Citizen journalists collaborate inside virtual communities. Within these forums, citizenship is quite literally do-it-yourself, reversing traditional journalistic norms where only a select few had the power to shape news content. Though these collectives typically reinforce traditional power structures, they can delegitimize them too through the visibility of their public opinions.[4] As the objectivity of professional journalists comes further into question, these forums have become increasingly visible and influential in making sense of current events.

The wealth of content produced by citizen journalists has done little to change the thinking of news corporations, still the most powerful influence over newsmaking. As the online editor of Great Britain's *The Sun* contends, readers crave "well-crafted" copy produced by a "trained and experienced" journalist, implying citizen journalists generate neither.[5] Slowly, however, traditional media is evolving. Enhancing the public's role in reporting draws in users and advertising dollars, regardless of the actual content produced, two results corporate media craves.[6]

While media executives may be slow to grasp the consequences of citizen journalism, professional journalists have not been. The visible criticism forum posts provide them has improved fact-checking. While many applaud this change, professionals believe this unfiltered contact encourages abusive discourse and empowers those with more developed writing skills, giving select users influence far beyond their knowledge, experience, or accuracy.[7]

If by digital democracy we think of a forum where users obtain citizenship and share power equally through presence and exercise free speech in conversation if not consensus-building, current technologies remain arguably the largest obstacle to its achievement. Technology produces a space for digital relationships, yet those who own the space threaten its arbitrary dissolution.[8] If the forum is denied access to the public sphere, it cannot, per Habermas, be democratic.[9] Though technology has weakened traditional intrastate controls, new, international networks of authority allow democratic forums only to the extent they coincide with market interests.[10] The result is best described by Zizi Papacharissi as a "commercially public medium."[11] Citizen journalism remains tilted toward commercial gain, not democratic discourse. Nowhere is this more visible than in the medium's most popular site, iReport.

iReport and Open Citizenship in Digital News Spaces

In 2006, CNN's iReport became the first major news site to embrace citizen journalism. It took over a year, however, until the site received footage of the April 2007 Virginia Tech shootings, for editors to appreciate how, with added freedom, users could break news and thereby increase page views. Consequently the site was subsequently spun off from CNN and users were given control over content and commentary. De facto vetting was eliminated.[12] Only a smattering of stories would be conspicuously labeled with the CNN-designed badge of authenticity, a necessary precursor for a story to appear on its affiliated networks. Democracy had made inroads.

With just under one million registered users as of 2011, iReport promises "to report and tell the story of an event together with its audience."[13] Blurring the lines between participant and producer, iReport's emphasis on group participation places it among the early adopters of the web's new generation of collaborative ventures that profit from the diversity of viewpoints online.[14] While its digital interactions require free registration, users gain the power to influence a mass audience through the site and CNN's worldwide networks. This may well encourage posts, for the desire to acquire celebrity status is as strong online as off.[15]

Four highly reported events from 2010—the April oil spill in the Gulf of Mexico, the immigration debate in Arizona, California's gay marriage debate, and the 9/11 mosque controversy in New York City—help reveal the dynamics behind iReport's do-it-yourself virtual communities.[16] These events all fueled numerous debates at the web's most popular citizen journalism site, which can serve as a means by which to better understand the relationship between power, discourse, civility, and democracy, speaking strongly to citizen journalism's present and future.

The Gulf Oil Spill

The explosion of a Deepwater Horizon oil rig in the Gulf of Mexico on April 20, 2010, began one of the worst environmental disasters in history, generating well over five hundred iReports. One of the first stories came from *capt1000*, on location with the Coast Guard.[17] His video of the burning rig produced two narratives, one focused on the loss of human life, another on the coming ecological disaster. Most approved of further drilling, hardly the subject that produced the report. This mentality resurfaced frequently, though the growing environmental damage did become a popular topic for unexpected reasons, shown in "Oiled Nest." Its focus, a picture of a sea turtle nest covered in oily seaweed, was labeled unnewsworthy and a fake. Aside from such slights, iReporters generally engaged in a civil debate on the importance of energy production and offshore drilling to the economy, once again tilting toward production over protection, concluding accidents were inevitable.[18]

Aside from consensus-making, the controversy provided an excellent chance to learn about user perceptions regarding freedom of speech at iReport. "Facebook Has Deleted Boycott BP" was a call-to-arms over the disappearance of an anti-BP group from the social media site.[19] Seventy-five iReporters jumped into the fray.[20] Some, believing corporate America was behind the group's deletion, wondered if CNN would censor the story. Others begged the network to investigate and outlined a boycott of Facebook. The open discussion of censorship and sanctions indicated that iReport's virtual community members recognized their ability to coordinate protests, the essence of democratic action. The naiveté of these same users, discussing the potential for CNN to censor the story *on its website*, shows a surprising lack of understanding regarding the power dynamics inside their virtual community.

Arizona's Immigration Debate

On April 23, 2010, Arizona Governor Jan Brewer enacted the nation's strictest immigration law, requiring legal immigrants to carry registration papers and affirming the right of police officers to check documentation.[21] One of the first iReports came from a protest outside Arizona's capital.[22] Vetted by CNN, it drew the most sizable commenter pool of any story examined in this report, eight hundred strong. Two styles of discourse emerged that demarked iReport's battle lines on immigration.[23] The first was a generally polite if absolutist interpretation regarding the economics of immigration. The second was crude and bigoted. "Wanna know why you can't find a person who supports the bill?," asked *Jfeul*. "Because they are all at work, you idiot." "If we don't stop [illegal immigration]," *sydonedave* wrote, "we won't have a country in a few years."[24]

This style of discourse continued in a vetted report by *Primeterre*. "These protesters are a bunch of racist nazis," concluded *hadjiladji*. *libshavetogo* was even terser: illegals "deserve no rights." Another claimed immigration was part of President Barack Obama's plan to destroy America. Even CNN drew criticism for vetting a "sympathetic" report.[25] Amid the vitriol of anti-protestor rhetoric, there was a brief discussion of immigration as a civil rights issue. Both arguments hearkened back to the 1960s, when Richard Nixon embraced a similar wave of indignation on his way to the presidency.[26]

At the end of July, a federal judge granted a preliminary injunction against the law.[27] "Arizona: Police Will Not be Allowed to Question Illegal Status!" expressed relief at the ruling, the author believing the new law would cause more problems than it solved. Anti-immigration advocates quickly shifted the board's tone. One attacked its author, *ANAV*, telling him, "Now you will continue to have more murders, raping of women, and crimes committed in Arizona committed by the protected illegals."[28] During a respite from personal attacks, a civil discussion broke out over just who was an illegal immigrant. While these debates raged, others contemplated President Reagan's earlier amnesty to illegals and its effect on President Obama.

Posters generally lauded the ruling, often using some form of anti-immigration rhetoric. The "new America," reported *cocroft* in a typical remark, "is a combination of Illegal Aliens and Multinational Citizens . . . Traditional Americans are invited to leave, die off or work for $.50 Cents an hour."[29] One commentator demanded that anyone waving a Mexican flag "get the heck out of here."[30] The irony in demanding the rule of law by denying one's civil rights (if by coincidence a protester is American) was lost in the tumult. Generally the law's purpose and intent was validated and its critics lambasted, but rarely answered.

Proposition 8

In November 2008, California voters approved Proposition 8 by a margin of 52 to 48 percent, overturning a California Supreme Court ruling legalizing gay marriage.[31] On August 4, 2010, a federal judge ruled the law unconstitutional.[32] iReporters sprung to life right after the announcement. Seventy-nine responded to *PDXSerric*'s ebullient report of the proposition's failure. The first rather civil and insightful strain of conversation considered the difference between marriage and civil unions, the oft-cited legal alternative to marriage. Others pondered the case's future as it likely worked its way up to the Supreme Court.[33] Aside from some angry comments about the judiciary infringing on popular sovereignty, discussion centered on what rights, if any, gay marriage threatened.

Another video iReport from the same day, "SF Lesbian Couple Tries to Get Married after Prop 8 Ruling," showed the civility within this virtual community was already under assault. Garnering 221 comments, iReport's virtual dialogue moved from debate over the value of majority rule versus constitutional law into utter demagoguery. To *jrsead*, homosexuals demanded through marriage rights that Americans "accept your deviant sexual lifestyle." *Davind* argued it would be "stupid" to give rights to people with a "behavior disorder." Discussion surprisingly calmed during a discussion of the 14th Amendment (guaranteeing citizens equal protection under the law). A secondary debate broke out regarding the power of states to define marriage, rather ironic given the 14th Amendment was an outcome of a conflict fought over the breadth of states' rights. This legal discourse faltered under a new barrage of extremist comments like those of *Jolat*, who compared homosexuality with incest and *jrsead*, who told gays

Muslims would slaughter them unless they voted for conservative Christian candidates. One poster did add some levity to these arguments, asking, "Where in the world did Cain find a wife?"[34] Insightful, respectful dialogue throughout mixed with incendiary rebukes that sought to shift debate from legality to absolutist moral doctrine. Intimidation, the enemy of all democratic forums, became the rule, not the exception.

TheVideoMan, interviewing California residents for a subsequent iReport, inadvertently revealed the effect of hate speech on this virtual community. His story, generally favorable to equal marriage rights, received nearly two hundred comments. Amid a mix of debate and hate, a new narrative emerged. As *PDXSerric* noted, "As you can see from the responses here and on similar reports, this is more evidence and support that matters of civil liberties and rights are not (and should not) be subject to a popular vote by a majority." *AlphaBrain*, in a comment straight out of the 1960s, argued that his peers must realize that equality cannot be legislated. By the time discussion ended, many agreed that marriage was best left out of politics entirely. As *JohnPhps* said, "If the majority always ruled, no minority would be free."[35] Democracy without checks and balances was very much in doubt.

The NYC Mosque

In May 2010 a group of investors announced they would open a mosque near ground zero of the 9/11 terrorist attacks in New York City. Three months later, President Obama publicly supported its construction, transforming the controversy from a local issue into a national debate over religion and 9/11.[36] Among the first to express his support for the president was *Satyendra*, in a webcam iReport. Since Muslim terrorists took down the towers in the name of Islam, one peer replied, a mosque near ground zero was tantamount to handing them a victory in the war on terror. Others like *Sshorty06111* equated critics with those who built Japanese internment camps in World War II. The story also provided a rare moment where racial politics intervened between users after *Satyendra*'s support was linked to his skin color. Among the polarizing voices moderates expressed hope the prospective mosque builders would consider the sensitive nature of the situation before making a final decision.[37] Unlike past debates about Prop 8 and immigration, here the law, which supports the right to build the mosque, faded to the background over a vague sense of the greater good.

Polite discourse, bigoted attacks, and reprisals continued their uneasy cohabitation in an iReport that equated the mosque's construction to "celebrating the [9/11] attacks." *grumpy457* added that "[M]uslims want to come here and kill people now." Several agreed. The anti-Islamic rhetoric lead "Indy609" to quote the Koran, contextualizing its calls for violence in the language of self-defense. As he explained, "I could not find a single word saying that Islam should be spread by the sword; but plenty of passages that say that if you are attacked for your beliefs, then fight like hell."[38]

Discourse took a decided turn a few days later. In "Mosque at Ground Zero. Are You Kidding Me?," debate first trended against the author's anti-mosque stance with references to the rule of law and the danger inherent in infringing upon one's freedom of religion and property rights. Extremism then pierced through reasoned discussion to link mosque builders (in a very peculiar, indirect way) to the president, allegedly engaged in anti-Israeli actions as part of a dastardly, un-American "plot" in Washington.[39] This conspiratorial trend was particularly visible in *SimpleCTZN*'s August 23 report. Decrying the ignorance of Americans spewing hate and misinformation, he asked, "Where have we gone wrong as a nation that we forget that a religion alone does not determine the value and rights of a person?" In an iReport that could be seen as a call to fight intolerance, citizen journalists responded with a bizarre mix of hate and 9/11 conspiracy theories.[40] The highly charged back-and-forth eventually transformed into a discussion of race and power after one poster claimed Obama's election, possible only with Oprah's help, proved that African Americans ran the country. Discussion had descended into the bizarre.

A Postmortem on Citizen Democracy, Circa 2010

Sifting through comments on each of these topics, some fascinating trends emerge that illuminate the present realities of citizen journalism. Three basic types of arguments filled iReport's pages. The most promising for democratic discourse were legal arguments. The government's role in overseeing economic development was a key topic on the Gulf spill. Anti-immigration advocates literally took a very black-and-white legal stance. For others, a law based on appearance was hardly equitable. Equal if not human rights were foremost on the mind of Prop 8 commentators. While some took the view that majority rule trumped constitutional authority, others cited the 14th Amendment to prove their point. As with immigration, the issue of whether states should have the right to legislate marriage took center stage, and the struct legal interpretations obscured the more complex underlying issues. With the varied legal views elsewhere, it was a bit surprising that both sides on the mosque issue acknowledged the project's legality.

When legal arguments failed to win converts, moral debates frequently took their place. With the majority accepting the legality of the mosque's construction, critics argued that human decency required its halt. Many interpreted gay marriage as a threat to Christian values, others believing equal rights for all was the only moral high ground. When it came to immigration, illegal became synonymous with immoral. Voices in defense of immigrants used surprisingly little moral language. iReporters exhibited a curious duality in their attitudes toward the Gulf spill. A palpable sympathy for workers affected by the tragedy did not consistently extend to the region's wildlife.

While respectful if not polite conversation was frequent and influential, extremism was the third argumentative style present in these stories. This is hardly a surprise. As Epstein and Reich argue, any system that mixes media with an indefinite authority is likely to produce a "war discourse."[41] The implications for citizen journalism are severe. The moment stereotypical language threatens the rights of others, democratic dialogue is imperiled; nowhere is incivility, especially hate speech, more visible on iReport than in discussions of ethnic and social groups.[42] Morality fueled this trend in arguments about Prop 8. Extremists argued that its legality ensured the decline of heterosexual marriage if not civilization. Immigration equaled a threat to America's future. Radicalism over the mosque centered on a select but vocal minority who equated Islam with terrorism. The least bitter debates related to the Gulf oil spill, the worst epithets hurled toward those favored environmentalism over energy production.

Most surprising about these bursts of extremism was their conservative nature. In the absence of any demographic data on iReport users, one can only speculate as to its meaning. It may be that other issues would encourage liberal fanaticism. There is also the oft-repeated belief that CNN is liberal, which might encourage conservatives to participate as an active opposition. I suspect, however, there is a more simple explanation. Immigration, sexuality, and religion are traditional subjects used by the right to indicate that the nation's future is threatened by an "other." Each of the topics had a very clear other that reflects the fears of the Far Right.

iReport and Citizen Journalism's Future

Given the potential for iReport to create a forum for a virtual democracy, the obvious divide between that ideal and reality raises important questions about the viability of citizen journalism as a whole. iReporters did encourage, if not provoke, readership and reaction, much like opinionated news programming.[43] At its best, this reflects one of citizen journalism's greatest strengths, its ability to foster a sense of independence and raise awareness. This must, however, be weighed against the role of hate speech to halt debate through intimidation and personal attacks.[44] Since iReporters face no threat to their public self from malicious postings, there is little incentive to curtail such behavior.[45] In the absence of strong checks and balances, anonymity remains both an asset and threat to democratic discourse. With only a small button available to report inappropriate comment, CNN's experts retain the power to censor. This may explain why vetted reports, which one might think would increase a story's credibility, were often considered the most biased. Users did not like to be reminded Big Brother was watching. The most democratic solution at the moment appears to be an in-house rating system controlled by users and already employed by citizen journalism sites like *Digg* that could discredit salacious posts while sustaining the virtual community's full participatory rights in iReport's oversight.[46] This would mean a significant loss of power for CNN, one the economics of journalism makes unlikely. Nonetheless, without an effective means of ensuring civility from the bottom up, the potential for a democratically achieved consensus will remain elusive.

The most important step in addressing the citizen journalism's limits, I argue, would also mark a significant evolutionary step in achieving a more democratic newsroom complete with essential checks and balances. The twenty-first-century journalist must, Jo Bardoel adds, sort out "relevant issues from an increasing supply of information in a crowded public domain" as the profession shifts from one of providing "content" to "context."[47] By summarizing all perspectives, evaluating evidence, and putting arguments in their historical context, news media's longtime role as a check against extremism might continue before citizen journalism inadvertently legitimizes fascist discourse over democratic debate.[48] To avoid this, citizenship rights to enter discussion over the professional narrative must remain open, ultimately increasing the sites where citizens might engage the newsmaking process.[49] As long as the unedited story and comments remained accessible and the summary piece not privileged, the hierarchal power structures of twentieth-century journalism should not be replicated.

Aside from its benefits in terms of making sense of discourse, this new twist on citizen journalism creates two products for the media corporation, the raw information feed behind the story, and the stylized final report.[50]

Without dollars to sustain infrastructure, citizen journalism is doomed, and this added layer of production might address citizen journalism's present faults while ensuring its future.

Conclusions

The potential for citizen journalism to allow free debate over news remains its most promising feature. Virtual debaters rarely questioned the nationality, race, or religion of their fellow community members. If in fact the digital divide is shrinking and potential citizenship in virtual communities continues to grow, traditional restrictions on access to discursive power may decline. Already there is evidence that nonwhite users experience a greater sense of community online than do white users.[51] To ensure an equitable discourse, however, professionals must acknowledge the legitimacy of citizen journalism. Showing equal respect to all participants is essential in disentangling information from persuasion in any discussion and ensuring open access. Otherwise, old structures of power will be reinscribed.

Human concerns aside, technology remains the greatest threat to full citizenship in these virtual communities. It mediates between the citizen and the digital forum but maintains, at least for now, familiar but hidden restrictions over content production As seen in iReport's discussions of censorship, users are blind to these restrictions, especially CNN's power, which included a site design linked to Western norms and values, making it discriminatory by design to non-Western cultures. These shortcomings must be addressed before they are too firmly established.

If we stand on the precipice of a post-national age where, as Mark Poster believes, the "netizen" will split his or her allegiance between the state and virtual communities, the coming years are essential in building cross-cultural and digital democratic structures before these spaces become another means of controlling and manipulating the body politic.[52] It would be inexcusable as well not to ask if media organizations want a virtual democracy. As long as advertising is linked to user views, media companies have a vested interest in pushing users to generate inflammatory versus informative content, as long as the former proves more salable.[53] This is a difficult barrier for users to overcome if they desire free and open access unless they control the technology.

The future of the medium is in the users' hands, specifically the silent majority that makes up the bulk of these virtual communities. Even the most commented stories on iReport drew posts from less than one one-thousandth of registered users, and this says nothing about the majority of web users who view without registering.[54] They may in time embrace the participatory aspects of the medium and in doing so reshape the discursive landscape by demanding greater control. The result could be an ever-expanding netizenship willing to discuss issues relevant to the body politic in forums open to all. On the other hand, as often happens in the brick-and-mortar world, users may accept their disempowerment, resulting in a virtual "Cyberia," as Andrew Jakubowicz calls the web.[55]

iReport's popularity speaks to the potential of citizen journalism to reshape the newsmaking process. It provides the public with a chance to personalize the news and shape a do-it-yourself democracy where all may speak, if not be heard. Its potential was confirmed during the 2009 post-election chaos in Iran when iReport received firsthand reports directing the world's attention to human rights violations there.[56] Examples like this underscore the potential of citizen journalism to act as a watchdog over authority gone amok. Nonetheless, CNN continues to doubt its ability to operate as a system of checks and balances in partnership with iReport's professionals. On its fifth birthday, the site reiterated its goal as "connecting the many voices and expertise and activity that you need to make a story come to life."[57] CNN remains the expert, its power unchecked. Users remain little more than iReport's foot soldiers.

For the moment, citizen democracy is best served walking the fine line between the anarchy of raw information streams and potentially infinite voices available online and the tyranny of media conglomerates and their structures of authority that collide within the virtual community. As long as traditional powers are left sorting through the cacophony of material on such sites, users will have room to carve out a niche within these established systems that could one day see citizen journalism reborn in its more free and democratic form, beyond the watchful eyes of corporate power.

Notes

1. Schudson 2004, 49.

2. Bruns, 2008, 174–177.

3. Barlow 2010, 53; Deuze 2009, 18–19; Bruns 2008, 177–178.

4. Song 2009, 7.

5. Thurman 2008, 140.

6. Shields 2008, 5; Dervin and Huesca 2004, 283.

7. Barlow 2010, 48; Thurman 2008, 140, 145; Ashman and Singer 2009, 235–239; Epstein and Reich 2010, 242.

8. Schuler 2004, 70–72; Schlove 1995, 11–17; Bardoel 1996, 293.

9. Habermas 2006, 73.

10. Shahin 2007, 15–20.

11. Papacharissi 2010, 124.

12. Probably less than 1 percent of stories are removed. Reyhan Harmanci, "Citizen Journalism Carries Unique Pitfalls; False Story on CNN's iReport Site Sent Apple Stock Tumbling," *San Francisco Chronicle*, October 5, 2008, A7; John P. Gamboa, "Putting the Pen in the Hands of Readers: CNN's New iReport Gives Consumers Opportunity," *The Daily Aztec*, February 21, 2008; "About CNN iReport," *iReport*, September 25, 2010, http://ireport.cnn.com/about.jspa#; Lila King, "Five Years of iReport," *iReport*, August 2, 2011, http://www.cnn.com/2011/IREPORT/08/02/5years/index.html?hpt=hp_bn.

13. King, "Five Years of iReport," *iReport*, August 2, 2011, http://www.cnn.com/2011/IREPORT/08/02/5years/index.html?hpt=hp_bn.

14. Johnson and Wiedenbeck 2009, 333–334; John Smith, "CNN Sets New Standard Online in Leads Competition," *Media News International*, February 1, 2010, http://www.mnilive.com/2010/02/cnn-sets-new-standard-online-in-leads-competition/.

15. Goode 2009, 1302.

16. Stories were chosen via basic search terms and iReport links to said stories. Approximately twenty stories were studied per topic, chosen based on quantity of user responses. The evidence below is representative of the general tenor of each topic. I will cite each story based on the date of first post.

17. "Rig Fire at Deepwater Horizon 4/21/10," *iReport*, April 22, 2010, http://ireport.cnn.com/docs/DOC-435316.

18. "Oiled Nest," *iReport*, July 16, 2010, http://ireport.cnn.com/docs/DOC-472856.

19. "Facebook Has Deleted Boycott BP, Leaving Almost 800,000 Fans Hanging," *iReport*, June 28, 2010, http://ireport.cnn.com/docs/DOC-466703.

20. A week earlier another iReport took CNN's Anderson Cooper to task for not asking the tough questions of an official associated with the cleanup. "Reporters Afraid to Ask Tough Questions These Days," *iReport*, June 19, 2010, http://ireport.cnn.com/docs/DOC-462398.

21. "What Does Arizona's Immigration Law Do?," *CNN*, April 23, 2010, http://articles.cnn.com/2010-04-23/politics/immigration.faq_1_immigration-reform-law-institute-immigrant-advocates-illegal?_s=PM:POLITICS.

22. "Just Moments after AZ Gov Signs Bill SB1070," *iReport*, April 23, 2010, http://ireport.cnn.com/docs/DOC-436053.

23. As with the Gulf spill, a few of these commentators take on CNN for vetting what they saw as a "biased" story, indicative of CNN's sympathies with the protesters.

24. "Just Moments after AZ Gov Signs Bill SB1070," *iReport*, April 23, 2010, http://ireport.cnn.com/docs/DOC-436053.

25. "Immigration Protest of Chicago Cubs vs. Diamondbacks," *iReport*, April 29, 2010, http://ireport.cnn.com/docs/DOC-438134.

26. For more on sixties anti-protestor actions, see Lytle 2006, 346–350.

27. "Legal battle looms over Arizona immigration law," *CNN*, July 28, 2010, http://articles.cnn.com/2010-07-28/us/arizona.immigration.law_1_arizona-immigration-law-illegal-immigrants-arizona-state?_s=PM:US.

28. "Arizona: Police Will Not be Allowed to Question Illegal Status!," *iReport*, July 28, 2010, http://ireport.cnn.com/docs/DOC-476636.

29. "Arizona Immigration Law: Read the Small Print," *iReport*, July 29, 2010, http://ireport.cnn.com/docs/DOC-476942.

30. "Protesters Break the Law," *iReport*, July 31, 2010, http://ireport.cnn.com/docs/DOC-477702.

31. Tamara Audi, Justin Scheck and Christopher Lawton, "California Votes for Prop 8," *The Wall Street Journal Online*, November 5, 2008, http://online.wsj.com/article/SB122586056759900673.html.

32. Bill Mears, "Proposition 8: Long road to the Supreme Court," *CNN*, August 5, 2010, http://www.cnn.com/2010/US/08/04/prop.8.next/index.html?iref=allsearch.

33. "Prop 8-Unconstitutional," *iReport*, August 4, 2010, http://ireport.cnn.com/docs/DOC-478844.

34. Presumably it was one of his sisters. "SF Lesbian Couple Tries to Get Married after Prop 8 Ruling," *iReport*, August 4, 2010, http://ireport.cnn.com/docs/DOC-479048.

35. "CA Prop 8 Stop the Hate," *iReport*, August 5, 2010, http://ireport.cnn.com/docs/DOC-47898.

36. Nicole Bilman, "Mosque to Go Up Near New York's Ground Zero," *CNN*, May 7, 2010, http://articles.cnn.com/2010-05-07/us/new.york.ground.zero.mosque_1_muslims-ground-zero-community-center?_s=PM:US; Dan Gilgoff, "Obama Throws Support behind Controversial Islamic Center," CNN, August 16, 2010, http://articles.cnn.com/2010-08-13/politics/obama.islamic.center.support_1_islamic-center-ground-zero-president-obama?_s=PM:POLITICS.

37. "Ground Zero Mosque No Problem," *iReport*, August 16, 2010, http://ireport.cnn.com/docs/DOC-482373.

38. "Mosque at Ground Zero is disgusting," *iReport*, August 17, 2010, http://ireport.cnn.com/docs/DOC-482675.

39. "Mosque at Ground Zero. Are You Kidding Me?," *iReport*, August 18, 2010, http://ireport.cnn.com/docs/DOC-482909.

40. "Americans, Conveniently Ignorant of Our Values," *iReport*, August 23, 2010, http://ireport.cnn.com/docs/DOC-484507.

41. Epstein and Reich 2010, 232.

42. Papacharissi 2004, 260, 274–275, 278.

43. Bruns 2008, 172–173; Carpenter 2009, 534; Shields 2008, 4–5; Toledo 2008, 8.

44. Epstein and Reich 2010, 228, 232–234.

45. Papacharissi 2004, 263.

46. Goode 2009, 1296.

47. Bardoel 1996, 297.

48. Hume 2004, 332.

49. Barabas 2004; 246; Epstein and Reich 2010, 243–244.

50. Deuze 2009, 22–23.

51. Murray and Weber 2004, 98; Harwood and McIntosh 2004, 216.

52. Poster 2002, 99–101.

53. King, "Five Years of iReport," *iReport*, August 2, 2011, http://www.cnn.com/2011/IREPORT/08/02/5years/index.html?hpt=hp_bn.

54. Deuze 2009, 24; John Smith, "CNN Sets New Standard Online in Leads Competition," *Media News International*, February 1, 2010, http://www.mnilive.com/2010/02/cnn-sets-new-standard-online-in-leads-competition/; Song 2009, 4.

55. Jakubowicz 2004, 203.

56. Shields 2008, 6.

57. King, "Five Years of iReport," *iReport,* August 2, 2011, http://www.cnn.com/2011/IREPORT/08/02/5years/index.html?hpt=hp_bn.

References

Ashman, Ian, and Jane B. Singer. 2009. User-Generated Content and Journalistic Values. In *Citizen Journalism: Global Perspectives,* ed. Stuart Allan and Einar Thorsen, 233–242. New York: Peter Lang Publishers.

Barabas, Jason. 2004. Virtual Deliberation: Knowledge from Online Interaction Versus Ordinary Discussion. In *Democracy Online: The Prospects for Political Renewal Through the Internet,* ed. Peter M. Shane, 239–252. New York: Routledge.

Bardoel, Jo. 1996. Beyond Journalism: A Profession between Information Society and Civil Society. *European Journal of Communication* 11 (3): 283–302.

Barlow, Aaron. 2010. The Citizen Journalist as Gatekeeper: A Critical Evolution. In *Public Journalism 2.0: The Promise and Reality of a Citizen Engaged Press,* ed. Jack Rosenberry, 45–55. New York: Routledge.

Bruns, Axel. 2008. The Active Audience: Transforming Journalism from Gatekeeping to Gatewatching. In *Making Online News: The Ethnography of New Media Production,* ed. Chris Paterson and David Domingo, 171–184. New York: Peter Lang Publishing.

Carpenter, Serena. 2009. How Online Citizen Journalism Publications and Online Newspapers Utilize the Objectivity Standard and Rely on External Sources. *Journalism & Mass Communication Quarterly* 85 (3): 531–548.

Dervin, Brenda, and Robert Huesca. 2004. Hypertext and Journalism: Audiences Respond to Competing News Narratives. In *Democracy and New Media,* ed. Henry Jenkins and David Thorburn, 281–308. Cambridge, MA: MIT Press.

Deuze, Mark. 2009. Journalism, Citizenship, and Digital Culture. In *Journalism and Citizenship: New Agendas in Communication,* ed. Zizi Papacharissi, 15–28. New York: Routledge.

Epstein, Dmitry, and Dor Reich. 2010. Citizen Journalism Online: Promise of an Alternative Conflict Discourse? In *Web Journalism: A New Form of Citizenship?* ed. Sean Tunney and Garrett Monaghan, 226–247. London: Sussex Academic Press.

Goode, Luke. 2009. Social news, citizen journalism and democracy. *New Media & Society* 11 (8): 1287–1305.

Habermas, Jurgen. 2006. The Public Sphere: An Encyclopedia Article. In *Media and Cultural Studies,* ed. Meenakshi Gigi Durham and Douglas M. Kellner, 73–78. New York: Blackwell.

Harwood, Paul G., and Wayne V. McIntosh. 2004. Virtual Distance and America's Changing Sense of Community. In *Democracy Online: The Prospects for Political Renewal Through the Internet*, ed. Peter M. Shane, 209–224. New York: Routledge.

Hume, Ellen. 2004. Resource Journalism: A Model for New Media. In *Democracy and New Media*, ed. Henry Jenkins and David Thorburn, 331–342. Cambridge, MA: MIT Press.

Jakubowicz, Andrew. 2004. Ethnic Diversity, 'Race,' and the Cultural Political Economy of Cyberspace. In *Democracy and New Media*, ed. Henry Jenkins and David Thorburn, 203–224. Cambridge, MA: MIT Press.

Johnson, Kristen, and Susan Wiedenbeck. 2009. Enhancing Perceived Credibility of Citizen Journalism Web Sites. *Journalism & Mass Communication Quarterly* 86 (2): 332–348.

Lytle, Mark Hamilton. 2006. *America's Uncivil Wars: The Sixties Era from Elvis to the Fall of Richard Nixon*. New York: Oxford University Press.

Murray, Sean, and Lori M. Weber. 2004. Interactivity, Equality and the Prospects for Electronic Democracy: A Review. In *Democracy Online: The Prospects for Political Renewal Through the Internet*, ed. Peter M. Shane, 95–108. New York: Routledge.

Papacharissi, Zizi A. 2004. Democracy online: civility, politeness, and the democratic potential of online political discussion groups. *New Media & Society* 6 (2): 259–283.

Papacharissi, Zizi A. 2010. *Democracy in a Digital Age*. Malden, MA: Polity Press.

Poster, Mark. 2002. Digital Networks and Citizenship. *Modern Language Association* 117 (1): 98–103.

Schlove, Richard E. 1995. *Democracy and Technology*. New York: Guilford Press.

Schudson, Michael. 2004. Click Here for Democracy: A History and Critique of an Information-Based Model of Citizenship. In *Democracy and New Media*, ed. Henry Jenkins and David Thorburn, 49–60. Cambridge, MA: MIT Press.

Schuler, Douglas. 2004. Reports of the Close Relationship between Democracy and the Internet May Have Been Exaggerated. In *Democracy and New Media*, ed. Henry Jenkins and David Thorburn, 69–84. Cambridge, MA: MIT Press.

Shahin, Jamal. 2007. The Reassertion of the State: Governance and the Information Revolution. In *The Resurgence of the State: Trends and Processes in Cyberspace Governance*, ed. Myrian Dunn et al., 9–34. Burlington, VT: Ashgate.

Shields, Mike. 2008. CNN: Power to the People. *Mediaweek* 18 (6). http://www.adweek.com/news/advertising-branding/cnn-power-people-94887 (accessed February 10, 2009).

Song, Felicia Wu. 2009. *Virtual Communities: Bowling Alone, Online Together*. New York: Peter Lang Publishing.

Thurman, Neil. 2008. Forums for citizen journalists? Adoption of user generated content initiatives by online news media. *New Media & Society* 10 (1):139–157.

Toledo, Elizabeth. 2008. Citizen journalism affects nonprofits. *PRWeek* 11 (17). http://www.prweekus.com/citizen-journalism-affects-nonprofits/article/109378/ (accessed February 10, 2009).

Contributors

Editors

Matt Ratto

Matt Ratto is an assistant professor in the Faculty of Information at the University of Toronto and Director of Semaphore Research Cluster on Mobile and Pervasive Computing. He also leads ThingTank Lab (http://www.thingtanklab.com), a nonprofit lab space and research project examining and designing the Internet of Things. Ratto's research examines how hands-on productive work—making—can supplement and extend critical reflection on the relations between digital technologies and society. This work builds upon the new possibilities offered by open source software and hardware, as well as the developing technologies of 3D printing and rapid prototyping. These technologies and the social collectives that create, use, and share them provide the context for exploring the relationship between "critical making" and "critical thinking."

Ratto received his PhD from the University of California, San Diego, in 2003, writing his dissertation on the social organization of the Linux development community. Following this, he completed a two-year postdoc at the Netherlands Institute for Scientific Information (NIWI), and in 2005 helped create the Virtual Knowledge Studio for the Humanities and Social Sciences in Amsterdam (VKS-KNAW). Ratto spent 2007 at the HUMlab, an innovative digital humanities laboratory located at the University of Umeå, Sweden, and moved to the University of Toronto in 2008. Recent publications include "Critical Making: Conceptual and Material Studies in Technology and Social Life," *The Information Society* 27 (4) (2011); "Open Design and Critical Making," in *Open Design Now: Why Design Cannot Remain Exclusive*, ed. P. Atkinson, M. Avital, B. Mau, R. Ramakers, and C.

Hummels (2011); and "The Ethics of Seamlessness: Resources and Future Directions," *International Review of Information Ethics* 8: Ethical Challenges of Ubiquitous Computing (2007).

Megan Boler

Megan Boler is Professor and Associate Chair of the Department of Theory and Policy Studies at the Ontario Institute of Studies in Education at the University of Toronto. She is Associate Faculty of the Center for the Study of United States and the Knowledge Media Design Institute also at UT. Her books include *Feeling Power: Emotions and Education* (1999) and *Democratic Dialogue in Education: Troubling Speech*; an edited collection, *Disturbing Silences* (2004); and *Digital Media and Democracy: Tactics in Hard Times* (2008). She has recently completed a three-year SSHRC-funded research project, "Rethinking Media, Citizenship and Democracy: Digital Dissent after 9/11." Her web-based productions include a study guide to accompany the documentary *The Corporation* (dir. Achbar and Abbott, 2003), and the multimedia website *Critical Media Literacy in Times of War*. Boler's essays have been published in such journals as *Educational Theory*, *Cultural Studies*, and *Women's Studies Quarterly*; recent publications include M. Boler, guest editor with Ted Gournelos, "Irony and Politics: User-Producers, Parody, and Digital Publics," *Electronic Journal of Communication* (September 2008), and M. Boler, "The Politics of Making Truth Claims: The Responsibilities of Qualitative Research," in *Methodological Dilemmas of Qualitative Research*, ed. Kathleen Gallagher (2008). She teaches philosophy, cultural studies, feminist theory, media studies, and social equity courses in the Teacher Education program and media studies at the Knowledge Media Design Institute, both at University of Toronto.

Contributors

Mike Ananny

Mike Ananny is an assistant professor at the University of Southern California's Annenberg School for Communication & Journalism, Affiliated Faculty with USC's Science, Technology and Society research cluster, and a Faculty Associate at Harvard's Berkman Center for Internet & Society. He studies the public significance and sociotechnical dynamics of networked news systems. He has held fellowships and scholarships with Stanford's Center on Philanthropy and Civil Society, the Pierre Elliott Trudeau

Foundation, the LEGO Corporation, and Interval Research. He was a founding member of Media Lab Europe's research staff, was a postdoc with Microsoft Research's Social Media Collective, and has worked or consulted for LEGO, Mattel, and Nortel Networks. He holds a PhD from Stanford University (Communication), an SM from the MIT Media Lab (Media Arts & Sciences), and a BSc from the University of Toronto (Human Biology & Computer Science). He has published in a variety of venues including *Critical Studies in Media Communication, International Journal of Communication,* the *Journal of Computer-Mediated Communication, American Behavioral Scientist, Television & New Media,* and the proceedings of the ACM's conferences on *Computer-Human Interaction* and *Computer Supported Collaborative Learning.* He is writing a book on a public right to hear in an age of networked journalism (MIT Press, forthcoming).

Chris Atton

Chris Atton is Professor of Media and Culture in the School of Arts and Creative Industries at Edinburgh Napier University, Scotland. His research specializes in alternative media, and his books include *Alternative Media* (2002), *An Alternative Internet* (2004), and *Alternative Journalism* (2008). He has made special studies of fanzines, the media of new social movements, and new media in Africa. He is currently researching how listeners make sense of and gain pleasure from avant-garde music and "difficult" forms of popular music.

Alexandra Bal

Alexandra Bal is an associate professor in the RTA School of Media at Ryerson University. She holds a PhD in Information and Communication Sciences from Paris University and is an associate researcher at the Maison des Sciences de l'Homme in Paris. She a researcher at the Experiential Design and Gaming Environments (EDGE) Lab at Ryerson, where she studies how people feel, move, congregate, and socialize around new media artifacts, with a particular focus on understanding how children's culture is changing with the use of digital technology. She is co-investigator on an SSHRC-funded grant project entitled "Voices from Digital Natives: Informal Learning and Sociable Media in Child and Youth Culture." She is leading a team of researchers who are working with Canadian children to understand and document the evolution of their use of digital media. She is also exploring whether the current online educational culture represents an evolution toward a de-schooled education system.

Devan Bissonette

Devan Bissonette is currently a lecturer in Comparative Cultural Studies at Northern Arizona University. He received his doctorate in 20th Century American Media History from Binghamton University in 2009. His most recent publication, "Visualizing the Limits of Democracy in the Silence of the Cold War: The Photography of *Life Magazine* and the Unraveling of the American Century," appeared in *Democratic Narrative, History, and Memory*, ed. Carole A. Barbato and Laura L. Davis (2012). Bissonette's current research interests include the study of visual news narratives and the consequences of anonymous discourse on free speech in cyberspace.

Catherine Burwell

Catherine Burwell is an assistant professor in the Faculty of Education at the University of Calgary, where she teaches courses on popular culture, media, and English language arts. Burwell's research interests include digital literacy, remix culture, and media education. Her most recent work examines young people's shifting attitudes to copyright and their influence on contemporary modes of cultural production. Burwell's work has been published in a variety of education, cultural studies, and communication journals, including *The International Journal of Cultural Studies* and *The Review of Education, Pedagogy and Cultural Studies*.

Red Chidgey

Red Chidgey (UK) is a feminist activist historian and holds a Postgraduate Diploma in Life History Research and an MA in Critical Theory at the University of Sussex, England. Zines and queers rock her world. With a grant from the Austrian Science Fund on feminist media production in Europe, she is currently drip-feeding her habit of interviewing feminist media producers and being endlessly inspired by the visions, working practices, and generosity of all the feminists that she meets.

Andrew Clement et al.

Brenda McPhail and Karen Louise Smith are PhD students in the Faculty of Information, where Jennette Weber is also a master's student. Andrew Clement is a professor in the Faculty of Information at the University of Toronto, where he coordinates the Information Policy Research Program. Joseph Ferenbok is a researcher and lecturer at the Institute of Communication, Culture and Information Technology. Alex Tichine is a senior developer and a master's student at the Faculty of Applied Science and Engineering at the University of Toronto.

Suzanne de Castell

Professor of Curriculum and Instruction in the Faculty of Education at Simon Fraser University, Suzanne de Castell produces work on literacy, technology, gender, educational game theory, research, design and development, and the multimodal analysis of communicative interaction. Recent coedited work includes *Worlds in Play: International Perspectives on Digital Games Research* (2008), *Loading . . . The Journal of the Canadian Game Studies Association*, work on design and development of educational games (*Contagion* and *A Baroque Adventure*), and recent publications on digital games and education, gender and gameplay and multimodal learning in informal and community settings.

Carl DiSalvo

Carl DiSalvo is an assistant professor in the School of Literature, Communication and Culture at Georgia Tech where he conducts design research concerning the role of interaction design in the public sphere. He received his PhD in Design in 2006 from Carnegie Mellon University. Prior to academia, he worked as a designer for many years, most notably at MetaDesign (San Francisco) and as a design consultant to the Walker Art Center's New Media Initiative. He is also a cofounder of DeepLocal, a design and technology firm that produces location-based products and services that foster civic engagement.

Kevin Driscoll

Kevin Driscoll is a doctoral student at USC Annenberg and works to encourage, support, and document cultures of everyday creativity. His recent research addresses the historicization of internet protocols, Wikipedia's changing editorial community, and the technical innovations of young people of color in hip-hop. Driscoll also supports open education initiatives as a member of the Students for Free Culture board of directors. He holds an MS in Comparative Media Studies from MIT and a BA in Visual Art from Assumption College, and he formerly taught mathematics and computer science at Prospect Hill Academy Charter School in Cambridge, MA.

Christina Dunbar-Hester

Christina Dunbar-Hester is an ethnographer who studies the intersection of technical practice and political engagement. She is currently developing a book manuscript based on her doctoral research, an examination of early twenty-first-century activism around low-power FM radio in the United States. She is also starting research on a new NSF-funded project on the gender-technology relation in activist technical projects, including advocacy to raise awareness about "diversity" issues in free software communities.

Miki Foster

Miki Foster is a video and new media artist and teaching artist specializing in social justice, video production, and new media education. She currently resides in Washington, DC, where she produces video and web content for Advocates for Youth, a national nonprofit working on youth mobilizing on sexual education. Her current artwork weaves audio and video narratives through craftwork and new/old networks of public display. She is the creator of Feminist Craft Corner and the producer/director of the public/web access television show Jerkwaterburg/Feminist Craft Corner. She completed her MFA in Digital Art/New Media at the University of California Santa Cruz in 2009 and holds a bachelor's degree from Evergreen State College.

Henry Jenkins

Henry Jenkins is the Provost's Professor of Communication, Journalism, Cinematic Arts, and Education at the University of Southern California. He is the author or editor of seventeen books, including *Textual Poachers: Television Fans and Participatory Culture*, *Convergence Culture: Where Old and New Media Collide*, and *Spreadable Media: Creating Meaning and Value in a Networked Culture*. Under a grant from the MacArthur Foundation, he and his research team are currently writing *By Any Media Necessary: Mapping Youth and Participatory Politics*. He blogs at henryjenkins.org.

Jennifer Jenson et al.

Jennifer Jenson is Professor of Pedagogy and Technology in the Faculty of Education. Her research and publication includes work on gender and technologies, gender and digital gameplay, players and identities in MMOGs (Massively Multiplayer Online Games) like World of Warcraft, Eve Online, and Rift, technology and education, and technology policies and policy practices in K–12 education in Canada. In addition, working with a team of people at York, Simon Fraser University, and Seneca College, she has designed and developed several educationally focused digital games, including a Baroque music game for the Tafelmusik Baroque Orchestra in Toronto. Negin Dahya is a senior doctoral candidate at York University, Faculty of Education. Her research explores postcolonial feminist theory in relation to digital media and learning with Muslim girls in low-income schools. Dahya's work examines how girls perceive and portray their local school and community through media production, and how engagement with different types of technology affect what students say and do. In addition, she is involved in the design and development of accredited university programs for refugees living in the Dadaab refugee camps, with a further interest on how ICT usage in education affects the educational experiences of girls and women in this context. Stephanie Fisher is a doctoral student at York University, Faculty of Education. Over the past six years she has worked with Jennifer Jenson (York) and Suzanne de Castell (UOIT), running several school-based video game clubs to examine the relationship between gender and play—specifically what, how, and under what conditions do girls/women play games. As a feminist intervention project, Fisher's dissertation work will highlight the ways preteen girls select and appropriate resources to construct subject positions that challenge their default subordinate status within digital games culture.

Yasmin B. Kafai

Yasmin B. Kafai is Professor of Learning Sciences at the Graduate School of Education at the University of Pennsylvania. Her research focuses on the study of design technologies in schools, community centers, and virtual worlds. Book publications include *Beyond Barbie and Mortal Kombat: New Perspective on Gender and Gaming* (2008) and *The Computer Clubhouse: Constructionism and Creativity in Youth Communities* (2009).

Ann Light

Ann Light is a professor in the School of Design at Northumbria University. Among other research, she has studied Digital Inclusion with the councils of South Yorkshire, completed five *Connected Communities* projects on participation, and helped set up a mobile phone innovation incubator with Makerere University in Uganda. Her interests include the social impact of technology and the politics of design, explored through design research such as Democratising Technology (www.demtech.qmul.ac.uk) and Fair Tracing (www.fairtracing.org). Drawing on this experience, she is currently working with the idea of Digital Interdependence: the potential for digital technologies to help build social structures and sustainable lifestyles for all.

Steve Mann

Steve Mann received his PhD degree from MIT in 1997, and is currently a tenured professor at the University of Toronto, where he teaches and does research in the Faculty of Applied Science and Engineering as well as the Faculty of Arts and Sciences. He is the inventor of the hydraulophone, a public water feature that is a fun and playful musical instrument similar to a woodwind instrument but using pressurized water instead of air. He is also a sculptor who builds hydraulophones as public art installations around the world. Mann is presently collaborating with a number of researchers including Ian Kerr, Canada Research Chair in Ethics, Law & Technology, University of Ottawa, who teaches a course on "Cyborg Law" that uses Mann's book. Mann, together with Kerr and others, are doing a SSHRC-funded project to study the ethics, law, and technology of anonymity, authentication, surveillance, and sousveillance, in addition to issues related to cyborg-law. The anonequity project is ongoing, and collaborator Kerr has also researched and lectured widely on implantable technologies.

Joel McKim

Joel McKim is a postdoctoral fellow at the University of Pittsburgh. He is currently working on a book length project entitled "Memory Complex: Competing Visions for a Post-9/11 New York." The project considers the intersection of memory, politics, and aesthetics at five distinct architectural sites connected to the events of September 11.

Owen McSwiney

Owen McSwiney studied architecture at University College Dublin, Ireland, and the Technical University Stockholm, Sweden. He has worked with architectural practices focused on cultural, residential, and restoration projects. He has collaborated with various community organizations to promote empowerment through self-build projects. His interests include vernacular construction, sustainability, craft, process, and travel.

Joshua McVeigh-Schultz

Joshua McVeigh-Schultz is a scholar and media maker whose work plays between the boundaries of documentary, performance, and design. He completed an MA in Asian Studies at UC Berkeley and an MFA at UCSC's DANM (Digital Arts and New Media) program. At UCSC he designed a mobile interface that crowdsources the traditional vox pop ("on the street") video interview. The project, "Synaptic Crowd: Vox Pop Experiments," attempts to mediate remotely distributed audiences as collaborative agents in the here-and-now of a public interview space. He recently started a PhD in Media Arts and Practice at the University of Southern California.

Graham Meikle

Graham Meikle is Senior Lecturer in Communications, Media and Culture at the University of Stirling in Scotland. His most recent book, coauthored with Sherman Young, is *Media Convergence: Networked Digital Media in Everyday Life* (2012). He is also the author of *Interpreting News* (2009) and *Future Active: Media Activism and the Internet* (2002), and coeditor, with Guy Redden, of *News Online: Transformations and Continuities* (2011).

Emily Rose Michaud

Emily Rose Michaud is an artist and activist working at the intersections of community development, civic participation, land use, public space, and urban ecology. In recent years, her experimental participatory and socially driven approach has resulted in a series of performances incorporating living "sproutfits," a guerrilla gardener's ensemble and electronic book designed to be reproduced and remixed by others, and the Roerich Garden Project, a three-year land art project in a post-industrial railyard turned urban meadow.

Kate Milberry

Kate Milberry is a postdoctoral fellow with a PhD from SFU's School of Communication. Her research examines the democratization of technology as a tool and technique for progressive social change. Her current work focuses on the relationship between social movements and the Internet, in particular, how tech activists use and develop free software to achieve broader goals of democracy, social and economic justice, equality, and environmental sustainability.

Jason Nolan

Jason Nolan is Assistant Professor in the School of Early Childhood Education and teaches in the Early Childhood Studies master's program at Ryerson University. He has previously held appointments at the University of Toronto and York. Nolan is autistic. He is director of the experiential design and gaming environment (EDGE) lab, and a professor in Early Childhood Studies at Ryerson University. He is also a faculty member in the joint Ryerson/York graduate program in Communication and Culture. Nolan graduated with a PhD in Critical Pedagogy from the Ontario Institute for Studies in Education in 2001, with a dissertation on virtual learning environments in education. His research focuses on adaptive design for children with disabilities, gaming/play, privacy/autonomy, sensory play, informal learning environments, virtual worlds, and the voices of "digital natives." His work has appeared in journals such as *Canadian Children*, *New Media & Society*, *Surveillance and Society*, and *Jeunesse: Young People, Texts, Cultures*. He is coeditor of *The International Handbook of Virtual Learning Environments*.

Kate Orton-Johnson

Kate Orton-Johnson is a lecturer in Sociology at the University of Edinburgh. Her research interests include the use of innovative methods in technologically mediated spaces, and she has published on the uses and challenges of virtual ethnography.

Kylie Peppler

Kylie Peppler is an assistant professor of Learning Sciences at Indiana University, Bloomington. An artist by training, Peppler engages in research that focuses on reconceptualizing the divide between formal and informal learning practices at the intersection of the arts, computation, and new media. Peppler completed her PhD at the University of California, Los Angeles (UCLA), studying the media arts practices of urban youth at a Computer Clubhouse in South Los Angeles.

David J. Phillips et al.

David J. Phillips holds a doctorate from the University of Pennsylvania's Annenberg School of Communication. He studies the political economy and social shaping of information and communication technologies, especially technologies of surveillance and identification. Michael Murphy and Karen Pollock hold Masters of Information from the University of Toronto.

Ian Reilly

Ian Reilly is an assistant professor in the Communication Studies Department at Concordia University. He received his PhD in Literary Studies from the University of Guelph. His research explores the intersections of politics, humor, civic engagement, and media activism. He teaches courses on mass media, Internet politics, media subcultures, telecommunications policy, and media history. He is currently at work on a book about—and in collaboration with—media activists the Yes Men.

Rosa Reitsamer

Rosa Reitsamer is an assistant professor at the Institute for Music Sociology at the University of Music and Performing Arts Vienna, Austria. She coedited the book *"They Say I Am Different . . ." Popularmusik, Szenen und ihre Akteure* (2011), and her monograph *When Will I Be Famous? The Do-It-Yourself Careers of DJs* was published in 2012. Her research addresses the questions of how agency is achieved in youth cultures and music scenes and how gender and ethnicity are negotiated by cultural producers.

Mandy Rose

Mandy Rose is Associate Professor and Director of the Digital Cultures Research Centre, University of the West of England. She researches the intersection between documentary and networked culture. Rose has led groundbreaking participatory media projects for the BBC including the Mass Observation inspired camcorder project, *Video Nation* (1994–2000), and *Capture Wales* (2001–2007), a pioneering digital storytelling project in the UK (BAFTA Cymru). She devised *Voices* (2004)—an early BBC foray into transmedia (Webby nominated) and executive produced *MyScienceFictionLife* (2006)—a collective history of British science fiction (Webby Honoree).

Rose's current production, "The Are You Happy? Project," revisits Jean Rouch's seminal 1960 documentary *Chronicle of a Summer* and explores the potential of HTML5 for the "creative treatment of actuality" (Grierson's definition of documentary).

Rose's research is reflected in the CollabDocs blog http://collabdocs.wordpress.com/ and via @CollabDocs on Twitter. She is a contributing editor to the i-Docs website.

Daniela Rosner

Daniela Rosner is an assistant professor of Human Centered Design and Engineering at the University of Washington. Her research combines design, computing, and fieldwork to reveal the social conditions and cultural values that shape and are shaped by digital technology. She has worked in design research at Microsoft Research, Adobe Systems, Nokia Research, as an exhibit designer at several museums, including the Adler Planetarium and Astronomy Museum, and as a lecturer at the California College of the Arts (CCA). She holds a PhD from UC Berkeley's School of Information, an MS in Computer Science from the University of Chicago, and a BFA from the Rhode Island School of Design in Graphic Design.

Yukari Seko

Yukari Seko is pursuing her doctorate in Communication and Culture at the York and Ryerson Universities' joint graduate program. Her academic interests are rather eclectic, including the psychosocial impacts of digital media use, online community, social performance, aesthetics of youth subculture, and the issues of identity negotiation and online technology. Her dissertation research examines photographic representations of self-injured bodies uploaded to social media websites, exploring the intersection between epistemological functions of social media and aesthetic-symbolic aspects of self-documentary photographs.

Lana Swartz

Lana Swartz is a doctoral student at USC Annenberg. Most of Lana's work is on money (and other regimes of value) as techno-social practice. At Annenberg, she has worked on the CivicPaths research collaborative and the new Media, Economics, and Entrepreneurship working group. In 2009, she completed a master's in Comparative Media Studies at MIT. Her thesis was on "fake" luxury fashion. There, she also developed a teachers' strategy guide and organized an unconference on cultural geography and new media literacies. As part of TeachForAmerica, she taught high school English in Houston, TX. She is the 2011–2012 Wallis Annenberg Graduate Research Fellow.

Elke Zobl

Elke Zobl is an assistant professor in the Department of Communication and director of the program area "Cultural Production & Contemporary Arts" at the University of Salzburg, Austria (http://www.w-k.sbg.ac.at/conart). She is currently conducting two research projects, namely "Feminist Media Production in Europe" and "P/ART/ICIPATE: Contemporary Arts Initiating Cultural and Social Change." She is the founder of the two online archives at www.grassrootsfeminism.net and www.grrrlzines.net and facilitates zine exhibits and workshops. Currently, she is editing an anthology on *Feminist Media: Participatory Culture, Networks and Cultural Citizenship.*

Index